Dennis J. Ireland (1952) is Editor of *The New Geneva Study Bible.* He received his Ph. D. in hermeneutics and Biblical Interpretation at the Westminster Theological Seminary, Philadelphia.

STEWARDSHIP
AND THE KINGDOM OF GOD

SUPPLEMENTS TO
NOVUM TESTAMENTUM

VOLUME LXX

STEWARDSHIP
AND THE KINGDOM OF GOD

*An Historical, Exegetical, and Contextual Study
of the Parable of the Unjust Steward in Luke 16:1-13*

BY

DENNIS J. IRELAND

E.J. BRILL
LEIDEN • NEW YORK • KÖLN
1992

Library of Congress Cataloging-in-Publication Data

Ireland, Dennis J.
    Stewardship and the kingdom of God: an historical, exegetical, and contextual study of the parable of the unjust steward in Luke 16:1-13 / by Dennis J. Ireland.
    p.   cm.—(Supplements to Novum Testamentum, ISSN 0167-9732; v. 70)
    Includes bibliographical references and indexes.
    ISBN 9004096000 (alk. paper)
    1. Unjust steward (Parable) 2. Bible, N.T. Luke XVI, 1-13—Criticism, interpretation, etc. I. Title. II. Series.
BT378.U5174   1992
226.8'06—dc20   92-15355
                                                      CIP

ISSN 0167-9732
ISBN 90 04 09600 0

PRINTED IN THE NETHERLANDS

CONTENTS

LIST OF ABBREVIATIONS USED

AB	Anchor Bible
ANQ	*Andover Newton Quarterly*
ASTI	*Annual of the Swedish Theological Institute*
ATR	*Anglican Theological Review*
AusBR	*Australian Biblical Review*
BAGD	W. Bauer, W. F. Arndt, F. W. Gingrich, and F. W. Danker, *Greek-English Lexicon of the NT*
BDB	F. Brown, S. R. Driver, and C. A. Briggs, *Hebrew and English Lexicon of the Old Testament*
BDF	F. Blass, A. Debrunner, and R. W. Funk, *A Greek Grammar of the NT*
BFCT	Beiträge zur Förderung christlicher Theologie
Bib	*Biblica*
BibLeb	*Bibel und Leben*
BibS(F)	Biblische Studien (Freiburg, 1895-)
BTB	*Biblical Theology Bulletin*
BZ	*Biblische Zeitschrift*
CBQ	*Catholic Biblical Quarterly*
CTM	*Concordia Theological Monthly*
ETL	*Ephemerides theologicae lovanienses*
ETR	*Etudes théologiques et religieuses*
EvT	*Evangelische Theologie*
ExpTim	*Expository Times*
FBBS	Facet Books, Biblical Series
HNT	Handbuch zum Neuen Testament
HTKNT	Herders theologischer Kommentar zum Neuen Testament
HTR	*Harvard Theological Review*
ICC	International Critical Commentary
IDB	G. A. Buttrick (ed.), *Interpreter's Dictionary of the Bible*
IDBSup	Supplementary volume to *IDB*
Int	*Interpretation*
JAAR	*Journal of the American Academy of Religion*
JB	*Jerusalem Bible*
JBL	*Journal of Biblical Literature*
JETS	*Journal of the Evangelical Theological Society*
JR	*Journal of Religion*
JSOTSup	Journal for the Study of the Old Testament—Supplement Series
JTS	*Journal of Theological Studies*
KJV	*King James Version*
MeyerK	H. A. W. Meyer, Kritisch-exegetischer Kommentar über das Neue Testament
NASB	*New American Standard Bible*
NCB	New Century Bible
NEB	*New English Bible*
NICNT	New International Commentary on the New Testament
NIGTC	The New International Greek Testament Commentary
NIV	*New International Version*
NovT	*Novum Testamentum*
NovTSup	Novum Testamentum, Supplements
NRT	*La nouvelle revue théologique*
NTD	Das Neue Testament Deutsch
NTS	*New Testament Studies*
RevExp	*Review and Expositor*

RHPR	*Revue d' histoire et de philosophie religieuses*
RNT	Regensburger Neues Testament
RSR	*Recherches de science religieuse*
RSV	*Revised Standard Version*
RTP	*Revue de théologie et de philosophie*
SBS	Stuttgarter Bibelstudien
ScEs	*Science et esprit*
SE	*Studia Evangelica*
SJT	*Scottish Journal of Theology*
SUNT	Studien zur Umwelt des Neuen Testaments
TDNT	G. Kittel and G. Friedrich (eds.), *Theological Dictionary of the New Testament*
THKNT	Theologischer Handkommentar zum Neuen Testament
TLZ	*Theologische Literaturzeitung*
TS	*Theological Studies*
TSK	*Theologische Studien und Kritiken*
TynBul	*Tyndale Bulletin*
TZ	*Theologische Zeitschrift*
UBSGNT	United Bible Societies *Greek New Testament*
VCaro	*Verbum caro*
WTJ	*Westminster Theological Journal*
ZNW	*Zeitschrift für die neutestamentliche Wissenschaft*

PREFACE

The following study is a slightly abbreviated version of my Ph.D. dissertation presented to the Faculty of Westminster Theological Seminary, Philadelphia, Pennsylvania, in 1989. Except for a few additions to the notes, no attempt has been made to include and interact with relevant literature that may have appeared or come to my attention in the meantime.

I wish to express my gratitude to several members of the faculty and staff of Westminster Seminary for their assistance in the course of my research and writing. The incisive comments and counsel, as well as scholarly model, provided by Professor Moisés Silva, first as dissertation adviser and then in the process of revision for publication, are very much appreciated. Professor Vern S. Poythress also took time from his schedule to read part of the first draft of several chapters and to offer a number of constructive suggestions. The patience and encouragement of Professor Richard B. Gaffin, Jr., in the formative stages of my work should also be acknowledged. My thanks go as well to Grace Mullen, Archivist at Westminster, for her efficient and cheerful assistance in securing many books and articles necessary for my research. Any errors of fact or judgment are, of course, my own responsibility.

Special thanks go to my family—my wife, Sandy, and sons, Jeremy, Joshua, Peter, and Timothy. Without their daily patience, encouragement, interest, and prayers, this work could never have been begun, let alone completed. To them I dedicate this book, with the hope that together we might be doers, as well as hearers, of the Word.

INTRODUCTION

The parables of Jesus have been the source of both fascination and perplexity ever since they were first pronounced almost two millennia ago. Very often the parables fascinate and attract the reader/hearer because profound spiritual truths are presented by means of down-to-earth, picturesque stories. At other times, however, these same stories perplex and even frustrate the reader/hearer because, for all their apparent simplicity, the impression lingers that something more is involved than meets the eye or ear, that there is a depth of meaning which one may not have completely grasped as yet. The following study is of one of the most perplexing of all Jesus' parables, that of the so-called unjust steward in Luke 16:1-13.[1] "This is," writes L. Morris, "notoriously one of the most difficult of all the parables to interpret."[2] This assessment is shared by many other scholars, past and present. The parable has been called the *crux interpretum* among the parables,[3] the "problem child of parable exegesis [Schwerzenskind der Parabelexegese],"[4] "the prince among the difficult parables,"[5] and "a notorious puzzle."[6] My goal in the following chapters is to bring the meaning of this enigmatic parable into progressively clearer focus by investigating it in terms of its various contextual levels.

It is a hermeneutical truism, disputed only by advocates of literary autonomy, that every text has a context. To understand a text properly one must interpret it in its context. This methodology is no less valid for the parables of Jesus than it is for any other text, biblical or otherwise,

---

[1] In referring to Luke 16:1-13 in this way I do not intend either to beg the question of the exact limits of the parable and its application(s), or to prejudge the steward's actions in the parable. At this point I am simply indicating the scope of my study and am doing so my means of the traditional title of the parable. Whether or not there is any cohesion among the verses of this passage and whether or not the steward's conduct was really unjust are matters to be discussed in chapter two. I have chosen to retain this title—the unjust steward—both because of its familiarity through long use (cf. especially the *KJV*) and its basis in the text itself (v. 8a: *kai epēinesen ho kyrios ton oikonomon tēs adikias*).

[2] L. Morris, *The Gospel according to St. Luke* (Tyndale New Testament Commentaries; Grand Rapids: Eerdmans, 1974) 245.

[3] A. Jülicher, *Die Gleichnisreden Jesu* (Tübingen: Mohr, 1910) 2.495.

[4] A. Rücker, "Über das Gleichnis vom ungerechten Verwalter, Lc 16:1-13," *BibS(F)* 17 (1912) 1.

[5] R. Stoll, "The Unjust Steward—A Problem in Interpretation," *Ecclesiastical Review* 105 (1941) 17.

[6] R. G. Lunt, "Towards an Interpretation of the Parable of the Unjust Steward (Luke xvi.1-18)," *ExpTim* 66 (1954-55) 335.

and it is the working assumption of the following study. The gospel writers have set the parables in particular contexts, ranging from the immediate to the broad; each of those contexts can play an important part in elucidating the meaning of the parable in question. I propose to examine the parable of the unjust steward in terms of its various contextual levels in Luke-Acts, beginning with the smallest or narrowest level (that of the pericope itself) and moving to the larger or broader level (that of Luke-Acts).[7]

Chapter one provides a history of the recent interpretation of the parable of the unjust steward (nineteenth and twentieth centuries) as background for the subsequent study. The pericope itself (Luke 16:1-13) is then considered in chapter two. More specifically, the parable itself is examined in terms of the application(s)/interpretation(s) attached to it. As will be seen, the exact limits and relationship of both the parable and the application(s) are matters of much debate. Among the questions to be considered are the following: What is the nature of the steward's actions toward his master's debtors? By whom and for what is the steward commended? How does one gain "friends" by "worldly wealth," who are these friends, and what is their role in one's reception into eternal dwellings? What, furthermore, is the relationship between vv. 1-9 and 10-13?

In chapter three the investigation of the parable is broadened to include its immediate and broader literary contexts. How does Luke 16:1-13 relate to and function within its immediate literary context in Luke 15 and 16? Why does Luke alone of all the gospel writers choose to include this parable, and why does he do so at this particular point? What role does our parable play, furthermore, in the broader literary context of the so-called "travel narrative" or central section of Luke's Gospel (9:51-19:44)? In chapter four I relate the parable to the theological context, in particular Luke's well-known emphasis on riches and poverty and Jesus' teaching on the kingdom of God. Is it really true, as L.T. Johnson alleges, "that although Luke consistently talks about possessions, he does not talk about possessions consistently"?[8] Does Jesus' proclamation of the kingdom of God as both present and future shed any light on the interpretation of this parable?

It is this last question of the eschatological dimension of the parable

---

[7] For practical reasons of length my discussion of context will be largely limited to Luke's Gospel, with only occasional reference to Acts.

[8] L. T. Johnson, *The Literary Function of Possessions in Luke-Acts* (Missoula, MT: Scholars Press, 1977) 130.

of the unjust steward to which special attention will be paid in the course of the following investigation. In conjunction with the theme of stewardship, I believe such an emphasis is one distinctive feature of, and justification for, this study. An eschatological approach to the parables is not new, of course; the eschatological background of the parables has been recognized and widely affirmed since the work of Dodd and Jeremias. I have become convinced, however, that many studies of this parable, including ones that admit the eschatological element, are one-sided. What is more, to my knowledge this parable has not been examined before from precisely the exegetical and contextual perspective I am proposing. Such a perspective can, I believe, shed valuable light on this parable of Jesus.

CHAPTER ONE

PUTTING THINGS IN PERSPECTIVE
A History of Recent Interpretation
of the Parable of the Unjust Steward

Given the central role context is to play in this study of the parable of the unjust steward, an appropriate place to begin is to set the study itself in context. To do so is the goal in the present chapter, and the means is a history of the recent interpretation of the parable. In the course of this chapter I will call attention to the difficulty of the parable itself, highlight the key interpretive issues involved, and point out suggestive ideas or approaches that in turn will be woven into the fabric of my own argument in subsequent chapters.[1] In this way it is hoped the reader will gain perspective on the entire study.

In attempting to offer a history of interpretation of any sort one is immediately faced with procedural questions. What chronological or historical parameters should be used? Then, how should the relevant studies within the chosen parameters be categorized? With respect to the first question, this chapter is limited to interpretations of our parable offered in the nineteenth and twentieth centuries. Since this investigation is not simply a history of interpretation, limits had to be drawn somewhere, from a purely practical standpoint alone. What is more, "the literature dealing with the parable of the unjust steward is staggering,"[2] and almost defies comprehensive systematization, whatever the parameters. Interpretations of the present century are included because a great deal has been written on our parable during this period which has not been surveyed elsewhere. To include only the twentieth century, however, seemed too narrow a limit, so the scope was extended to include the nineteenth century as well. After surveying the pertinent literature from both centuries, it became apparent that these historical parameters would be adequate for my purposes. The interpretations of the parable prior to the nineteenth century had already been handled by M. J. C. Schreiter's

---

[1] An abridgement of this chapter, along with a summary of the major conclusions of my study, can be found in *WTJ* 51 (1989) 293-318.

[2] L. J. Topel, "On the Injustice of the Unjust Steward: Luke 16:1-13," *CBQ* 37 (1975) 216.

history of interpretation published in 1803,[3] there is more than enough material available from the nineteenth and twentieth centuries, and these parameters have the added practical advantage of increasing the accessibility of the material.

Once the chronological or historical limits of this chapter were determined, the second major procedural question—that of categorization—had to be answered. If the question of parameters of the study is difficult, that of categorization of relevant material proves even more so. As even a quick glance at the literature reveals, the sheer volume of interpretations of the parable of the unjust steward even in the nineteenth and twentieth centuries is overwhelming. To illustrate, W. S. Kissinger, in the bibliographic section of his helpful book on the parables, lists 107 periodical articles alone on this parable which fall within our chronological parameters.[4] This statistic should indicate the difficulty of the task of categorization. One interpreter speaks of "the jungle of explanations of our parable [des Urwaldes der Erklärungen unserer Parabel],"[5] while another laments what he describes as "a wilderness of contradictory explanations and opinions."[6] When one adds to this state of affairs the almost limitless number of combinations of possible interpretations, the difficulty of systematic categorization is heightened even further. Many interpretations could justifiably be put in more than one category, and the danger of oversimplification looms large. How should one proceed?

To opt for a purely chronological approach, though convenient, appeared more confusing than helpful in attempting to convey the various major ways the parable of the unjust steward has been interpreted. To simply borrow A. Rücker's three categories—"Allegorical Interpretations Mostly of a Contemporary Kind," "Partial Elimination of Allegory Bound with Moralistic Interpretation," and "Newer Refusals of Allegory and Their Critique"—,[7] while again convenient, did not seem appropriate either. Among other things, Rücker's categories rest on the difficult and much-debated issue of just what constitutes allegory. To

---

[3] *Historico-critica explicationum Parabolae de improbo oeconomo descriptio, qua varias variorus interpretum super Lucae 16,1-13 expositiones digestas, examinatas, suamque ex Apocryphis Veteris Testamenti potissimum haustam exhibuit*, Lipsiae, 1803. Schreiter's work is cited by, among others, Rücker, "Gleichnis," 3-5, and M. Krämer, *Das Rätsel der Parabel vom ungerechten Verwalter, Lk 16:1-13* (Zurich: PAS-Verlag, 1972) passim.

[4] W. S. Kissinger, *The Parables of Jesus. A History of Interpretation and Bibliography* (ATLA Bibliography Series, No. 4; Metuchen, NJ: Scarecrow Press and The American Theological Library Association, 1979) 398-408.

[5] Krämer, *Rätsel*, 27.

[6] Stoll, "Problem," 18.

[7] Rücker, "Gleichnis," 6-26, 27-52, and 53-64, respectively.

use his categories would, therefore, have necessitated justifying why one interpretation was categorized as allegorical and another was not. Such a procedure would have taken me far beyond the scope and purpose of the present chapter. Rather than pursue either of these two approaches, I have chosen instead to organize the present chapter on the basis of how the steward's actions toward the debtors (Luke 16:5-7) are interpreted and what lesson Jesus draws from those actions. This approach is justified in view of the fact that the crux of this difficult parable is Jesus' apparent commendation (or condemnation) of criminal or immoral behavior on the part of the steward for imitation (or avoidance), in some way, by his disciples. What is the nature of the steward's actions, and in what sense are those actions to be imitated or avoided by Christians— i.e., what is being commended or condemned? This chapter is organized according to the answers given to these questions.

Two major headings will be used, with a number of subheadings under each. The interpreters under the first major heading all view the steward's actions toward the debtors as fraudulent or dishonest. A rather wide variety of conclusions about the lesson of the parable are drawn from that behavior. The first heading is divided into three subheadings: traditional (or monetary) interpretation, non-monetary interpretations, and negative example interpretation. Further subdivisions are made on the basis of different emphases.

The second major heading differs from the first in a fundamental way. Rather than viewing the actions of the steward as fraudulent, the interpreters under this heading understand the actions in question as directly commendable and exemplary, as basically honest, even righteous. A number of interpreters offer general ethical or moral interpretations of the steward's actions; many others stress the socioeconomic background of the parable. Each of these two emphases constitutes a different subheading. Additional nuances will be noted at appropriate points in the discussion.

I. Steward's Actions Fraudulent or Dishonest

A. Traditional (or Monetary) Interpretation

The most common (hence "traditional") interpretation of the parable of the unjust steward is probably that which regards the steward's actions toward the debtors as fraudulent or dishonest, but nevertheless draws a positive lesson from those actions. Very often that lesson relates to

Christian prudence or wisdom in the use of material possessions for spiritual goals and benefits.[8] The emphasis on the use of possessions (hence "monetary") distinguishes this interpretation from others to be considered in Part I.[9] So numerous are the interpreters who fall under this category and so nuanced are many of their interpretations that one must be content in a chapter such as the present with sketching the general and more widely held lines of argument. From time to time throughout this chapter, however, attention will be drawn to interpretive nuances which seem to be either especially suggestive or novel.

In order to avoid the difficulty of the praise in Luke 16:8a (*"ho kyrios* [the master? Jesus?] praised the unjust steward"), interpreters who explain the parable along the lines just outlined draw a distinction between different aspects of the steward's actions towards the debtors. The actions themselves are fraudulent, but the underlying wisdom, prudence, and foresight they display are praised and worthy of Christian emulation. A number of interpreters have emphasized this distinction. R. C. Trench, for example, contends that in telling the parable and praising the steward Jesus "disengages" the steward's "dishonesty from his foresight."[10] Jesus' purpose in doing so, Trench explains, is to provoke

---

[8] Of the 140 or so interpreters of the parable whom I surveyed, at least 50 understand it in this way. Included among them are the following, listed alphabetically: W. F. Arndt (*The Gospel according to St. Luke* [St. Louis: Concordia, 1956]); P. Bigo ("La richesse, comme intendence, dans l'Evangile, A propos de Luc 16:1-9," *NRT* 87 [1965] 265-71); B. S. Easton (*The Gospel according to St. Luke* [Edinburgh: T. & T. Clark, 1926]); L. W. Friedel ("The Parable of the Unjust Steward, Luke 16:1-13," *CBQ* 3 [1941] 337-48); N. Geldenhuys (*Commentary on the Gospel of Luke* [NICNT; Grand Rapids: Eerdmans, 1951]); F. Godet (*A Commentary on the Gospel of St. Luke* [5th ed.; 2 vols.; Edinburgh: T. & T. Clark, 1976]); W. Grundmann (*Das Evangelium nach Lukas* [THKNT, vol. 3; 2d rev. ed.; Berlin: Evangelische Verlagsanstalt, 1969]); B. A. Hooley and A. J. Mason ("Some Thoughts on the Parable of the Unjust Steward [Luke 16:1-9]," *AusBR* 6 [1958] 47-59); Krämer (*Rätsel*); M.-J. Lagrange (*Evangile selon Saint Luc* [7th ed.; Paris: Gabalda, 1948]); T. W. Manson (*The Sayings of Jesus* [London: SCM, 1949]); P.-H. Menoud ("Riches injustes et biens véritables," *RTP*, n.s., 31 [1943] 5-17); J. Pirot (*Paraboles et allégories évangéliques* [Paris: Lethielleux, 1949]); A. Plummer (*The Gospel according to S. Luke* [ICC; 5th ed.; Edinburgh: T. & T. Clark, 1922]); L. Ragg (*St. Luke* [Westminster Commentaries; London: Methuen, 1922]); K. H. Rengstorf (*Das Evangelium nach Lukas* [NTD, vol. 3; 6th ed.; Göttingen: Vandenhoeck & Ruprecht, 1952]); A. Schlatter (*Das Evangelium des Lukas* [2d ed.; Stuttgart: Calwer, 1960]); D. P. Seccombe (*Possessions and the Poor in Luke-Acts* [SUNT, ser. B, vol. 6; Linz, Austria: A. Fuchs, 1983]); C. H. Talbert (*Reading Luke. A Literary and Theological Commentary on the Third Gospel* [New York: Crossroad, 1982]); J. Wellhausen (*Das Evangelium Lucae* [Berlin: Reimer, 1904]); F. E. Williams ("Is Almsgiving the Point of the 'Unjust Steward'?" *JBL* 83 [1964] 293-97); and T. Zahn (*Das Evangelium des Lucas* [Leipzig: A. Deichert, 1913]).

[9] The term "monetary" is used for convenience' sake only and should not be construed as limiting the application of the parable to money alone. Material possessions in a broad sense are included.

[10] R. C. Trench, *Notes on the Parables of our Lord* (14th ed., rev.; London: Macmillan, 1882) 442.

his people "to a like prudence; . . . a holy prudence, and a prudence employed about things of far higher and more lasting importance."[11] Much the same point is made by F. Godet. Jesus did not scruple, Godet says, to use the example of the wicked for the purpose of stimulating his disciples. He continues.

> And in fact, in the midst of conduct morally blamable, the wicked often display remarkable qualities of activity, prudence, and perseverance, which may serve to humble and encourage believers. The parable of the unjust steward is the masterpiece of this sort of teaching.[12]

C. H. Pickar argues in similar fashion that the steward's prudence is praised, not his iniquity—"however bad, he provided for the future."[13] He concludes Christ holds up this prudence in providing for the future for imitation by his disciples.[14]

The distinction in view here is perhaps expressed most clearly by T. W. Manson. Entitling the parable (vv. 1-9) "The Clever Rascal," Manson contends that the difficulty which arises if Jesus (if he is *ho kyrios* of v. 8) praised the steward is "largely imaginary."[15] "Praise" of the steward's actions does not constitute moral approval of his plan by either his master or Jesus. Ethical judgment is passed on his plan in the epithet by which he is described in v. 8: "the dishonest/unjust steward [*ho oikonomos tēs adikias*]." It is the steward's astuteness that is praised, argues Manson. There is all the difference in the world, he suggests, between "I applaud the dishonest steward because he acted cleverly" and "I applaud the clever steward because he acted dishonestly." In this parable, according to Manson, the former is done, not the latter. "Whether it is the employer or Jesus that speaks [in v. 8], we must take the purport of the speech to be: 'This is a fraud; but it is a most ingenious fraud. The steward is a rascal; but he is a wonderfully clever rascal.'"[16] The point of the parable, continues Manson in a fashion very representative of the traditional interpretation, is found in v. 9 where Jesus counsels his followers to "use worldly wealth to gain friends" for themselves.

> If a bad man will take infinite trouble to get friends for his own selfish interests, the good man will surely take some trouble to make friends in a better way and for better ends. The point of this saying [v. 9] is rather that by disposing of worldly wealth in the proper way, one will have treasure in heaven.[17]

---

[11] *Parables*, 442.

[12] Godet, *Luke* 2.160-61.

[13] C. H. Pickar, "The Unjust Steward (Lk. 16:1-9)," *CBQ* 1 (1939) 251.

[14] "Steward," 252.

[15] Manson, *Sayings*, 290.

[16] *Sayings*, 292.

[17] *Sayings*, 292-93.

Like other synoptic parables, the parable of the unjust steward teaches by analogy,[18] or more specifically by an *a fortiori* argument.[19] J. M. Creed groups our parable with those of the so-called importunate friend (Luke 11:5-8) and the unjust judge (18:1-8) as parables which teach spiritual truth by analogy to reprehensible conduct.[20] He describes our parable as "a story from ordinary life in the world" which has "a counterpart in the spiritual world." "The emphasis falls," Creed continues, "upon the steward's 'prudence', and an analogous 'prudence' in another sphere is enjoined upon the disciples."[21] Taken with the subsequent sayings (vv. 9-13), the parable seems to be intended to commend prudence of a specific kind, that is, prudence in the use of wealth.[22] As the dishonest steward displayed prudence in earthly, temporal things for his own earthly future, so the disciples of Christ are to demonstrate an analogous prudence with earthly things for spiritual, eternal goals. Or, to put it in terms of an *a fortiori* argument, if the dishonest, fraudulent steward was prudent in his evil and temporal sphere of existence, how much more should Christians be prudent in their righteous and eternal sphere. As the steward used the time, opportunities, and resources still at his disposal before losing his position as steward, so Christians are to do likewise for spiritual purposes while they are still able to do so. Inherent in the analogy are differences and contrasts between the steward and Jesus' disciples. As R. Stoll expresses it, "The only similarity between them is in the matter of prudence and foresight, and even this is of a different nature and in a different order."[23]

If, on the basis of a distinction between different aspects of the steward's actions, the point of the parable is that Christians are to use their possessions and money with eternity in view,[24] how, more specifically, are they to do so, according to this parable? A. B. Bruce's suggestion that "the chief lesson" of the parable is "the duty of beneficence" summarizes well the answer many interpreters give to this question.[25] The prudent use of possessions commended in our parable is

---

[18] E.g., R. R. Caemmerer ("Investment for Eternity. A Study of Luke 16:1-13," *CTM* 34 [1963] 69-76), J. M. Creed (*The Gospel according to St. Luke* [London: Macmillan, 1930]), Krämer, and Trench.

[19] E.g., Grundmann, G. Krüger ("Die geistesgeschichtlichen Grundlegen des Gleichnisses vom ungerechten Verwalter," *BZ* 21 [1933] 170-81), Plummer, Pickar, and F. E. Williams.

[20] Creed, *Luke*, lxix.

[21] *Luke*, 201.

[22] *Luke*, 201.

[23] Stoll, "Problem," 26.

[24] Easton, *Luke*, 245.

[25] A. B. Bruce, *The Parabolic Teaching of Christ* (London: Hodder and Stoughton, 1882) 359.

to take the form of charity to the poor, in general, or almsgiving, in particular.[26] Fellow Christians may be especially in view as the intended recipients of this charity.[27] While this interpretation is shared by both Protestants and Catholics, the two groups of interpreters part company when it comes to the value or efficacy of such acts of charity. Luke 16:9, which is the center of controversy, reads as follows: "I tell you, use worldly wealth to gain friends for yourselves, so that when it is gone, you will be welcomed into eternal dwellings."[28] Many Catholic interpreters view the charity or almsgiving of this verse as in some way meritorious in itself and as being directly instrumental in the benefactor's eternal salvation. Pickar is representative when he says, "Alms given to the poor will be a means of attaining heaven."[29] Protestants have, not surprisingly, resisted such an interpretation. To do so several different tacks have been taken. The plural "friends" in v. 9 is, for example, interpreted as a reverential circumlocution for God himself,[30] in which case the beneficiaries of charity are not in view at all. Or, as others argue, if the beneficiaries are in view, their role is only that of welcoming their benefactors into heaven and/or of bearing witness to the genuineness of their benefactors' faith demonstrated and expressed in charity.[31] The details of these arguments on both sides will be discussed more fully in the next chapter. Suffice it to note at this point that very different theological conclusions are drawn from the same basic interpretation of

---

[26] E.g., Arndt (*Luke*, 357), Bigo ("Richesse," 268), Bruce (*Teaching*, 359), Godet (*Luke* 2.163-66), R. H. Hiers ("Friends By Unrighteous Mammon: The Eschatological Proletariat [Luke 16:9]," *JAAR* 38 [1970] 33-36), T. Hoyt, Jr. ("The Poor in Luke-Acts" [Ph.D. dissertation, Duke University, 1974] 160-61), T. G. Jalland ("A Note on Luke 16, 1-9," in *SE* I, ed. K. Aland et al. [Berlin: Akademie, 1959] 503-5), Johnson (*Function*, 157), D. F. Köster ("Analekten zur Auslegung der Parabel vom ungerechten Haushalter, Luk. 16:1ff.," *TSK* 38 [1865] 731), Krämer (in the second tradition-historical stage anyway; *Rätsel*, 134, 234), Lagrange (*Luc*, 434), F. J. Moore ("The Parable of the Unjust Steward," *ATR* 47 [1965] 103-5), P. Samain ("Le bon usage des richesses, en Luc XVI,1-12," *Revue Diocesaine de Tournai* 2/4 [1947] 334), Stoll ("Problem," 26), B. Weiss (*Die Evangelien des Markus und Lukas* [MeyerK; 8th ed.; Göttingen: Vandenhoeck & Ruprecht, 1892] 534), F. E. Williams ("Almsgiving," 293-97), and F. J. Williams ("The Parable of the Unjust Steward [Luke xvi.1-9]. Notes on the Interpretation Suggested by the Reverend R. G. Lunt," *ExpTim* 66 [1954-55] 371-72).

[27] This point is suggested by, e.g., Godet (*Luke* 2.165-66), J. C. K. von Hofmann (*Die Heilige Schrift*, vol. 8/1: *Das Evangelium des Lukas* [Nördlingen: Beck, 1878] 398, 400), Krämer (*Rätsel*, 234), and Zahn (*Lucas*, 576).

[28] *NIV*. Unless otherwise indicated, all biblical quotations are taken from the *NIV*.

[29] Pickar, "Steward," 252.

[30] E.g., Creed, *Luke*, 205; Grundmann, *Lukas*, 321; Manson, *Sayings*, 293; and Menoud, "Riches," 13.

[31] E.g., Arndt, *Luke*, 357; Caemmerer, "Investment," 71; Geldenhuys, *Luke*, 416; and Zahn, *Lucas*, 577. Caemmerer makes special note of Luther's interpretation of v. 9 that when we help the poor we demonstrate our faith and bear witness that we are heirs of eternal life. Cf. also O. Hof, "Luthers Auslegung von Lukas 16:9," *EvT* 8 (1948-49) 151-66.

the parable. This fact highlights, among other things, one of the interpretive issues at stake in the parable, i.e., the meaning of v. 9. It also illustrates the difficulty of categorizing interpretations.

According to the traditional interpretation of our parable a dishonest steward's wise or prudent response to the crisis of his impending dismissal is the basis for teaching on Christian stewardship of material possessions, especially for the benefit of the poor. Many interpreters associate, at least implicitly, the analogous crisis in the lives of Christians (and people in general) with the brevity and uncertainty of life. At best one only has a very brief time during which to use and dispose of one's possessions.[32] What is more, man is only a steward of goods entrusted to him by God and is not an owner anyway. The crisis in the face of which Christians are to respond with wisdom and prudence is that of their ever-impending death.[33] There are a number of interpreters, however, who relate this analogous crisis not so much to the brevity of life or to the imminence of death, but rather to the eschatological crisis occasioned by the coming (actual and/or imminent) of the kingdom of God in the person and ministry of Jesus. T. Hoyt, Jr., and D. P. Seccombe merit special mention for the suggestive ways they relate eschatology to stewardship of material possessions. Hoyt argues that by means of this parable people faced with the crisis of the kingdom are called upon to renounce earthly wealth for the sake of the poor.[34] Seccombe makes the relationship of eschatology and stewardship (or ethics) even more explicit. Describing Luke 16:1-13 as "a fundamental evaluation of possessions in light of the kingdom," he summarizes the meaning of the parable as "using possessions to actualize the values of the Kingdom in the present age by acts of humanitarian goodness."[35] Here the ideas of eschatology, possessions, and charity are combined in a way surpris-

---

[32] C. F. Nösgen (*Die Evangelien nach Matthäus, Markus und Lukas* [Nordlingen: Beck, 1886] 368) is more explicit than most on this point when he speaks of life being as uncertain as the steward's position. E. Riggenbach ("Zur Exegese und Textkritik zweier Gleichnisse Jesu," in *Aus Schrift und Geschichte* [Stuttgart: Calwer, 1922] 24) speaks of the disciples being in a situation similar to that of the steward of the parable. Earthly goods are at their disposal for only a short time—i.e., during their earthly lives— after which an accounting must be given.

[33] S. Goebel, "Die Gleichnisgruppe Luk. 15 u. 16, methodisch ausgelegt," *TSK* 48 (1875) 665, 669-70. Goebel's discussion of our parable on pp. 656-76 of this journal article is repeated in his commentary, *The Parables of Jesus: A Methodical Exposition* (Edinburgh: T. & T. Clark, 1883) 215-31.

[34] Hoyt, "Poor," 161.

[35] Seccombe, *Possessions*, 172. Others who emphasize eschatological crisis as the background of our parable include Hiers ("Friends," 32, 36) and Krämer (*Rätsel*, 67-68, 238).

ingly few other interpreters have done. In subsequent chapters I will contend that the eschatological background is important for a proper understanding of our parable.

Before leaving the traditional interpretation of the parable of the unjust steward, a few comments are in order about what might be called a contemporary-historical emphasis which some have given to the parable. It should be stressed that the scholars mentioned here interpret the parable along essentially the same lines as others who take the traditional approach. They have been singled out for attention here because of the way they relate (but do not limit) the teaching of the parable to Jesus' first-century audience and situation.

Several writers stress that our parable was intended especially for one or both of the two groups Luke reports as being in Jesus' company when the parable was first given: the publicans and "sinners" and/or the Pharisees and teachers of the law (15:1-2). Godet, A. Plummer, and B. S. Easton, for example, all emphasize the anti-Pharisaic character of both Luke 15 and 16, including our parable. Godet suggests that 16:1-13 keeps up "the contrast between the life of faith and pharisaic righteousness" begun in the previous chapter, especially in the parable of the lost son (15:11-32). He amplifies his suggestion by saying that in chapters 15 and 16 Jesus is challenging the "two chief sins of the Pharisees," pride and avarice. Godet believes the former sin is dealt with in the person of the elder son in the parable which concludes chapter 15, while the latter is handled in our parable.[36] The same basic approach to the parable is taken by Plummer. The two parables of chapter 16, he says, "like the previous three [in chapter 15] are directed against special faults [of the Pharisees and teachers of the law]. The former three combated their hard exclusiveness, self-righteousness, and contempt for others. These two [the unjust steward and the rich man and Lazarus] combat their self-indulgence."[37] Plummer is followed in his interpretation, though somewhat tentatively, by Easton who concludes that Plummer's suggestion is probably "the best explanation, even though vv. 1-8 are not designedly anti-Pharisaic."[38]

While Godet, Plummer, Easton, and others call attention to what they perceive to be the anti-Pharisaic pointedness of our parable, other interpreters relate the parable in a special way to the publicans and

---

[36] Godet, *Luke* 2.160. Cf. Luke 16:14 and also Matt 6:18-19 where Jesus passes from one of these "chief sins" to the other.

[37] Plummer, *Luke*, 380.

[38] Easton, *Luke*, 241.

"sinners" of 15:1. Both groups are included among the "disciples" to whom Luke reports the parable of the unjust steward was told (16:1). M. Dods and E. R. Stier, for instance, both argue that our parable in effect instructs converted or nearly converted publicans about their new duties as disciples. In Dods's view, the entire chapter teaches the publicans and rich among the disciples how their previously ill-gotten gains are now to be used.[39] Along the same lines, Stier says the parable is addressed to new disciples, especially publicans, telling them that the grace of God requires use of worldly goods for brotherly kindness.[40] This understanding of Luke 16:1-13 is conveyed in the title under which Stier discusses the pericope: "The Converted Sinner's Prudence in escaping from Punishment which yet threatens even him;—the unjust steward, true fidelity in the use of worldly goods."[41]

B. Non-monetary Interpretations

While many interpreters relate the message of our parable to the use of material possessions, a number of others disregard or deny the "monetary" note altogether. Sometimes an eschatological emphasis is present in such interpretations, sometimes it is not.

1. Eschatological Non-monetary Interpretation

As in the case of the traditional interpretation, a number of interpreters stress the eschatological background and teaching of our parable. This emphasis is particularly true of Luke 16:1-7 or 1-8, depending on where the parable proper ends and Jesus' application and/or subsequent redactors'

---

[39] M. Dods, *The Parables of our Lord* (Philadelphia: Westminster, 1904) 362-63.

[40] E. R. Stier, *The Words of the Lord Jesus* (8 vols.; Edinburgh: T. & T. Clark, 1880) 4.106.

[41] *Words* 4.163. Goebel makes much the same point as Dods and Stier. He insists that when our parable is taken with Luke 15, particularly with the parable of the lost son, it is a reminder to publicans and sinners who are now disciples that the seriousness of their repentance must be demonstrated through the use of their riches in God's service ("Gleichnisgruppe," 675-76). Since H. A. W. Meyer also relates the parable to the publicans, his rather novel interpretive twist can be mentioned here. Meyer (*Critical and Exegetical Commentary on the New Testament* [11 vols.; Edinburgh: T. & T. Clark, 1880]) suggests that the rich man of the parable represents mammon and the steward the disciples, especially those who were publicans before they followed Jesus. Before they became disciples they were servants of mammon. Meyer interprets the steward's actions in terms of v. 13 ("No servant can serve two masters"), which he takes as the key to the parable. Just as the steward of the parable was unfaithful to his master by his "knavish trick" (2.215) with respect to the debtors, so the disciples are to be prudent and "unfaithful" in breaking with their old master, mammon, in order to serve God (2.213, 226-27).

interpretations begin. Unlike the traditional interpretation, however, the eschatological message is not related to the use of possessions or money per se. Instead the parable is viewed in somewhat more general terms as a call for resolute action in the face of the eschatological crisis caused by the coming (present, imminent, and/or future) of the kingdom of God in the person and ministry of Jesus. This resolute action is usually explained as a positive response to Jesus. It is interesting and significant to note that whereas most interpreters who take the traditional approach connect vv. 1-13 and even in many cases argue for their essential unity, those who interpret our parable in non-monetary terms do so by separating vv. 1-7 or 1-8 from vv. 9-13. As will be pointed out later in this chapter, not a few of the latter interpreters concede that as the text now stands (vv. 1-13) the parable is about the right use of money or possessions. Such was not, however, the original meaning of the parable itself, these interpreters argue. Tradition or the early church has added vv. 8/9-13 to the parable in an effort to explain it, and in the process has either reinterpreted it altogether or at least seriously shifted its emphasis. I will say more on this matter later.

The eschatological non-monetary interpretation has some very prominent advocates. Among them are A. Loisy, M. Dibelius, C. H. Dodd, W. Michaelis, A. M. Hunter, J. D. Crossan, K. E. Bailey, and probably (though not certainly) D. O. Via, Jr. Loisy argues that the general meaning of the parable (which he limits to vv. 1-7) is the use of the present to prepare for the future, to assure oneself a part and place in the kingdom. In his view vv. 8-13 are attempts by the evangelist and perhaps subsequent redactors to make the application more specific by alluding to the charitable use of terrestrial goods in view of the kingdom of God. If the pericope were authentic (which it is not, according to Loisy) Jesus would not have limited kindness to alms, as he believes v. 9 does. Loisy concludes that as they now stand vv. 1-13 are "a rather feeble invention, and one must be content to see there a not very successful transposition of the parable of the unmerciful servant in Matthew [18:23-35]."[42]

Dibelius sees the steward as one who makes his future secure by one last deceit. His action is an example of decision, which when translated into eschatological terms offers doctrine and warning to the church of the disciples faced by "the great change." According to Dibelius, the parable itself contains "no exhortation for common life" (i.e., it has nothing to

---

[42] A. Loisy, Les Evangiles Synoptiques (2 vols.; Ceffonds: Pres Montier-en-der, 1908) 2.161. Loisy's approach is endorsed by M. Hermaniuk, La Parabole Evangelique (Paris: Desclee, de Brouwer, 1947) 248-49.

do with alms, etc.), but just such an exhortation now forms the conclusion in v. 9.[43] This conclusion, presumably added by tradition, emphasizes, strengthens, and transforms Jesus' words.[44]

The interpretation of Dodd deserves special mention here, if only
because of the watershed nature of his book on the parables. Dodd
believes vv. 1-7 constitute the parable and vv. 8-13 "a whole series of
'morals'" appended by the evangelist. He says, in words frequently
quoted and endorsed by others, "We can almost see here [in vv. 8b, 9,
and 11, which he has just quoted] notes for three separate sermons on the
parable as text."[45] Dodd goes on to suggest that v. 8a ("And *ho kyrios*
[which Dodd thinks is Jesus, not the master of the parable] praised the
steward") was added by the reporter of the parable, and was probably the
application of the parable in the earliest form of tradition. When taken
with this application, the point of the parable is to urge Jesus' hearers "to
think strenuously and act boldly" to meet their own momentous crisis
much as the unscrupulous steward had done to meet his.[46] As is intimated
in the title of Dodd's book itself, and as is made clear throughout the
book (and especially in the chapter on "The Kingdom of God" [pp. 21-
59]), this crisis is precipitated by the inbreaking of the long-expected
kingdom of God in the ministry of Jesus himself. It is in the context of
"realized eschatology,"[47] then, that Dodd interprets our parable.

The kingdom of God and realized eschatology also figure prominently in Hunter's interpretation of the parables, in general, and of our
parable, in particular. Hunter praises the work of both Dodd and J.
Jeremias (the latter of whom will be mentioned shortly) for putting "the
parables back into their true setting, which is the ministry of Jesus seen
as the great eschatological act of God in which God visited and redeemed
his people."[48] This background of realized eschatology, he believes,
forms "the true backcloth against which the parables of Jesus become
pregnant with point and meaning."[49] In another place in his writings on
the parables Hunter even goes so far as to contend that the theme of all
Jesus' parables is "the urgent issues of the Kingdom of God."[50] What is

---

[43] M. Dibelius, *From Tradition to Gospel* (London: James Clarke, 1971) 248.

[44] *Tradition*, 247.

[45] C. H. Dodd, *The Parables of the Kingdom* (rev. ed.; New York: Scribner's, 1961) 17.

[46] *Parables*, 17.

[47] *Parables*, 35.

[48] A. M. Hunter, "The New Look at the Parables," in *From Faith to Faith* (ed. D. Y. Hadidian; Pittsburgh: Pickwick, 1979) 193.

[49] "New Look," 193.

[50] "Interpreting the Parables. I. The Interpreter and the Parables. The Centrality of the Kingdom," *Int* 14 (1960) 73.

"the urgent issue" with which our parable deals? Hunter's answer is that it is among those parables which deal with the kind of men required for the kingdom, or, to put it in other terms, the qualities required of disciples.[51] The particular quality enjoined in our parable (vv. 1-8) is "practical prudence." In speaking of v. 8 ("And *ho kyrios* praised"), Hunter concludes that in these words of commendation Jesus "is saying in effect: 'Give me men who will show as much practical sense in God's business as worldlings do in theirs.'"[52] He also suggests in another context that in attempting to get back to the original meaning of the parables it is usually wise to ignore what he calls "generalizing conclusions." These conclusions, he believes, sometimes miss the real points of the parables to which they have been attached. Such is the case in Luke 16:10-13.[53]

If some interpreters, such as Dodd and Hunter, have emphasized (almost exclusively) the realized, present aspect of eschatology in their interpretations of our parable, others have focused on the future aspect instead. W. Michaelis is one such interpreter. Having concluded that the parable ends with v. 7 and that v. 8a is Jesus' own comment on the steward's actions, Michaelis emphasizes that the steward is praised not for his injustice but for his wisdom in understanding the seriousness of his situation, finding the only possible way out, and proceeding resolutely along that way.[54] He goes on to note that to be properly understood the parable must be transferred to the disciples' situation. In their situation they ought to show the same wisdom. "The disciples ought to clearly understand their position in view of the Last Day, and then with the same wisdom, the same consistency and resoluteness, ought to look after the securing of their future."[55] The mention of "the Last Day" puts the emphasis in Michaelis's interpretation upon the future aspect of eschatology. It should be noted that Michaelis also sees very little contact between vv. 1-8a and vv. 8b-13. Vv. 9-13, he suggests, may have been put together by Luke from various words of Jesus with the catchword "mammon." His purpose in doing so was to give Christians of his time instruction about how to behave with possessions and riches.[56]

---

[51] "Interpreting the Parables. III. The Gospel in Parables. The Men and the Crisis of the Kingdom," *Int* 14 (1960) 315-16.

[52] "Crisis," 317.

[53] *Interpreting the Parables* (Philadelphia: Westminster, 1960) 119.

[54] W. Michaelis, *Die Gleichnisse Jesu. Eine Einführung* (Hamburg: Furche, 1956) 227-28.

[55] *Gleichnisse*, 228.

[56] *Gleichnisse*, 228-29.

K. E. Bailey, J. D. Crossan, and D. O. Via, Jr., can also be mentioned here because of the distinctive twist they give to the position under discussion. Though different, these three scholars are related in that they emphasize a literary approach to our parable. Bailey argues that on literary grounds a clear separation can and should be made between vv. 1-8 and vv. 9-13. Vv. 1-8 make up the parable, which is an eschatological warning to sinners;[57] vv. 9-13 are a poem on the theme of mammon and God which has integrity of its own and which "should be read and interpreted apart from the parable that precedes it."[58] "When the two passages [vv. 1-8 and 9-13] are read as a single subject, both are put out of focus."[59] The subject of vv. 9-13, according to Bailey, is mammon, that of vv. 1-8 is eschatology. The lesson Bailey draws from the parable (vv. 1-8) is built on an interesting interpretation of the steward's plan and actions toward the debtors. Bailey argues that from the start the steward's plan with respect to the debtors was "to risk everything on the quality of mercy he has already experienced from his master." Rather than being tried and jailed by his master, the steward is instead simply dismissed, without even being scolded. Bailey takes this action as evidence of unusual mercy on the master's part which would not have been missed by the thoughtful listener/reader of the parable.[60] It was just this aspect of his master's nature that the steward counted on in executing his plan. "Because the master was indeed generous and merciful, he chose to pay the full price for his steward's salvation."[61] Bailey is not clear as to exactly how the master does so or where this point comes out in the parable. It may well be that he gets the point from the master's praise in v. 8. At any rate, the message for disciples is that "if this dishonest steward solved his problems by relying on the mercy of his master to solve his crisis, how much more will God help you in your crisis when you trust his mercy."[62] Bailey makes it clear that the disciples' crisis is that of the coming of the kingdom. Excuses will not avail. One's only option is to entrust everything to the mercy of God who will accept to pay the price for man's salvation.[63]

---

[57] K. E. Bailey, *Poet and Peasant and Through Peasant Eyes. A Literary-Cultural Approach to the Parables in Luke* (combined ed.; Grand Rapids: Eerdmans, 1983) 86.

[58] *Poet*, 110.

[59] *Poet*, 118.

[60] *Poet*, 98.

[61] *Poet*, 102.

[62] *Poet*, 105.

[63] *Poet*, 107. In similar fashion, M. Barth ("The Dishonest Steward and his Lord, Reflections on Luke 16:1-13," in *From Faith to Faith* [ed. D. Y. Hadidian; Pittsburgh: Pickwick, 1979] 65-73) argues that the real hero of the parable is not the steward, but the

J. D. Crossan also approaches our parable from a literary angle. He labels it a "servant parable," which in turn is a subdivision of the "parables of action." According to Crossan, the latter group of parables constitute the greatest number of extant parables and depict critical situations which demand resolute and firm action, prompt and energetic decision.[64] "The parables of action all challenge one to life and action in response to the Kingdom's advent."[65] The servant parables to which our parable belongs and which are a subdivision of the parables of action involve a master-servant relationship at a moment of critical reckoning.[66] Limiting the parable to vv. 1-7, Crossan describes it as "a carefully formed mini-drama" with three scenes. He makes it clear that he understands the steward's actions toward the debtors (vv. 5-7) negatively for he characterizes those actions as "further but calculated incompetence." "The cleverness of the steward," he suggests, "consisted not only in solving his problem but in solving it by means of the very reason (low profits) that had created it in the first place."[67] And what is the lesson in this parable for the listener/hearer? "Like a wise and prudent servant calculating what he must do in the critical reckoning to which his master summons him, one must be ready and willing to respond in life and action to the eschatological advent of God."[68] He then goes on to qualify this remark, somewhat enigmatically, by saying that the eschatological advent is that for which readiness is impossible because it shatters our wisdom and prudence.[69]

The interpretation of D. O. Via, Jr., can also be noted here, although his connection with the present subheading is perhaps tenuous. In common with Bailey and Crossan (and others), Via approaches the parables from a literary point of view. He also adds an existential perspective which makes categorizing his interpretation of our parable difficult. Literarily, Via classifies our parable as one of what he calls "the comic parables." More specifically, our parable belongs to the picaresque mode, defined by Via as "the story of a successful rogue who

---

master who was generous to his cheating steward. He is, then, a good and gracious lord, and the steward relied on this goodness as he carried out his plan. The wise person, Barth concludes, is one who puts everything on the good Lord and the riches of his grace. Paul's name for this action is justification by faith (p. 72).

[64] J. D. Crossan, *In Parables: The Challenge of the Historical Jesus* (New York: Harper and Row, 1973) 84.

[65] *Parables*, 119.

[66] *Parables*, 86.

[67] *Parables*, 111.

[68] *Parables*, 119-20.

[69] *Parables*, 120.

makes conventional society look foolish but without establishing any positive alternative."[70] Existentially, the parable says the present is a crisis because the future is threatening. The comic form in which the story is cast suggests man can overcome the danger by making appropriate response to the crisis. Via does admit that the crisis note points, albeit only "subsidiarily," to the same theme in Jesus' non-parabolic eschatological preaching (e.g., Mark 8:38; Luke 12:8-9; 17:22-30). Because of this admission I have included Via's interpretation at this juncture. He is quick to add, however (and hence my hesitancy), that because parables are autonomous aesthetic objects, one cannot simply isolate points of contact with non-parabolic teaching and ignore points of tension with such teaching. Via finds the latter in our parable as the character of the steward runs counter to Jesus' demand elsewhere for self-denial, purity, and love.[71] The tension thus created results in what Via terms "comic relief from dead seriousness, as the parable with a happy earthiness offers our tricky side a temporary fling." The more profound theological implication of this aesthetic effect may be, he suggests, that "our well-being does not rest ultimately on our dead seriousness."[72]

A few words are in order, before turning to the next category, about an approach which in effect bridges the eschatological non-monetary and the traditional (monetary) interpretations. Although many interpreters concede that Luke 16:1-13 ostensibly bears out the traditional interpretation outlined above, the situation is not that simple, they quickly add. The interpretation of the pericope is complicated, they contend, by the fact that the present text is really the product of tradition, the evangelist, or the early church. The point is that the collocation of the parable (the precise limits of which are variously defined) and the subsequent, editorial comments has at best shifted the emphasis of the parable and at worst misinterpreted it altogether. To understand the pericope properly, then, one must study it in terms of its constituent parts. Let me summarize the general lines of this argument in a bit more detail.

It perhaps bears noting here, before proceeding, that the differences between the traditional interpretation and this "bridging" one illustrate a key interpretive issue in our parable. That issue is where the parable ends and its application and/or explanation begins. The answer one gives to this question, discussed in more detail in the next chapter, affects

---

[70] D. O. Via, Jr., *The Parables: Their Literary and Existential Dimension* (Philadelphia: Fortress, 1967) 159.
[71] *Parables*, 161-62.
[72] *Parables*, 162.

significantly the conclusions one draws about the interpretation of the parable. Generally speaking, if the unity of vv. 1-13 (at least in subject matter, if not in actual fact) is maintained, the parable relates to the use of possessions or money. If, on the other hand, the unity is not maintained, this theme is seen as secondary or altogether extraneous, and the primary and original message of the parable must be deduced in other ways.

The interpretation of J. Jeremias is representative of this "bridging" approach. Jeremias understands vv. 1-7 to be the parable, with v. 8a being Jesus' application. He suggests that the parable and its application were originally addressed to the unconverted and served as a summons to resolute action in an eschatological crisis. This interpretation is essentially what I have called the eschatological non-monetary interpretation. With the addition of vv. 8b-13, however, the primitive church allegedly shifted the original emphasis of the parable from the eschatological to the hortatory, i.e., to the right use of money and a warning against unfaithfulness. At this point, the traditional interpretation enters the picture, and hence my description of this approach as "bridging." Much as Dodd before him, Jeremias would have us hear in vv. 8b-13 the voice of the primitive preacher drawing lessons from the parable. Unlike many others who believe a shift has taken place in our parable, Jeremias does not believe this shift has introduced a foreign element here. He reasons that the exhortation was implicit in the original form and the eschatological note has not been excised completely. The eschatological situation of the primitive church itself, after all, lent weight to the exhortations.[73] Jeremias does contend, however, that generalizing logia, such as vv. 10-13, were often added to parables as their conclusions. Though not necessarily unauthentic themselves, these logia more often than not obscured the original situation and blunted the conflict and sternness.[74] That very thing has happened, he believes, in the case of our parable.[75]

Before leaving Jeremias attention should be drawn to one further

---

[73] J. Jeremias, *The Parables of Jesus* (2d rev. ed.; New York: Scribner's, 1972) 46-48.

[74] *Parables*, 110, 112.

[75] Among others who espouse (with varying degrees of confidence in the present text) the same position that a shift from the eschatological to the hortatory has occurred, the following can be mentioned: D. Velte, "Das eschatologische Heute im Gleichnis vom ungerechten Haushalter," *Monatschrift für Pastoraltheologie* 27 (1931) 213-14; H. Zimmermann, "Das Gleichnis vom ungerechten Verwalter: Lk 16:1-9," *BibLeb* 2 (1961) 254-61; H.-J. Degenhardt, *Lukas—Evangelist der Armen* (Stuttgart: Katholisches Bibelwerk, 1965) 118-25; J. Dupont, *Les Beatitudes* (3 vols.; Paris: Gabalda, 1969-73) 3.118-22; W. E. Pilgrim, *Good News to the Poor. Wealth and Poverty in Luke-Acts* (Minneapolis: Augsburg, 1981) 125-29; and R. H. Stein, *An Introduction to the Parables of Jesus* (Philadelphia: Westminster, 1981) 106-11.

element of his interpretation, his observation about the element of
surprise in our parable. Jeremias suggests that in our parable Jesus was
apparently dealing with an actual case which had been indignantly
related to him.

> He deliberately took it as an example, knowing that it would secure redoubled
> attention, as far as his hearers did not know the incident. They would expect
> that Jesus would end the story with an expression of strong disapproval,
> instead of which, to their surprise, Jesus praises the criminal.[76]

Jeremias is not the first or the only one to have pointed out the element
of surprise in this parable.[77] Since he does give it some emphasis,
however, I have highlighted this element in connection with his interpretation. I will return to the element of surprise in the next chapter as an
important interpretive insight.

2. Non-eschatological Non-monetary Interpretations

a) General interpretation

A number of interpreters draw general lessons from our parable which
are unrelated to either the themes of possessions or eschatological crisis.
These interpreters agree that the parable calls for qualities displayed by
the unjust steward, although different names are used to describe those
qualities. Among the qualities frequently named are the following:
wisdom, foresight, consistency, decisiveness, resourcefulness, and prudence. According to A. Jülicher, for example, the parable (which he
limits to vv. 1-7) is not about the right use of riches (that comes in at v.
9). Instead the point of the parable is the resolute utilization of the present
as the prerequisite for a pleasant future.[78] Jülicher's general moral
interpretation, typical of all his interpretations of the parables, is endorsed by a number of other interpreters early in this century.[79]

---

[76] Jeremias, *Parables*, 182.

[77] Crossan, for example, says the parable moves away from "the expected normalcy"
(*Parables*, 104). Others who have noticed the element of surprise include G. Murray ("The
Unjust Steward," *ExpTim* 15 [1903-4] 307-10), G. A. Buttrick (*The Parables of Jesus* [New
York: Harper and Brothers, 1928]), D. R. Fletcher ("The Riddle of the Unjust Steward: Is
Irony the Key?" *JBL* 82 [1963] 15-30), and Stein (*Parables*).

[78] Jülicher, *Gleichnisreden* 2.511.

[79] E.g., R. Peters, "Der ungerechte Haushalter und die Gleichnisfrage," *Theologische
Zeitschrift aus der Schweiz* 17 (1900) 128-44; H. Weinel, *Die Gleichnisse Jesu* (Leipzig:
Teubner, 1905); and P. Fiebig, *Die Gleichnisreden Jesu im Lichte der rabbinischen
Gleichnisse des neutestamentlichen Zeitalters* (Tübingen: Mohr, 1912).

Somewhat more specifically, Rücker concludes that in our parable Jesus is recommending to his followers wisdom and decisiveness in caring for the future. They are to behave analogously in striving after heavenly goods.[80] Similarly, H. Firth speaks of "sanctified common sense" as the point of our parable, of the need for an astuteness in religion which corresponds to that found in business.[81] G. Murray describes the commended qualities as resolution and resource in religious matters,[82] while G. A. Buttrick uses the words foresight and resourceful zeal.[83]

W. O. E. Oesterley goes in a somewhat different direction when he argues that the keynote of the whole section, vv. 1-13, is consistency.[84] The steward was wicked from beginning to end, but at least he was consistent with his principles. Such consistency is, regrettably, more than can be said of many Christians. "Consistency is a virtue; being exercised in a wrong direction does not make it, *per se*, less a virtue."[85]

b) Contemporary-historical interpretation

A few interpreters who maintain a non-eschatological non-monetary interpretation of our parable add a contemporary-historical emphasis. Notable (and almost alone) here is R. G. Lunt. In his view the steward's actions are fraudulent but still convey a positive exhortation for Jesus' contemporaries. Lunt contends "that like the other parables of steward-ship and dismissal it is first to be understood in terms of the leadership of Israel in our Lord's day."[86] More specifically, he sees in the parable

---

[80] Rücker, "Gleichnis," 63. J. Schmid advocates much the same interpretation (*Das Evangelium nach Lukas*; RNT, vol. 3; 4th ed. [Regensburg: F. Pustet, 1960] 257-59). He contends the point of the parable (vv. 1-8) is wise provision for the future. Vv. 9-13 are added by Luke to apply the parable to the use of possessions.

[81] H. Firth, "The Unjust Steward," *ExpTim* 15 (1903-4) 426-27.

[82] Murray, "Steward," 307, 309.

[83] Buttrick, *Parables*, 118 and 120, respectively.

[84] W. O. E. Oesterley, "The Parable of the 'Unjust' Steward," *Expositor*, ser. 6, 7 (1903) 283.

[85] Oesterley, *The Gospel Parables in the Light of the Jewish Background* (New York: MacMillan, 1936) 199. Oesterley introduces the idea of money into his interpretation of our parable in his book on the parables. He still sees the primary purpose of vv. 1-13 as the inculcation of the need for consistency of life, but adds that its subsidiary teaching is about the danger of the love of money. The latter point is absent in his earlier article on the parable. On the basis of the argument of his book (even if money is only a subsidiary teaching), he might have been included under the traditional interpretation. Because of his overall emphasis on consistency, however, in both his article and book, I have chosen to include him here. This situation only illustrates the difficulty of and dangers inherent in any system of classifying interpretations.

[86] Lunt, "Expounding the Parables. III. The Parable of the Unjust Steward (Luke 16:1-15)," *ExpTim* 77 (1965-66) 135.

"a criticism of the high priests who have by their time-serving policy forfeited any title to spiritual leadership."[87] The debtors are taken to represent the publicans and sinners, and the reduction of debts "stands for" a relaxation of some of the ceremonial laws on which the Pharisees insisted.[88] By excluding vv. 9-13 as "the valiant but misleading glosses of an editor,"[89] Lunt draws the following conclusion about the parable: "It is not in fact then primarily about the right use of money nor about forcing one's way into the Kingdom, but it is about tolerance and charity and the things that are eternal." The parable asks for "a more liberal and considerate attitude" on the part of those who are stewards—i.e., in contemporary-historical terms, the religious leaders.[90]

C. Negative Example Interpretation

Thus far I have considered interpretations which draw positive lessons from negative evaluations of the steward's actions. As has been seen, the exact nature of the lessons varies considerably, but the interpreters are agreed that the actions themselves are fraudulent and dishonest. The actions themselves are not to be imitated by Jesus' disciples, but some quality revealed in the actions is (e.g., prudence). A fairly large number of interpreters, however, take quite a different approach to the parable. Instead of drawing a positive lesson from negative behavior, these individuals draw a *negative* lesson from negative behavior. The steward's actions must, therefore, be regarded as a warning, a negative example, for Christian disciples; those actions are an example of what disciples are *not* to do or be.

---

[87] "Interpretation," 335.

[88] "Interpretation," 336.

[89] "Parable," 136.

[90] "Interpretation," 336. As will be seen under the second major heading, a number of other interpreters draw much the same general conclusion from the parable, but do so by means of a very different interpretation of the steward's actions. Lunt has been included here rather than under the next major heading because he explicitly rejects efforts to vindicate or justify the steward's actions ("Parable," 132). The interpretation of G. V. Jones (*The Art and Truth of the Parables. A Study in their Literary Form and Modern Interpretation* [London: SPCK, 1964] 157-58) can also be noted here. Calling Luke 16:1-9 the parable of "the Fraudulent Steward," Jones includes it in his class of parables whose significance is limited to its particular historical reference. This classification is justifiable, he contends, on the grounds that Jesus is doubtless either referring to the Sadducees who were unfaithful stewards concerned to be on good terms with Rome, or to the disciples (or nation) who were not doing what the steward did: they failed to realize the seriousness of the situation and take appropriate action. Jones adds that despite the fact the parable as it stands in Luke's Gospel is addressed to an audience whose life-situation differs from that of the steward and of Jesus' audience, it takes on contemporary relevance because the need to decide what is to be done in an expanding field of situations is as real as when the parable was first spoken.

This approach to the parable can be explained more fully by citing representative interpreters. I do so under two subheadings. The first group draws their conclusions from the text as it now stands, hence the title, "Interpretations Based on the Present Text." These interpretations are in turn subdivided on the basis of whether or not a note of irony is detected in our parable. The second group arrives at what is also essentially a negative example interpretation. They do so, however, by various suggestions of textual confusion or corruption, hence the title, "Interpretations Based on Theories of Textual Confusion."

1. Interpretations Based on the Present Text

a) Non-ironical interpretation

In an 1827 article J. F. Bahnmaier espouses the position that the steward of our parable is a negative example. While himself rejecting an ironical interpretation of v. 8b, Bahnmaier admits that its exponents and he share the presupposition that the faithless steward is in no sense an example for Christians, not even with regard to his care for the future. Quite to the contrary, the steward is only a "detestable example [verabscheu-ungswürdiges Beispiel]," from whom nothing is to be imitated.[91] Bahnmaier suggests our parable contains the picture of pernicious self-help in contrast to the parable of the lost son in chapter 15 which portrays the way of real redemption.[92] Like a number of later interpreters,[93] Bahnmaier contends that v. 9 ("*Kai egō hymin legō*") introduces a contrast between the judgment of the swindled master in v. 8 and that of Jesus himself. Taking the *kai* with which v. 9 begins as a *kai adversativum*, he translates Jesus' opening words as "I, on the other hand." According to Bahnmaier, Jesus' intention is to exhort his followers, in contrast to the steward, to seek again to make friends with heaven through the faithful use of goods once gained by unjust ways.[94]

W. Milligan's argument runs in a similar vein. Instead of looking back to chapter 15, however, Milligan's concern is with the relationship between the parables of chapters 16 and 17. He concludes that the

---

[91] J. F. Bahnmaier, "Der ungerechte Haushalter Luc. 16:1ff. von Jesus keineswegs als Beispiel irgend einer Art von Klugheit aufgestellt," *Studien der evangelischen Geistlichheit Wirtembergs* 1 (1827) 34.

[92] "Haushalter," 41 n. 5.

[93] E.g., A. Feuillet, "Les riches intendants du Christ, Luc 16,1-13," *RSR* 34 (1947) 48, and Pirot, *Paraboles*, 312.

[94] "Haushalter," 46.

parables of both chapters treat the same subject from different sides—
i.e., "the odiousness of unfaithfulness and the value of faithfulness in the
stewardship with which we have been put in trust by God."[95] The keynote
of 16:1-13 is unfaithfulness against which Christians are thereby warned.
The opposite virtue, faithfulness, is inculcated in vv. 10-12.[96]

The work of H. Preisker may be cited as a third illustration of the
interpretation under discussion. Like many others already discussed,
Preisker distinguishes sharply between the parable (in his mind, vv. 1-
7) and secondary, subsequent additions and interpretations (vv. 8-13).
According to him, the parable describes man fallen under the power of
mammon.[97] The steward is not converted, but remains completely in the
embrace of mammon. The parable is, therefore, a sharp warning against
the serious danger of riches.[98]

Several interpreters combine the negative example interpretation
with a contemporary-historical emphasis. A. T. Cadoux, for example,
argues that the parables in general are weapons of controversy forged in
specific historical occasions.[99] When the original historical occasion
which first gave rise to a given parable is forgotten, however, the
meaning of the parable becomes unintelligible.[100] Such has happened,
Cadoux believes, in the case of our parable. The interpreter's job, then,
is to reconstruct the original historical occasion of the parable. Cadoux
limits our parable to vv. 1-7, and suggests the main point of the story is
"the way in which the steward tried to secure his own safety and comfort
at the expense of his trust."[101] The original application of the parable
describes people whose position had been rendered precarious by inat-
tention to trust. In an effort to secure their position these people had, by
an ostensibly liberal but dishonest use of their trust, succeeded in
currying the favor of those who were willing for a time to maintain them
in a position of ease and favor. Only the high priests answer this
description. "The high priestly office was," Cadoux explains, "held by
appointment of Rome and therefore they were inclined to barter the

---

[95] W. Milligan, "A Group of Parables," *Expositor*, ser. 4, 6 (1892 II) 126.

[96] "Parables," 114. Along the same lines as the latter point about contrasting faithfulness,
but with reference to v. 13 in particular, A. Descamps ("La composition littéraire de Luc XVI
9-13," *NovT* 1 [1956] 52) suggests that the verse contains an authentic word of Jesus taken
from another context. It was put here by Luke, Descamps believes, to complete unequivo-
cally the condemnation of the steward.

[97] H. Preisker, "Lukas 16:1-7," *TLZ* 74 (1949) 88.

[98] "Lukas 16:1-7," 90.

[99] A. T. Cadoux, *The Parables of Jesus: Their Art and Use* (London: Clarke, [1930]) 13.

[100] *Parables*, 26.

[101] *Parables*, 135.

national ideal and interests of a spiritual trust in order to get Roman favour and secure themselves in an office which their character would have otherwise lost for them."[102] This very bartering of one's trust is pictured in the actions of the steward of the parable, and is thereby condemned in the high priests. Having eliminated vv. 8-9 from consideration on various grounds,[103] Cadoux contends his interpretation of the parable is confirmed in vv. 10-13, all of which fit exactly the situation of both the steward of the parable and high priests.[104] Both had been unfaithful in little and big things, both were unfit for greater authority. Cadoux concludes that the parable gives "the half-pitying, half-contemptuous picture" of "the political astuteness of the high priestly party." Standing as it does immediately after the parable of the lost son with its condemnation of the scribes and Pharisees, our parable and its predecessor are Jesus' judgments on the two classes that combined to kill him.[105]

Much the same contemporary-historical point is made by A. R. Eagar. He describes vv. 1-13 as "sarcastic and political," giving Jesus' discussion of the causes of the fall of Jerusalem which he predicted. The actions of the steward portray the policy of the Jewish religious leaders of Jesus' day. They played fast and loose with God's law to preserve their temporal prosperity; they misused their trust from God; they evaded the spirit of the law by their traditions. They were servants of the Herods, especially with regard to the appointment of the high priests.[106] "Like the Unjust Steward they [the religious leaders] had lost their stewardship through unfaithfulness; like the Unjust Steward they were unfaithful to the end."[107] The political side of the national unfaithfulness is emphasized by the two contrasting qualities of faithfulness and single-hearted service in vv 10-13.[108] Both qualities were lacking in the steward and the Jewish leaders.

b) Ironical interpretation

The above mention of sarcasm by Eagar introduces a further interpretive nuance of which some have made a great deal. Not a few interpreters

---

[102] *Parables*, 135.
[103] *Parables*, 133-34.
[104] *Parables*, 134-36.
[105] *Parables*, 137.
[106] A. R. Eagar, "The Parable of the Unjust Steward," *Expositor*, ser. 5, 2 (1895) 465-66.
[107] "Steward," 467.
[108] "Steward," 467.

detect a note of irony in vv. 1-13, especially in vv. 8 and 9. These interpreters agree with others already cited in this subsection that the steward's actions are a negative example for Christians. They take the argument a step further by contending that Jesus conveys his warning message through irony. From the previous century, J. C. Reimpell, for example, argues that the parable (vv. 1-8 for him) is a warning mirror of the danger adhering to earthly, human wisdom of the sort displayed by the steward. V. 8b he takes as ironical, v. 9 as Jesus' application from the parable to earthly goods in the realm of Christian mercy, and vv. 10-13 as Jesus' positive demand for faithfulness from his own.[109] In the same century, W. B. Ripon offers a similar argument. He contends that the lesson of the parable is a caution against the shrewd but unscrupulous spirit which seeks self-interest at the cost of truth and principle.[110] This spirit is exemplified in the rulers and Pharisees of Jesus' day who lowered God's demands on man's allegiance and life as the steward had done with the bills of his master's debtors.[111] V. 9, Ripon suggests, is ironical. The force of the argument thus becomes as follows: the steward's actions opened the doors of tenants, but not those of heaven.[112] In this way Jesus condemns and shows the futility of a self-seeking, expedient spirit.

In the twentieth century the interpretation of our parable in terms of irony has found a number of exponents. J. F. McFayden, for one, rejects the general consensus of his day (he writes in 1925) that the parable refers to prudence in spiritual matters and/or the use of wealth. There are no other examples, he argues, of Jesus using a rascal as an example to be imitated. The alternative is irony, particularly in v. 9. This interpretation is confirmed by the unusual phrase "eternal tents" (*tas aiōnious skēnas*) in that verse. Since "tent" is the very symbol of that which is temporary, the phrase means "'The homes you will secure for yourselves in the other world by being generous with your ill-gotten gains will have only the eternity of tents'."[113] In other words, the benefits gained by actions such as the steward's are ephemeral at best, and he is held up "not as a model but as a warning."[114]

---

[109] J. C. Reimpell, "Das Gleichnis vom ungerechten Haushalter, Luk 16," *Zeitschrift für kirchliche Wissenschaft und kirchliche Leben* 1 (1880) 512-14. Reimpell's interpretation is endorsed by G. Jäger, "Noch einmal: Der ungerechte Haushalter," *Zeitschrift für kirchliche Wissenschaft und kirchliche Leben* 2 (1881) 111-12.

[110] W. B. Ripon, "The Parable of the Unjust Steward," *Expositor*, ser. 4, 7 (1893 I) 26.

[111] "Steward," 24-25.

[112] "Steward," 28.

[113] J. F. McFayden, "The Parable of the Unjust Steward," *ExpTim* 37 (1925-26) 536.

[114] "Steward," 536. McFayden also argues v. 9 is only one of several lessons Luke finds

Writing in 1938, A. King describes our parable as "a choice bit of satire"[115] which teaches not by resemblance but by contrast.[116] In his view, the key to the parable is v. 13: "No servant can serve two masters."[117] The steward of the parable is condemned for attempting precisely this kind of service. The parable, then, contains "one of the most biting indictments of worldliness ever made," and might well have begun with "The Kingdom of God is unlike . . ." King suggests Jesus told this parable to his disciples to impress upon them their new position. "Jesus would have them for a moment or two revisit the Far Country [cf. the lost son, chapter 15], where Mammon ruled, and see for themselves with undimmed eyes just the sort of thing they had left behind."[118] King summarizes the message of the parable in these words.

> What this Parable is calculated to bring home to us is just what we escape from when we pledge ourselves to Christ as servants of the Kingdom of God. As such we are definitely finished with the slack and devious ways of the Kingdom of Mammon. . . . This story reminds us that many of the things we have to give up are such as to make us unfeignedly thankful that we can give them up.[119]

G. Paul also uses the word sarcasm with regard to our parable. In particular, he describes v. 9 as "a piece of grim sarcasm, the tone of which was subsequently forgotten."[120] In words which recall other interpreters already discussed, Paul contends this parable and v. 9 especially have nothing really to do with money. "This is," he says, "a parable about the importance of decision. . . . If one has no wish to insure one's future with Jesus, then it is worth using every crooked means to get into the devil's good books, for there are no other choices and no other chances."[121]

P. G. Bretscher makes irony even more prominent in his interpretation of our parable. He puts his finger on what is perhaps the interpretive crux when he observes that vv. 8-9 are the opposite of what one would

---

in the parable. Others are contained in vv. 8b, 10-13. "Is not the obvious inference from all this that, by the time Luke wrote, people were just as much puzzled by the Parable as we are to-day, and that various sayings of Jesus had become attached to it as its interpretation?" (p. 536). This judgment is echoed by many before and after McFayden, and will be addressed in more detail in the next chapter.

[115] A. King, "The Parable of the Unjust Steward," *ExpTim* 50 (1938-39) 476.
[116] "Steward," 475.
[117] "Steward," 474.
[118] "Steward," 475.
[119] "Steward," 476.
[120] G. Paul, "The Unjust Steward and the Interpretation of Luke 16:9," *Theology* 61 (1958) 192.
[121] "Steward," 193.

expect Jesus to say, on the analogy of faith. The way out of this difficulty, he suggests, is to read here "the overtones of deepest irony" in Jesus' voice. In this way Jesus *does* in fact say the very opposite of what he actually means.[122] The force of Bretscher's argument is best conveyed by his own paraphrases of vv. 8-9. The meaning of v. 8a is expressed as follows.

> "You are surely clever!" he [Jesus] might say. "You have displayed real ingenuity, yes, the very highest wisdom this world knows—the wisdom of disguising your sin, pretending righteousness, shrugging off the anger of God, quieting a guilty conscience by gaining the approval of men, showing off a few good works to cover a heart full of evil."

V. 8b supplies Jesus' own commentary on such wisdom, also in irony. Bretscher continues his paraphrase.

> "Yes, this is a wisdom and cleverness the sons of light would not dream of. It is a damning cleverness, in fact, deceiving no one more than those who engage in it. The sons of light are not so clever."

V. 9 provides the climax.

> "Go ahead, then! Use all God's gifts to you for your own unholy and ungodly purposes! Use them to make friends of the sinners of this world! . . . Let them be your judges, let them open the gates of everlasting habitations to you!"

The implied conclusion, Bretscher argues, still paraphrasing Jesus, is "'You fool! They cannot do it! It is before God that you stand or fall, the God you ignored and despised. He will condemn you to the torments of hell.'"[123]

On Bretscher's reading of our parable as irony (especially in vv. 8-9), the lesson is "The Folly of Sinners Who, by Wisdom, Avoid Repentance."[124] He concedes that on a casual reading our parable does not sound like irony nor does it give any indication of such. He reminds us, however, that irony is conveyed by modulation of the voice and is, of course, lost in the written transmission (cf. the earlier remark of Paul). In that event only the context can point to irony in its written form.[125] Bretscher argues that the context does so here.[126]

Perhaps the most well-known and often-cited interpretation of our parable in terms of irony is that of D. R. Fletcher. The title of his 1963

---

[122] P. G. Bretscher, "The Parable of the Unjust Steward—A New Approach to Luke 16:1-9," *CTM* 22 (1951) 757.

[123] "Steward," 759.

[124] "Steward," 759.

[125] "Steward," 762.

[126] "Steward," 760.

article indicates his emphasis: "The Riddle of the Unjust Steward: Is Irony the Key?" He answers his own question in the affirmative. Fletcher is unpersuaded by various attempts to vindicate the steward's actions.[127] (Such attempts make up the second major heading of this chapter.) He also is convinced a "straight" reading of v. 9 does not fit the general tenor of Jesus' teaching about a radical distinction between his disciples and the world. Does Jesus really teach self-interest here, Fletcher asks, as he would on a "straight" reading?[128] No, irony is "the key" which "unlocks the riddle of the Unjust Steward." He cites what he believes are several other uses of irony by Jesus (e.g., Mark 2:17; Luke 15:7),[129] and then identifies the contrast in v. 9 between *tou mamōna tēs adikias* ("worldly wealth") and *tas aiōnious skēnas* ("eternal dwellings") as the clue to the meaning of the parable. The contrast is between mammon which will fail and the kingdom of God. Fletcher summarizes his argument in these words.

> The irony of Jesus' play on the story of the parable [in v. 9] is simply the utter irrelevance of the two concepts, mammon and its absorbing concerns over against the dwellings of God. "Make friends for yourselves," he seems to taunt: "imitate the example of the steward; use the unrighteous mammon; surround yourselves with the type of insincere, self-interested friendship it can buy; how far will this carry you when the end comes and you are finally dismissed?"[130]

Taken in this way the parable echoes the urgency and radical demand which are characteristic of Jesus' teaching, especially in the central section of Luke's Gospel. Fletcher sees the single theme of the whole passage (16:1-13) to be "a demand for faithfulness and obedience, particularly in the face of the corrosive influence of *ho mamōnas tēs adikias*."[131]

---

[127] Fletcher, "Riddle," 23.

[128] "Riddle," 24.

[129] "Riddle," 27-28.

[130] "Riddle," 29.

[131] "Riddle," 29-30. G. Sellin ("Studien zu den grossen Gleichniserzählungen des Lukas-Sonderguts. Die *anthrōpos-tis*-Erzählungen des Lukas-Sonderguts—besonders am Beispiel von Lk 10,25-37 und 16,14-31 untersucht," [Ph.D. dissertation, Münster, 1974]) synthesizes Fletcher's interpretation with that of F. E. Williams ("Almsgiving") to argue that vv. 1-8b are a "negative example for disciples" (p. 296) and vv. 9-13 an appendix providing the positive alternative—almsgiving (p. 298). In a note (p. 298 n. 1276) Sellin indicates that against both Fletcher and Williams, Jesus cannot be the author of Luke 16:1-13. Instead the verses must be explained completely from Luke's redactional motives. The essential correctness of Fletcher's ironical interpretation has also been affirmed recently by S. E. Porter ("The Parable of the Unjust Steward [Luke 16.1-13]: Irony *Is* the Key," in *The Bible in Three Dimensions: Essays in celebration of forty years of Biblical Studies in the University of Sheffield* [JSOTSup 87; ed. D. J. A. Clines, S. E. Fowl, and S. E. Porter; Sheffield: JSOT, 1990] 127-53).

Several interpreters agree our parable is ironical, but emphasize its contemporary-historical focus. F. Lenwood, for example, critiques and rejects "the ordinary explanation" (that the parable is about analogous cleverness in the affairs of the kingdom of God),[132] and offers his own theory instead: "The parable is really a criticism of the Pharisees by means of a story throwing the light of truth upon their methods."[133] As God's stewards, the Pharisees, fearing loss of their power, made concessions with respect to the strict law such as involved "an immoral cheapening of God's demands."[134] What Lenwood has in mind by concessions are the casuistic traditions of the Pharisees such as Corban. By such means the teachers were in effect, to use the imagery of the parable, writing fifty when one hundred was the debt men owe to God.[135] According to Lenwood, Jesus ironically praises the Pharisees in v. 8 because at such maneuvers "they are much nimbler that the real children of God." If v. 9 is connected at all to the parable (which he doubts), it is "an amplification of the irony of verse 8." Vv. 10-13 are judged to be "quite unconnected" to the parable. To meet the difficulty posed for his interpretation by the introduction of the parable (16:1: *pros tous mathētas*) Lenwood simply concludes that in adding these introductory words Luke had missed the point of the saying. The present-day interpreter can, therefore, he tells us, disregard the introduction.[136]

A second negative example interpretation which combines irony with a strongly contemporary-historical emphasis is that of R. Pautrel. He takes a slightly different interpretive tack by relegating v. 13 to the margin and making v. 15 the key verse.[137] He understands the master's praise of the steward (v. 8a) to mean the steward was not actually dismissed in the end. By his actions the steward managed to justify himself before his master as the Pharisees justified themselves before men (v. 15). The story is not finished, however, for either the steward or the Pharisees.[138] Pautrel detects a note of irony in v. 9, particularly in the phrase "eternal tents." He believes the conjunction of "tent," which

---

[132] F. Lenwood, "An Alternative Interpretation of the Parable of the Unjust Steward," *The Congregational Quarterly* 6 (1928) 366-68.

[133] "Parable," 368.

[134] "Parable," 368.

[135] "Parable," 369-70.

[136] "Parable," 368-69. This means of dispensing with the introduction of the parable has a modern ring to it, and will be dealt with in more detail in the next chapter. Note should be made of an editorial critique of Lenwood (by A. W. and E. Hastings) which appears in *ExpTim* 39 (1927-28) 532-33.

[137] R. Pautrel, "Aeterna Tabernacula (Luc, XVI, 9)," *RSR* 30 (1940) 315.

[138] "Tabernacula," 318-19.

characterizes a transitory habitation, with "eternal" can only be "an intentional shock."[139] The steward was able to deceive his master, but in the process submitted himself to perpetual blackmail by those whose bills were changed. Pautrel ranges the story in the cycle of "thieves embezzled." The contemporary-historical message of the story is plain. The Pharisees, more concerned as they are with the opinion of men than with serving God, have—like the steward of the parable—fixed themselves in a false position from which they are unable to escape. They have become prisoners of their roles. Their simulated holiness is, according to v. 15, an abomination to God. Pautrel concludes that from a logical and grammatical point of view the comparison of the parable is a positive one: like the steward, thus are the Pharisees. From a moral point of view, however, the lesson is a contrary example ("un exemple à rebours"), the force of which Pautrel conveys by means of Jesus' own words with respect to the Pharisees in Matt 23:3b: "But do not do what they do."[140]

2. Interpretations Based on Theories of Textual Confusion

All the interpreters in the above subdivision see the parable of the unjust steward as a negative example, and do so on the basis of the text as it now stands. Several other writers arrive at the same basic conclusion, but by a rather different route. Sensing the difficulty of the parable and finding other approaches unacceptable for one reason or another, several interpreters have theorized that the real meaning of the passage has been obscured in the process of the text's translation and transmission. These theories take several different forms.

a) Appeal to Aramaic setting

As long ago as 1919, H. F. B. Compston offered what he calls "a new view" of our parable. He suggests that *ek* in v. 9 ("Make friends for

---

[139] "Tabernacula," 320. Cf. the argument of McFayden summarized earlier in this chapter.

[140] "Tabernacula," 322-23. The ironical interpretation of our parable, though without a contemporary-historical emphasis, is also advocated by H. Clavier ("L'Ironie dans L'Enseignement de Jesus," *NovT* 1 [1956] 16). As is indicated by the title of his article, Clavier's concern is with Jesus' teaching more broadly than just our parable. He does cite our parable, however, as an example of Jesus' use of irony. Clavier's thesis is that irony is the explanation of many of the difficult sayings of Jesus, including Luke 16:1-13. He reads vv. 1-9 as irony, and vv. 10-13 as Jesus' lesson on fidelity and honesty. Also cf. J. A. Davidson, "A 'Conjecture' about the Parable of the Unjust Steward (Luke xvi.1-9)," *ExpTim* 66 (1954-55) 31.

yourselves *ek tou mamōna tēs adikias*") may well be the translation of the Aramaic *min*, one of the meanings of which is "away from," i.e., "without." Compston concedes that he has not found a similar use of *min* in Aramaic, but cites Job 19:26 (Hebrew) as a possible parallel. In any case, if this conjecture be admitted the sense of the exhortation in v. 9 becomes "Make friends *without* dirty money." This interpretation is something quite different from and in fact the opposite of the usual rendering of *ek* in v. 9. On Compston's reading the intended lesson is as follows: "Use foresight in spiritual things as did the tricky agent in things temporal. Be scrupulously honest in money matters; that goes without saying. You have, however, higher interests entirely, and those interests are spiritual."[141]

Virtually the same approach is adopted by R. B. Y. Scott, who offers his interpretation, however, without reference to Compston's earlier article. Scott does seek to bolster his argument by noting that *min* (Hebrew) is sometimes rendered by *ek* in the LXX (e.g., Num 15:24). The purport of our parable is similar to "lay up treasures in heaven." The steward, as a son of this world, did make friends by means of shrewdness in money matters. For the sons of light, however, there is a more excellent way, that indicated in vv. 9-13. Scott suggests v. 9 contains perhaps "another Semitism," the use of *waw* in an antithetical rather than a coordinate clause. In that event, v. 9 begins "But I say to you" and offers Jesus' judgment on the steward's actions in contrast to that (of the master?) found in v. 8.[142]

G. Schwarz offers a different approach, though still appealing to the Aramaic setting of the parable. Unlike Compston and Scott, who focus on v. 9, Schwarz contends that in v. 8 there has been a twofold translation error in the transmission of the parable from Aramaic to Greek. The errors involve the words *epēinesen* ("commended") and *phronimōs* ("shrewdly") in the present text (v. 8). Schwarz argues that "a striking peculiarity" of the Aramaic equivalents for both words (*brk* and *'rym*, respectively) is that both can be used in a good and bad sense. Among the possible meanings of *brk* (= *epēinesen*), he explains, is "to curse" and of *'rym* (= *phronimōs*) "cunning" or "deceitful." The alleged translation errors in v. 8 occurred when the Aramaic words meant by Jesus in a bad sense were taken by the translator in a good sense and rendered as such in Greek. Schwarz finds the basis for this error in v. 8b where the

---

[141] H. F. B. Compston, "Friendship without Mammon," *ExpTim* 31 (1919-20) 282.

[142] R. B. Y. Scott, "The Parable of the Unjust Steward, (Luke xvi. 1ff.)," *ExpTim* 49 (1937-38) 235. Cf. Bahnmaier's argument referred to earlier in the chapter.

adjective *phronimos* (= *'rym*) is clearly meant in a good sense. This good sense of *'rym* in v. 8b then reacted on what was meant as the bad sense of *'rym* in v. 8a and so caused two translation errors in v. 8a. According to Schwarz, the correct translation of what was meant in the original Aramaic is as follows: "And the master cursed the deceitful steward, because he had acted deceitfully." Schwarz adds that the master's judgment on his steward's actions would have hit home with those among Jesus' hearers who exercised the function of "stewards," i.e., the spiritual leaders of his time.[143]

b) Appeal to textual emendation

Like Compston and Scott, J. C. Wansey centers his explanation of the parable on the word *ek* in v. 9. He does so, however, not by reference to Aramaic but to Greek itself. He suggests that *ek* be emended to *ektos* [BAGD, "outside"], on the conjecture that a scribe omitted the letters *-tos*. If this emendation is correct, the sense of v. 9 is the same as that put forward by Compston and Scott above—"Make friends without mammon." In other words, in contrast to the steward, disciples are to let the basis of friendship be more trustworthy than monetary convenience. The parable, then, is not about stewardship but friendship. So fine a thing as friendship is not available by money. Wansey acknowledges the conjectural nature of his emendation, but feels it is natural enough to merit consideration.[144]

In summary, despite the diversity among the interpreters considered thus far, they at least agree that the steward's actions toward the debtors are fraudulent and dishonest. The actions themselves are not exemplary, and the lesson of the parable is to be found either in a quality exhibited in (but distinct from) those actions or in a total contrast to them.

As widespread as this general approach to the parable of the unjust steward is, it is not, however, the only possible approach. A very different one is the focus of Part II.

II. STEWARD'S ACTIONS JUST OR HONEST

Rather than distinguish between the dishonest and wise aspects of the steward's actions toward the debtors, a number of interpreters contend his actions are themselves just and honest and are, therefore, inherently

---

[143] G. Schwarz, "'. . . lobte den betrügerischen Verwalter'? (Lukas 16:8a)," *BZ*, n.f., 18 (1974) 94-95.

[144] J. C. Wansey, "The Parable of the Unjust Steward: An Interpretation," *ExpTim* 47 (1935-36) 39-40.

commendable. As such those actions serve as a more or less direct example for Jesus' disciples and/or other contemporaries. To express the substance of this approach in other terms, generally positive lessons are drawn from what is judged to be *positive* conduct by the steward.

The basic line of argument of this approach to the parable is to justify the changes the steward authorizes the debtors to make in their IOUs. The steward is thus vindicated of wrongdoing in those actions and the difficulty of the praise in v. 8 is alleviated. The commendation, whether by Jesus or the master, then becomes appropriate, even deserved. This vindication of the steward is achieved in a variety of ways. I have grouped them according to their stress either on charity or a similar ethical quality in the steward's actions or on the socioeconomic background of the parable. Neither category is mutually exclusive of the other; not infrequently they overlap.

A. Charity or Similar Quality Stressed

The earliest attempt to explain the parable by justifying the debt reductions is apparently that of D. Schulz.[145] Schulz argues that the changes were made in the presence of the master and could not, therefore, have been deceptive. Though a "son of this age" (v. 8b), the steward is praised for showing charity to the debtors. Jesus' demand to his disciples is that they use their temporal goods in analogous ways so as to give proof of their love for others and thus gain the friendship of God.[146] A similar but slightly different line of argument is taken by P. Brauns. He too believes the steward's actions took place in the presence of the master and could not have been deceptive, but then goes on to suggest that the steward, like Zacchaeus (Luke 19), repaid his master the amounts that were reduced with his own money. The steward thus made restitution to his master and was charitable to the debtors at the same time.[147] Therein lay his wisdom, "a wisdom of repentance [eine Klugheit der *metanoia*]."[148] Brauns's

---

[145] D. Schulz, *Über die Parabel vom Verwalter, Lk 16:1ff. Ein Versuch* (Breslau: J. Max, 1821). The description of Schulz's interpretation as the earliest of its kind is taken from Rücker, "Gleichnis," 33.

[146] *Parabel*, 103-6.

[147] P. Brauns, "Nun noch ein Auslegungsversuch von Lk 16:1-14," *TSK* 15 (1842) 1014-15. Others who explain the steward's actions as restitution include J. Grant ("The Unjust Steward," *ExpTim* 16 [1904-5] 240) and W. Arnott ("The Unjust Steward in a New Light," *ExpTim* 24 [1913] 510).

[148] "Lk 16:1-14," 1017. F. F. Zyro ("Neuer Versuch über das Gleichnis vom klugen Verwalter, Luk 16," *TSK* 5 [1831] 802-4) and J. Coutts ("Studies in Texts: The Unjust Steward, Lk 16:1-8a," *Theology* 52 [1949] 57-58) also characterize the steward's actions as acts of repentance.

argument that the steward's actions were carried out in the presence of the master and therefore were not deceptive is endorsed by Hölbe. He adds the suggestion, later offered and developed independently by others, that the steward reduced the debts by his own share and then handed over the documents. For this generosity he was praised. Hölbe regards the parable as a justification of the publicans many of whom, though unjustly slurred by the Pharisees, proved to be just and generous as the steward had been in similar circumstances.[149]

The contemporary-historical note in Hölbe's interpretation of our parable is sounded earlier in the nineteenth century by F. Schleiermacher. Schleiermacher describes our parable as a defense of tax collectors who had become Jesus' disciples. He also contends the steward was not guilty of the charges leveled against him and that the master dealt arbitrarily with the steward in dismissing him. Schleiermacher then goes on to interpret the parable in terms of the first-century circumstances. The rich man represents the Romans, the steward the tax collectors, and the debtors the Jewish people. If the tax collectors are charitable toward their own people (the Jews) with the money gained by their profession, the Romans will praise them in their hearts. When the Roman dominion ends and the kingdom of God begins, the tax collectors will be received into eternal dwellings.[150]

Much the same interpretation is offered by H. Olshausen later in the nineteenth century. Olshausen contends that when viewed in light of v. 13 ("No servant can serve two masters"), the steward's actions in vv. 5-7 depict service of the true Lord and despising of the false.[151] Such is what the publicans did when they used their wealth in service of God and their fellow men. The Pharisees, however, had not followed suit. The parable is, then, an implied defense of the publicans for having renounced previous allegiances and a rebuke of the Pharisees for refusing to do so. According to Olshausen, the express application for disciples is made in v. 9 ("Make friends for yourself")—they are to use mammon for spiritual and holy ends.[152]

If Hölbe and Schleiermacher emphasize the message of the parable for the publicans, and Olshausen the message for both the publicans and

---

[149] Hölbe, "Versuch einer Erklärung der Parabel vom ungerechten Haushalter, Lk 16:1ff.," *TSK* 32 (1858) 534-41.

[150] F. Schleiermacher, *Ueber die Schriften des Lukas* (Teil 1; Berlin: Reimer, 1817) 202-4.

[151] H. Olshausen, *Biblical Commentary on the New Testament* (6 vols.; New York: Sheldon, 1862) 2.64, 66.

[152] Olshausen, *Commentary* 2.63-70.

Pharisees, other interpreters have chosen to focus almost exclusively on the message for the Pharisees as the religious leaders of Israel. F. F. Zyro is one such interpreter from early in the last century. Although he removes vv. 1 and 14 of Luke 16 as Lucan glosses and brands the context as unreliable because secondary, Zyro nevertheless argues our parable has a sense and purpose similar to that of the lost son in chapter 15. Both parables, he believes, are aimed against the Pharisees, ours differing in that it is the more direct attack. On Zyro's reading of our parable, the rich man is God, the steward the Pharisees, and the debtors the Jewish people, especially the publicans. In acting as he does the steward of the parable displays love, mercy, and humility, all marks of true conversion and repentance. The main teaching of the parable, directed to the Pharisees and other religious leaders, is that without such actions and qualities justification and righteousness are not possible.[153] The steward's actions are, in a sense, the ideal to which the Pharisees should aspire.

Another interpreter in the nineteenth century who explains our parable as primarily a message to the Pharisees is G. Wiesen. He offers, however, a unique slant to the story. According to Wiesen, the steward is himself a rich man who has been unfaithful with goods entrusted to him, not by being a swindler, but by being a miser. The debtors are, Wiesen argues, debtors of the steward. When he reduces their bills, therefore, he is not acting fraudulently but rather showing charity.[154] Such actions bespeak the conversion of a miser. As Wiesen understands the parable, the steward is a humiliating example to the Pharisees who are similar to him only in their unfaithfulness, not his penance.[155]

In the present century, E. Kamlah also explains our parable in terms of its special significance for the Pharisees. He contends that "steward" (*oikonomos*) had a well-known metaphorical meaning which would have indicated at once to Jesus' hearers that the parable was about the Pharisaic teachers of the law. Kamlah sees the steward's conduct toward the debtors, then, as an example of and the standard for the appropriate conduct of these leaders. Like the steward, the Pharisees should, among other things, lighten the burdens of their subordinates and also humble themselves.[156] Up to the time of the parable's telling they were doing

---

[153] Zyro, "Versuch," 788-92, 804.

[154] G. Wiesen, *Die Stellung Jesu zum irdischen Gut mit besonderer Rücksicht auf das Gleichnis vom ungerechten Haushalter* (Gütersloh: Bertelsmann, 1895) 72-73, 75.

[155] *Gleichnis*, 72, 75, 84.

[156] E. Kamlah, "Die Parabel vom ungerechten Verwalter (Luk. 16:1ff.) im Rahmen der Knechtsgleichnisse," in *Abraham unser Vater* (eds. O. Betz, M. Hengel, and P. Schmidt; Leiden: Brill, 1963) 282-84, 287-88, 292-94. It is interesting to note in passing that whereas

neither, but were instead isolating themselves from sinners to keep themselves pure and making obedience unattainable by their detailed traditions. When seen in this way, our parable becomes "a parabolic polemic against the pharisaic casuistry."[157]

Another way in which the steward's actions have been vindicated and the difficulty of the praise alleviated is by explaining those actions in terms of forgiveness. Within the historical parameters of this chapter, this approach is advocated by B. K. Jensen as long ago as 1829 and by L. J. Topel as recently as 1975.[158] A summary of each will illustrate the approach. Jensen begins by dismissing Schleiermacher's interpretation that the parable is a defense and instruction of publicans who had attached themselves to Jesus.[159] He then argues on the analogy of other parables that the master is God, the grace of whom is shown in the praise of v. 8a. In the context of chapters 15 and 16, furthermore, our parable is an instruction for all bystanders about the pardon of sinners. Whether or not the steward's actions in remitting the debts were within his rights as steward, Jensen does not say. What is important for his argument is that the steward was showing forgiveness to others, something quite in keeping with the exhortation to forgive so frequently on Jesus' lips. Jensen's point is that such forgiveness will bring God's blessing to the contrite sinner who by such acts to others gives expression to his own need of and desire for God's grace.[160]

Topel, in the opening pages of his article on our parable, makes it clear that his goal is to publicize the work of F. Maass.[161] Maass's basic point

---

Kamlah regards the steward's actions as a positive example of what the Pharisees should have done (i.e., reduce the ceremonial laws), other interpreters already mentioned (e.g., Eagar ["Steward," 465-66] and Lenwood ["Parable," 368]) see those actions as an indictment of what they were doing (i.e., evading the spirit of the law by their traditions).

[157] Kamlah, "Parabel," 294. Kamlah's interpretation is heartily endorsed by Krämer (Rätsel, 70-74). Degenhardt (Lukas, 118) also interprets the parable, at least as originally given, as an exhortation to the religious leaders to act wisely by alleviating the burden they had placed on the people of God. He admits, however, that the text as it now stands is about the right conduct of disciples with possessions (p. 125). H. S. Marshall ("The Parable of the Untrustworthy Steward [Luke xvi.1-13]. A Question Reopened," ExpTim 39 [1927-28] 120-22) also explains the parable as an indictment of pharisaic casuistry, although he does so less clearly than the others mentioned here.

[158] Other writers who have stressed forgiveness as the teaching of our parable include F. G. Dutton ("The Unjust Steward," ExpTim 16 [1904-5] 44: "the wisdom of man's forgiving"), and Coutts ("Steward," 54-60: repentance expressed in charity in the form of forgiving debts).

[159] B. K. Jensen, "Über der Gleichnis vom ungerechten Haushalter," TSK 2 (1829) 700-703.

[160] "Haushalter," 700-709.

[161] Topel, "Steward," 217; F. Maass, "Das Gleichnis vom ungerechten Haushalter, Lukas 16:1-8," Theologia Viatorum 8 (1962) 173-84.

is that the steward's reductions of the debts convey a command to forgive which from the prevailing human standpoint of justice appears "unjust."[162] Topel takes up this point,[163] and attempts to set it in a redaction-critical context.[164] At the earliest stage of tradition, Topel argues, the parable (16:1-8) was an exhortation to Christians to act decisively in the eschatological crisis. At a later stage Luke's addition of his own theology of sharing with the poor (16:9, 10-13) introduced the monetary note. When the whole unit on riches (16:1-13) was, in the final redaction, added to chapter 15, the theological motif of forgiveness (already inherent in the parable) was made explicit and was completed.[165] Topel makes much of the forgiveness theme in chapter 15[166] and in 17:1-4. In this context, the presumption is that our parable relates to the same theme, and Topel contends it does. In reducing the debts as he does, the steward of the parable forgives. The point of the parable, in its Lucan context, is that forgiveness involves the generous use of money, particularly in the form of almsgiving to the poor.[167] "Being faithful to this kind of justice," Topel concludes, "is what makes the Christian steward trustworthy with true wealth and an heir of the kingdom."[168]

B. Socioeconomic Background Stressed

Perhaps the most common way to justify the steward's actions toward the debtors is by appealing to the socioeconomic background of the parable. The basic line of argument of this approach is as follows. A steward (*oikonomos*) in ancient Near Eastern societies had much greater

---

[162] Maass, "Gleichnis," 179.

[163] "Steward," 223-27.

[164] "Steward," 217-23.

[165] "Steward," 226-27. The redactional distinctions just outlined make Topel difficult to categorize. As already noted, the same difficulty applies to others who draw similar distinctions (e.g., Jeremias and Krämer). The difficulty in categorizing Topel's interpretation is compounded by his lack of clarity about how the steward's actions are to be understood. On the one hand, he critiques J. D. M. Derrett's approach (discussed under the next subheading) on a number of points (p. 218 n. 13), and stresses the steward's injustice as a key element of the parable (p. 227). In this respect, he implies the steward's actions were fraudulent or dishonest, at least as far as his master was concerned. On the other hand, however, Topel's basic point is that the steward's actions represent the forgiveness which Christians are asked to exercise. Forgiveness is something which often appears "unjust" to human eyes, but which reveals higher, divine justice. In this respect, the word "unjust" is being used in an almost ironical sense. Since the positive lesson of forgiveness is Topel's main emphasis, I have included him here, although not without reservations.

[166] He describes chapter 15 as containing three parables on "rejoicing in forgiveness of one another as God rejoices in forgiving" ("Steward," 221).

[167] "Steward," 220-21, 226.

[168] "Steward," 227.

discretionary rights and powers than his modern, Western counterpart. As long as the steward remained in office he had almost complete control in the management of his master's property and affairs. In particular, it was within his authority to fix and collect rents from tenants, transact sales and purchases with traders, and otherwise run the estate of his master. Against this background the actions of the steward of our parable take on a different character. When he has the debtors reduce the amounts of their bills he is in actual fact acting quite within his rights as steward. Technically and legally he is not defrauding his master at all. If anything, the steward is the only one to suffer financial loss from the transactions. At long last he is displaying charity and honesty, and for such actions he is commended.

A review of representative exponents of this approach will clarify it further, as well as bring out various interpretive nuances. I begin with several earlier interpreters whose socioeconomic emphasis is implicit but not pronounced, and move to those in whom the emphasis is stronger.

J. J. van Oosterzee is among the earliest interpreters to appeal, albeit implicitly, to the socioeconomic background of the parable to vindicate the steward.[169] Oosterzee's suggestion is that the steward had been extracting more from the debtors than he actually turned over to his master, perhaps using the difference to support a wanton lifestyle. In the face of threatened dismissal the steward responds by having the debtors enter lower amounts on their IOUs. In Oosterzee's view, the records have not thereby been falsified, but represent instead the lease amounts previously reported and submitted to the master by the steward. In other words, the amounts on the tenants' leases and the amounts actually collected and passed on to the master finally agree. The steward's actions toward the debtors are an abandonment of his earlier dishonesty.[170] Although he does not elaborate, Oosterzee also implies the steward's actions involve compensation for past damages.[171] He understands the parable as an effort by Jesus to lead both publicans and Pharisees to "prudent foresight." Jesus wants to remind the former of their duty as

---

[169] J. J. van Oosterzee, *The Gospel according to Luke*, vol. 8 in J. P. Lange's *Commentary on the Holy Scriptures Critical, Doctrinal and Homiletical* (12 vols.; Grand Rapids: Zondervan, 1960). The first edition of Oosterzee's commentary came out in 1859.

[170] *Luke*, 245-46. Essentially the same interpretation is advocated by C. E. van Koetsveld (*Die Gleichnisse des Evangeliums* [Leipzig: F. Jansa, 1904] 233-39; the first Dutch edition came out in 1886) and M. Evers (*Die Gleichnisse Jesu* [4th ed.; ed. H. Marx; Berlin: Reuther & Reichard, 1908] 82-89; cf. Evers's earlier monograph on the parable, *Das Gleichnis vom ungerechten Verwalter* [Krefeld: G. Hohns, 1901]).

[171] Oosterzee, *Luke*, 247. Cf. the interpretations of Brauns, Hölbe, Grant, and Arnott referred to earlier.

disciples to make restitution wherever possible, and, at the same time, to warn the latter of their status as stewards for whom a day of reckoning is coming.[172]

Oosterzee's approach is endorsed and developed by F. Nägelsbach. Nägelsbach rejects Reimpell's interpretation of our parable as a warning example (mentioned earlier in this chapter), and agrees with Oosterzee that the steward's reductions represent excess rent he had been charging.[173] Once again there is in the steward's actions a special message for the publicans, who are to recognize themselves in the picture of a steward who had previously misused his position. As the steward had become wise, so they are to use mammon in support of brotherly love and as a means to eternal salvation.[174]

The essence of Oosterzee's and Nägelsbach's approach to our parable is found in the well-known and oft-cited article of M. D. Gibson. Writing just after the turn of this century, Gibson tentatively offers a suggestion which, she says, has not occurred "to any of our learned commentators."[175] Arguing on the analogy of "Eastern customs" at the beginning of the twentieth century, she believes the steward of the parable had been overcharging the tenants and pocketing the difference. So typical, she asserts, is this practice in Oriental societies even in the twentieth century that many listeners, upon hearing the parable of the unjust steward, would understand the situation intuitively and no explanation would be needed. "They would know that the steward, in telling the cultivators to write less in their bills than he had originally demanded from them, was simply renouncing his own exorbitant profits, without in any way defrauding his master."[176]

---

[172] Oosterzee, *Luke*, 245.

[173] F. Nägelsbach, "Noch einmal das Gleichnis vom ungerechten Haushalter," *Zeitschrift für kirchliche Wissenschaft und kirchliche Leben* 2 (1881) 481, 483.

[174] "Gleichnis," 484, 486. Nägelsbach adds a theological flavor to his interpretation when he explains Luke 15 and 16 in terms of justification and sanctification, respectively (p. 482). Much the same interpretation as that of Oosterzee and Nägelsbach is advocated in the twentieth century by, among others, A. Wright ("The Parable of the Unjust Steward," *The Interpreter* 7 [1911] 279-87) and L. Fonck (*Die Parabeln des Herrn im Evangelium* [4th ed.; Innsbruck: F. Rauch, 1927] 680-90). Wright argues that when the steward is accused and dismissed (falsely, Wright believes) he prepares for the future by reducing the accumulated arrears of his master's debtors. Since the debts are the result of excessive rent in the first place, to remit a large part of them "will only be rendering tardy justice" (p. 283). The steward is commended for redressing a longstanding grievance and for rescuing his master's name from serious reproach (p. 284). Fonck suggests the steward may have charged the tenants higher sums than were actually turned over to the master. It is this excessive rent that the steward reduces.

[175] M. D. Gibson, "On the Parable of the Unjust Steward," *ExpTim* 14 (1902-3) 334. Either she has in mind only British commentators or she is unaware of the earlier interpretations of Oosterzee, Nägelsbach, Koetsveld, and Evers.

[176] "Steward," 334.

Gibson's "almost casual suggestion"[177] has been endorsed, developed, and modified by many interpreters. W. D. Miller, for example, agrees with Gibson's suggestion, and explains that in the process of giving up his own profits the steward does a generous thing to the tenants, a just thing to his master, and a sacrificial thing with regard to himself. As a result, foes are turned to friends and the steward's circumstances are altered for the better. Thus understood, the parable contains a double lesson of wisdom (in turning foes to friends) and of self-sacrificing repentance (in throwing oneself on the master's/God's mercy).[178]

P. Gächter has played an important role in disseminating and elaborating Gibson's socioeconomic vindication of the steward in our parable. In an article published in 1950, the title of which reveals his approach ("The Parable of the Dishonest Steward after Oriental Conceptions"), Gächter puts his finger on the main difficulty in our parable. He asks, "How can Jesus make villainy an example for his followers?"[179] "Did Jesus, who otherwise knew so well how to speak to the hearts of men, really propose a parable which necessarily strikes one as touching on what according to all standards of morals is wrong?"[180] In the face of this difficulty, which, in his judgment, other interpretations are unable to explain satisfactorily, Gächter argues for the essential correctness of Gibson's interpretation. He does so in more socioeconomic detail than Gibson, especially in a 1963 article. Our problem with the parable, he believes, is in our Western-oriented interpretation of it. If, however, we were to listen to it with the ears of an Oriental, we would discover it corresponds feature for feature to life, the praise included. The rich man of the parable, Gächter explains, is a large landowner who lives in a city, perhaps Damascus or Beirut. As an absentee landlord the man must engage the services of a steward to manage the estate for him. The steward of his Palestinian holdings is not paid for his efforts, but instead holds the estate under lease. According to the terms of this lease the

---

[177] This evaluation is Bailey's (*Poet*, 88). Bailey is, incidentally, very critical of Gibson (and others who have followed her) for misreading the cultural background.

[178] W. D. Miller, "The Unjust Steward," *ExpTim* 15 (1903-4) 333-34. Much the same endorsement is given by E. Hampden-Cook ("The Unjust Steward," *ExpTim* 16 [1904-5] 44). Labelling Gibson's suggestion "conceivable," Hampden-Cook argues the steward's actions in reducing the overcharges are not trickery and dishonesty, but repentance and justice—at least outwardly. There should be little wonder, therefore, that the steward is commended. Hampden-Cook also adds that the steward's behavior is constantly illustrated in the East in his own day (he writes as a missionary in India).

[179] P. Gächter, "The Parable of the Dishonest Steward after Oriental Conceptions," *CBQ* 12 (1950) 121.

[180] "Conceptions," 123.

steward must give a definite sum to his master yearly which he in turn collects from sub-lessees. In keeping with the usual practice, however, the steward requires the sub-lessees or tenants to pay him much more for their manorial rights than was necessary for him to meet the terms of his own lease. The excess is his personal income. In reducing the tenants' IOUs, then, the steward is actually giving up his own income, not defrauding his master or the tenants.[181] Gächter concludes that in Jesus' application of the parable in vv. 8b-9 he "brings home to his disciples how they should detach themselves from riches, apply it to their brethren in need, and thus secure for themselves an eternal reward."[182]

The major contribution to the socioeconomic vindication of the steward's actions is made by J. D. M. Derrett. The significance and seminal nature of Derrett's work lies in his attempt to root our parable firmly in first-century *Jewish* soil. Unlike other interpreters before him who were content to explain the parable by means of cultural parallels that were either non-Jewish (e.g., Gächter argues on the basis of Indian parallels), or twentieth century, or both (e.g., Gibson), Derrett takes pains to base his interpretation on Jewish law and practice at the time the parable was first told by Jesus. Derrett begins by stressing the "utter incompatibility" between Roman or Greek law and Jewish law, at least insofar as the treatment of servants is concerned. Under the former, for example, a steward accused of wrongdoing would not simply be dismissed as the steward of the parable is, but would be punished. The steward's dismissal fits Jewish law and practice instead. Derrett notes that this incompatibility explains why non-Jews had difficulty in understanding the parable and why some Christians misunderstood it. "Why Luke retained it [the parable] without providing the key to the meaning is not entirely clear."[183] That key, according to Derrett, lies in the Jewish

---

[181] Gächter, "Die Parabel vom ungetreuen Verwalter (Lk 16:1-8)," *Orientierung* 27 (1963) 150. In this connection, mention can also be made of the similar but apparently independent suggestions of J. Steele and G. Gander. Steele, in an almost passing remark, suggests the steward is giving up his own legitimate profits which had been figured into the amounts due on the bills ("The Unjust Steward," *ExpTim* 39 [1927-28] 236). Gander thinks the steward's renunciation of his own unjustly acquired profits is intended by Jesus as a condemnation of Israel's religious leaders ("Le procédé de l'économe infidèle, décrit Luc 16:5-7, est-il répréhensible ou louable?" *VCaro* 7 [1953] 128-41, esp. 130, 134-35, 140-41). Gander (p. 130) credits G. Chastand (*Etudes sociales sur les paraboles évangéliques* [Toulouse: Societe d'édition de Toulouse, 1925] 68-72) with having opened "another way" of interpreting our parable when he suggested the steward voluntarily deprived himself of excess and unjustly acquired profits.

[182] "Conceptions," 131. Gächter's interpretation is followed by, among others, J. Volckaert ("The Parable of the Clever Steward," *Clergy Monthly* 17 [1953] 332-41) and E. H. Kiehl ("The Parable of the Unjust Manager in the Light of Contemporary Economic Life," [Th.D. dissertation, Concordia Seminary, 1959]).

[183] J. D. M. Derrett, "Fresh Light on St Luke XVI. I. The Parable of the Unjust Steward,"

laws of agency and usury.[184] The steward, acting for his master as an agent with "the most comprehensive authority,"[185] had been lending money at interest to fellow Jews and had concealed it in the bills by means of Pharisaic casuistry.[186] Morally our steward was a transgressor, but legally he was secure, "so long as his contracts hid the fact that the loan was usurious."[187]

Against this background the steward's actions toward the debtors take on a different light. If the contracts were in fact usurious, the amounts reduced may well correspond to the usurious portion of the debts (plus insurance).[188] In this case, the steward "was acting righteously, and making amends."[189] "On dismissal his duty towards his master faded before the practical necessity to recognize his duty towards God. He decided to obey the creator instead of his creature."[190] Derrett also suggests that by remitting the usurious part of the debt the steward was in effect giving up his own money. "Any release of rabbinical usury would, therefore, be a payment out of the steward's own pocket."[191] He goes on to argue that the steward's actions as his master's agent would be seen by the debtors as an act of the master himself.[192] The master, in order to preserve this unexpected and undeserved reputation as a pious man, not only praised the steward, but adopted and ratified his actions.[193]

What, according to Derrett, is Jesus' point in telling this story? The story is not precisely exemplary, he observes; the message is not exactly,

---

NTS 7 (1960-61) 200 (= *Law in the New Testament* [London: Darton, Longman & Todd, 1970] 51; pp. 48-77 of this book repeat the argument of his article). A later article by Derrett on Luke 16:6 may be an effort to respond to just this problem ("'Take Thy Bond . . . and Write Fifty' [Luke xvi.6]. The Nature of the Bond," *JTS*, n.s., 23 [1972] 438-40). There he concludes, on the basis of a number of demotic and Greek parallels, that Luke's readers would understand that the IOUs included additional sums. These sums could be demanded in Hellenistic courts but were against the spirit of OT law (pp. 439-40). I. H. Marshall (*The Gospel of Luke* [NIGTC; Exeter: Paternoster, 1978]), who himself judges Derrett's interpretation "feasible" for the first century (p. 615) and as having "most to be said for it" (p. 617), wonders whether a non-Palestinian audience ignorant of this background would have understood the point. "Perhaps Jesus intended the full meaning," Marshall suggests, "but the subsequent tradition failed to do so and hence the less adequate interpretation [i.e., that which says the steward acted corruptly throughout] came to dominate exegesis from a very early date" (p. 615).

[184] Derrett, "Steward," 200.
[185] "Steward," 204. See pp. 201-4 for Derrett's discussion of agency.
[186] "Steward," 204-9, 214.
[187] "Steward," 209.
[188] "Steward," 209, 214-15.
[189] "Steward," 209.
[190] "Steward," 215.
[191] "Steward," 209.
[192] "Steward," 210.
[193] "Steward," 216-17.

"Go and do likewise." The steward and master are not, after all, children of light. Derrett summarizes the meaning of the parable in these words.

> The meaning is that, since worldly people both by training and instinct act, in some crises, upon the assumption that God's standards are the right standards, and deal with worldly property single-mindedly according to their prevailing principles (i.e., *mammon*-directed with all, or God-directed with all) we may learn a lesson from their reactions both as to the validity of God's standards, respect for which is planted even in them by Nature, and as to the applicability of those standards to every department of life and every sphere of activity.[194]

Derrett's interpretation of the actions of the steward in our parable has been followed by many interpreters, too many in fact to discuss each here.[195] One interpreter who does deserve mention, however, is J. A. Fitzmyer. His interpretation of our parable is noteworthy because of the way in which he combines socioeconomic vindication of the steward's actions with the eschatological and monetary notes referred to earlier. Fitzmyer argues that in the Lucan context the parables of chapters 15 and 16 (particularly those of the lost son, the unjust steward, and the rich man and Lazarus) form a group of parables which give instruction on the use of wealth. With regard to Luke 16:1-13, Fitzmyer distinguishes between the parable itself (vv. 1-8a) and the multiple Lucan conclusion (vv. 8b-13).[196] "The unity of the story of the Dishonest Manager should not be stressed," he insists.[197] When it comes to the interpretation of the parable Fitzmyer follows Derrett's approach. The steward renounced usury and in the process relinquished his own profits. This action was hardly

---

[194] "Steward," 219.

[195] Among those who explicitly endorse Derrett's approach the following might be cited, in chronological order: H. Zimmermann ("Verwalter," 257-58), A. C. Thiselton ("The Parables as Language-Event: Some Comments on Fuchs's Hermeneutics in the Light of Linguistic Philosophy," *SJT* 23 [1970] 459-60), Morris (*Luke*, 245-46), E. E. Ellis (*The Gospel of Luke* [NCB; Grand Rapids/London: Eerdmans/Marshall, Morgan & Scott, 1974] 199), Marshall (*Luke*, 614-16, with some reservations), and S. J. Kistemaker (*The Parables of Jesus* [Grand Rapids: Baker, 1980] 228-31). It is perhaps worthy of note that the rudiments of Derrett's position seem to have been anticipated by C. B. Firth ("The Parable of the Unrighteous Steward [Luke xvi.1-9]," *ExpTim* 63 [1951-52] 93-95). On the basis of points of contact with Indian society which he had observed, Firth suggests the steward in our parable remitted interest. Firth does not develop this suggestion further, nor does he relate it to first-century Jewish society as does Derrett. Attention should also be drawn to J. A. Findlay's interpretation (*Jesus and His Parables* [London: Epworth, 1950] 82) that what the steward did in reducing the debtors' bills was forfeit his own commission. The steward was thus the only party who suffered in the transaction. Derrett's conclusion that the steward remitted his own usurious profits is virtually repeated by M. D. Goulder ("The Chiastic Structure of the Lucan Journey," in *SE* II [ed. F. L. Cross; Berlin: Akademie, 1964] 198), but without reference to Derrett.

[196] J. A. Fitzmyer, "The Story of the Dishonest Manager (Lk 16:1-13)," *TS* 25 (1964) 24-26. He argues that vv. 8b-9, 10-12, and 13 represent respectively "three different ways in which the early Church moralized the parable" (p. 38, following Dodd, *Parables*, 17).

[197] "Manager," 30.

dishonest, and since his master was not cheated of anything that was really his he commends the steward's prudence in view of the impending dismissal.[198] The manager is, suggests Fitzmyer, a model for Christians who are expected to grasp the dramatic situation of the kingdom and the crisis it brings. "It is a situation which calls for a prudent use of one's material wealth."[199]

III. SUMMARY/CONCLUSIONS

The foregoing history of the recent interpretation of the parable of the unjust steward is at best one of several possible ways to organize the relevant literature. To review this history as I have presented it the reader is referred to the Table of Contents. The sheer number of interpretations canvassed above, as well as the many possible overlaps among them, highlight the difficulty of the parable in a striking, if not overwhelming and at times disheartening, fashion. A number of key interpretive issues have also surfaced in the course of the foregoing survey. Among them are the following: the relationship of the parable to the context, particularly Luke 15; where the parable ends and its applications/interpretations begin; the identity of *ho kyrios* in v. 8a; the teaching in vv. 8-9 especially; and the cohesion (or lack thereof) between vv. 1-8/9 and 9/10-13.

While not every interpretation mentioned above can be valid, some emphases and suggestions do appear to offer particular insight for the interpretation of this difficult parable. These emphases will be woven into the fabric of my interpretation in the subsequent chapters. They include the eschatological crisis motif, the stewardship of material possessions, the context of controversy with the Pharisees and the teachers of the law, and the element of surprise.

With this chapter as background, let us now turn our attention to a detailed exegetical study of Luke 16:1-13.

---

[198] "Manager," 34-36. The same interpretation of our parable is offered by Fitzmyer in *The Gospel according to Luke (X-XXIV)* (AB, vol. 28a; Garden City: Doubleday, 1985) 1097-98, 1100-1101.

[199] "Manager," 37. The combination of socioeconomic vindication with eschatological and monetary notes also characterizes Marshall's interpretation of the parable (*Luke*, 614-22).

CHAPTER TWO

EXEGESIS OF LUKE 16:1-13

The focus of the present chapter is an exegetical discussion of Luke 16:1-13 itself. The sheer number of interpretations already seen in the first chapter is striking testimony to the difficulty of this pericope. "The story and the context in which it stands," writes W. Grundmann, "belong to the most controversial problems of Lucan exegesis."[1] "Few passages in the Gospel [of Luke]," I. H. Marshall notes, "can have given rise to so many different interpretations" as this one.[2] Fully cognizant of the difficulties and variety of interpretations of this passage, the thesis I will argue in this chapter is as follows: the parable of the unjust steward (Luke 16:1-9) and the verses attached to it (vv. 10-13) together deal with the matter of the Christian's wise use of money, possessions, and/or material goods. The background for this teaching is the coming of the kingdom of God. To express the thrust of Luke 16:1-13 more succinctly, the passage might be entitled "Christian Stewardship in an Eschatological Key" or "Stewardship and the Kingdom." In subsequent chapters this message will be related to the larger Lucan contextual levels.

The focus of the present chapter will be restricted for the most part to Luke 16:1-13. As indispensable as the literary context is for the interpretation of the passage (i.e., Luke 15 and 16 and the central section of Luke's Gospel), full treatment of that context will be deferred until the next chapter. In addition, discussion of connections with other relevant verses, passages, themes, and theology in Luke will be kept to a minimum. The reasons for proceeding in this admittedly artificial fashion are both practical and methodological. On the practical side, the number and complexity of the major interpretive issues associated with Luke 16:1-13 are such that the present chapter promises to be long enough without also considering here other levels of context. On the methodological side, since many interpreters of our parable minimize, disregard, or reject the context anyway, I will in this chapter examine the passage on its own terms as much as possible. I will show that even on its own terms, that is, temporarily isolated from its Lucan context, Luke 16:1-13 is about the faithful stewardship of material possessions against

---

[1] Grundmann, *Lukas*, 316.
[2] Marshall, *Luke*, 614.

an eschatological background. When the contextual levels of the parable are widened in subsequent chapters, the teaching of the parable will be brought into sharper focus and my overall thesis confirmed.

The approach adopted for this chapter is to concentrate attention on the key interpretive issues in Luke 16:1-13, the majority of which are in vv. 8-13.

I. REVIEW OF LUKE 16:1-7

Whatever differences interpreters may have about Luke 16:8-13, almost all agree that vv. 1-7 at least are part of the parable of the unjust steward. In this part of the chapter I will set the stage for Part II by reviewing the main and (dare I say?) noncontroversial features of the story in vv. 1-7.

It should be noted at the outset that despite all the interpretive difficulties associated with Luke 16:1-13, the authenticity of the parable itself is seldom questioned. Although the precise limits and context of the parable of the unjust steward are variously defined, almost everyone believes it was spoken by Jesus.[3] Many would agree with the judgment that the very difficulty of the parable "guarantees its authenticity."[4] In D. R. Fletcher's words, "It hardly seems plausible that an apocryphal parable involving such obvious difficulties of interpretation should have been incorporated by the early Christian community into its traditions of the parables of Jesus."[5] As we approach this parable, then, its authenticity is not in question. Most interpreters operate on the assumption that the parable is from Jesus, even though they may differ widely as to its exact limits and meaning. Although the authenticity of the parable itself is unquestioned and the main flow of the action is clear, interpreters still disagree about the meaning of some of the details of the story. In what follows, I will note these differences, but will not pause to discuss them carefully since they do not, for the most part, significantly affect the interpretation of the parable as a whole.

Luke 16:1-7 tells the story of a steward who, faced with dismissal, shrewdly provides for his future. Luke introduces the parable in 16:1a with these words: "*Elegen de kai pros tous mathētas.*" Ostensibly Luke's

---

[3] Many interpreters see Luke's hand in parts of this pericope, especially in vv. 8-13. Sellin seems alone in wanting to attribute the entire passage to Luke ("Studien," 298 n. 1276).

[4] Stein, *Parables*, 106. This judgment is especially true for those interpreters who see the parable extending at least as far as v. 8a. The difficulty, to be discussed in Part II, arises when the steward's actions in vv. 5-7 are praised (apparently) in v. 8a.

[5] "Riddle," 15.

introduction connects our parable in some way with the scene in chapter 15 (*elegen de kai*) and indicates that the parable is directed primarily to Jesus' disciples. Since the significance of this introduction is disputed, however, further discussion of it will be delayed until the next part of the chapter.

Following Luke's introduction, the two main characters of the parable—a certain rich man and his steward—are brought on the stage at once in v. 1b. The conditions presupposed here are apparently those common in Galilee in the first century. "The *plousios* is probably to be regarded as the owner of a large estate who lives abroad and is represented by a steward."[6] The steward (*oikonomos*), acting as the rich man's agent with considerable legal powers, is charged with the management of the entire estate in the owner's absence.[7] Whatever the precise financial arrangements between the two men,[8] it quickly becomes apparent that all is not well between them (vv. 1c-2).

The steward is accused (by whom we are not told) of "wasting" (*hōs diaskorpizōn*, v. 1c) the rich man's property. Given the fact that he is then dismissed rather than arrested or made to pay compensation, the allegation against him is probably not embezzlement but rather carelessness and neglect of duty.[9] We are not told explicitly whether or not the accusations are true, and the matter is not decided by *hōs*.[10] More telling,

---

[6] Jeremias, *Parables*, 181. So also Grundmann, who speaks of latifundium (*Lukas*, 317), and Marshall (*Luke*, 617). The largeness of the man's estate is deduced from the size of the debts in question in vv. 5-7. Bailey, however, takes exception to this evaluation of the rich man when he writes that "the wealthy, distant, foreign, ruthless landowner is unknown in the synoptic parables" (*Poet*, 90). He argues instead that the rich man was a man of noble character who was a respected member of the community, not an absentee landlord (p. 94).

[7] For a detailed discussion of the responsibilities and rights of a Jewish agent, see Derrett, "Steward," 201-4, and Oesterley, "Steward," 275-76 (= *Parables*, 193-94).

[8] This point is a matter of debate which has implications for the understanding of the steward's actions in vv. 5-7. On the one hand, Bailey, for example, argues that the steward was a salaried official who no doubt made extras "under the table." These amounts were not, however, reflected in the signed bills (*Poet*, 94). On this basis Bailey concludes that the actions described in vv. 5-7 are fraudulent. Kiehl, on the other hand, represents the position that the steward is unsalaried and is expected to care for himself by his own measures. Whatever he can get above the annual amount owed to the rich man as rent is the steward's own gain ("Parable," 107). Kiehl's conclusion is that the actions of vv. 5-7 are not fraudulent. These interpretations of vv. 5-7 will be discussed in Part II.

[9] Zahn, *Lucas*, 572; Geldenhuys, *Luke*, 414 n. 4, 415; and Marshall, *Luke*, 617. Klostermann suggests the steward is charged with bad business management (*Lukas*, 524). Fonck calls attention to the fact that *diaskorpizō* is the same word used of the lost son in 15:13 (*NIV*, "squandered"), and concludes that the steward's mismanagement may be the result of his efforts to maintain an opulent, wanton lifestyle (*Parabeln*, 680). Degenhardt suggests the steward may have been guilty of being too generous to others with his master's property (*Lukas*, 165).

[10] Jülicher, *Gleichnisreden* 2.496; Marshall, *Luke*, 617; and Weiss, *Lukas*, 530 n. (unnumbered).

perhaps, is the steward's silence when confronted by his master about the accusations (v. 2) and his subsequent soliloquy about his predicament (vv. 3-4). Many interpreters see in these features of the story an indirect admission of guilt.[11] It may well be, however, that whether or not the accusations are true is ultimately only a secondary matter of little real importance. What is important is that the master apparently believes the accusations and loses confidence in the steward's fitness to continue managing the estate.[12] In v. 2 the rich man calls in the steward[13] and gives him notice of his dismissal.[14] Despite differences of opinion among interpreters about when the steward's dismissal becomes effective,[15]

---

[11] Among the interpreters who see indicting significance in the steward's silence in v. 2 are Bailey, *Poet*, 97 (the silence is "supremely significant" in an Oriental context); Lagrange, *Luc*, 431; Loisy, *Evangiles* 2.157; and Michaelis, *Gleichnisse*, 226. Weiss (*Lukas*, 531) and Zahn (*Lucas*, 571) detect a consciousness of guilt in the soliloquy of vv. 3-4, while Loisy suggests the reflections of the steward in these verses indicate neither the remorse of the guilty nor the revolt of the falsely slandered (*Evangiles* 2.158).

Mention should perhaps also be made at this point of several interpreters who contend the accusations against the steward are false. Among those who hold this opinion are Hölbe, "Parabel," 534; Köster, "Haushalter," 727; Schleiermacher, *Lukas*, 202-3; and Wright, "Parable," 282.

[12] This point is stressed by Jülicher, *Gleichnisreden* 2.496; Lagrange, *Luc*, 431; and Schmid, *Lukas*, 257.

[13] The clause *kai phōnēsas* [BAGD, *phōneō*, 2.b.: "call to oneself," "summon"] *auton eipen autōi* (v. 2) would seem to speak against the rich man being an absentee landlord and in favor of his being a local resident. An alternative explanation might be that the dismissal is pronounced during one of the rich man's visits to his estate.

[14] Jülicher is no doubt right when he says the rich man's question to his steward in v. 2 (*Ti touto akouō peri sou;*) is not a real one in the sense that he is uncertain about or doubts the accusations. Instead it is an "animated expression of indignation" (*Gleichnisreden* 2.497 [cf. Acts 14:15]). Meyer explains the syntax of the question as the result of the contraction of a relative clause with an interrogative clause (*Commentary*, 216). Marshall (*Luke*, 617) suggests that for *ti touto* we are to understand *estin*; M. Zerwick and M. Grosvenor (*A Grammatical Analysis of the Greek New Testament* [rev. ed. in 1 vol.; Rome: Biblical Institute Press, 1981] re. Luke 16:2) and Creed (*Luke*, 203) offer the fuller equivalent *ti estin touto ho*.

[15] Interpreters are divided on whether the steward is fired on the spot or whether his dismissal is to become effective after he turns over the accounts. Bailey represents the former view. On the analogy of life in conservative Middle Eastern villages today, Bailey argues that in our parable the steward's authority is terminated immediately. Because it takes some time for word of his dismissal to get out, however, the steward has room to maneuver, which he does in vv. 5-7. Bailey suggests the steward's soliloquy in vv. 3-4 is given on his way to get the accounts to surrender them to the rich man (*Poet*, 96-97). Other interpreters who believe the steward is fired on the spot include Jülicher, *Gleichnisreden* 2.498; Topel, "Steward," 217 n. 8; and Wright, "Parable," 282. The alternate view, that the steward's dismissal is a process and not immediate, is argued by, for example, Marshall. While he speaks of the steward's "summary dismissal" (*Luke*, 617), Marshall believes the present tense of the verb *aphaireitai* in v. 3 signifies a process of dismissal which is not completed until the steward has had time to set down the accounts (p. 618). Derrett views the dismissal as effective from the moment the accounting is rendered ("Steward," 204). Zahn suggests there is a double purpose for the accounting called for in v. 2—to convict the steward and to prepare for his successor (*Lucas*, 571).

almost all are agreed that the rich man's decision is final and irrevocable (*ou gar dynēi eti oikonomein*, v. 2b).[16] The accounting called for in v. 2 (*apodos ton logon tēs oikonomias sou*) is at best intended as preparation for the steward's successor.

The crisis note sounded in v. 2 is strengthened in vv. 3-4. Here the steward's predicament is conveyed by means of a soliloquy, a feature not uncommon in parables (cf., e.g., Luke 12:17; 15:17-19).[17] Judging from the steward's own reflections in v. 3, he has no illusions he will be reinstated by his master, but seems to regard his dismissal, whether already completed or imminent, as certain (*ho kyrios mou aphaireitai tēn oikonomian ap' emou*). The more obvious options open to him are ruled out rather quickly. He is not strong enough for manual labor (*skaptein ouk ischyō*), he is too proud to beg (*epaitein aischynomai*). His future seems hopeless indeed. Suddenly[18] an idea occurs to him—"I know what I'll do" (*NIV*), he says. The hearer/reader is not told in v. 4 what that idea is, but has to wait until it is executed in vv. 5-7. As Krämer observes, this feature of the story catches the attention and lifts the curiosity of the hearer.[19] What *is* clear from v. 4b, however, is that the steward's goal is not to change his master's mind or to have the decision reversed. Rather the steward hopes his plan will secure the hospitality of others (*hina . . . dexōntai me eis tous oikous autōn*)[20] when he loses his position (*hotan metastathō ek tēs oikonomias*).[21]

---

[16] "Almost all" are agreed on this point, but a few interpreters take the position that the dismissal is only threatened and will be reversed if the accusations are proven false by the accounting (e.g., Hölbe, "Parabel," 535; Oosterzee, *Luke*, 245). Plummer notes that the phrase *apodos ton logon*, commonly understood of the final accounting for surrender of the stewardship, might mean instead the account to investigate the charges against the steward. In any event, Plummer concludes that "the steward, knowing that he cannot disprove the charges, regards this demand for a reckoning as equivalent to dismissal" (*Luke*, 382). A number of interpreters believe the steward is not dismissed in the end, that the master's decision to dismiss him is reversed because of the steward's prudent response to his crisis (e.g., Coutts, "Steward," 56; Oosterzee, *Luke*, 245; Pautrel, "Tabernacula," 318-19; Pirot, *Paraboles*, 316; and Wiesen, *Gleichnis*, 76).

[17] Marshall, *Luke*, 618.

[18] Suddenness is probably the force of the aorist *egnōn* in v. 4 (Creed, *Luke*, 203; Marshall, *Luke*, 618; and Plummer, *Luke*, 383). Plummer calls attention to E. W. Burton's *Syntax of the Moods and Tenses in New Testament Greek* §45. There Burton discusses "The Dramatic Aorist," which, he explains, is "sometimes used of a state of mind just reached, or of an act expressive of it. The effect is to give to the statement greater vividness than is given by the more usual Present." Burton illustrates this usage of the aorist by *egnōn* in Luke 16:4. It may be that the translators of the *NIV* sought to convey the idea of suddenness through their punctuation of vv. 3b-4a: "I'm not strong enough to dig, and I'm ashamed to beg—I know what I'll do . . . "

[19] Krämer, *Rätsel*, 67.

[20] The subject of *dexōntai* is the debtors of vv. 5-7 (Marshall, *Luke*, 618, and Plummer, *Luke*, 383).

[21] Hölbe ("Parabel," 535) takes the aorist subjunctive *metastathō* as proof the dismissal

The steward's plan unfolds in vv. 5-7. He calls in each one[22] of his master's debtors and authorizes them to reduce their debts.[23] Two such transactions, typical of the steward's dealings with all the debtors, are described in vv. 5-7. The motive for these actions has been revealed already in v. 4; the steward expects that the debtors whom he helps will express their gratitude by receiving him into their homes when he is unemployed. The exact nature of the steward's actions here is a matter of much debate and will be discussed more carefully in Part II. At this point, however, a few comments about background details are in order.

Interpreters are divided over the identity of the debtors (*chreopheiletai*). Some take them to be tenants who live on the master's estate and who pay a fixed portion of their crops in rent.[24] This explanation seems plausible given the steward's position and the fact the bills (*ta grammata*, vv. 6-7) of the two representative debtors are stated in terms of natural goods, that is, oil and wheat. Other interpreters, however, explain the debtors as merchants who have received goods from the estate on credit and who have given promissory notes in their own handwriting to the steward.[25] Among the reasons given in support of this position are the

---

is conditional, not categorical. Jülicher (*Gleichnisreden* 2.499), on the other hand, denies the element of conditionality here, arguing instead that the force is purely temporal as, e.g., in Luke 9:26 and 21:30-31 (= "as soon as" or "when").

[22] The phrase *hena hekaston* can be taken in two ways. Depending on how it is taken, the stress falls either on the idea that all the debtors are summoned or that each is dealt with secretly. In favor of the first emphasis, Easton argues this phrase means "without exception," not "one by one," despite his concession that the steward naturally would seek privacy in his interviews (*Luke*, 242). Zerwick and Grosvenor (*Analysis*) render the phrase as "each and every," *NIV* and *NASB* as "each one." *RSV* and *NEB*, on the other hand, apparently favor the second emphasis (i.e., secrecy), for they both translate the phrase "one by one." A number of interpreters have stressed the element of secrecy in the transactions, although not necessarily basing it on this phrase (e.g., Bailey, *Poet*, 99; Schmid, *Lukas*, 257; and Zahn, *Lucas*, 572). Perhaps too much should not be made of this phrase since the ideas of inclusiveness and secrecy are a matter of emphasis and are not mutually exclusive. After all, as noted by Easton above, the steward could have called in all debtors ("each one") and, because of the nature of the transactions, dealt secretly with them ("one by one"). Goebel ("Gleichnisgruppe," 660) has few followers when he suggests the debt reductions are carried out in the presence of the other debtors.

[23] The first debtor owes one hundred baths of oil (*hekaton batous elaiou*, v. 6), which is reduced to fifty, and the second one hundred cors of wheat (*hekaton korous sitou*, v. 7), which is reduced to eighty. These measures are Hebrew measures (cf. 1 Kgs 5:11), which, it should be noted, Luke does not explain or translate for his non-Jewish audience. (Might this fact not be another indication of, among other things, the authenticity of the parable?) The bath is a liquid measure equal to between eight and nine gallons (BAGD), while the cor is a dry measure of between ten and twelve bushels (BAGD). In typical Teutonic fashion (as one of my professors once observed), Jeremias calculates that the oil owed by the one debtor is the yield of 146 olive trees and the wheat the yield of one hundred acres (*Parables*, 181).

[24] E.g., Bailey, *Poet*, 92; Fonck, *Parabeln*, 683; Krämer, *Rätsel*, 45; Michaelis, *Gleichnisse*, 228; Nägelsbach, "Gleichnis," 483; and Wright, "Parable," 281-82.

[25] E.g., Godet, *Luke* 2.163; Goebel, "Gleichnisgruppe," 659; Marshall, *Luke*, 618; Smith, *Parables*, 108; and Weiss, *Lukas*, 531.

facts that the debtors can write[26] (*grapson*, vv. 6-7, presumably something tenants would be unable to do) and that the debts are so large[27] (one
hundred baths of oil and one hundred cors of wheat, presumably too
much to be owed by tenant farmers). As interesting as such discussions
may be for the background of our parable, Jülicher is surely correct when
he calls such a debate "superfluous."[28] Although tenant farmers seems
the more likely explanation (for the reasons given above), the exact
identity of the debtors makes absolutely no difference in the interpretation of the parable.

Another matter of background detail over which interpreters are
divided is the debt reductions authorized by the steward. Here I have in
mind the differences in the amounts and the relative proportions of those
reductions, not the morality of the actions themselves (the latter will be
discussed in Part II). The first debtor has his debt reduced from one
hundred to fifty baths of oil, the second from one hundred to eighty cors
of wheat—reductions of fifty and twenty percent, respectively. One
explanation of the differences is that they are further evidence of the
steward's arbitrariness and unscrupulousness with his master's property.[29] Another is that the differences are an indication of the steward's
discernment; in each case he tailors his liberality to get the same result.[30]
A third explanation is that the differences are simply literary or artistic
variations which bear no special significance.[31] Finally, there is the
explanation that the reductions are equal in value (about five hundred
denarii each) though different in size and proportion of the total debt.[32]
However one explains the differences, the size of the debts involved (and
only two of several debtors are mentioned) indicates the estate is very
large, the debtors themselves are relatively rich and important men,[33] the
obligations are heavy, and/or Jesus possessed "the oriental story-teller's
love of large numbers."[34]

Thus far in Luke 16:1-7, we have seen a steward who, faced with the
prospect of dismissal from office, responds decisively to ensure his

---

[26] Creed, *Luke*, 204, and Lagrange, *Luc*, 433.

[27] Summers, *Luke*, 189.

[28] Jülicher, *Gleichnisreden* 2.500. Cf. the similar judgments of Grundmann, *Lukas*, 318,
and Schmid, *Lukas*, 257.

[29] Plummer, *Luke*, 383, and Zahn, *Lucas*, 573.

[30] Godet, *Luke* 2.163.

[31] Creed, *Luke*, 204; Easton, *Luke*, 242; Klostermann, *Lukas*, 525; Peters, "Haushalter,"
136; and Weiss, *Lukas*, 532.

[32] Bailey, *Poet*, 101; Bugge, *Haupt-Parabeln*, 442; Grundmann, *Lukas*, 318; Jeremias,
Parables, 181; Rengstorf, *Lukas*, 192; and Schmid, *Lukas*, 257.

[33] Bailey, *Poet*, 99.

[34] Jeremias, *Parables*, 34.

future by reducing the amounts owed by his master's debtors. Judging from the steward's soliloquy in v. 3 and his directions to at least the first debtor in v. 6 (*Dexai . . . kai kathisas tacheōs grapson . . .*),[35] he takes the dismissal seriously and responses accordingly. As we read on we are perhaps surprised to discover that the outcome of the steward's actions is not revealed in this parable, at least not in so many words. Instead, having seen his plan in action in vv. 5-7, we read next in v. 8a that the steward is praised by *ho kyrios* (his master or Jesus?) for having acted "wisely" or "shrewdly" (*phronimōs*, BAGD). This statement brings us to the much more thorny interpretive issues to be discussed in Part II. It bears noting here that almost every interpretation of our parable assumes the steward's plan is successful, that is, he is eventually received into the homes of the debtors. The only exception to this assumption would be those interpreters who believe the steward's actions resulted in his reinstatement by his master, thus making reliance on the hospitality of others unnecessary.[36] In all other interpretations, however, it is assumed he is dismissed and that the praise (whether ironic or sincere) is an indication of success. Without the presumption of success, the parable loses most of its impact.

II. KEY INTERPRETIVE ISSUES

Having reviewed Luke 16:1-7, in which the notes of crisis and response are prominent, we are now in a position to consider the more substantive interpretive issues in this parable. The vast majority of these issues arise in vv. 8-13. For the most part the following discussion treats the issues as they come up in the text.

A. Audience, v. 1

One issue of importance for the interpretation of the parable of the unjust steward arises in the opening words of Luke 16. That issue is the

---

[35] Although most interpreters take the adverb *tacheōs* with *grapson* rather than *kathisas* (e.g., Bailey, *Poet*, 99; Easton, *Luke*, 242; Lagrange, *Luc*, 433; and Weiss, *Lukas*, 532), Jülicher is right when he contends it makes little difference which it modifies since *kathisas* and *grapson* ought to coincide temporally (*Gleichnisreden* 2.501; cf. Loisy, *Evangiles* 2.159 n. 1). The steward's instructions to the first debtor indicate his awareness of the urgency of his situation, if not also the clandestine, dishonest nature of the transaction itself. On the assumption the steward's actions are dishonest (a matter to be discussed in a subsequent section), Bailey suggests that *tacheōs grapson* ("write quickly") is "a crucial key to a proper understanding of what is going on." The steward "must finish before the master finds out what he is doing, but also before the renters themselves find out that it is all dishonest" (*Poet*, 99 n. 50).

[36] Coutts, "Steward," 56; Pautrel, "Tabernacula," 318-19; Oosterzee, *Luke*, 245; and Wiesen, *Gleichnis*, 76.

audience to whom Jesus addresses the parable. Stein lists the audience as one of four "serious problems" connected with our parable.[37] In Luke 16:1 we read these words: *Elegen de kai pros tous mathētas*. Ostensibly, this introduction implies or indicates several things. First, it implies that the parable is in some sense almost a sequel to the three parables in chapter 15. Second, it indicates that, whatever the message of the parable is, it is primarily directed by Jesus to his disciples. I will discuss this introduction more carefully later in this section of the chapter. Before doing so, however, consideration should be given to various objections raised against taking this introduction at face value. Not a few interpreters contend Luke's words are misleading or at best irrelevant for the interpretation of our parable, and can, therefore, be disregarded or rejected.[38] What are some of the arguments advanced to support such a conclusion, and what can be said in response?

1. Objections to Luke's Introduction

Sometimes Luke's introduction to our parable is disregarded because the point of the parable is judged to be irrelevant for the disciples. This argument can take several forms, depending on one's decisions about the point of the parable. If the point is the wise use of money or possessions, then, some would argue, the parable cannot be to the disciples since they were not rich.[39] Directions to them about the use of riches would be out of place. The parable must, therefore, be directed to a different audience than Luke's words indicate. If the point is resolute action in a crisis, then, others would say, as Jeremias does, "it would hardly have been addressed to the disciples, but rather to the 'unconverted', the hesitant, the waverers, the crowd."[40] Both forms of the argument that the parable is irrelevant for disciples disregard Luke's introduction.

In response, it can be said that the first form of the argument—Jesus'

---

[37] Stein (*Parables*) lists the problems on p. 106, and discusses the matter of audience on p. 110.

[38] Among the interpreters who so treat Luke's introduction are Jeremias, *Parables*, 47; Lenwood, "Parable," 368-69; Loisy, *Evangiles* 2.156; Lunt, "Parable," 335; Via, *Parables*, 157; Weiss, *Lukas*, 529; and Wiesen, *Gleichnis*, 67.

[39] Degenhardt, *Lukas*, esp. 27-39 and 105-12 (cited by Krämer, *Rätsel*, 130 n. 211), and Wiesen, *Gleichnis*, 83.

[40] Jeremias, *Parables*, 47. Stein quotes these words as support for his own suggestion that Luke may here be taking material originally addressed to a hostile audience (such as the Pharisees and scribes) and applying it to Jesus' followers (*Parables*, 110). In similar fashion, Via believes Luke transforms this parable into a "disciple parable" (*Parables*, 157).

disciples were not rich—is an overgeneralization which fails to consider some important material in the Third Gospel. While many of Jesus' disciples were no doubt poor, we cannot conclude from this fact that all were. In Luke 8:1-3, for example, we read of some women who were accompanying Jesus on his itinerant preaching ministry, supporting him and his entourage from their possessions. This fact suggests that at least these women were anything but poor. Zacchaeus also comes to mind in this connection (19:1-10). As a chief tax collector he was a wealthy man when he became a disciple. There is no reason to assume he did not remain wealthy, even after giving half his possessions to the poor and promising to make restitution to anyone whom he had cheated. Another relevant factor is the presence of tax collectors in 15:1-2. If, as I will argue shortly, the scene is the same in Luke 15 and 16, and if some tax collectors were disciples of Jesus, there is merit to the suggestion that our parable is directed at least in part to these individuals. Some of them were no doubt wealthy like Zacchaeus, and may well have been in need of instruction on how to use their ill-gotten gains now that they were disciples.[41] Our parable may provide just that instruction.

The argument that our parable cannot be to disciples if it is a summons to resolute action in a crisis appears as something of a *non sequitur*. It is hard to understand why such a summons necessarily excludes disciples. Is not such a summons just as relevant and necessary for disciples as it is for "the 'unconverted', the hesitant, the waverers, the crowd"? It may be that the logic behind this argument is that disciples have already acted resolutely in following Jesus. As a result of their commitment to Jesus already, the particular call to resolute action in our parable is not directed to them. Even if this reasoning lies behind the objection in question, I remain unpersuaded. Such an argument fails to recognize that there were many would-be followers of Jesus, many who may have looked like disciples but, in the final analysis, were not (cf. Luke 8:7, 14; 9:57-62; 13:22-30). True discipleship involves following Jesus to the end; it necessitates a series of resolute responses as the disciple takes up his cross daily and follows Jesus (9:53; 14:27). If discipleship is of this character, it is hard to see why a summons to resolute action here in our parable is judged irrelevant for disciples. As will be argued in due course, the point of the parable is that the wise, faithful use of material possessions is evidence of the genuineness of one's discipleship.

---

[41] Among the writers who emphasize this point are W. Arnot, *The Parables of our Lord* (London: T. Nelson, 1865; repr. Grand Rapids: Kregel, 1981) 454; Arnott, "Steward," 509; Dods, *Parables*, 362; Meyer, *Commentary*, 211; and Stier, *Words* 4.102.

In addition to the above arguments against the Lucan introduction based on the subject matter of the parable, another objection emphasizes the context of the parable. Given the prominence of the Pharisees and scribes in Luke 15 (cf. vv. 1-3) and 16:14-31, the conclusion is drawn that 16:1-13 must be directed to them as well.[42] On this reading our parable combats either the Pharisees' casuistry[43] or their attachment to earthly goods.[44] In an anti-pharisaic context such as Luke 15 and 16, so the argument goes, a change of audience to the disciples in the middle hardly seems appropriate.

What can be said about this argument? First, this argument must be credited for its attention to context, even though, in my judgment, an unwarranted inference is drawn from it that our parable is not to the disciples or that the context itself is artificial. As will be argued in the next chapter, the backdrop for the parable of the unjust steward *is* Jesus' controversy with the Pharisees and scribes. Second, this argument ignores the broader literary structure of the so-called central section of Luke's Gospel (9:51-19:44). One of the characteristic features of that section, to be elaborated in the next chapter, is the alternation between opponents and disciples. Suffice it to say here, the change in audience itself is not sufficient grounds for rejecting Luke's introduction.

2. Luke's Introduction

Having considered some objections to Luke's introduction and having found them far from compelling, let me now look more carefully at the introduction itself. As noted at the outset of the discussion of the audience, Luke's introduction to the parable of the unjust steward suggests that, whatever the message, it is primarily directed by Jesus to his disciples. It is also in some sense a sequel to the three parables in chapter 15. Let me establish these points exegetically.

The opening phrase of Luke 16:1, *elegen de kai*, expresses at least

---

[42] Kamlah, "Parabel," 294; Lenwood, "Parable," 369; Loisy, *Evangiles* 2.156; and Wiesen, *Gleichnis*, 67.

[43] The interpretation of the parable as a polemic against Pharisaic casuistry can take very different forms. One approach views the steward's actions to the debtors in the parable as a positive model to be followed by the Pharisees—i.e., they are to relieve the burden on the people by reducing the ceremonial laws (e.g., Kamlah, "Parabel," 294, and Lunt, "Parable," 336). Another approach understands the same actions of the steward in exactly the opposite way. Instead of a positive model of what the Pharisees should do, the parable is viewed as an indictment of the Pharisees for having reduced God's claim on men by their casuistic practices (e.g., Lenwood, "Parable," 369-70).

[44] Loisy, *Evangiles* 2.156.

conceptual continuity between what has been said in chapter 15 and what is about to be said in chapter 16. The imperfect, *elegen*, in particular, conveys this sense. As Topel points out, all nine uses of *elegen de* in Luke connect what follows the phrase with what precedes it.[45] The idea of continuity between Luke 15 and 16 is also expressed by the conjunction *kai*. Many interpreters would agree with Zahn's explanation that *kai* in Luke 16:1 indicates a change of persons addressed without a change of scene.[46] On the occasion of 15:1-2 Jesus *also* has something to say to his disciples.[47] Jesus has addressed three parables to the grumbling Pharisees and scribes in chapter 15; he now (16:1) turns his attention to his disciples. The disciples *also* need instruction to make God's will clear to them.[48] In addition, there may be truth to the suggestion that the *kai* points to the fact the Pharisees are still in the background (cf. 16:14).[49] Jesus directs this parable to the disciples in the hearing of the Pharisees. Although the parable is especially for the disciples, it has significance (as a warning) for the Pharisees as well.[50]

The parable of the unjust steward is, according to Luke, spoken *pros tous mathētas*. That it is addressed to Jesus' disciples has already been touched on in the discussion of objections to Luke's introduction; a few further words of clarification are, however, perhaps in order. As Luke uses the word, "disciples" is broader than just the twelve apostles (cf. 6:17; 17:1, 5; 18:31; 19:37), though it includes them (9:54), and is distinct from the crowds (12:54; 14:25). The disciples are Jesus' followers, not simply the sum total of all those in his presence on any given occasion. They are the multitude of earnest hearers anxious for salvation.[51] To these people Jesus speaks the parable of the unjust steward.

To summarize my discussion of the audience of our parable, I have argued that objections to Luke's introduction are not compelling, and

---

[45] Topel, "Steward," 222 n. 34. The nine uses of *elegen de* in Luke are 5:36; 9:23; 10:2; 12:54; 13:6; 14:7, 12; 16:1; 18:1.

[46] Zahn, *Lucas*, 570 n. 77. Creed, *Luke*, 203; Geldenhuys, *Luke*, 414 n. 1; Klostermann, *Lukas*, 524; and Plummer, *Luke*, 381, are among the interpreters who so explain the significance of the conjunction.

[47] Zahn, *Lucas*, 570.

[48] Schlatter, *Lukas*, 362-63.

[49] Hooley and Mason, "Parable," 51.

[50] Marshall, *Luke*, 617.

[51] Goebel, "Gleichnisgruppe," 656. If, as I have argued, Luke's introduction does connect chapters 15 and 16, one may conclude from 15:1 that many tax collectors and sinners are numbered among Jesus' disciples. Many interpreters see special significance in our parable for the tax collectors in particular (e.g., Goebel, "Gleichnisgruppe," 656; Arnot, *Parables*, 454; Arnott, "Steward," 509; Dods, *Parables*, 362; Kiehl, "Parable," 66; Meyer, *Commentary*, 211; Olshausen, *Commentary* 2.67; Oosterzee, *Luke*, 245; and Stier, *Words* 4.102).

that there are good reasons for taking Luke's introduction to our parable at face value. On that basis, the primary audience of our parable is the disciples, and the general scene is the same as that in chapter 15.

B. The Identity of ho kyrios, v. 8a

Despite differences about certain details of the story in Luke 16:1-7, most interpreters agree those verses are part of Jesus' original parable. The situation changes when we come to v. 8, a verse which one writer describes as "full of thorns" and as having "mountains of difficulties."[52] The first issue one encounters in this verse is the identity of *ho kyrios* by whom the steward is praised. In this context the noun is ambiguous insofar as it could refer to either the master of the parable or to Jesus himself. If *kyrios* refers to the master, v. 8a is still part of the story itself and constitutes Jesus' report of the *master's* response to his steward's plan. If *kyrios* refers to Jesus, the story itself ends at v. 7, and v. 8a is then Luke's account of *Jesus'* response to and application of the steward's actions. This matter is part of the larger issue of the original ending of the parable which includes vv. 8-13. Since a discussion of that larger issue at this point would involve a discussion of each of those verses, I will treat that issue as I come to it in each verse. For the time being, however, the focus of attention will be on the identity of *ho kyrios* in v. 8a. Our decisions on this matter will determine at least whether or not the original parable includes v. 8a.

1. Jesus

What are the arguments pro and con for each of the interpretations of *ho kyrios*? Let us consider first the interpretation which identifies *kyrios* as Jesus.[53] One of the arguments given to support this identification is the absolute use of this noun in Luke. Since, according to Jeremias's calculations, *ho kyrios* is used at least seventeen times in Luke to refer to Jesus, probability is in favor of 16:8 being the eighteenth such use.[54]

---

[52] Krämer, *Rätsel*, 139 and 237, respectively.

[53] The representatives of this interpretation include Cadoux, Ellis, Gander, Hunter ("Crisis"), Jeremias, Jülicher, Kiehl, Klostermann, Lenwood, Loisy, Menoud, Michaelis, Paul, Rengstorf, Riggenbach, Rücker, Schmid, Smith, Weiss (*Lukas*), and Wellhausen.

[54] Jeremias, *Parables*, 45 n. 82. Ellis (*Luke*, 199) and Riggenbach ("Gleichnisse," 19) draw the same conclusion. Rücker ("Gleichnis," 60) approaches the word from a slightly different angle. He notes that every time *kyrios* = master in Luke 16:1-7 it is made clear by the addition of a pronoun, either personal (vv. 3, 5—*mou*) or reflexive (v. 5—*heautou*). Since there is no pronoun in v. 8a, however, Rücker concludes the absolute use here favors *kyrios* being Jesus.

Frequently cited in this connection is the analogy of Luke 18:6.[55] "Above all," writes Jeremias, "the analogy of 18.6 suggests that the *kyrios* in 16.8 is Jesus; since it is clear that in 16.8 [*sic*, 18:6] with the words *eipen de ho kyrios* the judgement of Jesus is inserted into a parable . . . and yet there occurs here, too, in 18.8 a *legō hymin* of Jesus [cf. 16:9, *kai egō hymin legō*]."[56] On this analogy, Luke 16:8a also is taken to be "the judgement of Jesus" inserted into our parable.

Another argument offered in favor of identifying *ho kyrios* as Jesus in 16:8 is the improbability of the master praising the man who cheated him. Dodd refers to such a possibility as "palpably absurd,"[57] B. T. D. Smith calls it "incredible."[58] The logic of human nature, then, allegedly precludes identifying *ho kyrios* as the steward's master. Some interpreters also contend the parable itself gives no indication the master ever gets wind of the steward's actions.[59] The parable presupposes the master does not find out, Schmid contends, for only then would the steward's conduct deserve the judgment "wise."[60]

2. The Steward's Master

What can be said in favor of the alternate identification of *ho kyrios*, i.e., the steward's master? How do the advocates of this identification support their position?[61] My answer will be framed largely in terms of responses to the arguments just outlined for identifying *ho kyrios* as Jesus.

One argument for identifying *ho kyrios* of v. 8a with the master of the parable is the use of *kyrios* three times in the parable for the master (vv.

---

[55] This verse is cited by, among others, Ellis, *Luke*, 199; Jeremias, *Parables*, 45; Klostermann, *Lukas*, 525; Menoud, "Riches," 9; Rengstorf, *Lukas*, 192; Riggenbach, "Gleichnisse," 20; and Wellhausen, *Lucae*, 86.

[56] Jeremias, *Parables*, 45.

[57] Dodd, *Parables*, 18.

[58] Smith, *Parables*, 109. Other interpreters who stress the improbability of praise from the master include Jeremias, *Parables*, 45 ("How could he [the master] have praised his deceitful steward?"); Loisy, *Evangiles* 2.161; Michaelis, *Gleichnisse*, 227; Nägelsbach, "Gleichnis," 484; and Paul, "Steward," 189.

[59] Smith, *Parables*, 109, and Riggenbach, "Gleichnisse," 19. Who, Menoud wonders, would inform the master ("Riches," 9)?

[60] Schmid, *Lukas*, 258.

[61] Those who identify *ho kyrios* as the master include Arndt, Arnot, Bahnmaier, Bailey, Bruce, Buttrick, Dods, Drummond, Easton, Fitzmyer, Fonck, Gächter, Geldenhuys, Hiers, Hoffmann, Hooley and Mason, Kögel, Köster, Krämer, Lagrange, Lunt, Marshall, Meyer, Oosterzee, Schulz, Sellin, Stein, Stier, Trench, Via, Weiss (*The Life of Christ* [2 vols.; Edinburgh: T. & T. Clark, 1883] 2.252; in *Lukas* [532] Weiss argues for Jesus), Wiesen, Wright, and Zahn.

3, 5). Without an indication of a change of usage in v. 8a, the natural presumption is that the use in this verse is the same as in the preceding ones.[62] As Bailey argues, the use of *ho kyrios* elsewhere in Luke may not be as decisive for Luke 16:8 as many suggest. Bailey points out that within the parabolic material of Luke the numerical weight of Jeremias's argument from the absolute use of *kyrios* "vanishes." The reason is that in the parables *ho kyrios* three times means master (12:37; 12:42b; 14:23) and two times Jesus (12:42; 18:6).[63] When viewed from this perspective, the statistics are inconclusive. It should also be stressed that in the uses of *ho kyrios* in parables the context makes it clear to whom the word refers. In the other such uses there is no confusion or ambiguity as there is in Luke 16:8a. This fact can be illustrated from Luke 18:6, the oft-cited analogy to 16:8a. In Luke 18 it is clear from the context that the parable ends in v. 5 because v. 6 shifts to indirect speech. It is also clear that *ho kyrios* in v. 6 is Jesus because the noun is not used in the parable. In the parable of chapter 18 the actors are a judge and a widow, not a master (*kyrios*) and his steward. In other words, in the alleged analogy of 18:6 there is no other way to interpret *kyrios* than as a reference to Jesus. The analogy between 16:8a and 18:6 is, therefore, "far from exact."[64] These considerations suggest *ho kyrios* in 16:3, 5, 8a, has the same meaning in each case, i.e., the steward's master.

In defending the identification of *ho kyrios* as the master the alleged improbability of the victimized master's praise must be considered. This argument from human nature is, it will be remembered, often used to support identifying *kyrios* as Jesus here. To be sure, it is surprising and even, at first glance, improbable that the steward is praised. This feature of the story is surprising, however, on either interpretation of *ho kyrios*. In either case, some sort of qualification or explanation is required. This

---

[62] This argument is articulated clearly by Stein, *Parables*, 107. Among others who emphasize the presumptive force of *kyrios* in vv. 3, 5 for v. 8a are Marshall, *Luke*, 620; Schulz, *Parabel*, 56; and Sellin, "Studien," 292. A possible response to Rücker's argument for *kyrios* = Jesus on the basis of the pronouns in vv. 3, 5 ("Gleichnis," 60, referred to above) might be that the use of pronouns in v. 8a to identify *kyrios* as the master would have been stylistically awkward (so Krämer, *Rätsel*, 172).

[63] Bailey, *Poet*, 103. Bailey adds (p. 103 n. 71) that since in our parable Luke is dealing with traditional material (cf. the historic present in v. 7 [*legei*] and the untranslated weights and measures in vv. 6-7), "one must be extremely cautious about drawing conclusions based on Lucan stylistic peculiarities" (pp. 103-4). While this point is well taken, its force may be weakened somewhat by the fact that the very matter of the limits of the traditional material is in debate. If the traditional material is confined to vv. 1-7, as many contend, Bailey's argument is irrelevant for the use of *ho kyrios* in v. 8.

[64] Stein, *Parables*, 107. Fitzmyer ("Manager," 28 n. 8) makes the same point: "However, the situation in chap. 16 is not the same as that in chap. 18. There is an earlier mention of *kyrios* in 16:3, 5, whereas there is nothing similar in Lk 18."

matter is the focus of the next section of the chapter. At this point I submit that praise by the master is not ruled out simply because it is surprising. It may well be that the surprising nature of the master's praise is an intentional feature of the parable, used to arrest the attention and stimulate the thinking of Jesus' hearers and Luke's readers. There are, furthermore, several different ways to explain the steward's actions and/ or the master's praise so that the praise is at least conceivable, if not expected. According to one approach to the parable, for example, the master applauds his steward because he returns to legal dealings. According to another, the master admires the foresight and prudence displayed by his steward, even if the actions themselves are fraudulent. In view of these and other explanations of the master's praise (to be discussed more fully later), the objection of improbability is, to use Marshall's word, "weak."[65]

The striking shift to the first person in v. 9 (*Kai egō hymin legō*) is often cited as proof that *ho kyrios* in v. 8a must be the master. The reasoning is that since the introductory formula of v. 9 indicates a change of speaker (now Jesus), the master must be the one who praises the steward in v. 8a.[66] Jeremias himself acknowledges the force of this argument, although he quickly dismisses it. At the outset of his discussion of our parable Jeremias observes that "the change of subject (*kai egō hymin legō*) at the beginning of v. 9 seems to point decisively to the conclusion that the lord of the parable is intended [by *kyrios* in v. 8a]."[67] This fact is a difficulty for his own interpretation of *kyrios* (= Jesus). His way out of the difficulty is to explain vv. 9-13 as sayings that have been added to the parable.[68] This explanation eliminates any argumentative force in the opening words of v. 9 for the interpretation that *kyrios* is the master. *Ho kyrios* is, therefore, Jesus, despite appearances to the contrary in the present text. Jeremias's remarks raise issues that will be discussed in Part II (e.g., the relationship of vv. 9-13 to the parable). The point to be made here is simply that when taken at face value v. 9 suggests *ho kyrios* in v. 8a is the master, not Jesus.

---

[65] I. H. Marshall, "Luke xvi.8—Who Commended the Unjust Steward," *JTS*, n.s., 19 (1968) 617. The same can also be said of the argument from the silence of the parable about the master's discovery of his steward's actions. Such an argument overlooks the fact that economy is a feature of the parables. Silence about details in a parable is thus a weak basis of argument.

[66] The change of speaker in v. 9 is stressed by Stein, *Parables*, 107. Others who use the introduction of v. 9 as evidence for identifying *kyrios* in v. 8a as the master include Geldenhuys, *Luke*, 414 n. 10; Lagrange, *Luc*, 433; Schulz, *Parabel*, 56; and Sellin, "Studien," 292.

[67] Jeremias, *Parables*, 45.

[68] *Parables*, 45-46.

If, for the sake of argument, *ho kyrios* is the master in v. 8a and Jesus speaks in direct speech in v. 9, what are we to make of v. 8b? Does not the fact that Jesus is the speaker in v. 8b ("For the people of this world are . . . "), as most admit, minimize the force of the change of subject in v. 9 and, in turn, support taking *kyrios* in v. 8a as Jesus, as some contend?[69] The matter is complicated, and full discussion will be delayed until the next section. At this point, however, attention may be drawn to an explanation of the problem which might allow v. 9 to retain at least some of its force for interpreting *kyrios* in v. 8a as the master. This explanation is that in vv. 8-9 we have a mixture of indirect and direct speech.[70] If v. 8b is indirect speech and v. 9 direct, Jesus could still be the speaker in both and the master the one who praises the steward in v. 8a.[71] While this explanation leaves the door open for *kyrios* being the master, it does not, however, establish the identity of *kyrios*. On the basis of a mixture of indirect and direct speech either interpretation is possible. The ambiguity suggests that too much stress should not be placed on the introduction of v. 9 for the identification of *kyrios* as the master in v. 8a. The identity of *kyrios* must be decided on other grounds.

Another argument sometimes advanced in support of *kyrios* = the master is that the parable is a torso if it ends at v. 7 and v. 8a is the application. Fitzmyer expresses this opinion as follows: "Without v. 8a the parable has no real ending. From the beginning the reaction of the master to the manager's conduct is expected; it is finally given in v. 8a."[72]

---

[69] Among the interpreters who would so contend are Jülicher, *Gleichnisreden* 2.503; Menoud, "Riches," 9; Rengstorf, *Lukas*, 192; Riggenbach, "Gleichnisse," 19; and Smith, *Parables*, 110.

[70] This explanation of the grammatical structure of vv. 8-9 is developed by I. H. Marshall, "Steward," 617-19. Cf. also Wellhausen, *Lucae*, 86. Marshall's conclusion is that the question of who commended the steward must be answered on other grounds than that the transition from v. 8 to v. 9 is grammatically difficult (p. 619). The mixture of indirect and direct speech allows for either interpretation. On the analogy of Luke 5:14, where there is a mid-sentence shift from indirect to direct address, Schmid uses this grammatical point to argue that *ho kyrios* is Jesus in 16:8a (*Lukas*, 259).

[71] Marshall comes to this conclusion (*Luke*, 619-21).

[72] Fitzmyer, "Manager," 27 (cf. *Luke* 2.1096). Bailey cites this remark with approval (*Poet*, 104), and attempts to support it on the basis of literary structure (p. 104 n. 75). He classifies our parable as a "parabolic ballad," and concludes that this form requires "that the master be the master of the story." His explanation is as follows. "Stanza seven [v. 8] balances stanza one [v. 1] as we have noted [pp. 95-96]. In stanza one the reader is introduced to a rich man and an unfaithful steward. In the balancing stanza, stanza seven, the form requires and the listener/reader expects a return to the rich man and his dishonest steward." Via also argues that the reaction of the master is expected in our parable, and that *kyrios* is, therefore, the master, not Jesus. Like Bailey, he reaches this conclusion on the basis of literary form. "The logic of the literary mode to which the parable belongs," says Via, "calls for 16:8a to have been an original part of the parable" (*Parables*, 157). The literary mode or form he detects here, however, is quite different than that suggested by Bailey. Via

Along much the same lines, Stein contends that if *kyrios* is Jesus, the parable ends at v. 7 with "great abruptness and without any real conclusion." The parable therefore requires v. 8a as its conclusion.[73] If so, *ho kyrios* must be the master of the parable.[74]

On the basis of the evidence cited above, nothing demands Jesus is *ho kyrios* in v. 8a, and several considerations favor the master (e.g., the use of *kyrios* in vv. 3, 5, the introduction of v. 9, and the "decided abruptness"[75] if the parable ends with v. 7). While this conclusion does not, of course, answer the more important questions about the relationship of verses vv. 1-8a to vv. 8b-13 or the nature of the master's praise, it does, however, establish that v. 8a is an original part of the parable and that the parable of the unjust steward includes at least vv. 1-8a. This decision is, I believe, a step in the direction of properly understanding the parable.

C. The Nature of the Praise, v. 8a

Having argued the case for identifying *ho kyrios* in v. 8a as the master, the more weighty issue of his praise of the steward can now be considered. In vv. 1-7 we are told of a steward who, faced with the prospect of losing his job, authorizes his master's debtors to reduce their bills, in hopes that they will someday reciprocate with hospitality. In v. 8a we read Jesus' "short rendering of the essential contents"[76] of the master's response to those actions: "*kai epēinesen ho kyrios ton oikonomon tēs adikias hoti phronimōs epoiēsen.*" Given the ostensibly dishonest and fraudulent nature of the steward's actions, we would expect to read/hear of further punishment or at least condemnation by the injured party. Instead, much to our surprise, the master praises his steward! This unexpected praise has rightly been labeled "the root problem"[77] in the interpretation of our parable, and is responsible for the great variety of interpretations offered. The difficulty caused by this praise is not alleviated by either interpretation of *kyrios*. Whether *kyrios* is Jesus or

---

contends that our parable belongs to "the picaresque mode," which "tells the story of a successful rogue who makes conventional society look foolish but without establishing any positive alternative" (p. 159). According to Via, it is the element of success in the picaresque mode that suggests 16:8a is an original part of the parable (p. 161).

[73] Stein, *Parables*, 107. Other interpreters who make the same point include Bailey, *Poet*, 104 (quoting Fitzmyer, "Manager," 27); Marshall, *Luke*, 620; and Sellin, "Studien," 292.

[74] This interpretation of *ho kyrios* is reflected, Stein notes (*Parables*, 107 n. 28), in most modern translations: e.g., *RSV, NEB, NIV, NASB,* and *JB*.

[75] Marshall, *Luke*, 620.

[76] Zahn, *Lucas*, 574.

[77] Morris, *Luke*, 245.

the master, "the surprise is that the steward is congratulated on his stratagem."[78] On either interpretation the problem remains of how the steward can be praised and thereby be used as an example for Jesus' disciples.[79] This problem is the focus of the present section.

1. The Meaning of epaineō

Since the praise is the crux of our parable, perhaps the place to begin our discussion is with the verb itself in Luke 16:8a—*kai epēinesen ho kyrios*. The verb *epaineō* is used five other times in the NT, once with regard to God (Rom 15:11, a quote from Ps 117:1) and the rest with regard to men (I Cor 11:2, 17, 22 [twice]). Its most common meaning is "to praise" (*NASB*, Luke 16:8a), "to commend" (*KJV*, *RSV*, *NIV*), "to applaud" (*NEB*).[80] Whatever else is made of the verb, it very likely indicates that the steward's stratagem is successful, that he is eventually received by the debtors.[81] Manson is right that the master's praise is not necessarily moral approval,[82] but the verb does express approval or admiration in some sense (unless it is used ironically). This approval is clarified and delimited in the clause *hoti phronimōs epoiēsen* to which I will come shortly. For the moment, mention should be made of further nuances found in the verb *epaineō* by some interpreters.

Derrett, for example, writes that "the exact force of *epēinesen* seems to have escaped commentators." His own suggestion is that the use of the word in Greek in general (he cites Liddell and Scott) supports the implication of adopting, sanctioning, ratifying, as well as approving and

---

[78] Fletcher, "Riddle," 28.

[79] In this sense Schmid is right when he concludes that it makes no material difference whether *kyrios* in v. 8a is Jesus or the master. Even if *kyrios* is the master, it is still Jesus himself who, through the mouth of the master, emphasizes the exemplary feature of "wisdom" in the steward's actions (*Lukas*, 259).

[80] A novel and opposite interpretation of *epēinesen* is offered by Schwarz ("Verwalter," 94-95; see chapter one, Part I.C.2.b). Postulating two translation errors from Aramaic to Greek in v. 8a, Schwarz contends that Jesus actually finishes the parable with the master *cursing* the *deceitful* steward. Although this approach ends the parable (rather prosaically, I might add) on a note perhaps expected by most readers, to my knowledge no one writing on our parable since 1974 has seriously considered it, much less endorsed it. Fitzmyer even describes Schwarz's interpretation as "farfetched" (*Luke* 2.1101).

[81] Topel, "Steward," 218-19. A few interpreters have gone a step further and argued on the basis of the praise that the steward is not dismissed in the end but reinstated by his master. Among those who so interpret this feature of the parable are Pautrel, "Tabernacula," 318-19; Pirot, *Paraboles*, 316 (the steward comes back in favor); Via, *Parables*, 157 (the praise indicates an improved situation); and Wiesen, *Gleichnis*, 76 (the praise bespeaks a change of mind).

[82] Manson, *Sayings*, 292.

commending.[83] When the master *epēinesen* his steward, therefore, he not only commended him *hoti phronimōs epoiēsen*, but at the same time officially ratified, adopted, and endorsed the steward's actions. In so doing, the master is in effect recognizing the new bills authorized by the steward.[84]

While there may be merit to Derrett's suggestion, it may be heavily colored by his desire to alleviate the difficulty of the praise by vindicating the steward's actions themselves. Those who stress this nuance of the verb also explain the steward's actions as honest, even righteous. If the steward's actions arc *not* honest, however, it is hard to see how this nuance could be present here. In other words, one's judgment about the nature of the steward's actions will affect whether or not one sees this particular nuance of ratification in the verb.

Other interpreters detect an eschatological nuance in the verb *epaineō* here. Bailey, for example, calls attention to "the eschatological usage of the Greek word" (he has in mind not so much the verb as the noun [*epainos*]) in the NT. Bailey quotes approvingly Preisker's comment about the eschatological significance of the noun,[85] and notes that, despite the few occurrences of "the verb form" in the NT, "the idea of a divine master offering approval in an eschatological setting is present in Matthew [25:21, 34]."[86] "Thus the Greek word," Bailey concludes, "on the level of the story itself, carries the meaning of simple approval of what the steward has done. At the same time, on a theological level this word provides additional evidence for interpreting the parable as being primarily concerned with eschatology."[87]

Because I share Bailey's conviction that the parable is "primarily concerned with eschatology," his interpretation of *epaineō* is attractive. I am, however, reluctant to endorse it wholeheartedly because his argument is based more on the usage of the noun than the verb. In addition to the fact that none of the eleven NT occurrences of the noun are in the Gospels (thus a parallel within Jesus' own teaching is lacking), none of the other five NT occurrences of the verb have a clear eschatological nuance. Bailey's observation about Matthew 25:21, 34 may be more to

---

[83] Derrett, "Steward," 210 n. 3.

[84] In addition to Derrett ("Steward," 216), the nuance of ratification in the verb is advocated by, among others, Degenhardt, *Lukas*, 118; Fitzmyer, "Manager," 37, and *Luke* 2.1101 (tentatively); and Morris, *Luke*, 248.

[85] "'*epainos*' signifies the acceptance or approval of the righteous by God alone in the Last Judgment" (H. Preisker, "*epainos*," *TDNT* 2.587, quoted by Bailey, *Poet*, 107).

[86] Bailey, *Poet*, 107.

[87] *Poet*, 107.

the point given the eschatological notes of dismissal, accounting, and crisis in our parable. The parallel is, however, conceptual rather than verbal, and has little force in an argument based on the usage of Greek words, as Bailey claims his argument is.

In view of the foregoing considerations, it seems best to take *epēinesen* as indicating simply the master's praise, commendation, or approval of his steward's actions. If there is an eschatological nuance here it comes more from the context of the story itself than from this verb alone. This conclusion does not, of course, answer the question of how or why the steward is praised. Of some consequence for that answer is the epithet by which Jesus describes the steward in v. 8a. In summarizing the master's response to his steward's actions Jesus says the master praised *ton oikonomon tēs adikias*. What is the meaning of this unusual phrase? Its meaning will cast light on the master's praise.

2. The Meaning of ho oikonomos tēs adikias

Grammatically, this phrase is to be explained as an instance of the use of the genitive for the adjective as in Hebrew.[88] Zerwick and Grosvenor call the genitive "a 'Hebrew genitive' standing for [the] adj[ective] *adikos*";[89] Blass-Debrunner-Funk term it "the genitive of quality."[90] The words *tēs adikias* are best translated, therefore, as an adjective: "the unjust steward" (*KJV*), "the unrighteous steward" (*NASB*), or "the dishonest steward" (*RSV, NEB*) or "manager" (*NIV*).[91] The noun *adikia* itself usually means "wrongdoing, unrighteousness, wickedness, injus-

---

[88] Other such uses in Luke include *tous artous tēs protheseōs* (6:4), *tou mamōna tēs adikias* (16:9), and *ho kritēs tēs adikias* (18:6).

[89] Zerwick and Grosvenor, *Analysis*. In his Greek grammar (*Biblical Greek* [Rome: Pontifical Institute, 1963] §40) Zerwick explains this description of the genitive (also called "attributive" or "qualitative"). It is, he says, due to the fact that "its scope and use in Biblical Greek is extended, owing to Semitic influence, to many expressions in which the Greeks used not a genitive but an adjective." He cites the phrase under discussion here and *ho mamōnas tēs adikias* ("unjust gain"; "worldly wealth," *NIV*) in v. 9 as among the best-known examples of this usage. Zerwick then adds these words of caution: "There is a danger that this manner of speaking may mislead those unaccustomed to it into reading some recondite sense into a genitive which in reality corresponds to some quite ordinary adjective."

[90] BDF §165. "The genitive of quality provides in many combinations an attributive which would ordinarily be provided by an adjective: *ho mamōnas tēs adikias* Lk 16:9 = *ho adikos mamōnas* 11. Hebrew usage is thus reflected, in that this construction compensates for the nearly non-existent adjective." Others who interpret the genitive in the same way include Creed, *Luke*, 204; Degenhardt, *Lukas*, 117; Goebel, "Gleichnisgruppe," 661; Grundmann, *Lukas*, 32; Marshall, *Luke*, 620; Plummer, *Luke*, 383 (= "a characterizing genitive"); and G. Schrenk, "*adikia*," *TDNT* 1.155 (= the Hebrew genitive of definition).

[91] At this point passing mention should be made of the dissenting argument of H. Kosmala ("The Parable of the Unjust Steward in the Light of Qumran," *ASTI* 3 [1964] 114). He insists

tice" (BAGD). Its use here to qualify *ho oikonomos* denotes Jesus' criticism of the steward in some respect, even as he reports the master's response. Differences of opinion arise, however, as to what aspect of the steward's behavior warrants this description. Is he described in this way because of the earlier behavior in v. 1 for which he is dismissed, or because of his actions to the debtors in vv. 5-7? One's decision on this question has important implications for understanding the nature of the praise.

a) Reference to v. 1 or vv. 5-7?

A number of interpreters point to the accusations of mismanagement lodged against the steward in v. 1 as the basis for Jesus' characterization of him by *ton oikonomon tēs adikias* in v. 8a. Degenhardt is representative of this approach. The steward is called "*oikonomos tēs adikias*," Degenhardt writes, "because of his earlier, dishonest, probably self-seekingly exploitive management, not because of his present reduction of debt [in vv. 5-7] which in no place in the parable is reprimanded, but on the contrary is praised."[92] On this approach the steward's *adikia* includes inefficiency and probably dishonesty, both of which characterized his earlier conduct, not that toward the debtors in vv. 5-7. This explanation often figures in arguments to alleviate the difficulty of the master's praise by vindicating the steward from dishonesty in vv. 5-7.[93]

Although this argument appears plausible to some, my own judgment is that it is weak. As much as inefficiency and dishonesty may have been typical of the steward's management of his master's goods before his dismissal, his *adikia* is still not established clearly enough in vv. 1-2 to justify this characterization in v. 8a.[94] In addition, as Stein notes, the characterizing genitive is not needed in v. 8 since it is clear which steward is in view. If, however, something in vv. 3-7 reveals a quality of dishonesty in the steward which is central to the parable, the descrip-

---

tēs adikias is a "genitival [*sic*] expression," not the equivalent of an adjective. The steward is not dishonest or fraudulent per se, Kosmala contends, but *tēs adikias*, i.e., he belongs to a certain category of people. I will come back to Kosmala again because, although I believe he is wrong in denying the adjectival force of the genitive here, his overall point is valid and helpful in understanding the phrase in question.

[92] Degenhardt, *Lukas*, 118.

[93] Others who interpret the epithet in v. 8a as a reference to v. 1 include Derrett, *Law*, 55 (the steward is so described because of inefficiency and dishonesty); Firth, "Steward," 426 (inefficiency); Fonck, *Parabeln*, 685; Kiehl, "Parable," 112 (neglect of property); Kistemaker, *Parables*, 232; and Oosterzee, *Luke*, 246 (earlier and now abandoned dishonesty).

[94] Stein, *Parables*, 109, and Topel, "Steward," 218 n. 13.

tion becomes necessary. On this basis Stein concludes it is "reasonable" that *tēs adikias* would be omitted in v. 8a if it did not refer to the actions in vv. 5-7.[95] Rather than tie the epithet to more remote and inexplicit verses (1-2), it seems much more natural to connect it with the actions described in the immediately preceding verses (i.e., 5-7). While this consideration alone does not decide the question of the steward's actions in the latter verses, it strongly suggests (if *adikia* here has its usual force) that those actions are being branded dishonest.

If *ton oikonomon tēs adikias* in v. 8a is not a reference to the steward's actions in vv. 1-2, it must then refer to those in vv. 5-7, where the steward authorizes his master's debtors to reduce the amounts they owe. If, as seems natural, *tēs adikias* describes the steward in terms of those actions, then the phrase in question is an important, albeit passing, indictment of the steward. Thus understood Jesus here gives his ethical judgment about the steward's plan.[96] While Jesus reports (and endorses) the master's commendation of his steward for prudence or shrewdness, he at the same time condemns the actions themselves by means of this phrase.[97] In this way the praise is qualified significantly. The shrewdness for which the steward is commended (and which presumably disciples are to emulate, unless vv. 8-9 are ironical) is to be distinguished or isolated from the dishonesty of his actions.

b) Eschatological nuance

In seeking to understand the master's praise of his steward, two interpretations of the phrase *ton oikonomon tēs adikias* have been considered thus far. One explanation connects the phrase to the steward's conduct hinted at in vv. 1-2, the other (more likely) explanation connects it to the conduct described in some detail in vv. 5-7. Yet another line of thought merits consideration at this point, that of an eschatological nuance in *tēs adikias*. Very influential in this regard is an article by H. Kosmala which, as its title indicates, investigates "The Parable of the Unjust Steward in the Light of Qumran." The phrase *tēs adikias* figures prominently in this article. As noted already, Kosmala rejects interpretations which render the phrase as simply an adjective (e.g., "unjust," "dishonest," or "fraudu-

---

[95] *Parables*, 109.

[96] Manson, *Sayings*, 292.

[97] Stier, *Words* 4.181. The actions of vv. 5-7 are not unrelated to the accusations in v. 1. As Plummer observes, there is no hint that the fraud of vv. 5-7 (if that is what it is) is a new departure (*Luke*, 382). Although *adikia* is primarily a reference to the actions of vv. 5-7, there is a sense in which it embraces the steward's whole career and character.

lent"). Instead, the "genetival [*sic*] expression," as he calls it, assigns the steward "to a certain group or category of people: he belongs to this world as opposed to the children of light . . . It is this world which, with all its wealth and its people serving mammon, is *tēs adikias*."[98] On the basis of parallels drawn between Qumran and the NT, Kosmala comes to the following conclusion: "The expression *oikonomon tēs adikias*, therefore, describes a man who is completely bound up with this world in which *adikia* is the ruling principle."[99] Implicit in this epithet, then, is the eschatological dualism between this world/age and the next so characteristic of NT eschatology, in general, and Jesus' own teaching, in particular. This dualism is explicit in v. 8b where Jesus speaks of "the sons of this age" and "the sons of light."

Kosmala's argument for an eschatological nuance in *tēs adikias* is frequently cited and endorsed by others.[100] There are a number of points in its favor. First, in addition to possible Qumran or NT parallels, there is the fact, pointed out by Ellis, that *adikia* occurs in three Lucan passages (13:27; 16:8, 9; and 18:6). At least two of the three occurrences of the noun are in parables (the latter two references), and all are in eschatological contexts.[101] This fact suggests its use here may be eschatological, too. Second, an eschatological nuance in *tēs adikias* fits the note of eschatological urgency so vividly portrayed in the steward's situation in the parable. Third, and perhaps most telling of all, there is explicit eschatological dualism in v. 8b—"the sons of this age"/"the sons of light." Unless these expressions are being used ironically, they are strong evidence that eschatology is central to our parable. An eschatological nuance in Jesus' description of the steward is, therefore, not unlikely.

Having agreed an eschatological nuance is likely in the phrase *ton oikonomon tēs adikias*, I hasten to add that Kosmala's argument needs to be qualified at an important point. Kosmala insists that *adikia* assigns

---

[98] Kosmala, "Steward," 114-15.

[99] "Steward," 115.

[100] E.g., Ellis, *Luke*, 199; Krämer, *Rätsel*, 149; Marshall, *Luke*, 620; and Sellin, "Studien," 296. The substance of Kosmala's argument seems to have been anticipated by J. Kögel in 1914 ("Zum Gleichnis vom ungerechten Haushalter, Bemerkungen zu Luk. 16:1-13," BFCT 18 [1914] 581-612). Kögel describes *adikia* as almost a technical term emphasizing that the one so referred to is a member of this evil world. It is used, he says, in a contrasting sense to a member of the heavenly world (p. 590). Later in the same article he writes that *oikonomos tēs adikias* is not a statement about the steward himself or his character, but only a contrast of the kind of world to which he belongs (p. 597). Apparently Kosmala came to his conclusion independently of Kögel, for Kögel's article is not cited by him. As long ago as 1892, Weiss called attention to *adikia* as the essence of this age under the dominion of the devil (*Lukas*, 532).

[101] Ellis, *Luke*, 199.

the steward to the category of the worldly, without passing judgment on the morality of his actions. Although Kosmala's basic point about category is well taken, his formulation of it is, as Krämer observes, exaggerated. The steward is not qualified loosely as Kosmala's argument would suggest, but according to a very graphic story in which his worldly qualities are revealed in his actions.[102] The words *tēs adikias* brand the steward as worldly all right, but it does so precisely because he acts as he does. In the context of the parable, *adikia* can, therefore, assign the steward to the category of the worldly while at the same time condemn his actions as dishonest or unjust.

While conclusions reached thus far in the discussion of the nature of the master's praise have implications for our understanding of that praise (e.g., *tēs adikias* qualifies the praise significantly), it remains to be seen how a dishonest steward can be commended at all. This problem brings me to the phrase *hoti phronimōs epoiēsen* in v. 8a.

3. The Meaning of hoti phronimōs epoiēsen

a) General definition of adverb

Jesus reports that when the master learned of the steward's actions (as presumably he did) he praised him *hoti phronimōs epoiēsen*. This clause is important for several reasons. It provides the ground or basis of the praise,[103] it significantly qualifies the praise itself, and it highlights the point of comparison (or contrast, if used ironically) between the steward and Christian disciples. The adverb *phronimōs*, occurring only here in the NT, means "wisely, shrewdly" (BAGD). *NASB* and *NIV* render it as the latter, *KJV* as the former, *NEB* as "astutely," and *RSV* as the noun "prudence." On the assumption that "the original Aramaic word in the story was *hokmah*," Bailey concludes that the steward is praised for, quoting G. Fohrer, the "cleverness and skill deployed in self-preservation."[104] This conclusion is endorsed by Stein, who stresses the non-moral nature of the steward's prudence (to use the noun). The quality does not necessarily demand honesty or godliness. The steward had "the

---

[102] Krämer, *Rätsel*, 149 n. 38. Krämer goes on in the same note to offer the interesting suggestion that the Greek translator (of a presumed Aramaic source) may have kept the genitive construction because the adjective construction in Greek would have emphasized too one-sidedly the evil in the steward's actions (i.e., the moral quality) to the detriment of the religious (i.e., the eschatological) which is actually in the foreground here.

[103] Manson, *Sayings*, 292, and Stein, *Parables*, 110 n. 37.

[104] Bailey, *Poet*, 106, quoting Fohrer, "*sophia*," *TDNT* 7.484.

cunning cleverness," as Stein puts it, to prepare for the future in light of the crisis facing him.[105] In view of these considerations, as well as the stated goal of the steward's actions to be received by the debtors (v. 4), the commended quality might be defined as "decisive provision for the future at a critical moment." The steward is praised by his master for the wisdom or shrewdness of his actions. If Jesus is not speaking ironically, he too echoes the praise.

b) Ethics of steward's actions in vv. 5-7

To define the steward's wisdom in general terms does not, however, resolve the difficulty of the master's praise. One's interpretation of precisely what is being commended (or condemned) by Jesus in this parable depends in large measure on prior decisions about the ethics of the steward's actions toward the debtors in vv. 5-7. It is, therefore, important to consider those actions more carefully if we are to understand the master's praise.

(1) Fraudulent and dishonest actions
As simple as it may seem, one factor in favor of understanding the steward's actions as fraudulent and dishonest is that at first blush they strike the listener or reader in just that way. When the parable is heard or read, the first impression is that the steward is cheating his master to further his own interests. One has only to look at the history of interpretation to verify the truth of this observation. The vast majority of interpreters of our parable, until the present century at least, have understood the steward's actions in this way. If the steward's actions did not appear so dishonest, the master's praise would present no difficulty, and the many discussions of the parable (including this one) would be unnecessary. It may be, of course, that the difficulty is simply the result of reading the parable through Occidental rather than Oriental eyes, a possibility I will evaluate shortly. The fact of the matter is, however, that the steward's actions *appear* dishonest, at least to the Western reader/

---

[105] Stein, *Parables*, 111, citing both Fohrer and Bailey approvingly. In similar fashion, Plummer explains this adverb as "a shrewd adjustment of means to ends. It is the man's prompt *savoir faire* that is praised" (*Luke*, 384). Among other nouns or phrases used for the quality commended here by Jesus are the following: "astuteness" (e.g., Manson, *Sayings*, 292, and Tillmann, "Verwalter," 181); "cleverness" (Hooley and Mason, "Parable," 53; Lagrange, *Luc*, 434; and Loisy, *Evangiles* 2.160 ["habileté"]); "foresight" (Buttrick, *Parables*, 118); "prudence" (Pickar, "Steward," 251; Summers, *Luke*, 190; and Trench, *Parables*, 441 [Trench uses both this word and the former one]); "wisdom" (Rengstorf, *Lukas*, 192); and "wise provision for the future" (Grundmann, *Lukas*, 320, and Schmid, *Lukas*, 257).

listener and perhaps to Luke's Gentile audience as well. The steward's actions demand some explanation, even if it is that they are not really dishonest after all.

The impression of dishonesty is strengthened by the phrase *ton oikonomon tēs adikias* in v. 8a, discussed above. The most natural way to take this phrase is as a description of the steward in terms of the actions in the immediately preceding verses (5-7). The epithet expresses, therefore, Jesus' own passing but poignant judgment about the ethics of the steward's actions toward the debtors. He hereby pronounces the steward and his actions *adikia*—dishonest, unjust, worldly.

If the steward's behavior toward the debtors is dishonest, how then is the praise in v. 8a to be explained? As I have noted, this problem exists for either interpretation of *kyrios*, and really forms the interpretive crux of the whole parable. Under the assumption that the steward's actions are fraudulent, there are two major explanations of the praise. One draws a distinction between the dishonesty and the wisdom of the actions, the other detects irony in Jesus' voice.

(a) Distinction between dishonesty and wisdom of actions

One way to account for the troublesome praise is to draw a distinction between the steward's actions and the wisdom displayed in them. The actions themselves are fraudulent and dishonest, but the wisdom underlying them is praiseworthy.[106] Jesus' focus is on the latter, as the phrase *hoti phronimōs epoiēsen* in v. 8a indicates. While Jesus reports and echoes the master's praise he at the same time introduces a significant qualification by means of this phrase. The steward is praised for his wisdom or shrewdness in decisively providing for the future at a critical moment, not for the fraudulent or dishonest means he utilizes to do so. The distinction is an important one. As Manson observes, there is all the difference in the world between praising the dishonest steward because he acted cleverly (our parable) and praising the clever steward because he acted dishonestly.[107] The latter would be difficult to conceive on either interpretation of *kyrios*. The former is, however, quite within the realm of possibility, even from the victimized master. The master, himself a man of the world, recognizes and admires shrewdness when he sees it,

---

[106] Among the many interpreters who maintain such a distinction are Buttrick, *Parables*, 118; Grundmann, *Lukas*, 320; Hooley and Mason, "Parable," 53; Lagrange, *Luc*, 434; Loisy, *Evangiles* 2.160; Manson, *Sayings*, 292; Pickar, "Steward," 251; Plummer, *Luke*, 384; Rengstorf, *Lukas*, 192; Schmid, *Lukas*, 257; Stein, *Parables*, 111; Summers, *Luke*, 190; Tillmann, "Verwalter," 181; and Trench, *Parables*, 441.

[107] Manson, *Sayings*, 292.

and cannot help but commend his steward for it.[108] It should be noted again, however, that the praise is for shrewdness, not dishonesty. Through the mouth of the master, Jesus commends shrewdness for emulation by his disciples in their own analogous situation. Jesus' exhortation to his disciples is "Be as wise as the steward, but let your wise care be for eternity."[109]

A possible objection to the line of argument just outlined is that it involves, in J. Drury's words, "the use of the bad man to make a good point."[110] According to several writers, the improbability of Jesus' doing so is decisive against interpreting our parable as a positive exhortation to prudence. Lenwood, for example, asks, "Is it probable that Jesus would have drawn a lesson of the need for holy prudence from a story in which the arresting impression is one of fraud?"[111] He answers in the negative. In a similar vein, McFayden argues there is no other instance of Jesus using a rascal as an example to be imitated.[112] In the face of this difficulty both he and Lenwood, and others, opt for detecting irony in Jesus' voice. I will consider that alternative in a few moments. Before doing so, however, let me address the objection itself.

The objection that it is unlikely Jesus would have used a bad man to make a good point is not persuasive. As a number of interpreters point out, on a few occasions Jesus *does* deduce his teaching from the behavior of bad men.[113] In Smith's words, "The parable of the Unjust Steward,

---

[108] "Clearly, the tactics were unscrupulous," explains Murray, "and yet they compelled admiration of a kind. The master was a man of the world himself, and he had enough humour to note his servant's wit" ("Steward," 308). Cf. Bruce, who speaks of the master bestowing on the steward's actions "a sort of humorous laudation" (*Teaching*, 367), and Dods, who says that although the plan was "thoroughly unprincipled and dishonest," the master "had humor enough to enjoy the man's cleverness, candor enough to praise his prudence" (*Parables*, 366-67). The plausibility of this explanation of the master's praise increases when one considers the fact, noted by Bailey, that "an Oriental master is often pleased that a servant is clever enough to outwit him" (*Poet*, 103 n. 68).

[109] Stier, *Words* 4.168.

[110] J. Drury, *Tradition and Design in Luke's Gospel* (London: Darton, Longman & Todd, 1976) 78.

[111] "Parable," 367.

[112] McFayden, "Steward," 536. This objection is echoed by Bretscher, "Steward," 760-61.

[113] Creed, *Luke*, lxix; Köster, "Haushalter," 734; Marshall, *Luke*, 614; Murray, "Steward," 307; and Stier, *Words* 4.165. Bailey makes an interesting cultural observation which may also explain how a dishonest man can be used as an example. He suggests that the middle Eastern peasant at the bottom of the economic ladder finds a parable such as this one "pure delight." "Nothing pleases him more than a story in which David kills a Goliath" (*Poet*, 105). Eastern listeners/hearers would, therefore, have found nothing startling in this particular feature of the story. What would be of surprise to them, Bailey goes on to note, is that the hero of the story (the steward) is *criticized* as "unrighteous" and called a "son of darkness" (v. 8b) (p. 105).

whose conduct goes from bad to worse, is only the most outstanding of
a class of parables, the use of which appears to be a unique and striking
feature of Christ's teaching."[114] The parables of the importunate friend
(Luke 11:5-9) and the unjust judge (18:1-7) may be two other examples
of this class. All three parables are similar insofar as they include an *a
fortiori* argument.[115] This argument is explicit in the context of the
parable of the importunate friend (especially 11:13, "*posōi mallon*"),
and is implicit in the parable of the unjust judge (18:6, "*Akousate ti ho
kritēs tēs adikias legei*") and in our parable as well. If the reluctant friend
and the unjust judge finally gave in and granted the respective requests
made of them, *how much more* will God answer the prayers of his
children. If the dishonest steward displayed wisdom at a critical moment
in his evil and temporal sphere of existence, *how much more* should
Christian disciples do so in their righteous and eternal sphere. The same
sort of argument is also implicit in 16:9, as we will see. The *a fortiori*
argument in all three parables serves to illuminate truth by contrast.[116] It
also highlights the features of analogy and contrast in parabolic teaching.
In our parable, as the phrase *hoti phronimōs epoiēsen* indicates, "the
emphasis falls upon the steward's 'prudence', and an analogous 'prudence' in another sphere is enjoined upon the disciples."[117] Disciples are
to imitate the steward in decisively providing for the future, but their own
means of and motives for doing so are to be different than the steward's.
As will be argued in a subsequent section of this chapter, the form the
disciples' wisdom is to take is made clear in v. 9. At this point it is to be
remembered that the steward and his actions are judged *adikos*. Although this parable is "a story from ordinary life in the world" which has
"a spiritual counterpart in the spiritual world," its characters still "no
more serve to immediate edification than the reluctant friend (xi.8) or the

---

[114] Smith, *Parables*, 109. Smith turns this unusual feature of the parable to positive
advantage for the genuineness of the parable. "The fact that we do not expect such a tale to
be used to enforce a religious lesson appears to be an almost unanswerable argument in favor
of the authenticity of this parable" (p. 109).

[115] If no parallel be admitted between these two parables and ours, ours could still
constitute a class of its own. While such uniqueness would demand added caution in the line
of argument being defended here, it would not in itself be decisive against it.

[116] Köster, "Haushalter," 734. Köster adds that in parables of this type misinterpretation
is guarded against through additional remarks. In the case of our parable, I will contend, that
function is served by vv. 9-13. Among the interpreters who have called attention to the *a
fortiori* argument in our parable are Bailey, *Poet*, 105; Buttrick, *Parables*, 124 n. 17;
Grundmann, *Lukas*, 321 (re. v. 9); Hiers, "Friends," 33 (re. v. 9); Kögel, "Gleichnis," 597;
Krüger, "Grundlagen," 181 (*a minori ad maius* is the key to the parable); Pickar, "Steward,"
252 (he notes that Augustine interpreted the parable in this way); and F. E. Williams,
"Almsgiving," 294.

[117] Creed, *Luke*, 201.

unjust judge (xviii.2)."[118] The analogy between the conduct of the steward in our parable and that expected of Christians is, therefore, an important but strictly limited one. *What* the steward does is commended (he provides for the future at a critical moment), *how* he does so is not (by dishonest and fraudulent means).

(b) Irony

The other major explanation of the praise of the dishonest steward takes a very different interpretive tack. Rather than drawing the distinction outlined above, it detects irony in Jesus' voice. The advocates of this approach agree that the steward's actions described in vv. 5-7 are indeed fraudulent and dishonest, but they deny that a positive lesson is drawn from those actions in either v. 8a or vv. 8b-9. Quite to the contrary, these interpreters are convinced Jesus is actually, by means of irony, condemning the steward's maneuvers even though he appears to be commending at least some aspect of them. Instead of a model of prudence, then, the steward is from beginning to end a warning example to disciples of how *not* to act. On this reading, irony is implicit in the verb *epaineō* (*ho kyrios* is usually assumed to be Jesus), and is even more pronounced in *phronimōs* in v. 8a and the related adjective *phronimōteroi* in v. 8b. Both the adverb and adjective are taken to have "a lightly scornful or derogatory overtone," much as the words "shrewdness" or "cleverness" have in English.[119] Irony is, therefore, present in vv. 8-9 (most exponents of this approach focus on vv. 8b-9.)[120]

What can be said in response to this approach to our parable? Most advocates of other approaches routinely dismiss this one with little or no explanation, if they even mention it at all. Such treatment fails to reckon with the plausibility of this interpretation, at least in its broad outlines. On occasion Jesus does seem to utilize irony to make his point. "Examples are rare," Bretscher admits, "but they do exist."[121] He cites three other instances of Jesus' use of irony (Matt 23:32; 26:45; Luke 13:33);[122]

---

[118] Creed, *Luke*, 201.

[119] Fletcher, "Riddle," 23. As support Fletcher cites Paul's use of the adjective in a derogatory sense (e.g., Rom 11:25; 12:16; 1 Cor 4:10; 2 Cor 11:19 [BDF §495 (2) describes the latter as irony of "the sharpest kind"]). Of the latter two uses Fletcher explains that "Paul calls these Christians *phronimoi* with heavy irony, referring to their vaunted wisdom . . ." (p. 23). According to Fletcher, a similar sense is present in Luke 16:8. Fletcher's interpretation is endorsed by, among others, Sellin ("Studien," 294, 296).

[120] For a fuller summary of this approach, see chapter one, Part I.C.1.b).

[121] "Steward," 761.

[122] "Steward," 761.

Fletcher calls attention to Mark 2:17 (// Luke 5:31-32) and Luke 15:7.[123]
Limited though the precedent is, it does suggest our parable could be
irony, too. Another factor which adds plausibility to this approach is
what Bretscher calls its "powerful unity of thought." "Here the lesson is
clear and simple: 'The Folly of Sinners Who, by Wisdom, Avoid
Repentance'."[124] Such simplicity enhances the attractiveness of this
explanation.

As plausible as this approach may appear, it is not without serious
difficulty. The major difficulty I find is its subtlety. As even Bretscher
himself admits, our parable does not sound like irony or give any
indication of it in the course of a casual reading. Irony is not the obvious
explanation. Because irony is conveyed by modulation of voice, however, it is readily lost in the written word. "Only the context can point to
such irony in its written form."[125] While Bretscher thinks such is the case
in our parable, many, myself included, are not so sure. In the case of
Paul's use of *phronimos* appealed to by Fletcher, irony *is* clear from the
context, as, for example, in 1 Cor 4:10. In that verse Paul dramatizes the
boastful pride of some of the Corinthian Christians by contrasting them
with the apostles: "We are fools for Christ, but you are so wise in Christ!"
Irony is unmistakable in this case (cf. 1 Cor 1:18-2:5; 2 Cor 11:19). In
the case of Jesus' alleged use of irony, sometimes the context does
suggest irony. In Luke 15:7, for instance, Jesus concludes the well-
known parable of the lost sheep with these words: "I tell you that in the
same way there is more rejoicing in heaven over one sinner who repents
than over ninety-nine righteous persons who do not need to repent." The
reference to "ninety-nine righteous persons" could very well be ironical,
as Fletcher, among others, suggests.[126] Self-righteous persons are condemned by that parable. The context of Jesus' controversy with the
Pharisees and scribes (cf. 15:1-2) makes irony probable there. Such is
not clearly the case, however, in our parable. There is nothing in the

---

[123] Fletcher, "Riddle," 27-28. Further examples are given by Clavier, "Ironie," 9-12. Cf.
also BDF §495 (2).

[124] Bretscher, "Steward," 759.

[125] "Steward," 762.

[126] "Before God there are none such; but there are those who think themselves righteous
and who despise 'sinners'" (Fletcher, "Riddle," 28). Cf. also Plummer, *Luke*, 369, and L.
Schottroff and W. Stegemann, *Jesus and the Hope of the Poor* (Maryknoll, NY: Orbis, 1986)
34-35. Other interpretations of the reference to "righteous persons" in Luke 15:7 are,
however, possible. Among other possibilities are the following: Jesus is referring to those
who are righteous in the OT sense (e.g., Godet, *Luke* 2.146-47 ["Levitically and theocratically
speaking" (146)], and perhaps also Marshall, *Luke*, 602 ["God is, after all, also pleased with
the righteous (1:6)"]), or this statement is a typical (Lucan) way of exaggerating for the sake
of emphasis God's joy over a repentant sinner (Fitzmyer, *Luke* 2.1078).

context itself to point to irony. Instead irony seems to have suggested itself because of the difficulty of explaining the praise in v. 8 or Jesus' exhortation in v. 9. Difficulty alone, however, is no proof of irony, especially if, as I am arguing, other plausible explanations are available. Such explanations make resorting to irony unnecessary.

Despite the wide differences between the two major explanations just outlined, both agree the steward's behavior itself is fraudulent and dishonest. Another interpretation, to which we now turn, takes an altogether different view of the steward's conduct. It too has its own interpretive implications for the content of the steward's wisdom, the nature of the praise, and the point of the parable.

(2) Just and honest actions

A number of interpreters have attempted to resolve the difficulty inherent in the master's (or Jesus') praise by exonerating the steward of wrongdoing in vv. 5-7. Not only is the steward innocent of fraud or dishonesty in reducing the debts, but his actions are even just and honest. Rather than distinguish different aspects of the steward's actions, this group of interpreters contends the actions themselves are commendable. In this case, the steward's praiseworthiness consists not only in his wisdom per se, but also in the very form his wisdom takes. Jesus commends the steward's honesty and even charity, as well as his preparedness, for imitation by his disciples.

As noted in chapter one, the usual means of vindicating the steward is to explain his actions in terms of first-century socioeconomic practices. The details and nuances of this approach have already been presented there and need not be rehearsed here. The basic line of argument is that the steward of our parable is acting quite within the rights of his position when he authorizes the debt reductions. The reductions themselves represent usurious overcharges and/or his own commission hidden in the bills. His actions are, therefore, honest, just, and charitable, and for this reason he is commended.

This approach to our parable, especially as articulated by Derrett and Fitzmyer, has been greeted with considerable scholarly enthusiasm. In favor of this approach are its apparent feasibility in terms of first-century Palestinian circumstances and its ability to alleviate neatly the difficulty created by the praise in v. 8a. It is, however, not without its weaknesses. Those weaknesses warrant discussion if we are to come to a conclusion about the question of the steward's actions and the meaning of his commendation.

One objection to this interpretation of the steward's actions is the description *ho oikonomos tēs adikias* (v. 8a). Those interpreters who explain the steward's actions as just are forced to attribute this description to his earlier behavior (vv. 1-2) rather than to that toward the debtors (vv. 5-7). This explanation of the phrase is not, however, the most natural one, as has already been argued. The phrase instead constitutes Jesus' own passing, but clear, indictment of the steward's actions in vv. 5-7 as dishonest and fraudulent.

A second objection, raised by Bailey, calls the validity of this interpretation into question on cultural grounds. Bailey's criticism is directed especially against Gibson's early and "almost casual suggestion" that the steward merely subtracts his "cut" from the bills.[127] His comments apply equally well to later versions of this approach, including that of Derrett.[128] Bailey agrees with Gibson's assumption (subsequently documented by Derrett from the Mishnah) that officially the steward receives a fee from the renters for acting as his master's agent. In addition, suggests Bailey (on the basis of modern village customs), the steward likely receives "a little something 'under the table' from most, if not all, of his master's renters. A token amount is considered legitimate and honorable."[129] Only if he demands too much is he criticized. What is of particular significance for the interpretation of the steward's actions in our parable is that, according to Bailey, these "extras" do not appear in the accounts. They are strictly "under the table." What is recorded on the bills is known to the master and the public at large, and must be delivered to the master.[130] The debtors would be aware of any inflation of the bills, and could appeal to the master himself, unless he is "a partner-in-crime" (something Bailey denies). If the debtors have been cheated by 20-50% of their bills, they would bitterly hate the steward. According to Bailey, once such a steward loses his position he will be forced to leave the community. "No further deception, even if it is to their economic advantage, will lead those debtors to welcome him into their homes."[131] These considerations suggest there are significant cultural obstacles to interpreting the steward's actions in our parable as honest and just.

A third objection that could be lodged against taking the steward's

---

[127] Bailey, *Poet*, 88, referring to Gibson, "Steward," 334.
[128] Derrett, "Steward," 198-219 (= *Law*, 48-77).
[129] Bailey, *Poet*, 89.
[130] *Poet*, 89-90. Stein cites Bailey's argument as a "decisive criticism" of attempts to vindicate the steward (*Parables*, 109).
[131] *Poet*, 90.

actions as honest is that such an approach robs the parable of its element of surprise, or what might be called its "shock factor." As Crossan notes, this parable is a "deliberately shocking story."[132] When the parable is read or heard it invariably shocks the reader/listener; it grabs attention and forces further reflection (cf. the parable of the vineyard workers in Matt 20:1-16). The history of interpretation itself bears testimony to this fact. It may well be that this feature of surprise or shock, caused particularly by the master's praise of his steward, is a deliberate part of Jesus' pedagogy.[133] If so, this feature would be lost or dulled if the steward's actions are honest and readily recognized as such by Jesus' audience. If honest, the master's (and Jesus') praise comes as no surprise at all; it is quite expected. We would have been surprised, in fact, if he was not commended! While this rhetorical feature does not settle the question of the morality of the steward's actions in vv. 5-7, it must be given more serious consideration than it often receives. I concur with Lunt's conclusion: "All attempts to explain away or gloss over the dishonesty of the steward seem to me to impoverish the characteristically bold analogue."[134] The master's surprising praise of his dishonest steward serves to focus attention on the one quality Jesus wants to commend to his disciples here, i.e., wisdom with regard to the future.

A fourth and final (and in my mind, decisive) objection against interpreting the steward's actions as honest is the question whether Luke's non-Jewish readers would have gotten the point. This problem is recognized even by representatives of the approach in question. Derrett, for example, notes that the heavily Jewish background of the parable accounts for the perplexity of non-Jews. He then admits, "Why Luke retained it without providing the key to the meaning is not entirely clear."[135] Marshall, who himself judges Derrett's interpretation "feasible" for the first century and as having "most to be said for it,"[136] wonders, however, whether a non-Palestinian audience ignorant of the socioeconomic background would have understood the actions as hon-

---

[132] Crossan, "The Parable of the Wicked Husbandmen," *JBL* 90 (1971) 465.

[133] Seccombe suggests the master's unexpected judgment may be meant to provoke shock in the hearers and thus to invite them to closer consideration of the steward's actions (*Possessions*, 161 n. 106, 162). Although he identifies *ho kyrios* as Jesus, Jeremias also calls attention to the element of surprise in our parable (*Parables*, 182). Others who have noted this element include Murray ("Steward"), Buttrick (*Parables*), Fletcher ("Riddle"), and Stein (*Parables*).

[134] Lunt, "Expounding," 134.

[135] Derrett, "Steward," 200. As noted in chapter one (n. 183), a later article by Derrett on Luke 16:6 ("Bond") may be his response to just this problem.

[136] Marshall, *Luke*, 615, 617, respectively.

est. Marshall's own tentative explanation is that "perhaps Jesus intended the full meaning [i.e., that the steward's actions are legal and praiseworthy], but the subsequent tradition failed to do so and hence the less adequate interpretation [i.e., that the steward acted dishonestly throughout] came to dominate exegesis from a very early date."[137] While this possibility cannot be ruled out entirely, its hypothetical nature makes it no more plausible than the interpretation which draws a distinction between the steward's dishonest actions and his wisdom. Unless Luke himself has also missed Jesus' point, it seems just as reasonable to assume that the present form of the parable contains the necessary information for the reader to understand the main point.[138] Otherwise, it is difficult to account for Luke's inclusion of this parable at all, the point of which his Gentile readers would likely miss.

Having considered the alternate interpretations of the steward's actions in Luke 16:5-7, my own judgment, in summary, is that the weight of probability favors the interpretation that those actions as dishonest. The steward is thus commended not for the actions themselves, but rather for the underlying wisdom displayed in those actions. Given the stated goal of his actions ("I know what I will do so that, when I lose my job here, people will welcome me into their houses" [v. 4]), the steward's wisdom consists in his decisive provision for the future at a critical moment. Christian disciples are to imitate him in this regard in their own analogous situation.

c) Eschatological nuance

Before closing the discussion of the master's praise, a final point needs to be made with respect to the clause currently under discussion, *hoti phronimōs epoiēsen*. As has been noted already, an eschatological nuance is present in the crisis motif of the story itself and perhaps also in the noun *adikia*; several interpreters detect the same nuance in the verb *epēinesen*. In addition, an eschatological nuance is very likely present in the key words *phronimōs/phronimos*. Although the adverb occurs only here in the NT, the corresponding adjective is used fourteen times. Sometimes, as noted in the earlier discussion of irony, the adjective is used in a derogatory sense (e.g., by Paul: 1 Cor 4:10; 2 Cor 11:19; Rom 11:25; 12:16). In the Gospels, however, it is used in a different, more positive sense. All nine Gospel uses of the adjective are attributed to

---

[137] *Luke*, 615.
[138] This point is stressed by Stein, *Parables*, 109.

Jesus, all are in "parables or parabolic sayings,"[139] and all but one of those uses are clearly eschatological in nature (Matt 7:24; 24:45 [// Luke 12:42]; 25:2, 4, 8, 9; Luke 16:8).[140] The predominant usage of the adjective in the Gospels connotes the ideas of preparedness and watchfulness, in particular for the coming of the Son of Man. It is used to describe "those who have grasped the eschatological position of man,"[141] and who have reacted accordingly. In reporting and endorsing the master's praise of his steward, Jesus is making just this point. The steward acted *phronimōs*, he grasped the urgency of his situation and reacted wisely to do something about it, even if his actions were dishonest. In this narrow but important respect the unjust steward is a model for Christian disciples. They, too, are to grasp their own analogous eschatological situation in view of the coming of the kingdom of God.[142] They, too, are to respond *phronimōs*. The specific form their wise response is to take is, I will argue, indicated by Jesus in v. 9.

D. Verse 8b

Luke 16:8b reads, "*hoti hoi huioi tou aiōnos toutou phronimōteroi hyper tous huious tou phōtos eis tēn genean tēn heautōn eisin*"—"For the people of this world are more shrewd in dealing with their own kind than

---

[139] G. Bertram, "*phronimos*," *TDNT* 9.234.

[140] The exception seems to be Matt 10:16 where Jesus says to the Twelve, as he sends them out to preach and heal, "I am sending you out like sheep among wolves. Therefore be as shrewd [*phronimoi*] as snakes and as innocent as doves." Whether or not the adjective has an eschatological nuance in this verse, the second half of the verse is often cited as a parallel to the quality being commended in our parable (e.g., Hooley and Mason, "Parable," 53; Olshausen, *Commentary* 2.68; and Zahn, *Lucas*, 574). The two occurrences of the adjective in Luke are telling examples of its overwhelmingly eschatological use in the Gospels. The whole context of its first Lucan occurrence in 12:42 is that of watchfulness for the coming of the Son of Man (12:40). "The faithful and wise steward [*ho pistos oikonomos ho phronimos*]" (12:42) is the one found doing his master's will when he returns (12:43). Also telling for an eschatological nuance in the adverb *phronimōs* is the (comparative) use of the adjective in 16:8b (*phronimōteroi*). As will be argued in more detail at a later point in this chapter, the strongly eschatological overtones of v. 8b ("the sons of this age"/"the sons of light") color the meaning of both the adjective and adverb.

[141] Bertram, "*phronimos*," *TDNT* 9.234. Preisker defines the adjective in the same way, but believes the adverb is used differently in Luke 16:8a ("Lukas 16:1-7," col. 89). Jeremias, however, argues for the eschatological nuance in the adverb here as well (*Parables*, 46). Cf. also Bailey, *Poet*, 106, and Fitzmyer, *Luke* 2.1102. The eschatological force of the adverb was recognized earlier by Velte ("Heute," [1931] 214).

[142] "The manager stands for the Christian confronted with the crises that the kingdom brings in the lives of men" (Fitzmyer, "Manager," 32 n. 21; cf. *Luke* 2.1102). "The clever, resolute behaviour of the man when threatened by imminent catastrophe should be an example to Jesus' hearers" (Jeremias, *Parables*, 46).

are the people of the light." The following issues in this verse merit examination: its speaker and original connection with the parable, the subjects of the comparison, and the nature of the comparison.

1. The Speaker and Original Connection to vv. 1-8a

Almost everyone is agreed that the words of v. 8b are *not* those of the master. The eschatological dualism here between "the sons of this age" and "the sons of light" is out of place in the mouth of one who is himself a son of this age and for whom the distinction would have little meaning.[143] The natural assumption of many interpreters, then, is that Jesus is the speaker in v. 8b. The usual corollary of this assumption is that v. 8b is an original part of the parable. This conclusion is not shared by everyone, however, a number of interpreters arguing instead that v. 8b is secondary. Among the alternate explanations of the origin of this verse are that it is a pre-Lucan interpretation of the parable,[144] Luke's own remark,[145] or an independent logion of Jesus appended here by Luke or his source.[146] None of these explanations are particularly compelling, for the following reasons.

First, the fact that the thought here is Palestinian and not Hellenistic favors Jesus as the speaker.[147] While this fact does not prove Luke could not have used terminology such as "the sons of this age" and "the sons of the light," the Palestinian precedent or background for the terminology does, however, call into question the need to seek a source other than Jesus himself. If Jesus *could* have spoken these words, why explain them as Lucan? The Jewish flavor of the terminology in v. 8b fits with the untranslated measures in the story itself (*batos* [Heb. *bath*], v. 6, and *koros* [Heb. *kor*], v. 7), and both features suggest Luke is transmitting traditional material here. At least as far as the Palestinian background of the terminology in v. 8b is concerned, then, there is reason to believe the words originate from Jesus himself.

A second argument against interpreting v. 8b as secondary, particularly as an appended independent logion, is the relative obscurity of the

---

143 Hiers, "Friends," 33 n. 16; Tillmann, "Verwalter," 179; and Zahn, *Lucas*, 575.

144 Degenhardt, *Lukas*, 119, and Via, *Parables*, 156.

145 Dodd, *Parables*, 17; Schmid, *Lukas*, 258; and Tillmann, "Verwalter," 179.

146 Fitzmyer, "Manager," 28, and perhaps also Michaelis, *Gleichnisse*, 228-29.

147 This point is stressed by Marshall on the basis of the usage of the expression "the sons of light" in the Qumran literature (*Luke*, 621). Degenhardt also notes this expression is good Palestinian usage, but draws the conclusion Luke knew and used it, rather than Jesus (*Lukas*, 119 n. 29).

verse. Is it really plausible that these words (even if they are authentically Jesus') had an independent existence, that they circulated at least for a time without this or any context? Would they be intelligible on their own? Such a prospect seems most unlikely. The obscurity of the words demands a context, and, as will be demonstrated in the remainder of this section, they fit as well in their present context as anywhere else in the NT. The parable, with its account of the steward's shrewd behavior, provides a vivid and apt illustration of the very quality in which "the sons of this age" surpass "the sons of (the) light." Nothing is gained by postulating another context or an independent existence for these words. They can, therefore, be taken as an original part of the parable.[148]

Having concluded v. 8b is original and Jesus is the speaker, its connection with the parable, particularly with v. 8a, needs careful consideration. In the latter verse Jesus concludes the parable on a surprising note by reporting that when the master discovered the dishonest steward's plan he commended him for the wisdom or foresight of his actions. Jesus then continues in v. 8b, "*hoti hoi huioi tou aiōnos toutou phronimōteroi . . .*". While the precise sense of *hoti* here is not altogether clear, most interpreters understand it as explicative.[149] V. 8b is thus Jesus' own commentary on the parable. Here he explains and justifies the master's praise in v. 8a,[150] as well as reveals his own purpose in telling the parable.[151] The force of the conjunction, and thus the sense of the connection between vv. 8a and 8b, is perhaps best conveyed by Plummer: "'He [the master] was justified in praising his shrewdness, because'; or,

---

[148] At least passing mention should be made at this point of yet another argument offered in support of the originality of v. 8b. It is put forward by Bailey, and is based on the literary form of the parable itself. Bailey contends that since the three lines of the last stanza (v. 8) balance the three of the first stanza (v. 1), v. 8 as a whole must be part of the original telling (*Poet*, 107-8; cf. pp. 95-96 for an outline of the "parabolic ballad" form of the parable). Although I agree with Bailey's conclusion that v. 8b is original, his line of reasoning on the basis of literary form is not persuasive, primarily because of its implications for v. 9. If vv. 1-8 are a self-contained literary unit, v. 9 cannot be original. As will be noted in the next section, Bailey uses a similar literary argument with respect to vv. 9-13 to separate sharply the latter verses from vv. 1-8. If, however, a case can be made for the position that v. 9 is original to the parable, as I think can be, both of Bailey's literary forms become suspect.

[149] Wellhausen (*Lucae*, 86) suggests the second *hoti* of v. 8b is equivalent to the Hebrew *lemor* and thus introduces direct discourse. Very few have adopted this interpretation, Krämer being about the only exception (*Rätsel*, 170). (Fitzmyer [*Luke* 2.1108] says I. H. Marshall ["Steward"] also tries to support Wellhausen's interpretation, but Marshall explicitly dismisses it [p. 618].) Easton notes the difficulty of the second *hoti*, and although he suggests "because" is the simplest explanation, he concludes no explanation is really satisfactory (*Luke*, 242).

[150] Derrett, "Fresh Light on St Luke XVI. II. Dives and Lazarus and the Preceding Sayings," *NTS* 7 (1960-61) 365; Fonck, *Parabeln*, 688; Lagrange, *Luc*, 434; Marshall, *Luke*, 621; and Zahn, *Lucas*, 775.

[151] Geldenhuys, *Luke*, 415, and Volckaert, "Steward," 337.

'I cite this example of shrewdness, because'."[152] Either way, v. 8b makes it clear that Jesus endorses the master's praise (unless, of course, he is speaking ironically). The verse also indicates that the point of comparison between the steward and Jesus' disciples is wisdom or foresight, not dishonesty. V. 8b thus serves as a corrective to possible misunderstanding of the master's commendation.[153]

At the same time, Jesus begins in v. 8b to apply the point of the parable to the disciples. He does so in an unexpected fashion. "While the disciples were chuckling over the surprising issue of the story," writes Buttrick, "Jesus turned on them—humor in His eyes, and love, and holy purpose—and drove home the sharp truth: 'For . . . '."[154] Jesus says, in effect, that the disciples can learn something positive from this steward, dishonest though he was. In v. 8b he picks up on the wisdom or foresight exhibited by the steward, and focuses attention on this quality as one in which the disciples are outdone by people like the steward. All too often, Jesus says, "the sons of this age" are shrewder or wiser (*phronimōteroi*) than his own disciples. Although, as we will see, the comparison is not intended absolutely, it nonetheless serves as both a rebuke of and exhortation for his disciples. At least some of them are in need of the teaching of this parable.[155]

2. The Subjects of the Comparison

In Luke 16:8b Jesus compares "the sons of this age [*hoi huioi tou aiōnos toutou*]" and "the sons of the light [*tous huious tou phōtos*]." According to Sellin, the eschatological dualism of this comparison stamps the whole parable, including v. 9.[156] The noun *huioi* with the genitive is the common Semitic expression for "people belonging to a particular class,"[157] "those who share the characteristics of" someone or something.[158] One class of people, of which the steward and the master are members, belongs to "this age." This phrase, much used in the theology of Jesus'

---

[152] Plummer, *Luke*, 384. Godet writes, "*Wisely*: Yes, adds Jesus, it is quite true. For . . ." (*Luke* 2.164). Arndt conveys the sense as follows: "The dishonest steward won praise for his prudence because it is a fact that the sons of this world are . . . " (*Luke*, 356).

[153] Bailey, *Poet*, 107.

[154] Buttrick, *Parables*, 120.

[155] Menoud, "Riches," 10.

[156] Sellin, "Studien," 295.

[157] Marshall, *Luke*, 621.

[158] Geldenhuys, *Luke*, 414 n. 12, quoting H. K. Luce, *Luke*. Zerwick (*Biblical Greek* §42) explains that *huios* followed by the genitive expresses "a certain intimate relation to a person or thing." In Luke 16:8b, the relation is to "this age" or "the light."

day, denotes the present world as the time of transitoriness, imperfec-
tion, sin, and death. As such it stands in contrast to the *aiōn mellōn* (cf.
Luke 18:30; 20:34-36).[159] "This age" is the present world outside Christ
and under the power of Satan.[160] It is characterized by *adikia* (cf. v. 8a).
"The sons of this age," then, are "those who belong entirely to this
present age, as contrasted with those who look for the age to come."[161]
They are "those who live for this world, whose heart is attached to what
this earth affords in the way of comforts, enjoyments, and satisfactions."[162]
Their outlook is entirely conditioned by this world. They are "the
worldly,"[163] "unbelieving worldlings."[164] The whole expression *hoi
huioi tou aiōnos toutou* is, therefore, first and foremost an "eschatological
category-title [Kategoriebezeichnung]" for those who have not (yet)
embraced the gospel.[165]

The other class of people mentioned by Jesus in v. 8b are "the sons
of the light [*tous huious tou phōtos*]." It is to this group that the disciples
belong. Unlike the previous phrase, which occurs in the NT only here and
in 20:34,[166] the phrase "the sons of the light" has been shown to have been
used by the Qumranians as a self-designation.[167] Whatever the nature of
the influences of Qumran on Christianity,[168] Jesus' use of this particular
phrase here distinguishes people who belong to the age to come from
those who belong to the present age. If the present age is characterized
by darkness, the age to come is characterized by light. Light is probably
used here in a soteriological and ethical sense as the opposite of impurity
and sin.[169] It is the opposite of the *adikia* which characterizes the
steward's actions and his whole worldly sphere of existence (cf. v. 8a).
The sons of light are those who have embraced the gospel of the kingdom
as preached by Jesus, and who, as a result, belong to the age to come.
Their whole sphere of existence is now different. Their goals, methods,

---

[159] Jülicher, *Gleichnisreden* 2.504.

[160] Geldenhuys, *Luke*, 414 n. 13. Cf. John 12:31; 14:30; 17:15; Gal 1:4; 1 John 5:19.

[161] Creed, *Luke*, 204.

[162] Arndt, *Luke*, 356.

[163] Zerwick and Grosvenor, *Analysis*, re. Luke 16:8. Cf. *NEB* ("the worldly") and *NIV*
("the people of this world").

[164] Geldenhuys, *Luke*, 414 n. 13.

[165] Krämer, *Rätsel*, 154.

[166] Krämer, *Rätsel*, 153.

[167] Marshall, *Luke*, 621; e.g., 1 QS 1:9 and 1 QM 1:3. Cf. also Grundmann, *Lukas*, 320.
This phrase is not used by the rabbis, however, a fact explained by Krämer as deliberate
avoidance of terminology being used by Qumranians and Christians alike (*Rätsel*, 153).

[168] P. Benoit ("Qumrân et Le Nouveau Testament," *NTS* 7 [1960-61] 276-96) qualifies
the dependence of Christianity on Qumran at a number of significant points. Included in his
discussion (pp. 288-90) are the expressions under consideration here.

[169] Kögel, "Gleichnis," 593.

and values are no longer earthbound or worldly, but "other-worldly."[170] The phrase *tous huious tou phōtos* also denotes, therefore, an eschatological category. It is one more indication that our parable is, to use Bailey's words, "primarily concerned with eschatology."[171]

3. The Meaning of the Comparison

The meaning of the comparison in v. 8b has already been touched on in the discussion of the original connection of the verse with the preceding verses. Here I want to develop the point a bit further. The sons of this age are, Jesus says, *phronimōteroi* than the sons of light. Simply put, the worldly make better provision for their future that Christian disciples do for theirs. Jesus' statement, which no doubt took the disciples by surprise, should not, however, be taken in an absolute sense as if worldly people surpass Jesus' disciples always and in every respect. As Wiesen reminds us, Jesus' judgment here is valid when the groups as wholes are considered; it is not meant without exception.[172] The comparison is limited to the matter of wisdom or foresight with regard to the future. What is more, there is a qualitative difference in the wisdom of the two groups of people. The latter point is made in at least two ways. First, it is implicit in the two spheres of existence themselves to which the respective groups belong. One sphere is characterized by *adikia*, the other by light. The goals, methods, and values of each are very different. Wisdom or foresight in one sphere, therefore, will take a different form than it does in the other. Second, the qualitative difference between the wisdom of worldly people and that of Christian disciples is explicit in the qualifying phrase *eis tēn genean tēn heautōn*. Worldly people are wiser, yes, but only "in relation to" (*NASB*) or "in dealing with" (*NIV* and *NEB*)[173] "their own kind [*genea*]."[174] This phrase indicates that the

---

[170] "The other-worldly" is in fact Zerwick's and Grosvenor's name for "the sons of the light" (*Analysis*, re. Luke 16:8); it is also the translation of the phrase in the *NEB*.

[171] Bailey, *Poet*, 107.

[172] Wiesen, *Gleichnis*, 78.

[173] The preposition *eis* is used here in the sense of "for," "to," "with respect or reference to" (BAGD, s.v., 5). Cf. Schulz who calls attention to this meaning of *eis*, citing 9:62; 12:21; and 14:35 as other examples of the same use in Luke (*Parabel*, 73).

[174] The word *genea*, which literally means those descended from a common ancestor (a "clan"), came to be used for "race" or "kind" generally (BAGD, s.v., 1). As Weiss notes, the word denotes not a temporally detached group but one which is intrinsically of the same kind (*Lukas*, 533 n.). A *genea* is a group of contemporaries animated by the same feelings (Lagrange, *Luc*, 434), "men who agree in some respect, who share the same ideals" (Zerwick and Grosvenor, *Analysis*), "the like-minded" (Krämer, *Rätsel*, 157-58). In this respect, the constituent members of a given *genea* resemble a family, race, or people.

"surprising commendation" of v. 8a is "limited to the prudence of the children of this world in their dealings with one another, and does not refer to their relations with God."[175] Within their own sphere of existence and towards people who share the same outlook the worldly often exercise more foresight than do Christians in their respective interests and affairs.[176] Christians can learn something from worldly people at this point. As exemplary as the wisdom of the worldly may be, it is, however, in the final analysis only short-sighted and ephemeral. Wisdom for the Christian disciple must be of a different nature and order.[177]

The comparison between the sons of this age and the sons of light is, then, restricted to one point, that of wisdom. Any praise for the sons of this age in v. 8b is only "ironically bitter praise."[178] This fact does not, however, remove the sting of Jesus' words for his disciples. Qualified though the comparison between the two classes of people is, v. 8b is still "a plain criticism"[179] of the disciples. "It is a sigh of regret, the expression of a truth, but a regrettable truth."[180] Jesus upbraids his disciples for being less alert to their eschatological situation than a dishonest, worldly steward who faced the prospect of dismissal. To put it in other terms, disciples are often less wise in their own world than a businessman in his.[181] "The world is better served," writes Trench, "by its servants than God is by his."[182] Perhaps behind Jesus' censure stands the lukewarmness

---

[175] Jeremias, *Parables*, 46. Other exegetes who call attention to the delimiting function of this phrase include Easton, *Luke*, 243; Goebel, "Gleichnisgruppe," 663; Kögel, "Gleichnis," 593; Krämer, *Rätsel*, 160; Meyer, *Commentary*, 220; and Zahn, *Lucas*, 575.

[176] Since Jesus is making a general observation about both classes of people, the most natural way to read this phrase is to connect it with both groups (so, e.g., Wiesen, *Gleichnis*, 78). The worldly are wiser in their sphere of existence than Christians in theirs. This assumption seems to be shared by most interpreters, although a few restrict the reference of the phrase to "the sons of this age" (e.g., Creed, *Luke*, 204; Jeremias, *Parables*, 46 n. 84; and Meyer, *Commentary*, 221). While the main focus of the application of the parable for Christians may be their mutual relations with other Christians (Godet, *Luke* 2.164-65; Jülicher, *Gleichnisreden* 2.505; Plummer, *Luke*, 384; and Zahn, *Lucas*, 575), the application is not limited only to other Christians. Jesus is making a general point about wisdom or foresight in the affairs of and among the citizens of the respective spheres; he is not carefully delimiting the area in which the application is to be made by his disciples.

[177] Arnot, *Parables*, 453; Jülicher, *Gleichnisreden* 2.503; and Stoll, "Problem," 24-25.

[178] Krämer, *Rätsel*, 163.

[179] Kosmala, "Steward," 118. While the vast majority of interpreters regard v. 8b in this way, there have been a few dissenters. Arndt, for example, argues v. 8b is "purely descriptive" of the worldlings' adroitness, with no censure intended (*Luke*, 357). Cf. also Bruce, *Teaching*, 368-69. Almost all other interpreters who deny v. 8b is a criticism of the disciples do so on the basis of alleged irony in Jesus' words (e.g., Bretscher, "Steward," 759, and Lenwood, "Parable," 368).

[180] C. L. Mitton, "The Unjust Steward," *ExpTim* 64 (1953) 308.

[181] Seccombe, *Possessions*, 163.

[182] Trench, *Parables*, 443.

and halfhearted commitment of some of his disciples. Jesus may be addressing himself to followers who remain attached to the things of the world, who may, like the Pharisees, be trying to serve both God and mammon (cf. vv. 13-14). His words may have special relevance for the tax collectors and other rich people among his disciples for whom the problem of halfheartedness may be particularly acute.

While Jesus here rebukes his disciples for being outdone by the world, he at the same time exhorts them to greater wisdom or foresight in their affairs. Not only should they be shamed by the conduct of worldly people in this regard, they should also learn a lesson. Jesus' words are, therefore, a censure *and* an imperative. Implicit in Jesus' words is an *a fortiori* argument.[183] If worldly people make provision for their temporal future, how much more should Christians do so for their eternal future. Hunter expresses well the imperative force of Jesus' words when he writes that Jesus is saying in effect, "Give me men who will show as much practical sense in God's business as worldlings do in theirs."[184] This lesson is, in general terms at least, the point of our parable.

The specific form the disciples' wisdom is to take is not indicated in v. 8b. Jesus points out the disciples' need for greater wisdom and spurs them to it, but he does not say in this verse precisely how that wisdom should be expressed. This fact has led many interpreters to explain the point of the parable as an exhortation to wisdom (either generally or eschatologically) without reference to the use of money or possessions.[185] In order to do so, of course, the original connection of v. 9 to our parable must be denied. As will be argued in the next section, there are, however, adequate grounds for taking v. 9 as an original part of the parable. If that is true, the "disappointing truth" of v. 8b is not Jesus' last word on his disciples' conduct; in v. 9 he adds positive teaching.[186] I will show that in v. 9 he applies the point of the parable (wisdom) to the disciples' faithful use of earthly possessions for the benefit of others. V. 8b thus functions as "the point of transition,"[187] "the pivot,"[188] between the parable and its direct positive application. As such it serves an important role in our parable.

---

[183] F. E. Williams, "Almsgiving," 295.

[184] Hunter, "Crisis," 317.

[185] See my discussion of "Non-monetary Interpretations" in chapter one.

[186] Menoud, "Riches," 11.

[187] Trench, *Parables*, 440.

[188] "Der Angelpunkt," Krämer, *Rätsel*, 168. Others who have called attention to this function of v. 8b include Derrett, "Dives," 365, and Volckaert, "Steward," 336, 337 n. 9.

To summarize Luke 16:8b, Jesus begins here to apply the parable of the dishonest but shrewd steward to his disciples. He does so in an unexpected and startling fashion. He rebukes his disciples for too often showing less wisdom and foresight in eternal matters than worldly people like the steward do in temporal matters. In the process he also seeks to spur them to exercise more wisdom in the affairs of their own sphere. V. 8b thus serves as a transition between the parable and its application by showing the disciples their need of such teaching, and also leading them to the direct positive application of the parable in v. 9.

E. Verse 9

The exegetical difficulties of our pericope continue in Luke 16:9. The many issues of this thorny verse will be discussed under three headings: the connection of v. 9 with vv. 1-8, the meaning of the basic exhortation in v. 9a, and the meaning of the purpose clause in v. 9b.

1. The Connection to vv. 1-8

Most interpreters agree that Luke 16:9 deals with the use of material possessions and money.[189] There is considerable difference of opinion, however, when it comes to the question of whether or not this verse is an original part of the parable. (The question of originality extends to vv. 10-13 as well, the focus of the next section of this chapter.) This issue is an important one because it affects how one interprets the basic point of the parable. Simply put, if v. 9 is not original, the point of the parable relates to wisdom or prudence (either general or eschatological); if it is original, the use of money is introduced into the application.

a) Objections to original connection

Jeremias is representative of those who deny that Luke 16:9 is an original part of the parable to which it is now attached. Although he concedes v. 9 seems to be the point of the parable, he doubts that it was such originally. Among the reasons Jeremias gives for separating v. 9 from the parable are the following. First, "the abrupt transition" from the third

---

[189] About the only exceptions to this statement are some of the interpreters who detect irony in Jesus' voice. In their understanding, v. 9 is not about the use of money, but is rather an indictment of Pharisaic casuistry. Paul, for example, contends v. 9 is original but has nothing to do with money ("Steward," 192-93). Cf. also Ripon ("Steward," 25).

person in v. 8 to the first person in v. 9 (*kai egō*) is taken as proof of "a join between the two verses." According to Jeremias, the explanation of this transition is that several sayings (vv. 9-13) have been added to the parable.[190] Second, Jeremias contends that in v. 9 "we have an entirely different application of the parable from that which is given in v. 8a."[191] In v. 8a, which Jeremias takes to be Jesus' original application of the parable, the steward is an example because of his "prudent resolution." V. 9, however, "looks like an appeal to a sacrificial, sociable attitude,"[192] and the steward is an example "on account of his wise use of money: he used it to help others."[193] Jeremias concludes that as the primitive church applied the parable to the Christian community, "it shifted the emphasis from the eschatological to the hortatory application."[194] "A summons to resolute action in a crisis" originally addressed to the "unconverted" was thus transformed into "a direction for the right use of wealth" by disciples.[195]

What can be said in response to these arguments? First, although the transition from v. 8 to v. 9 is striking, there are ways to account for it other than concluding it is an editorial seam. As I will soon argue more fully, the words *kai egō hymin legō* introduce Jesus' own application of the parable. Second, Jeremias's assumption that "a summons to resolute action in a crisis" cannot have been spoken to disciples must be called into question. Since this point has already been made in connection with

---

[190] Jeremias, *Parables*, 45-46. Even among interpreters who deny an original connection between v. 9 and the parable, there are different ways to explain the origin of v. 9 and the text as it now stands. Many interpreters believe that in vv. 9-13 Luke has put together Jesus' words from other contexts and appended them here (e.g., Bailey, *Poet*, 116-17; Descamps, "Composition," 49-50; Grundmann, *Lukas*, 319; Michaelis, *Gleichnisse*, 229; Peters, "Haushalter," 142; Schmid, *Lukas*, 259; and Via, *Parables*, 156). Others suggest the combination of verses may have occurred in the pre-Lucan tradition (e.g., Ellis, *Luke*, 198). Still others regard v. 9 as Luke's own conclusion added here to make the meaning of the parable more specific (e.g., Loisy, *Evangiles* 2.161; Topel, "Steward," 220; and Weiss, *Life*, 256 n. 1). The estimation of the quality of Luke's redactional work ranges from that of "a rather feeble invention" (Loisy, *Evangiles* 2.161) to that of "artistic editing" (Topel, "Steward," 220 n. 20). For further details and nuances of the various explanations of the origin of v. 9 by those who deny its originality here, see Krämer, *Rätsel*, 125-26.

[191] *Parables*, 46. Much the same point is made by Schmid, *Lukas*, 259.

[192] *Parables*, 46.

[193] *Parables*, 47.

[194] *Parables*, 47-48.

[195] *Parables*, 47. Mention can also be made of Bailey's literary argument against an original connection between vv. 1-8 and v. 9. It will be recalled that Bailey contends *for* the originality of v. 8b on the basis of the literary form of vv. 1-8 (*Poet*, 107-8). The same argument implies v. 9 is *not* original. Bailey makes this point explicit when he uses the literary form of Luke 16:9-13 ("a carefully constructed poem with three stanzas on the single theme of mammon and God" [*Poet*, 110]) to maintain the unity of those verses *and* a sharp division between them and vv. 1-8 (pp. 110-18). If, however, a case can be made for the originality of v. 9, Bailey's arguments on the basis of literary forms become suspect.

the audience of the parable, I will not repeat it here. Suffice it to say that if the parable *was* originally addressed to the disciples, as v. 1 indicates, then v. 9 need not be separated from the parable on the grounds that the audience of the parable has changed. Both v. 9 and vv. 1-8 are addressed to the same audience, that is, to disciples.

The third objection to Jeremias's separation between vv. 1-8 and v. 9 is that the application of v. 9 need not be viewed as "entirely different" from that of v. 8a. To be sure, "a direction for the right use of wealth" (v. 9) is more specific than "a summons to resolute action in a crisis" (v. 8a), but does that make them "entirely different"? Such a conclusion seems neither compelling nor necessary. Why must the hortatory be separated in such rigid fashion from the eschatological? Why, to be more specific, must we assume that the coming of the kingdom has so little to do with the use of material possessions and money? It is my contention, to be developed more fully in a subsequent chapter, that in vv. 1-9 Jesus in fact grounds the hortatory on the eschatological. It is precisely because the kingdom of God is inaugurated in Jesus' person and ministry that he here directs his disciples to use their possessions wisely. In short, eschatology has important practical implications for ethics. Jeremias himself acknowledges as much, although he attributes v. 9 to the primitive church's application of the parable and not to Jesus himself. Having concluded that the church's addition of vv. 9-13 shifted the emphasis of the parable from the eschatological to the hortatory, Jeremias adds the following caveat.

> It would, however, be erroneous to assume that by its hortatory application the primitive Church introduced an entirely foreign element into the parable. *Exhortation is already implicit in the original form of the parable, for Jesus' command to be resolute and make a new start embraces the generosity of v. 9, the faithfulness of vv. 10-12, and the rejection of mammon in v. 13.* Thus, by the hortatory application the parable is not misinterpreted, but 'actualized'.[196]

If exhortation is in fact "implicit in the original form of the parable," why cannot Jesus himself have applied it in the specific ways indicated by Jeremias? There is no good reason to doubt that he did so, at least in v. 9, the focus of our concern here.

---

[196] *Parables*, 48; emphasis added.

b) Arguments for original connection

Thus far I have considered and responded to arguments against an original connection between the parable and v. 9. Marshall is surely right when he judges these and similar arguments "weak."[197] Several arguments can be offered in favor of v. 9 being original.

First, there is the introductory formula with which v. 9 begins: "*Kai egō hymin legō.*" As already seen, some interpreters take these words as evidence of an editorial seam.[198] Others see them as an indication of a sharp contrast between the judgments of the master and Jesus on the steward's actions.[199] Although there is an element of contrast in v. 9, the best way to understand the opening words of the verse is to regard them as "a solemn conclusion,"[200] as Jesus' warning to his hearers that what he is about to say is of great importance.[201] Thus understood, the master's praise of his steward in v. 8a is balanced by Jesus' exhortation to his disciples in v. 9. Jesus puts himself affirmatively on the side of the master (*kai egō*) and puts the disciples on the level of the steward (*hymin*).[202] The point is that the disciples are to earn similar commendation in spiritual matters.[203] Their commendation is similar, yet also different. While Jesus compares his disciples to the steward, he at the same time draws an implicit contrast.[204] If the master, himself a worldly man, praised his

---

[197] Marshall, *Luke*, 622.

[198] E.g., Bailey, *Poet*, 110; Jeremias, *Parables*, 45-46; and Via, *Parables*, 156.

[199] Feuillet, "Intendants," 31; Pirot, *Paraboles*, 312-13; and Summers, *Luke*, 190. Bahnmaier ("Haushalter," 46) speaks of *kai adversativum* in v. 9 ("I, on the other hand"), and Scott ("Steward," 235) postulates a "Semitism," i.e., the use of *waw* to introduce an antithetical rather than coordinate clause ("But I say to you"). On this reading the sense is, "The master praised the dishonest steward, yes; but I, on the other hand, say to you."

[200] Krämer, *Rätsel*, 132. Particularly noteworthy in this connection are several uses of *legō hymin* to conclude parables, e.g., Luke 15:7, 10; 18:8, 14. Even more striking is the fact that in Luke 11:9 the application is linked to the parable by means of virtually the same phrase as in 16:9—*kagō hymin legō.*

[201] Volckaert, "Steward," 338. This note of emphasis seems to be the force of the equivalent phrase *legō hymin*, which, according to Bailey (*Poet*, 110 n. 105), occurs thirty-eight times in Luke's Gospel (e.g., 10:12, 24; 11:51; 12:4-5, 27; 13:3, 5).

[202] Hiers, "Friends," 33; Krämer, *Rätsel*, 132; Meyer, *Commentary*, 221; Plummer, *Luke*, 385; and Zahn, *Lucas*, 576. As far as "the abrupt transition" (Jeremias, *Parables*, 45) to the first person in v. 9 is concerned, this feature can be explained in terms of a mixture of indirect and direct speech (cf. Luke 5:14). This explanation is offered by Marshall ("Steward," 617-19; *Luke*, 619-21; cf. Fitzmyer, *Luke* 2.1108, for a rebuttal). Against Jeremias, who takes the transition as an indication of a seam between vv. 1-8 and 9, Topel refers to 16:9 as "an emphatic change of person" akin to Matt 5:22-44 ("Steward," 218 n. 11).

[203] Plummer, *Luke*, 385.

[204] Among those who have called attention to the element of contrast in the opening words of v. 9 are Gächter, Hiers, and Stier. Gächter describes the argument of v. 9 as "*qal wachomer*," and offers the following summary: "Jesus brings home to his disciples how they should detach themselves from riches, apply it to their brethren in need, and thus secure for

dishonest steward for acting wisely, how much more should disciples strive to earn the commendation of God. As has been stressed already, Christ's disciples are to take a lesson from the foresight and wisdom of the worldly steward, but they are to employ different means for different ends in a different sphere of existence. To anticipate subsequent arguments, disciples are to invest their possessions and money better than the steward did his master's. They are to use their possessions for eternal purposes.

A second argument in favor of v. 9 being original is the existence of several parallels between it and earlier verses. The most striking and frequently noted of these parallels are found in vv. 4b and 9b. The steward's *hina hotan metastathō* (v. 4) is paralleled by Jesus' *hina hotan eklipēi* (v. 9), *dexōntai me* (v. 4) by *dexōntai hymas*, and *eis tous oikous autōn* (v. 4) by *eis tas aiōnious skēnas* (v. 9).[205] Other less striking parallels between v. 9 and earlier verses have also been noticed, among them the use of "goods" (*ta hyparchonta*, v. 1, and *ho mamōnas*, v. 9), the echo of v. 8 in the use of the phrase *tēs adikias* in v. 9, and the "sons of the light" in v. 8 which leads naturally to "you" in v. 9.[206] Unless these parallels be explained as "signs of artistic editing,"[207] when taken together they "make it unlikely that vs. 9 was simply tacked onto the parable."[208] The threads binding v. 9 to vv. 1-8 are, therefore, numerous and strong enough to make separating v. 9 arbitrary.[209] They tie v. 9 to the parable and suggest that in this verse we have Jesus' original application of the parable.

Arguments of a more negative nature can also be given to support the originality of v. 9. Krämer offers at least three. First, without v. 9 the

themselves an eternal reward. This is the natural end to a perfect parable" ("Conceptions," 131). Hiers speaks of "an implicit 'how much more'" in the opening words of v. 9 ("Friends," 33), and Stier of a perfect correspondence between this introduction and the *posōi mallon* of 11:13 (*Words* 4.165). The dual elements of comparison and contrast in Luke 16:9 may account for the striking emphasis on the pronouns—*kai egō hymin legō*, "And *I* say to *you*." According to Topel's statistics, only two of the forty-two uses of *legō hymin* in Luke have *egō* (11:9 and here; "Steward," 218 n. 11). On Bailey's count, *hymin legō* (with the pronoun first) occurs only in the two verses cited by Topel and 6:27 (*Poet*, 110 n. 105). In 16:9 Jesus is comparing and contrasting his disciples to the steward of the parable; to do so he stresses both pronouns.

[205] Among the many exegetes who stress the parallels between vv. 4 and 9 as evidence for the latter verse being an original part of the parable are Bigo, Feuillet, Hiers, Hooley and Mason, Samain, Tillmann, Wellhausen, F. J. Williams, and Zahn.

[206] These parallels and several others are noted by Hiers, "Friends," 32-33.

[207] This view is put forward by Topel ("Steward," 221 n. 20), specifically in contrast to Hiers (cf. the previous note).

[208] Hiers, "Friends," 33.

[209] Tillmann, "Verwalter," 182.

point of the parable as prudent action remains inappropriately vague for a popular preacher like Jesus. Second, without v. 9 the parable has no expressed practical application. Third, there is no other context in the NT where v. 9 fits better than here.[210] While in themselves not decisive, when taken with the positive considerations noted above these arguments too point to the original connection of v. 9 with the parable.

There is, in conclusion, no good reason to doubt, and several good reasons to believe, that v. 9 is an original part of the parable of the unjust steward. V. 9 is Jesus' conclusion to the parable, his practical application, expressing a direct positive exhortation for his disciples. As will be seen, Jesus here commends wisdom of a specific kind, that is, in the use of mammon.[211] His disciples are to use their possessions and money for spiritual purposes as wisely as the worldly do for material aims.[212] Such an exhortation would certainly have had special significance for the converted tax collectors and other rich people among Jesus' disciples.[213]

2. The Basic Exhortation, v. 9a

Jesus' basic exhortation to his disciples is given in v. 9a—"heautois[214] poiēsate philous ek tou mamōna tēs adikias." Jesus probably frames his instruction in these terms to continue the imagery of the parable where the dishonest steward made friends for himself (especially v. 4). Most interpreters identify the friends in v. 9 as the poor who are to be helped by works of charity, particularly almsgiving.[215] The scope of charitable

---

[210] Krämer, Rätsel, 132-33. With respect to the last argument, Fletcher argues along the same lines that it is unlikely v. 9 would have been preserved in early tradition as an isolated logion. He writes, "The saying is not self-contained; it leans on the parable" ("Riddle," 20). The same argument could be used for v. 8b as well. F. J. Williams, who also thinks v. 9 belongs to the parable, contends the verse "is difficult enough not to have been 'invented'" ("Steward," 371).

[211] Creed, Luke, 201. Others who stress v. 9 as a specific application of the wisdom commended in v. 8a include Fonck, Parabeln, 699; Goebel, "Gleichnisgruppe," 664; Menoud, "Riches," 11; and Schmid, Lukas, 259.

[212] Morris, Luke, 249.

[213] Among the interpreters who emphasize this point are Dods, Parables, 371; Fonck, Parabeln, 699; and Stier, Words 4.171.

[214] The third person plural reflexive pronoun is used here for the second person form (Zerwick and Grosvenor, Analysis; cf. Zerwick, Biblical Greek §209). Its position is emphatic—"In your own interest make friends" (Plummer, Luke, 385; cf. Marshall, Luke, 621, and Meyer, Commentary, 222).

[215] E.g., Arndt, Luke, 357; Descamps, "Composition," 50; Grundmann, Lukas, 321; Hoyt, "Poor," 160-61; Johnson, Function, 157; Jülicher, Gleichnisreden 2.507; Krämer, Rätsel, 105, 219; Marshall, Luke, 621; Morris, Luke, 249; Plummer, Luke, 385; Seccombe, Possessions, 169; and Zahn, Lucas, 578. Other writers identify the friends as God or angels (e.g., Ellis, Luke, 200; Jeremias, Parables, 46 n. 85; Manson, Sayings, 293; Meyer, Commentary,

activity is certainly not restricted to alms alone; Jesus' exhortation includes all works of mercy and charity to those in need.[216] Other Christians may be especially in view as the intended recipients.[217] Such acts of charity bespeak true Christian wisdom. While admittedly not explicit, this interpretation of v. 9 will be borne out and clarified by the wider contextual levels of the parable to be considered in subsequent chapters.

The means by which the friends are to be made is indicated in the phrase *ek*[218] *tou mamōna tēs adikias*. The noun *mamōnas*, which is from Aramaic, occurs in the NT only four times, all on the lips of Jesus (here, 16:11, 13, and Matt 6:24 [the latter two verses are parallels]). Although the etymology of the word is uncertain,[219] its frequent use in the literature of the rabbis and of Qumran makes it clear that it means material possessions, property in the sense of movable effects, especially money.[220] Mammon is money in the widest sense, possessions of all kinds, wealth in any form.[221] The derogatory sense which the word eventually acquired in Judaism is recognizable in Jesus' own use of it.[222] This sense is particularly clear in the present verse where *mamōnas* is qualified by the phrase *tēs adikias*. This phrase, which also occurs in the preceding verse with *oikonomos*, is an instance of the so-called "Hebrew genitive."[223]

221; and Schmid, *Lukas*, 260) or as personified almsdeeds (e.g., Fiebig, *Gleichnisreden*, 211, and F. E. Williams, "Almsgiving," 295). Rengstorf contends that the closeness of our verse to Luke 12:33 (a matter to be discussed in a subsequent chapter) makes a special interpretation of friends in 16:9 unnecessary (*Lukas*, 193).

[216] Arndt, *Luke*, 357; Degenhardt, *Lukas*, 123; Jensen, "Haushalter," 709; Stoll, "Problem," 26; and Seccombe, *Possessions*, 169.

[217] Among those who stress other Christians as the recipients of the commended charity are Bugge, *Haupt-Parabeln*, 445; Hofmann, *Lukas*, 397; Krämer, *Rätsel*, 105; and Zahn, *Lucas*, 576, 578. Stier calls attention to the universal scope of the exhortation since we do not know who might one day become a Christian (*Words* 4.189).

[218] The preposition *ek* is used here to "introduce the means which one uses for a definite purpose, *with*" (BAGD 3.f., where in addition to our verse Luke 8:3 is cited as an example; cf. also Acts 1:18). Cf. *NASB* and *RSV*: "by means of." Attempts to give the preposition quite a different sense, either by connecting it to the Aramaic *min* ("without," e.g., Compston ["Friendship," 282] and Scott ["Steward," 235]), or by postulating textual corruption (*ek* was written for an original *ektos* [adv., "outside"], e.g., Wansey ["Steward," 39-40]), have met with little acceptance.

[219] For a summary of the various explanations that have been offered for the etymology of this word, see F. Hauck, "*mamōnas*," *TDNT* 4.388 n. 2. According to Krämer, most exegetes opt for a derivation from the root '*mn* (*Rätsel*, 78; see n. 3 for a list of representative exponents). In that case the basic sense is "that on which one relies" (so, e.g., Fonck, *Parabeln*, 688; Grundmann, *Lukas*, 321; and Marshall, *Luke*, 621), from which a semantic shift to "money, possessions" would not be difficult (Fitzmyer, *Luke* 2.1109).

[220] Krämer, *Rätsel*, 80.

[221] Kosmala, "Steward," 116, and Marshall, *Luke*, 621.

[222] Hauck, "*mamōnas*," *TDNT* 4.389, and Krämer, *Rätsel*, 81.

[223] See the earlier discussion of this construction under "The Meaning of *ho oikonomos tēs adikias*."

Here, as in v. 8, the noun *adikia* in the genitive is used as an adjective, and the expression can be translated "unrighteous mammon" (*RSV*; cf. v. 11 where the adjective *adikos* is actually used with this noun). While interpreters generally agree on the construction itself, "the big question," to use Krämer's words, is what Jesus means by this unusual expression.[224] The answers that have been given are too numerous to discuss them all here.[225] Several of them, however, should be mentioned because of the frequency with which they are met in the literature on our parable and/or because of the element(s) of truth they contain.

One explanation of Jesus' use of the expression "unrighteous mammon" emphasizes the unrighteousness and injustice often associated with the acquisition of wealth, as was supposedly the case with the steward.[226] On this understanding, Jesus is here counselling his disciples, especially those who are converted tax collectors, on the proper use of "ill-gotten gains."[227] Another explanation is that this expression focuses more on the way wealth is used than on the way it is acquired. The use of wealth not infrequently involves unrighteousness, and hence this description of *mamōnas*.[228] A third explanation views the expression as a reference to the deceptive and/or transitory nature of wealth.[229] Wealth is uncertain and unstable; to trust in it is to trust a lie.[230] It cannot provide true happiness.[231]

As many elements of truth as these explanations may contain, none of them fully accounts for Jesus' use of *ho mamōnas tēs adikias* in Luke 16:9. There is yet another explanation of this epithet which in a sense is

---

[224] Krämer, *Rätsel*, 81.

[225] Krämer, e.g., organizes the different explanations of the phrase *ho mamōnas tēs adikias* into no less than ten categories (*Rätsel*, 81-94).

[226] This meaning of the phrase is stressed, e.g., by Bigo, "Richesse," 270; Bruce, *Teaching*, 373; Grundmann, *Lukas*, 321; Hauck, "*mamōnas*," *TDNT* 4.390; and Morris, *Luke*, 249.

[227] Manson, *Sayings*, 293.

[228] Arndt, for example, calls it "sin-producing money" because it is often used for the wrong purposes (*Luke*, 357). Other exponents of the interpretation that the use of money is primarily in view here include Arnot, *Parables*, 458; Oosterzee, *Luke*, 247; and Ragg, *Luke*, 217.

[229] Degenhardt, *Lukas*, 122; Feuillet, "Intendants," 35; Köster, "Haushalter," 728; Riggenbach, "Gleichnisse," 21-22; Schlatter, *Lukas*, 368; Schlögl, "Die Fabel vom 'ungerechten Reichtum' und der Aufforderung Jesu, sich damit Schätze für den Himmel zu sammeln," *BZ* 14 (1917) 42; and Schrenk, "*adikia*," *TDNT* 1.157. In support of this position attention is often drawn to v. 11 (*ho adikos mamōnas* is contrasted with *to alēthinon* ["true," "dependable," "genuine," "real," BAGD]) and Matt 13:22//Mark 4:19 (Jesus speaks of the deceitfulness of riches [the Lucan parallel, 8:14, omits *hē apatē*]).

[230] Trench, *Parables*, 447.

[231] Schlögl, "Fabel," 42.

broader than those just mentioned and can even embrace them.[232] If the word *adikia* has an eschatological nuance in v. 8a (*ho oikonomos tēs adikias*), as already suggested, there is good reason to believe it has the same nuance in v. 9. Just as *tēs adikias* in v. 8 places the steward in the category of people who belong to this present world/age, "the ruling principle" of which is *adikia*,[233] so here the phrase marks wealth as belonging to the same age. When viewed from the perspective of the age to come, *mamōnas tēs adikias* is wealth "which belongs to this evil world";[234] it is "worldly wealth."[235] As part of God's creation wealth and material possessions are not, of course, inherently evil. As one of the influences of this age,[236] however, as one of the "main driving forces" of "a world alien and antagonistic to God,"[237] wealth in all its forms shares in the unrighteousness of this age. As such it is destined to fade with this age,[238] as the third explanation above emphasizes. As a component of life in a fallen world, as an instrument of worldly men, it will be acquired and used in worldly ways. Many times the acquisition and use of wealth will involve *adikia*, unrighteousness and injustice. What is more, as v. 13 indicates, the pursuit of wealth and wholehearted allegiance to God are mutually exclusive. Here in v. 9, therefore, Jesus exhorts his disciples to press wealth into service for the kingdom of God of which they are citizens. They are to do so by using it to help those in need. Herein is true wisdom. The eschatological background of Jesus' exhortation, as well as the specific form of activity enjoined here, will be made clearer in subsequent chapters.

3. The Purpose Clause, v. 9b

In v. 9b Jesus gives the purpose of or reason for his exhortation in v. 9a. "Use worldly wealth to gain friends for yourselves," he says, "*hina hotan eklipēi dexōntai hymas eis tas aiōnious skēnas*." The reader is struck at once by the unmistakable parallels between this clause and v. 4b. The latter verse reads, "*hina hotan metastathō ek tēs oikonomias dexōntai me*

---

[232] On several occasions in his discussion of the various interpretations of this phrase, Krämer calls attention to the overlap and combination of some of them (e.g., *Rätsel*, 87 n. 59, and 89 n. 65). Many of the interpretations of this phrase, including the three just outlined, are not mutually exclusive.

[233] Kosmala, "Steward," 116.

[234] Jeremias, *Parables*, 46 n. 86.

[235] Jalland, "Note," 504, and Marshall, *Luke*, 621. Cf. *NEB* and *NIV*.

[236] Jülicher, *Gleichnisreden* 2.506.

[237] Krämer, *Rätsel*, 95.

[238] This point is noted by Rengstorf, *Lukas*, 193, and Seccombe, *Possessions*, 165.

eis tous oikous autōn." As argued already, these parallels are evidence
for the authenticity and originality of v. 9 as a whole. Jesus here uses the
phraseology of the story to enforce the moral lesson of the parable.[239] In
doing so Jesus sets up an analogy and a contrast between the steward and
his disciples. The clauses of both verses outline the purpose or goal of
the actions of the respective parties. In both cases the goal is to provide
wisely for the future. In the case of the steward, however, that future is
only temporal and earthly; in the case of the disciples it is different, as
will be seen.

There are several exegetical difficulties in Luke 16:9b. Those difficulties revolve around the following words or phrases: *hotan eklipēi,*
dexōntai, and *tas aiōnious skēnas.*

a) hotan eklipēi

Jesus exhorts his disciples to make friends for themselves by means of
"worldly wealth" in order to provide for the time *hotan eklipēi.* The
meaning of the verb *ekleipō,* three of the four NT uses of which are in
Luke's Gospel (here, 22:32, and 23:45), is "fail," "come to an end," "give
out," "grow dark" (BAGD). While most interpreters agree that the
subject here is *ho mamōnas tēs adikias* (v. 9a),[240] there is substantial
difference of opinion as to the meaning of *hotan eklipēi* itself. Two major
interpretations have been offered.[241] The majority view is that Jesus is
here alluding to the hour of death when money is no longer of any value
or use to the individual.[242] Sometimes quoted in support of this position
is Luke 12:20, where God says to "the rich fool," "this very night your
life will be demanded from you." The alternate view, espoused by a
relatively small number of interpreters, is that the phrase is an allusion

---

[239] Arnot, *Parables,* 464. Oosterzee observes that the form of the promise in v. 9b is
borrowed from v. 4 (*Luke,* 246).

[240] This interpretation is reflected in most modern translations: e.g., "when it is gone"
(*NIV*), "when it fails" (*RSV* and *NASB*), "when money is a thing of the past" (*NEB*).

[241] Krämer lists a third interpretation, which views the phrase in question as a reference
to the loss or giving away of riches in the lifetime of the owner (*Rätsel,* 97). I have omitted
this interpretation from discussion because it has had so few advocates in the history of
interpretation (Krämer [p. 97 n. 88] cites Degenhardt and Olshausen as its advocates).

[242] Bruce, *Teaching,* 370; Dupont, *Beatitudes* 3.120-22; Feuillet, "Intendants," 36 n. 1;
Geldenhuys, *Luke,* 414 n. 16; Grundmann, *Lukas,* 321; Jülicher, *Gleichnisreden* 2.507;
Klostermann, *Lukas,* 526; Lagrange, *Luc,* 435; Morris, *Luke,* 249; and Schmid, *Lukas,* 260.
This interpretation is explicit in the variant reading *eklipēte* ("you come to an end, die"; cf.
KJV, "when ye fail") which is noted by several interpreters (e.g., Feuillet; Grundmann;
Oesterley, *Parables,* 200; and Plummer, *Luke,* 385), but not by the two major modern Greek
NTs. The vastly superior attestation of *eklipēi* accounts for the rejection of the variant.

to the parousia.[243] At the eschatological end of the present age worldly wealth will come to an end and will be replaced by treasures in heaven.

As popular and plausible as the majority view may be, it is open to question on several points. First, the pronounced eschatological undertone of the parable, to which attention has been called on a number of occasions, suggests that *hotan eklipēi* is also eschatological. To interject individual eschatology here seems arbitrary and unwarranted. Second, in the phrase in question Jesus seems to be referring to the time when worldly wealth itself comes to an end, when it ceases to be of use and value in the ultimate sense. If so, this fact points to the parousia, to the end of the present age, rather than the death of the individual. Third, the expression *tas aiōnious skēnas* at the end of v. 9 is also relevant here. If, as will be argued, this expression refers to the eschatological consummation, it too supports my contention that *hotan eklipēi* is eschatological.[244] In view of these arguments, I concur with the minority interpretation that *hotan eklipēi* refers to the end of the present age, to the parousia. It should be stressed, however, that one's conclusions about this particular phrase do not significantly affect the interpretation of v. 9. Whether the allusion is to death or the parousia, the force and urgency of Jesus' exhortation remains the same. Worldly wealth is, at best, precarious.[245] Jesus' disciples must, therefore, use it wisely (that is, for others) while they can. To do so, moreover, in some way has a bearing on one's reception in the age to come, a point which brings me to the second disputed phrase in v. 9b, *dexōntai hymas*.

b) dexōntai hymas

Two issues arise with respect to this phrase—the subject of the verb, and the relationship between the action exhorted in v. 9 and this reception. Interpreters of our parable seem fairly evenly divided on the identification of the subject of the verb *dexōntai* in v. 9. One group explains the third person plural as a circumlocution for God's name.[246] It is God alone

---

[243] Krämer (*Rätsel*, 98 n. 97) lists as representatives of this view only Weiss, Jeremias, Martin-Achard, himself (in an earlier article and in his monograph), and less decisively Kosmala. To this list I can add only A. J. Mattill, Jr. (*Luke and the Last Things* [Dillsboro, NC: Western North Carolina Press, 1979] 37-39) and Meyer (*Commentary*, 224-25).

[244] The eschatological coloring of *hotan eklipēi* by *tas aiōnious skēnas* is emphasized by Krämer, *Rätsel*, 99, and Meyer, *Commentary*, 224.

[245] Pirot, *Paraboles*, 307.

[246] E.g., Creed, *Luke*, 205; Geldenhuys, *Luke*, 414 n. 17; Grundmann, *Lukas*, 321; Jeremias, *Parables*, 46 n. 85; Krüger, "Grundlagen," 175 n. 1; Manson, *Sayings*, 293; Marshall, *Luke*, 622; Menoud, "Riches," 13; Morris, *Luke*, 249; Oesterley, *Parables*, 200;

who does the receiving in question. Several instances of a similar usage of a third person plural verb in Luke are cited as evidence (e.g., 6:38, 44; 12:20, 48; 14:35). A second group of interpreters contends that the subject is the friends of v. 9a, that is, the beneficiaries of Christian love and mercy.[247] While the latter understanding is the more natural of the two,[248] either interpretation encounters difficulty when it comes to the matter of the relationship between the action exhorted in v. 9a and the reception spoken of in v. 9b. If the subject of *dexōntai* is God, how does the action exhorted in v. 9a relate to God's reception? If friends is the subject, what role do they play in the reception *eis tas aiōnious skēnas*? Since these questions are related, they can be discussed together.

Several interpreters read v. 9 as teaching the merit of good works and/ or the intercession of those helped.[249] In effect, the charitable use of wealth plays an important role in gaining salvation. This explanation has not been a viable one, however, for many interpreters, Protestants in particular. These interpreters emphasize instead the analogy of faith in interpreting this verse. Since the time of Luther,[250] "the Protestant explanation" of the difficulty in v. 9 is that the good works enjoined here are testimony to and demonstration of faith which itself is the only means of salvation. Like other good works, the charitable use of wealth will be rewarded by God.[251]

Ragg, *Luke*, 217; and Talbert, *Reading Luke*, 155. This interpretation may be reflected in the *NIV* ("you will be welcomed") and *NEB* ("you may be received").

[247] E.g., Arndt, *Luke*, 357; Bugge, *Haupt-Parabeln*, 446-47; Feuillet, "Intendants," 37; Godet, *Luke* 2.165; Hofmann, *Lukas*, 400; Hoyt, "Poor," 161; Jülicher, *Gleichnisreden* 2.506-7; Lagrange, *Luc*, 435; Oosterzee, *Luke*, 246; Smith, *Parables*, 112; Stier, *Words* 4.188; and Zahn, *Lucas*, 577. This interpretation is reflected in the *KJV*, *NASB*, and *RSV* ("they").

[248] In favor of taking the friends as the subject are the following considerations. First, as Jülicher suggests (*Gleichnisreden* 2.506-7), the parallel with v. 4 (where the subject of the verb is the debtors in vv. 5-7) suggests the subject of the verb in v. 9b is the beneficiaries of the disciples' actions. Second, in the other allegedly analogous uses of the third personal plural in Luke, the context makes it clear that those usages are impersonal and/or a circumlocution for God. In those cases, no other possible subjects are present; there is no ambiguity as there is in our verse. The friends of v. 9a is the natural subject of the verb *dexōntai* in v. 9b.

[249] E.g., Fonck, *Parabeln*, 690; Riggenbach, "Gleichnisse," 24; and Stoll, "Problem," 26.

[250] See Hof, "Luthers Auslegung." Cf. also Krämer's excursus on the dogmatic difficulties in this verse for Protestants (*Rätsel*, 111-19). Krämer devotes particular attention to Luther's explanation of Luke 16:9.

[251] Arndt, *Luke*, 357-58; Arnot, *Parables*, 460-61; Caemmerer, "Investment," 71; Drummond, *Teaching*, 321; Jalland, "Note," 505; Kiehl, "Parable," 126; Marshall, *Luke*, 622; Stier, *Words* 4.193; and Zahn, *Lucas*, 577. Since, strictly speaking, the argument from the analogy of faith takes us beyond the limits of Luke 16:1-13 itself, it is perhaps permissible at this point to call attention to v. 15. There Jesus makes it clear that one's heart attitude, not simply external actions (even alms), is what counts with God. Good works, even if sincerely motivated, are not in themselves sufficient grounds for salvation.

If the subject of *dexōntai* is friends, the latter interpretation needs to be nuanced further.[252] The explanation often given is that the (Christian) recipients of charity will welcome their (Christian) benefactors into heaven, and/or they will testify to the genuineness of their benefactors' faith as evidenced in their good works.[253] If poor Christians do have a role in their benefactors' welcome *eis tas aiōnious skēnas*, it will only reflect the verdict of the Judge;[254] they will act only in conjunction with God.[255] It should also be remembered that Jesus is here teaching by means of a parable, not making precise and complete theological statements. The form and imagery of the promise in v. 9 is borrowed from v. 4, and should not, therefore, be made the basis of doctrinal formulations apart from the clear, unambiguous teaching of Jesus.[256]

c) eis tas aiōnious skēnas

Jesus promises that people who make friends for themselves by means of worldly wealth will be received *eis tas aiōnious skēnas*. What is the meaning of this unusual phrase? The phrase *aiōnioi skēnai*—variously translated as "eternal dwellings" (*NIV*; *NASB* adds the definite article), "an eternal home" (*NEB*), or "the eternal habitations" (*RSV*)—occurs nowhere else in the NT, OT, or rabbinic literature. Krämer concludes from this fact that it originates with Jesus and is thus of great importance for determining the origin of v. 9.[257] The phrase is unusual, even paradoxical,[258] because it combines "apparent opposites."[259] The word

---

[252] Godet refers to the service of poor Christians to their benefactors as "perhaps the most difficult question in the explanation of the parable" (*Luke* 2.165).

[253] Arndt, *Luke*, 357; Geldenhuys, *Luke*, 416; and Zahn, *Lucas*, 577.

[254] This point is made by W. P. Paterson, "The Example of the Unjust Steward," *ExpTim* 35 (1923-24) 393.

[255] Topel, "Steward," 220 n. 24. Topel concludes from this fact that the third person plural can serve as the equivalent of a theological passive. Though beyond the scope of this study, it at least bears mention that many interpreters point to Matt 25:31-46 (esp. v. 40: "whatever you did for one of the least of these brothers of mine, you did for me") as the best explanation of Luke 16:9. Among those who have noted the connections between Luke 16:9 and Matt 25 are Dods, *Parables*, 374; Drummond, *Teaching*, 322; Godet, *Luke* 2.165; Hooley and Mason, "Parable," 56; Jülicher, *Gleichnisreden* 2.507; Krämer, *Rätsel*, 105; Oosterzee, *Luke*, 247; Plummer, *Luke*, 385; Trench, *Parables*, 449; and Wiesen, *Gleichnis*, 81. There are affinities to the thought of reward for helping the needy in Luke 14:13-14.

[256] "The meaning which we attribute to the parable [i.e., any parable] must be congruous with the interpretation of His own ministry offered by Jesus in explicit and unambiguous sayings, so far as such sayings are known to us; and in any case it must be such as to fit the general view of His teaching to which a study of the non-parabolic sayings leads" (Dodd, *Parables*, 19).

[257] Krämer, *Rätsel*, 100.

[258] "Paradoxical" is Bruce's description (*Teaching*, 370).

[259] Oesterley, *Parables*, 200. "The oxymoron in *aiōnious skēnas* is intentional," writes

skēnē itself ("tent," "dwelling" [BAGD]) usually epitomizes that which is temporary, but here, in combination with the adjective *aiōnios*, seems to refer to something permanent. The imagery may be that of the tents of Abraham or of the wilderness wanderings which is being transferred here to the life to come. In that case, the life to come is being represented under the image of a glorified Canaan.[260] It may also be, as Michaelis argues, that behind the use of *skēnē* here stands the LXX usage (for *mishkān*, "dwelling-place, 'tabernacle'" [BDB]) where the word took on the character of the lasting. "The idea of God's abiding presence," Michaelis writes, "was especially connected with the concept of the shekinah in later Judaism."[261]

Most interpreters understand the phrase *aiōnioi skēnai* as a reference to eternal life. This interpretation is often nuanced further, the reception *eis tas aiōnious skēnas* being either reception into heaven[262] or the consummated kingdom of God.[263] In view of the eschatological character of the rest of v. 9 and of the parable as a whole, the latter interpretation seems more probable.[264] Either way, however, the emphasis of the phrase is on the secure future of God's people in his presence. This emphasis stands in sharp contrast to the future of the steward in the parable. According to v. 4, the steward's hope is that he will be received into *tous oikous autōn*, the debtors' homes. According to v. 9, the prospect for the disciples is that they will be received into *tas aiōnious skēnas*.[265] The contrast between the destinies of the two groups is intentional. Among

---

Easton (*Luke*, 245). Some interpreters regard the apparent contrast of the terms in this expression as evidence of sarcasm or irony in v. 9 and the whole parable (e.g., Eagar, "Steward," 463; McFayden, "Steward," 536; and Pautrel, "Tabernacula," 320, 322-23).

[260] Godet, *Luke* 2.166. Other exegetes who call attention to possible OT allusions in this expression include Bruce, *Teaching*, 370; Mattill, *Last Things*, 39; Meyer, *Commentary*, 225; Weiss, *Lukas*, 534; and Wiesen, *Gleichnis*, 80.

[261] Michaelis, "*skēnē*," *TDNT* 7.378-79. This interpretation is endorsed tentatively by Marshall, *Luke*, 621. Jülicher, *Gleichnisreden* 2.506, and Pirot, *Paraboles*, 308, also regard *skēnai* as a reference to the dwelling of God.

[262] Feuillet, "Intendants," 36; Pirot, *Paraboles*, 310; Samain, "Richesses," 332; and Wiesen, *Gleichnis*, 80. Krämer implies this interpretation is the majority view, so widely held in fact that he thinks it unnecessary to list its representatives (*Rätsel*, 101 n. 104). As Krämer also observes, this particular interpretation is often associated with the reception of the individual into heaven at death (p. 101).

[263] Jeremias, *Parables*, 46 n. 88; Krämer, *Rätsel*, 102; Meyer, *Commentary*, 225; Michaelis, "*skēnē*," *TDNT* 7.378; and Seccombe, *Possessions*, 168.

[264] Michaelis, e.g., says we are to assume the word *skēnai* "shares in the eschatological character of the saying [i.e., v. 9]" ("*skēnē*," *TDNT* 7.378). This assumption also applies to the phrase as a whole.

[265] This contrast in vv. 4 and 9 has been noted by many interpreters, among them Goebel, "Gleichnisgruppe," 666; Hiers, "Friends," 32; Jülicher, *Gleichnisreden* 2.506; Kistemaker, *Parables*, 233; Michaelis, "*skēnē*," *TDNT* 7.379 n. 62; Plummer, *Luke*, 386; Schmid, *Lukas*, 260; Schulz, *Parabel*, 90-91; Stoll, "Problem," 26; and Volckaert, "Steward," 339.

other things, Jesus wants to make it clear that his disciples are to act in a different manner and for different goals than did the steward of the parable. Much more is at stake in the use of wealth and possessions than provision for life in this world.

V. 9 is, in summary, Jesus' own positive and practical application of the parable of the unjust steward. It is in a real sense "the key to the meaning" of the parable.[266] Here Jesus tells his disciples how and why they can practice in their own sphere of existence the wise preparation for the future which the steward exercised in his. Jesus says in effect that true wisdom is to use money with eternity in view,[267] "to use wealth in the service of love."[268] Unlike the unjust steward who at best provided only for his earthly future, acts of charity by disciples will bear interest in eternity.[269] Jesus' exhortation is, I have also argued, eschatologically conditioned.

F. Verses 10-13

Having discussed the parable of the unjust steward in Luke 16:1-9, we come now to the final verses of the passage, vv. 10-13. In one sense, these verses are less controversial than vv. 1-9. Most interpreters would agree, for instance, that vv. 10-13 teach faithfulness and wholehearted service of God. Interpretive difficulties arise, however, over the question of the relationship of vv. 10-13 to the parable. That question will be considered in this section. The teaching of vv. 10-13 as a whole will also be summarized and the individual verses themselves treated briefly.

1. The Relationship to vv. 1-9

The relationship between vv. 10-13 and 1-9 is a matter of considerable debate. The reasons for this debate include the parallels between vv. 10-12 and the parable of the talents (Matt 25:20-30 and Luke 19:17-26), between v. 13 and Matt 6:24, and the subject matter of vv. 10-13. Two different basic explanations of the relationship between vv. 10-13 and 1-9 are offered. One explanation is that vv. 10-12/13 are original to the parable of the unjust steward.[270] The other is that these verses are

---

[266] Plummer, *Luke*, 380.
[267] Easton, *Luke*, 245.
[268] Pilgrim, *Good News*, 129.
[269] Stier, *Words* 4.193. Kistemaker calls such acts of charity "spiritual investments" (*Parables*, 234).
[270] This view is held, e.g., by Feuillet, "Intendants," 32, 43; Geldenhuys, *Luke*, 417;

secondary.[271] The many variations and nuances of these two explanations preclude detailed discussion here.[272] Without defending it in detail, it seems very likely that vv. 10-13 are at the very least authentic words of Jesus. This point is conceded even by many who explain these verses as secondary.[273] The terse style of vv. 10-12 is characteristic of Jesus' teaching, and the parallels with undisputed sayings of Jesus (cf. Matt 25 and Luke 19) suggest these verses were not simply composed by Luke or someone else in the early church. The view that at least vv. 10-12 are a unit (i.e., they were spoken together on the same occasion) is also defensible. The unity of vv. 10-12 is likely in light of the strict parallelism within these verses (a matter to which I will return) and the relative obscurity and vagueness of vv. 11-12 themselves.[274] Just as v. 9 leans on vv. 1-8, so vv. 11-12 lean on v. 10.

In view of the considerations just outlined, vv. 10-13 can be regarded as authentic words of Jesus, and at least vv. 10-12 as having been spoken together. Whether or not vv. 10-13 are original to the parable of the unjust steward is another question, one which will never be answered conclusively. On the one hand, there is no compelling reason to believe these verses could not have been original to our parable. Clear verbal connections exist, for example, between them and the parable (*mamōnas*, vv. 9, 11, 13, and *adikia/adikos*, vv. 8-11). In addition, the conceptual and logical relationships between vv. 1-9 and 10-13 can be plausibly explained, as I will show. On the other hand, there is no reason—even on a high view of Scripture—to insist on the originality of vv. 10-13 here.

Godet, *Luke* 2.168; Kiehl, "Parable," 75; Martin-Achard, "Notes," 139; Menoud, "Riches," 14; Pautrel, "Tabernacula," 315; Pirot, *Paraboles*, 311-12; Plummer, *Luke*, 384-85; Samain, "Richesses," 333; Schlatter, *Lukas*, 363, 368; Schulz, *Parabel*, 111; and Zahn, *Lucas*, 576. I have referred to these verses as 10-12/13 because some who maintain the original connection of vv. 10-12 to the parable regard v. 13 as secondary (e.g., Feuillet; Pautrel; and Schlatter [Schlatter treats v. 13 apart from vv. 1-12; see *Lukas*, 547-48]).

[271] E.g., Bugge, *Haupt-Parabeln*, 449; Fitzmyer, "Manager," 29-30, and *Luke* 2.1105-6; Gächter, "Conceptions," 131 n. 40; Jeremias, *Parables*, 46, 110-11; Krämer, *Rätsel*, 218, 224, 231-33; Loisy, *Evangiles* 2.164; Marshall, *Luke*, 623; Schmid, *Lukas*, 259; and Sellin, "Studien," 291. At the risk of overgeneralization, these verses are usually viewed as authentic words of Jesus which have been appended to the parable by either Luke or the tradition he uses. Very often v. 13 is regarded as itself a secondary addition to vv. 10-12.

[272] For more details see Krämer, *Rätsel*, 184-233. Krämer observes that although interpreters who take these verses to be secondary agree they originally had nothing to do with the parable, there are wide differences regarding their origin, composition, conformity to the parable, and function in the present context (p. 184). He then discusses each of these issues (pp. 184-92). The variations among the advocates of the originality of vv. 10-12/13 are not as diverse (cf. pp. 192-212). Krämer's own interpretation is found on pp. 212-33.

[273] Krämer, *Rätsel*, 184.

[274] The latter argument is advanced by Krämer, *Rätsel*, 215-16. He uses it, however, to argue that vv. 10-12 are the creation of an early Christian teacher which was later added to the parable (pp. 218, 224).

It is quite possible that Luke (or pre-Lucan tradition) has here appended words of Jesus from another context in order to elucidate this enigmatic parable. If, as many today are willing to acknowledge, Luke is to be credited with considerable literary and theological skill, the question of the originality of these verses is not one of ultimate interpretive significance. The interpretation of the parable itself does not depend in a substantive way on the originality of vv. 10-13. The question of the originality of these verses can, therefore, be left open.

My own approach in what follows is to interpret vv. 10-13 in their present canonical context without trying to decide the question of their originality. Whatever difficulties this approach may have, it is certainly less precarious than attempting to interpret these verses in isolation and/or in terms of some other hypothetical context. Regardless of whether or not these verses originally belonged to this parable, the fact is they are now connected with it. If they are not original, their present canonical position suggests that at the very least Luke (or the tradition he follows) saw some legitimate connection or relationship between them.[275] In what follows, I will seek to unfold that relationship briefly. A good case can be made for the view that vv. 10-13 fit well here, even if they were not originally part of the parable.

2. Summary of vv. 10-13 in Terms of the Parable

A good place to begin to unfold the meaning of vv. 10-13 in their present context might be to summarize their teaching in terms of the parable. How do they relate to vv. 1-9, how do they fit here? The exegetical foundation for this summary will be supplied in the next subsection.

As vv. 10-13 now stand they seem intended to supplement the parable of the unjust steward (vv. 1-9) by elaborating on the wise use of material possessions (cf. *mamōnas* in vv. 11 and 13). Vv. 10-13 "overload the teaching," as Easton puts it, but carry on the moral. They also guard against misunderstanding the commendation in v. 8.[276] These verses

---

[275] Cf. the catchwords *mamōnas* and *adikia/adikos* in vv. 9, 11, 13, and 8-11, respectively; the lack of transition between vv. 9 and 10; and the conjunctions *oun* in v. 11 and *kai* in v. 12.

[276] Easton, *Luke*, 246. Many interpreters, not all of whom take vv. 10-13 as original, have made the same point about a corrective function served by these verses in their present context. Those who do so include Bailey, *Poet*, 110, 117; Bugge, *Haupt-Parabeln*, 449; Creed, *Luke*, 202; Goebel, "Gleichnisgruppe," 674; Jensen, "Haushalter," 711; Klostermann, *Lukas*, 527; Köster, "Haushalter," 729; Loisy, *Evangiles* 2.163; Plummer, *Luke*, 384-85; Schmid, *Lukas*, 260; Smith, *Parables*, 112; Stier, *Words* 4.170; Trench, *Parables*, 450; and Wellhausen, *Lucae*, 88.

bring out "with unmistakable clarity" that the parable is not a commendation of dishonesty.[277] In contrast to the steward who was wise but
dishonest and unfaithful, Jesus' disciples are to be wise *and* faithful.[278]
Since one's use of wealth has some bearing on one's eternal destiny (v.
9), faithfulness is a manifestation of true wisdom. What is more,
faithfulness in the stewardship of earthly possessions is a test of basic
commitment, of whom one serves. How one uses possessions is crucial
because it is the testing ground for the kingdom, the place where ultimate
loyalties are revealed.[279] One's conduct in externals, in the use of wealth,
indicates whether one serves God or money in his heart; it shows whether
he will inherit the kingdom of God.[280] "Putting too high an evaluation on
earthly possessions," Arndt explains, "means that one does not care for
the heavenly treasures, that is, that one is at heart an unbeliever."[281]
Faithfulness with worldly wealth is, therefore, vitally important for
disciples. In the context of the parable and particularly v. 9, faithfulness
entails using possessions to help those in need. Such faithfulness bears
witness that one has grasped the eschatological situation, that one is a
citizen of the kingdom, that one is truly a disciple of Jesus.

3. Exegetical Comments

With the foregoing summary of the meaning and function of vv. 10-13
in mind, the exegetical basis can now be provided. In v. 10 Jesus (on the
assumption these verses are at least authentic) gives a general principle

---

[277] Arndt, *Luke*, 358.

[278] A number of interpreters have emphasized the note of contrast between the unfaithfulness of the steward and the faithfulness which disciples are to exhibit (e.g., Ellis, *Luke*,
198; Feuillet, "Intendants," 47; Fletcher, "Riddle," 21; Friedel, "Steward," 347; Grundmann,
Lukas, 319; Lagrange, *Luc*, 436; and Marshall, *Luke*, 622). Along the same lines, not a few
interpreters refer to the steward as a negative, deterrent example for disciples (e.g.,
Descamps, "Composition," 51; Jeremias, *Parables*, 47; Jülicher, *Gleichnisreden* 2.512;
Schmid, *Lukas*, 260; Sellin, "Studien," 291; and Weiss, *Lukas*, 535).

[279] Pilgrim, *Good News*, 129. Pilgrim contends that vv. 1-9 make the same point. The
probationary use of wealth, if it might be called that, is illustrated by Godet from human life.
Just as a rich father trains and tests his son's character by starting him off with small
responsibilities, so God lets us use earthly goods. How these are handled in both cases
reveals one's fitness for bigger responsibilities (*Luke* 2.169-70). Godet concludes that these
verses (especially 11-12) contain "the entire philosophy of our earthly existence" (p. 170).
Godet's explanation is followed by Plummer, *Luke*, 387. In similar fashion, though not
clearly dependent on Godet, Ragg describes earth as "a school for heaven: we develop our
moral and spiritual faculties by the way we use our wealth" (*Luke*, 217).

[280] Ellis, *Luke*, 198.

[281] Arndt, *Luke*, 359.

from human experience. "He who is faithful[282] in a very little thing is faithful also in much; and he who is unrighteous[283] in a very little thing is unrighteous also in much" (*NASB*). Faithfulness or dishonesty is of a piece. Because of the general nature of this principle, v. 10 may at first glance appear quite unrelated to vv. 1-9. Such an appearance is dispelled by vv. 11-12, where, by means of rhetorical questions, the principle of v. 10 is specifically applied to the use of "worldly wealth" (*en tōi adikōi mamōna*, v. 11). The implications of this specific application, as well as the formal parallelism of these verses, will be considered in a moment. At this point it should be noted that in vv. 11-12 an inference is drawn (*ei oun*, v. 11; *kai ei*, v. 12) from the negative side of the principle in v. 10.[284] To summarize both verses in terms of v. 10, "If then you have not been faithful in a very little thing, who[285] will entrust[286] you with much?" The inference is that no one would do so because an unfaithful person could only be expected to misuse such a trust as well. Unfaithfulness in a very little thing—here in the use of worldly wealth—disqualifies a person from bigger responsibilities and blessings. The reason, as v. 13 will make clear, is that unfaithfulness, particularly in the use of worldly wealth, reveals ultimate loyalties and heart attitudes.

Having outlined the line of thought in vv. 10-12, let me now consider more carefully the implications of the application in vv. 11-12. The formal parallelism between these two verses is striking and noteworthy. It can perhaps best be seen by setting the parallel clauses one under the other.

---

[282] "*ho pistos*." According to Feuillet, this adjective (repeated four times in vv. 10-12), as well as the verb *pisteusei* in v. 11, brings out the stewardship theme which runs throughout vv. 10-12 and the whole parable ("Intendants," 33).

[283] *adikos*, "unjust," "dishonest," "untrustworthy" (BAGD). Because of the parallel between vv. 10b and 11 (cf., *ei . . . pistoi ouk egenesthe*, v. 11), the sense of untrustworthiness or unfaithfulness seems prominent in the adjective in v. 10b. The idea of dishonesty is present as well (cf. *NEB, NIV, RSV*). *adikos* recalls the use of the related noun (*adikia*) in the parable, in v. 8 qualifying the steward and in v. 9 mammon.

[284] Although the positive side is no doubt implicit here, it is striking, nonetheless, that in vv. 11-12 Jesus focuses on the negative side of the principle, on the prospect and consequences of unfaithfulness. Perhaps he does so because he is talking especially to those disciples who have been unfaithful (so Feuillet, "Intendants," 39). Or, it may be that because the Pharisees are in the background (cf. v. 14), Jesus wants to counteract the influence of their unfaithfulness on his disciples and to call the Pharisees themselves to repentance. The latter suggestion will be developed in the next chapter.

[285] Marshall suggests that behind the *tis* of Jesus' question is God (*Luke*, 623).

[286] The verb in v. 11 is *pisteusei* and in v. 12 *dōsei*. In view of the parallelism of these two verses, the verbs are virtual synonyms here (Krämer, *Rätsel*, 224). Marshall suggests the contrast in vv. 11-12 between the tense of these verbs (both future) and that of *egenesthe* (aorist) indicates that the bestowal in question is something that awaits the age to come (*Luke*, 623).

ei oun/ en tōi adikōi mamōna/ pistoi/ ouk egenesthe, (v. 11a)
kai ei/ en tōi allotriōi / pistoi/ ouk egenesthe, (v. 12a)
to alēthinon/ tis hymin/ pisteusei; (v. 11b)
to hymeteron/ tis hymin/ dōsei; (v. 12b)

Although not strictly parallel, these verses also correspond to v. 10b (cf. *ho en elachistōi adikos* and *en pollōi*). The significance of these observations is that the parallel members of each side of the antitheses (*en elachistōi, en tōi adikōi mamōna, en tōi allotriōi;* and *en pollōi, to alēthinon, to hymeteron*) are essentially synonyms.[287] This fact could be helpful hermeneutically, if we can discover a specific point of reference among them. Such is found, I would argue, in v. 11 where the general principle of v. 10 is concretely applied to the use of *ho adikos mamōnas,* "worldly wealth" (*NIV*). The latter expression ties v. 11 (and by implication vv. 10 and 12 as well)[288] to v. 9 (cf. *ek tou mamōna tēs adikias*). So close in fact is this verbal connection and so unique are the expressions themselves that, unless *ho adikos mamōnas* is a creation of Luke or an early Christian teacher, it is hard to imagine or postulate a better context than this one for at least v. 11. The point again is that if vv. 10-12 are not original to the parable, they at least fit well here and postulating another context is unnecessary.

On account of the parallelism of vv. 10-12, the expression *ho adikos mamōnas* in v. 11 implies that the otherwise vague terms *elachistos* (v. 10) and *to allotrion* (v. 12) are also references to worldly wealth. In v. 10, then, worldly wealth is described as *elachistos,* "a very little thing" (*NASB*). This description emphasizes the relative insignificance of material possessions and warns the disciples against overrating their value.[289] Worldly wealth is also characterized in v. 12 as *to allotrion,* that which belongs to someone else or that which is foreign.[290] On either

---

[287] Krämer, *Rätsel,* 218.

[288] In addition to this parallelism, cf. my earlier remarks about the probable unity of vv. 10-12. What is true of one of these verses also applies to the others.

[289] Geldenhuys, *Luke,* 414 n. 19.

[290] Most interpreters and translations seem to take *to allotrion* in v. 12 as a reference to man's role as a steward of material possessions. Wealth belongs to God; it is only entrusted to men. Among the interpreters who espouse this approach are Arndt, *Luke,* 359; Marshall, *Luke,* 623; Meyer, *Commentary,* 228; Morris, *Luke,* 250; Oosterzee, *Luke,* 248; Plummer, *Luke,* 387; Samain, "Richesses," 333; Schmid, *Lukas,* 261; Summers, *Luke,* 191; and Wiesen, *Gleichnis,* 83. Among the translations which understand the word in the same way are the *NEB* ("what belongs to another"), *NIV* ("someone else's property"), and *NASB* and *RSV* ("that which is another's"). In this interpretation the note of stewardship is prominent. There is, however, another way of looking at the word. That way is to regard *allotrion* as emphasizing the fundamentally foreign or alien nature of worldly wealth when seen from the perspective of a citizen of heaven. As part of God's creation wealth is a gift of God, yet it

interpretation the point is the same: disciples are stewards, not owners, and as such they must be faithful.

In contrast to the expressions in the first halves of vv. 10-12 stand *en pollōi*, *to alēthinon*, and *to hymeteron* in the second halves of the respective verses. The antithetical nature of the parallelism in these verses suggests that these terms are synonyms for that which is the opposite of worldly wealth. In that case the terms all refer to heavenly treasures. Stier is right when he observes that the antitheses of these verses resolve into one great antithesis, that between the earthly and the heavenly, the temporal and the eternal.[291] In v. 11 the antithesis is expressed as that between worldly wealth and *to alēthinon*, "true riches" (*NIV*). These riches have been defined as treasures in heaven,[292] the goods of the messianic kingdom,[293] the kingdom of God itself.[294] In contrast to worldly wealth, true riches are "real," "genuine"; they are neither illusory nor passing.[295] They correspond to *hai aiōnioi skēnai* of v. 9.[296] In v. 10 true riches are described as *pollōi*, "much." If in the first half of that verse worldly wealth is characterized as insignificant, this half depicts true riches, treasures in heaven, as among God's greatest blessings. In v. 12 they are called *hymeteron*,[297] "that which is your own" (*NASB, RSV*), "your own property" (*NIV*). This word portrays treasures

---

still belongs to this present evil age. It is *adikos*, according to v. 11 (cf. v. 9, *ho mamōnas tēs adikias*). Although according to v. 11 its use is in some sense a means to true riches, wealth itself is not to be confused with true riches. This approach, in which the eschatological note is prominent, is represented by Jülicher, *Gleichnisreden* 2.509; Kögel, "Gleichnis," 595; Manson, *Sayings*, 294; Seccombe, *Possessions*, 171 (he denies the stewardship motif here); and perhaps also Creed, *Luke*, 205, and Smith, *Parables*, 112.

Given the parallelism in vv. 11-12 and the eschatological nuance in the formally different but semantically equivalent expression *ho mamōnas tēs adikias* in v. 9, the weight of probability favors the latter approach. Perhaps the two approaches are somehow complementary, or at least not mutually exclusive. BAGD seems to imply as much by using both senses side by side. Luke 16:12 is cited under the substantive *allotrios* ("other people's property" [1.b.α.]), and the meaning in our verse is then explained as "the wealth of this world is foreign to the Christian."

[291] Stier, *Words* 4.197. Because of the eschatological nuance in the semantically equivalent epithet in v. 9 (*ho mamōnas tēs adikias*), the fundamental antithesis of vv. 10-12 might also be expressed as the contrast between this age and the next.

[292] Arndt, *Luke*, 359; Manson, *Sayings*, 294; Plummer, *Luke*, 386; Wiesen, *Gleichnis*, 83.

[293] Weiss, *Lukas*, 535. Meyer describes these riches as the salvation of the kingdom of Messiah (*Commentary*, 228).

[294] Ellis, *Luke*, 198.

[295] Seccombe, *Possessions*, 171.

[296] Feuillet, "Intendants," 40. Krämer also calls attention to this correspondence with v. 9 (*Rätsel*, 217-18).

[297] "The reading *hēmeteron* (B L *al*) has the appearance of being a later theological refinement (='belonging to the Father and the Son'), expressing the divine origin of the true riches (ver. 11)—as is also expressed by the Marcionite reading *emon*. It may be, however,

in heaven as the disciples' inalienable possession.[298] What is striking is that in these verses, as in v. 9, one's use (or misuse) of worldly wealth has a bearing on the inheritance.

On the basis of the specific application in v. 11 and the parallelism of vv. 10-12, my conclusion is that vv. 10-12 stand in close relationship with the parable, especially v. 9. As has already been noted, this relationship is more than simply a verbal one. A conceptual correspondence is discernible, for example, between the two series of parallels in vv. 10-12 and the two halves of v. 9. What is more, one can even describe the former verses as the counterpart of the latter on the basis of the emphasis in vv. 11-12 on the negative aspect of the principle enunciated in v. 10, i.e., unfaithfulness. If the point of v. 9 is that the charitable use of worldly wealth (faithfulness) has some positive bearing on one's eternal destiny, the point of vv. 10-12 is that unfaithfulness (lack of charity) has a negative bearing. To express it another way, if v. 9 is a positive exhortation to charity, vv. 10-12 are a warning about the consequences of a lack of charity. In vv. 10-12 Jesus tells his disciples that if they are not faithful with worldly riches, they will not be entrusted with true riches. As will be argued in the next chapter, the parable of the rich man and Lazarus in Luke 16:19-31 graphically illustrates this truth.

Luke 16:13 is the well-known statement about serving two masters. Because of both the verbatim parallel between this verse and Matt 6:24[299] and the generality of all but its final sentence, v. 13 is often distanced from vv. 1-12, if not separated altogether.[300] As with vv. 10-12, I am leaving aside the question of the originality of this verse and am interpreting it in its present context. Whether or not v. 13 is original to

---

that, owing to the constant scribal confusion between *y* and *ē* (in later Greek the two vowels came to be pronounced alike), copyists who wrote *hēmeteron* intended *hymeteron*—for in the context the correct antithesis to 'another's' is 'yours'" (B. M. Metzger, *A Textual Commentary on the Greek New Testament*).

[298] Marshall, *Luke*, 624.

[299] The only difference between the two versions of the saying is that Luke's has an added *oiketēs*, "house slave," "domestic" (BAGD). Whether this word is authentic or editorial, it has the effect of connecting the principle of v. 13 to the parable, the main character of which is an *oikonomos*. The word also fits the stewardship motif of vv. 10-12.

[300] Fitzmyer says v. 13 has nothing to do with the parable ("Manager," 38); Jeremias calls it an isolated logion (*Parables*, 47); Jülicher (*Gleichnisreden* 2.513) and Schmid (*Lukas*, 261) see no connection here with the steward; Schlatter discusses v. 13 separately from vv. 1-12 (the former verse in *Lukas*, 547-48); and Wansey describes it as an "otherwise irrelevant apophthegm" ("Steward," 40). It should be pointed out, however, that some interpreters argue for the originality of v. 13 here. Among those who do so are Derrett, "Dives," 367; Martin-Achard, "Notes," 139-40; Meyer, *Commentary*, 213; Olshausen, *Commentary* 2.72; and Plummer, *Luke*, 387. For a full discussion of the various approaches to the originality of v. 13, see Krämer, *Rätsel*, 226-33.

the parable and/or to vv. 10-12, Luke or the tradition he uses apparently did not view it as out of place here. As already indicated in the previous subsection, a logical connection can be established between v. 13 and the preceding verses.

In v. 13 we have what Easton calls the "final generalization"[301]—one cannot serve two masters. This common-sense principle is explained on the basis of mutual exclusiveness, and is then applied to serving God and *mamōnas*. The repetition of *mamōnas* at the end of v. 13 immediately connects the verse, at least verbally, with vv. 10-12 and with the parable (cf. v. 9). In v. 13 wealth is personified and depicted as a rival to wholehearted service of God. It is on the basis of the principle that one cannot serve two masters that the disciples are challenged in the parable to use their wealth for others. V. 13 also indicates why the use of wealth is tied to one's eternal future: "One's use of wealth points to whom one serves."[302] The way one handles possessions expresses concretely the quality of one's response to God.[303] On the one hand, to use them for the benefit of others is an expression of wholehearted love and service of God. One does so because his affection is reserved for God.[304] In short, charity is motivated by love for God. On the other hand, however, to fail to serve God in this way strongly suggests one does not really love God at all. To be unfaithful with wealth is to be enslaved to it, and one cannot at the same time serve God. V. 13 is, therefore, a call for the right use of wealth in the service of God.[305] It is also a warning against the love of money.[306] "No vice is more exacting," writes Plummer, "than avarice."[307] As will be argued in the next chapter, it is this fact of human existence, illustrated in the actions and attitudes of the Pharisees, that prompts our parable to the disciples in the first place. If so, v. 13 fits very well in its present Lucan context, even if it was not original.

Luke 16:10-13, in summary, enforces the teaching of vv. 1-9 by warning of the consequences of neglecting to help those in need. Such neglect is unfaithfulness, it is bad stewardship, it is evidence that one's ultimate loyalties are misplaced. A person who is unfaithful with material possessions in this way cannot expect to be received *eis tas aiōnious skēnas*.

---

[301] Easton, *Luke*, 245.
[302] Talbert, *Reading Luke*, 155.
[303] Johnson, *Function*, 158.
[304] Menoud, "Riches," 14.
[305] Pilgrim, *Good News*, 129.
[306] Plummer, *Luke*, 387, and Seccombe, *Possessions*, 172.
[307] *Luke*, 387.

III. Conclusions

In Part I of this chapter attention was focused on Luke 16:1-7, verses which are universally accepted as belonging to the parable of the unjust steward. The purpose of that discussion was to set the stage for Part II by reviewing the main features of the story itself as narrated in those verses. In the process of that review several interpretive differences were highlighted, most of which arise from the socioeconomic details of the story. In vv. 1-7 Jesus narrates the story of a steward who, faced with dismissal by his master, provides for his future by ingratiating himself with his master's debtors. He does so by authorizing them to reduce the size of their debts. The ethics of the steward's actions, as well as the surprising praise of which we read in v. 8, are hotly debated issues which have significant implications for the interpretation of the parable. These and similar issues were my concern in Part II.

In Part II I argued that the parable of the unjust steward (the original limits of which extend at least as far as v. 9) is addressed by Jesus to his disciples. The story itself concludes on the surprising and attention-getting note in v. 8a that when the master learned of his steward's actions (as presumably he did) he praised or commended him for having acted so wisely. Although Jesus indicates that the actions themselves were not praiseworthy, he nevertheless echoes the master's praise and focuses attention on the wisdom or foresight of the steward's actions. It is for the purpose of inculcating this quality in his disciples that Jesus tells the parable. This point is made more explicit in v. 8b, where, to judge from the negative tone, Jesus both indicts and exhorts his disciples. In the matter of wise provision for the future, worldly people like the steward often outdo disciples in their respective affairs and interests. The disciples can, therefore, learn a lesson even from a dishonest steward. In the affairs and interests of the kingdom they are to show a wisdom analogous to that shown by the worldly steward. In v. 9 Jesus applies the lesson of the parable to the use of material possessions. True wisdom, he says in effect, is to use worldly wealth for the benefit of others in need. Such actions give evidence of genuine faith, and have a bearing on one's eternal destiny. An eschatological note reverberates throughout the entire parable and extends into vv. 10-13 as well.

The teaching of the parable in vv. 1-9 is reinforced in vv. 10-13. Whether or not these verses were an original part of the parable, I contend they at least fit well here. There is, consequently, no reason or grounds for postulating a different context for them. The emphasis in vv.

10-13 is on the consequences of faithful or unfaithful stewardship of worldly wealth; neither asceticism nor total renunciation is in view. The negative emphasis in particular in vv. 10-12 suggests these verses are meant to serve as the counterpart of the positive exhortation in v. 9. Here Jesus devaluates, or better, revaluates worldly wealth, and in the process makes it clear that unfaithfulness disqualifies a person from greater responsibilities and blessings. V. 13 crowns the argument by indicating that how one uses worldly wealth is crucial because it reveals ultimate loyalties.

This chapter has been limited as much as possible to Luke 16:1-13 itself. Other relevant verses, passages, themes, and theology were introduced only when absolutely necessary. While such an admittedly artificial procedure cannot alone do justice to the parable, it can demonstrate, as I think it has in this chapter, that even temporarily isolated from its broader Lucan context the parable of the unjust steward treats the faithful, prudent use of material possessions. At a number of points, however, this procedure inevitably resulted in less than full treatment of the teaching of the parable. It also left a remnant of questions which warrant more detailed discussion if we are to understand the parable properly. The most important of these questions are the literary context of Luke 16:1-13, the relationship of the teaching in the parable to Jesus' teaching on riches elsewhere in Luke-Acts, and the eschatological background of the parable. The first of these questions will be dealt with in the next chapter, the second and third in chapter four. In this way the teaching of the parable of the unjust steward will be set in its proper Lucan context.

CHAPTER THREE

THE LITERARY CONTEXT

Having treated the history of interpretation of the parable of the unjust steward (chapter one) and the exegesis of Luke 16:1-13 itself (chapter two), in the present chapter the discussion of the parable will be broadened by examining its literary context. In particular, two levels of literary context for the parable will be considered, the immediate literary context of Luke 15:1-32 and 16:14-31 and the broader literary context of the so-called travel narrative or central section of the Third Gospel (9:51-?).[1] The goal of this chapter is to show how these contextual levels affect the interpretation of our parable and enhance our understanding of it.

I. IMMEDIATE LITERARY CONTEXT

A. Luke 15:1-32

1. Discussion of Luke 15

Perhaps the most natural place to begin a consideration of the literary context of the parable of the unjust steward is with Luke 15. This procedure seems justified, even dictated, by Luke's introduction to the parable in 16:1. As was argued in chapter two in connection with the audience of the parable, the opening words of Luke 16 (particularly *Elegen de kai*, 16:1) suggest that at the very least the parable is to be understood as having been spoken on the same occasion as the three well-known parables of chapter 15. There is a change of audience in 16:1 (*pros tous mathētas*; cf. 15:1-3), to be sure, but the Lucan setting remains the same. This continuity between Luke 15 and 16:1-13 implies not only that our parable is spoken at the same time and under the same circumstances as chapter 15, but also that a deeper relationship exists between the two chapters. In the following paragraphs it will be argued that that

---

[1] Both the name and exact limits of this large section of Luke's Gospel are disputed matters about which I will say more in my treatment of the broader literary context of the parable.

relationship is thematic or conceptual in nature. If so, our parable is to be seen as in some sense a sequel to chapter 15. To establish this connection it is necessary to examine briefly the setting and content of chapter 15 itself.

The setting of Luke 15 is one of controversy between Jesus and the religious leaders of Israel.[2] The note of controversy is sounded in vv. 1-3. Luke tells his readers that on one occasion the Pharisees and scribes were grumbling and complaining (*diegongyzon*, v. 2)[3] because Jesus was receiving and eating with the tax collectors and sinners who had gathered to listen to him (vv. 1-2). Jesus' response to their criticism (*eipen de pros autous*, v. 3) takes the form of three parables, the lost sheep (vv. 4-7), the lost coin (vv. 8-10), and the lost son (vv. 11-32). The basic thrust of his response will be outlined in a few moments. At this juncture, however, it is to be emphasized that Luke sets the parable of the unjust steward in the context of this controversy with Israel's religious leaders. Jesus responds to his critics in chapter 15, and then, according to 16:1, turns his attention to his disciples and, as was argued in chapter two, instructs them about the wise use of material possessions (16:1-13). Even in that instruction controversy is not far from the surface, as 16:14-31 indicate. The Pharisees are still in the background as Jesus instructs his disciples in vv. 1-13 (*Ēkouon de tauta panta hoi Pharisaioi*, v. 14), and their sneers (*exemyktērizon auton*, v. 14) perpetuate the controversy and lead to further rebuke from Jesus (vv. 15-31). Although our parable is addressed to the disciples, it must be viewed against this larger context of controversy. When it is, the question then arises how the instruction to the disciples in chapter 16 is related to the controversy with the Pharisees and scribes in chapter 15. That question moves us from the setting to the teaching of Luke 15.

The three parables of the lost sheep, coin, and son are well-known and much loved by Christians the world over. It is not my intention to discuss them in any detail here since to do so would take me beyond the scope of the present chapter and is, in fact, unnecessary. Two basic points about the teaching of Luke 15 should be sufficient to establish the existence of a thematic or logical connection between our parable and Luke 15. Those points are, first, the three parables in Luke 15 are Jesus' vindication of

---

[2] As will be seen, this note of controversy is very prominent and important throughout the larger section of Luke's Gospel to which both chapters 15 and 16 belong.

[3] BAGD amplifies the meaning of the verb *diagongyzō* by the addition of the adverb "aloud" in parenthesis; Zerwick and Grosvenor (*Analysis*) explain the actions in question as directed "to one another" (*dia-*).

his own attitude and actions towards sinners, and, second, the three parables are at the same time an indictment of the Pharisees and scribes. Let me develop each of these points briefly and then relate them to our parable.

Jesus' purpose in the parables of the lost sheep, coin, and son is to vindicate his own attitude to the poor and needy.[4] At the risk of oversimplification, the substance of Jesus' parabolic response to his critics is that the people whom he receives are the very kind whom God himself earnestly seeks and, on the condition of repentance, joyfully accepts. This point is made rather clearly in v. 7. "I tell you,"[5] Jesus says in concluding the parable of the lost sheep, "that in the same way [as in the parable] there is more rejoicing in heaven over one sinner who repents [*epi heni harmartōlōi metanoounti*] than over ninety-nine righteous persons [*epi . . . dikaiois*] who do not need to repent." The same point is repeated in the conclusion of the parable of the lost coin (v. 10) and then depicted in the father's joyful response to the return of his prodigal son (vv. 20-24).[6] Spoken by one who himself was receiving tax collectors and sinners, these three parables say, in effect, that Jesus' own actions and attitudes toward such people mirror, even express, the actions and attitudes of God himself. Jesus' defense is, in the words of Pilgrim, "simply this: he acts as God would act. His acceptance of outcasts and sinners reflects God's acceptance and forgiveness."[7] In this light the grumbling criticism of the Pharisees and scribes against Jesus becomes a self-indictment of their own attitudes. Jesus reverses their expectations and standards of righteousness.[8] They were apparently convinced that heaven was reserved only for people like themselves; Jesus shows them in the three parables of Luke 15 that it is open to repentant sinners. In the final analysis, then, they are the ones who stand condemned, not Jesus.

The underlying note of condemnation in Jesus' teaching is the second matter to which attention should be called in Luke 15. In the process of vindicating himself Jesus at the same time condemns the faults of his critics. In Luke 15 particular attention seems focused on their self-

---

[4] Marshall, *Luke*, 614.

[5] *legō hymin*; cf. 16:9, *kai egō hymin legō*.

[6] Cf. *euphranthōmen*, v. 23, and *euphrainesthai*, v. 24, with *chara* in vv. 7, 10. Cf. also *hēmarton*, vv. 18, 21. God's joyful reception of repentant sinners is the common theme of all three parables.

[7] Pilgrim, *Good News*, 81.

[8] The reversal motif, implicit in the three parables of Luke 15, is explicit in 16:15, 19-31, verses to be discussed in due course. The motif is prominent in Luke's Gospel.

righteous pride that fostered their contempt for the people whom Jesus welcomed and gave rise to their criticism of him. One can almost hear their contempt for others in the words of their complaint in v. 2: "*Houtos hamartōlous prosdechetai kai synesthiei autois.*" The pride of Jesus' critics also comes out in v. 7, a verse quoted in the previous paragraph. What is significant in this verse for the present discussion is Jesus' reference to "ninety-nine righteous persons who do not need to repent [*dikaiois hoitines ou chreian echousin metanoias*]." These words are not to be taken as a concession that some people are righteous enough as to have no need of repentance.[9] Rather, the words are probably better understood as Jesus' ironic criticism of the Pharisees and scribes for regarding themselves as righteous when in fact they were not righteous at all.[10] The pride of Jesus' critics surfaces more explicitly in the person of the elder son in the parable of the lost son (vv. 25-32). The elder son's complaints against his father for being too generous to his wayward brother echo those of the Pharisees and scribes against Jesus for receiving sinners.[11] Jesus thus turns the tables on his critics and uses their own criticisms against them. He shows them that their own attitudes toward others are as deplorable and indefensible as those of the elder son toward his brother.

With these two observations about Luke 15 in mind (i.e., that Jesus here vindicates himself and condemns his critics), it can now be suggested how chapters 15 and 16 are related. It is my contention that Jesus' polemic against the faults of the Pharisees and scribes in Luke 15 is continued in 16:1-13 and that herein lies the basic connection between the two chapters. To be more specific, Luke 15 combats the pride of the Pharisees and scribes, while chapter 16, including our parable, confronts their avarice or greed.[12] This suggestion has been made by several

---

[9] The word *dikaioi* here recalls Luke 5:32 and also anticipates 16:15 ("*Hymeis este hoi dikaiountes heautous*") and 18:14 ("*katebē houtos [the tax collector] dedikaiōmenos...par' ekeinon [the Pharisee]*"). In each of those verses the self-righteousness of the Pharisees and scribes is condemned. The same sense seems intended in Jesus' use of the word here in Luke 15.

[10] Recall the mention of this interpretation of Luke 15:7, as well as other possibilities, in the discussion of irony in chapter two.

[11] "The likeness [of the elder son's reaction in vv. 28-30] to the Pharisees is unmistakable. We can easily imagine the elder brother saying of his father, 'This man receives sinners and eats with them' (15:2)" (Morris, *Luke*, 243).

[12] I am aware that the generalized negative portrait of the Pharisees presented here and throughout this study seems incompatible with available extra-biblical literature and may in fact be somewhat one-sided. While it is not my purpose to enter the extensive contemporary discussion of first-century Pharisees, the following qualifications of the negative portrait are to be understood throughout my discussion. First, the characterization does not apply to every Pharisee (cf. Luke 23:51 [if Joseph of Arimathea is a Pharisee] and Acts 15:5). Second,

interpreters. Godet, for example, argues that Luke 16:1-13 continues "the contrast [begun in chapter 15] between the life of faith and pharisaic righteousness." The two chapters together treat "the two chief sins" of the Pharisees, pride and avarice. According to Godet, the former sin is the subject of Luke 15, the latter is the subject of 16:1-13.[13] Plummer makes much the same point. He suggests all five parables in Luke 15 and 16 (the three in chapter 15, ours in 16:1-13, and the rich man and Lazarus in 16:19-31) are to be understood as directed against "special faults" of the Pharisees. The three parables of Luke 15 combat their "hard exclusiveness, self-righteousness, and contempt for others," the two in Luke 16 their "self-indulgence."[14] This explanation of the connection between Luke 15 and 16:1-13 eases the otherwise "painfully sharp" transition from the one chapter to the other,[15] and it accounts well for the introduc-

Jesus' condemnation of the Pharisees' hypocrisy (cf. 12:1) is not tantamount to condemnation of their motives. What is at issue (at least in Luke's Gospel) is a discrepancy between their teaching and their actions. Third, given the polemical purpose of Jesus and the Evangelists, a "balanced" or "objective" historical reconstruction of the Pharisees is not to be expected in or demanded of the biblical texts. For a helpful discussion of the apparent contradiction between the biblical and extra-biblical portraits of Pharisaism, see M. Silva, "The Place of Historical Reconstruction in New Testament Criticism," in *Hermeneutics, Authority, and Canon* (ed. D. A. Carson and J. D. Woodbridge; Grand Rapids: Zondervan, 1986) 109-21, from which the above qualifications are drawn (pp. 115-16).

[13] Godet, *Luke* 2.160.

[14] Plummer, *Luke*, 380. Plummer's interpretation that Luke 16:1-13 continues the anti-pharisaic theme of chapter 15 is endorsed by Easton. Easton concludes Plummer's suggestion is probably "the best explanation [of the connection between chaps. 15 and 16], even though vv. 1-8 are not designedly anti-Pharisaic" (*Luke*, 241). While Easton may be technically correct on this last point insofar as our parable is not spoken directly to the Pharisees, they are still very much present and probably in Jesus' mind as he speaks to his disciples (cf. 16:14 and my observation in the previous chapter about the force of *kai* in 16:1). In a real sense, then, the parable of the unjust steward is a "two-edged sword" (Hooley and Mason, "Parable," 51), exhorting the disciples and, at the same time, warning the Pharisees.

    Mention should also be made at this point of other interpreters who recognize a connection between Luke 15 and 16 similar to the one under discussion, even if the connection is qualified or rejected. Loisy, for example, explains that, at least for the people responsible for the combination of the parables in Luke 15 and 16, the last three parables in particular (the lost son, the unjust steward, and the rich man and Lazarus) are a sort of trilogy against the Pharisees. Chapter 15 is an apology for Jesus' own actions while chapter 16 is a direct attack against his critics (*Evangiles* 2.156). Loisy himself believes this link is artificial, but he at least concedes that these parables have an anti-pharisaic function in the text as it now stands. Jülicher also notes there is a certain "inner connection" between Luke 15 and 16. Among other things, the former chapter is defensive while the latter is offensive (*Gleichnisreden* 2.495-96). When it comes to interpreting our parable, however, Jülicher regards this connection as insignificant ("eine starke Harmlosigkeit," p. 496). Lunt describes Luke 16:1-13 as "the penultimate member in a series of parables mainly critical of the Pharisees." He dismisses Plummer's suggested connection as "ingenious but not very convincing," but adds that a negative judgment (i.e., that there is no connection at all between the chapters) would do less than justice to Luke's usual literary skill. His own suggestion is that "the thread that runs through the whole series is Luke's compassionate concern with those who in the world's eyes are less than respectable" ("Expounding," 132).

[15] The description of the transition is Easton's (*Luke*, 241).

tion of the theme of money and possessions in our parable. That our parable is spoken against the background of the Pharisees' greed also seems confirmed, as will be seen, by Luke's comment in 16:14 that the Pharisees are "lovers of money [*philargyroi*]" and by the parable of the rich man and Lazarus in vv. 19-31.[16]

2. Impact of Luke 15 on Interpretation of 16:1-13

The above arguments about the connection of Luke 15 and 16 indicate that the immediate literary context of Luke 15 casts valuable light on the interpretation of the parable of the unjust steward. The polemic nature of Jesus' apologetic in chapter 15 sharpens his teaching to the disciples in 16:1-13 and gives it a note of urgency. His teaching about the beneficent use of possessions in 16:1-13 does not arise in a vacuum, but is motivated by a real threat to the disciples' wholehearted service of God. It is a threat exemplified in the Pharisees. They cannot serve God and mammon, Jesus warns his disciples in v. 13. Serving mammon or greed (the former is a rather good explanation of the fundamental nature of the latter) and serving God are mutually exclusive loyalties and pursuits. It may be that the temptation to try to reconcile the two loyalties was felt with special keenness by those disciples who were or had been tax collectors. In any event, in the context of the anti-pharisaic polemic of Luke 15, our parable provides the antidote to the threat of greed posed by the example and influence of the Pharisees. The antidote is to use one's possessions for the benefit of others. The consequences of failing to do so, of being greedy, are brought out by Luke in 16:14-31, the next component in the immediate literary context of our parable.

B. Luke 16:14-31

1. Discussion of Luke 16:14-31

The verses which follow our parable in Luke 16 fall rather neatly into two

---

[16] Several other explanations of the connection between Luke 15 and 16 merit mention. With various nuances, Bretscher ("Steward," 760), Coutts ("Steward," 56), Goebel ("Gleichnisgruppe," 675), Goulder ("Structure," 199), and Stier (*Words* 4.467) all argue the common theme of chapter 15 and at least 16:1-13 is repentance. Jensen ("Haushalter," 709) and Topel ("Steward," 221-23) explain that the link between the chapters is forgiveness. Still others suggest the connection lies in the misuse or wasting of possessions by both the prodigal son and the unjust steward (e.g., Fitzmyer, "Manager," 25; Grundmann, "Fragen der Komposition des lukanischen 'Reiseberichts'," *ZNW* 50-51 [1959-60] 267; Koetsveld,

parts, vv. 14-18 and vv. 19-31. The former verses treat "The Law and the
Kingdom of God,"[17] the latter are the well-known parable of the rich man
and Lazarus. The purpose of this section is to show that both parts are
logically and thematically related to each other and to vv. 1-13. The basic
thesis to be argued is that Luke 16:14-31 continues and amplifies the
polemic against greed which is the background for Jesus' teaching in vv.
1-13. The controversy with the Pharisees in Luke 15 comes to the
foreground again in 16:14-31 and the latter verses are directed to and
against those opponents. At the same time, however, these verses serve
to reinforce Jesus' teaching in vv. 1-13 by warning the disciples of the
consequences of trying to serve God and mammon, of being lovers of
money, of not using their material possessions for the poor. As in earlier
discussions, the issue with which I am concerned here is not so much
whether these verses were originally spoken together and in this context,
but rather what they mean in their present Lucan context.

a) Luke 16:14-18

Luke 16:14-18 are very difficult verses, often noted for their "apparent
unrelatedness" both to the context (especially vv. 1-13) and to each
other.[18] Marshall, for example, observes that the connection between
these five verses and the preceding and following verses is far from
obvious. What is more, the connection between vv. 14-15 ("Reproof of
the Pharisees") and vv. 16-18 ("The Law and the Kingdom of God") is,
in Marshall's opinion, artificial.[19] In a similar vein, Ellis refers to Luke
16:14-18 as "a rag-bag collection of sayings" joined by the theme of
reversal.[20] Whatever one thinks about these particular conclusions, there
is little question that an extra measure of caution and reserve is warranted
in the interpretation of these verses. There is a fragmentary and terse

---

Gleichnisse, 247; Köster, "Haushalter," 726; Menoud, "Riches," 15; and Rengstorf, *Lukas*,
191). While the latter feature is not the most obvious one in the story of the prodigal son and
probably should not be emphasized in the interpretation of that parable, it is still striking that
two of the three uses of the verb *diaskorpizō* by Luke occur in the parables of the lost son
and the unjust steward (15:13 and 16:1, respectively; the other Lucan occurrence is in 1:51
where the verb is used more figuratively of scattering or dispersing people).

[17] This title is from *UBSGNT*.

[18] Seccombe, *Possessions*, 178.

[19] *Luke*, 624-25; the titles of the pericopae are from pp. 624 and 626, respectively.

[20] *Luke*, 202. Ellis makes a major break in his outline of Luke's central section at Luke
16:14, 16:14-18:14 being "Teachings of Messiah: The Coming of the Kingdom" (p. 200).
He admits the teachings of the latter section continue themes in the preceding one and that
there is little indication in the text itself that 16:14-18:14 is even a separate section. Luke
may intend 13:22-18:14 be viewed as one unit, Ellis suggests.

character to them, perhaps because they are the summary of a much longer discourse.[21] Luke 16:14-18 resembles "the peaks of a mountain chain," to use Godet's illustration; the interpreter's job is to reconstruct the bases of the mountains and the valleys between them.[22] To do so, one must, of course, read between the lines, and what follows is an attempt to do so. I will not offer an exhaustive exegetical study of Luke 16:14-18, but will rather summarize the thrust of these verses and suggest how they may relate to each other and to the context.[23] My goal in the always risky business of conjecture is to make a plausible case for a basic conceptual or thematic unity in the present text. In the interests of convenience, Luke 16:14-18 will be discussed in two subsections, vv. 14-15 and vv. 16-18.

(1) Luke 16:14-15

The controversy with the Pharisees, explicit in Luke 15 and underlying the teaching to the disciples in 16:1-13, resurfaces in 16:14. The Pharisees' grumbling in 15:2 now becomes ridicule or scorn,[24] and, as in Luke 15, the rest of this chapter (16:15-31) constitutes Jesus' response to his critics. In a real sense v. 14 is the introduction to the rest of the chapter and is also the pivotal link between vv. 1-13 and vv. 15-31. In v. 14 Luke connects the Pharisees with Jesus' teaching about mammon in vv. 1-13 by noting that they "were listening to all these things" and were "lovers of money" (NASB).[25] Ēkouon de tauta panta suggests the occasion introduced here in v. 14 is the same as that of vv. 1-13,[26] which in turn is the same as in chapter 15. The Pharisees, to whom Jesus speaks directly in the three parables of chapter 15, are in the background as he speaks to the disciples in 16:1-13. The Pharisees were listening to "all

---

[21] This suggestion is made by, among others, Godet, *Luke* 2.171, and Lagrange, *Luc*, 438. Godet seems to attribute the summary to Luke's source(s) and even uses the disjointed character of these verses as "proof of conscientious fidelity" on Luke's part (p. 174). Lagrange, on the other hand, seems to believe that Luke himself is responsible for the summary character of these verses, but adds that Luke probably put them here with some concern for context. The question of who summarized the discourse in vv. 14-18 (if these verses even are a summary) cannot be decided with any certainty and is really a secondary matter at best.

[22] *Luke* 2.174.

[23] R. J. Karris speaks of the relation of 16:14-18 to vv. 1-13 and 19-31 as "a relatively unexplored question" ("Poor and Rich: The Lukan *Sitz im Leben*," in *Perspectives on Luke-Acts* [ed. Talbert] 121-22).

[24] Fitzmyer, *Luke* 2.1113.

[25] J. L. Resseguie, "Instruction and Discussion in the Central Section of Luke: A Redaction Critical Study of Luke 9:51-19:44" (Ph.D. dissertation, Fuller Theological Seminary, 1978) 138.

[26] Plummer, *Luke*, 387.

these things [*tauta panta*]," Luke says, referring to the parable of the unjust steward and perhaps especially to Jesus' teaching in v. 13 about the incompatibility of serving God and mammon.[27] What the Pharisees heard caused them to ridicule and sneer at Jesus (*exemyktērizon auton*). The reason for this reaction, Luke tells his readers, is the Pharisees are "lovers of money [*philargyroi hyparchontes*]."[28] Although several interpreters object that this characterization of the Pharisees does not accurately reflect the historical situation or better fits the Sadducees than the Pharisees,[29] most interpreters are satisfied that it has adequate basis in tradition.[30] This almost passing comment by Luke is very significant for it "throws into relief the main idea" of our parable and of Luke 16 as a whole,[31] i.e., the use of material possessions and money. The adjective *philargyros* ("fond of money, avaricious" [BAGD]) links v. 14 with vv. 1-13 (cf. *mamōnas*, vv. 9, 11, 13, and *agapaō*, v. 13), and thereby confirms that the parable of the unjust steward is related to the topic of possessions. To judge from Luke's explanation of the motivation of the Pharisees' reaction, the Pharisees at least understood the parable and its application as bearing on this topic. The connotation of greed in *philargyros* ("who were covetous," *KJV*) also lends weight to the earlier suggestion that the common denominator in Luke 15 and 16 is the faults of the Pharisees, in particular that their avarice is behind Jesus' teaching to the disciples in 16:1-13. In addition, *philargyros* ties vv. 1-13 to the remaining verses of Luke 16, where, as will be seen, the issue is also the use (or misuse) of material possessions.

Having established a plausible connection between vv. 1-13 and v. 14, it might be helpful to explore that connection more carefully before considering Jesus' response which begins in v. 15. What is there in the teaching in Luke 16:1-13 that so offends the Pharisees and brings forth

---

[27] Fitzmyer, *Luke* 2.1112. On the assumption of the composite nature of Luke 16, Fitzmyer also suggests v. 13 (with its reference to loving and serving mammon) may account for the introduction of the Pharisees in v. 14. Whether or not Fitzmyer's assumption about the nature of Luke 16 is correct, his basic point about the relationship between v. 14 and vv. 1-13 is well taken.

[28] Grundmann explains that Luke grounds the Pharisees' ridicule on their love of money (*Lukas*, 322). Zahn says this description of the Pharisees is Luke's explanation why the parable and its application (vv. 1-13) provoked the Pharisees' ridicule (*Lucas*, 579).

[29] E.g., Easton, *Luke*, 247; Lunt, "Expounding," 133; and Manson, *Sayings*, 295.

[30] E.g., Plummer, *Luke*, 387; Rengstorf, *Lukas*, 195; Summers, *Luke*, 192; and R. C. Tannehill, *The Narrative Unity of Luke-Acts*, vol. 1: *The Gospel according to Luke* (Philadelphia: Fortress, 1986) 181. The latter interpreter notes this charge against the Pharisees has some basis in tradition (cf. Luke 11:39 and 20:47 with Matt 23:25 and Mark 12:40), but has been emphasized by Luke.

[31] F. W. S. O'Neill, "The Unjust Steward," *ExpTim* 16 (1904-5) 240.

their scorn? Can we, in other words, be more specific about the connection Luke might see between vv. 1-13 and the Pharisees' reaction in v. 14? I believe we can, albeit tentatively. At least part of the explanation for the Pharisees' scorn may be that they saw no conflict between piety and possessions, God and mammon, such as Jesus teaches, especially in v. 13.[32] In their minds there was nothing incompatible in serving both God and mammon; they apparently had managed to reconcile the love of God and money.[33] Perhaps one way they managed this reconciliation was by regarding "their wealth as a special blessing for their careful obedience to the Law" and themselves, then, as "an abiding proof of the connexion between riches and righteousness."[34] Such an assumption would account for their ridicule. On the basis of such an assumption the teaching of vv. 1-13 (especially v. 13) would be a *non sequitur*, perhaps made all the more illogical by Jesus' own poverty.[35] "How easy it is for Jesus to preach about riches as he does," we can imagine them thinking, "when he has so little of those riches himself!" On the Pharisees' premise of a direct relationship between riches and righteousness, it may be, moreover, that "they had their own explanation of the reason why a Rabbi who was poor declaimed against riches."[36] In any event, if this conjecture about Luke's understanding of the background of the Pharisees' reaction is correct, it lends credibility to Talbert's suggestion that vv. 14-31 are an attack on the Pharisees' assumptions about wealth.[37] Such an attack would serve as a warning to any of Luke's own readers who may share these or similar assumptions.

Jesus' response to the ridicule of the Pharisees begins in v. 15 (*kai eipen autois*), and, since there is no change of scene or audience until 17:1, continues to the end of chapter 16. The Pharisees' reaction to Jesus' teaching induces him to expose their folly more clearly.[38] In v. 15 Jesus offers "a probing contrast"[39] between outward appearances and reality,

---

[32] Ellis, *Luke*, 203. Other exegetes who explain the Pharisees' ridicule in terms of their reaction to the teaching in v. 13 include Rengstorf, *Lukas*, 195, and Tannehill, *Unity*, 181.

[33] Dods, *Parables*, 381.

[34] Plummer, *Luke*, 387-88. This explanation is offered by many interpreters, among them Derrett, "Dives," 367; Dods, *Parables*, 381; Geldenhuys, *Luke*, 420 n. 1; Lagrange, *Luc*, 439; Loisy, *Evangiles* 2.156; Summers, *Luke*, 192; Talbert, *Reading Luke*, 156; and Volckaert, "Steward," 341.

[35] Godet (*Luke* 2.171), Koetsveld (*Gleichnisse*, 246), and Zahn (*Lucas*, 579-80) all emphasize the poverty of Jesus and his disciples as the cause for the Pharisees' scorn in v. 14.

[36] Plummer, *Luke*, 388.

[37] *Reading Luke*, 156.

[38] Dods, *Parables*, 381.

[39] The phrase is Fitzmyer's (*Luke* 2.1112).

between the opinions and values of men and of God. Jesus accuses the Pharisees of self-righteous pride and hypocrisy—"You are the ones who justify yourselves [*Hymeis este hoi dikaiountes heautous*] in the eyes of men." "Jesus' words imply," writes Fitzmyer, "that the Pharisaic attitude toward money is rooted in something deeper, in a quest for an image of uprightness before others."[40] We are not told here how the Pharisees maintained this image, but in the present context it is likely that their attitude toward money played a part in and is the background for Jesus' charge. Perhaps Jesus has in mind their equation of riches and righteousness which allowed them to parade as just men blessed by God with riches.[41] Or it may be, as some have suggested, that Jesus here alludes to his critics' penchant for ostentation in almsgiving attested in other synoptic tradition.[42] In any event, Jesus characterizes (and implicitly criticizes) the Pharisees as those who value their righteous image in the eyes of other people and who strive to maintain that image.

Jesus goes on to make it clear, however, that God is not fooled by appearances; "but God knows your hearts," he says to them (v. 15). Here the hypocrisy of the Pharisees' actions and attitudes, perhaps especially with regard to money, comes more into the open. The implication of Jesus' statement, which echoes a familiar OT idea (cf. 1 Sam 16:7; 1 Kgs 8:39; 1 Chr 28:9; Prov 24:12), is that the Pharisees' piety is "but empty show."[43] The Pharisees are hypocrites because their outward piety, however projected and maintained, conceals their proud and greedy hearts.[44] Prosperity, then, is "an ambiguous sign—only a knowledge of the heart can tell for sure whether or not one is righteous."[45] On the latter basis the Pharisees are not righteous at all and, furthermore, stand under the judgment of God. Inner attitudes are what count with God, not mere appearances, certainly not riches, not even formal acts of righteousness like almsgiving.[46] If the Pharisees were aware of this essential require-

---

[40] *Luke* 2.1113.

[41] Volckaert, "Steward," 341. Karris suggests Luke 16:1-31 as a whole may be Luke's argument against rich Christians whose cultural conditioning against concern for the poor was being reinforced by an appeal to wealth as a sign of God's favor ("Poor," 122-23).

[42] Creed, *Luke*, 206, and L. Sabourin, *L'Evangile de Luc* (Rome: Editrice Pontificia Universita Gregoriana, 1985) 283. Cf. Matt 6:1-4.

[43] Fitzmyer, *Luke* 2.1113.

[44] Marshall, *Luke*, 613.

[45] Talbert, *Reading Luke*, 156.

[46] Easton objects to the description of the Pharisees in v. 14 as "lovers of money" on the grounds that the Pharisees emphasized the importance of alms (*Luke*, 247). This objection misses the point, however, of Jesus' statement in v. 15. If almsgiving is one element of the background here, the point is not whether the Pharisees give alms, but rather how and why they do so. God knows their motives, and the implication of v. 15 is that their motives are not acceptable. This conclusion is confirmed by Luke 11:39, 41-42, where Jesus indicts the

ment of religious life, they apparently were not living up to it. Perhaps some Christians or would-be Christians in Luke's own day were guilty of the same thing.

In the last clause of v. 15 Jesus reveals the danger in striving to justify oneself before other men. He also gives the basis for the divine judgment implicit in his previous statement. The Pharisees stand condemned "for [*hoti*] that which is highly esteemed among men is detestable in the sight of God" (*NASB*). Here is the reversal motif we saw in Luke 15 (God receives sinners, not the "righteous") and that recurs in 16:19-31, especially vv. 19-26. In the present context, "that which is highly esteemed among men [*to en anthrōpois hypsēlon*]" may have specific reference or application to mammon or the love of it.[47] In God's eyes this human value is "detestable," it is an "abomination [*bdelygma*]." This word recalls OT language, particularly with regard to idol worship (e.g., 1 Kgs 11:5, 7).[48] The point of Jesus' use of the word here may be "that love of money is exalted by men but in the mind of God it is idol worship."[49] To express it another way, "coveting mammon is the real abomination in God's sight."[50] Serving mammon (loving money) and serving God are, therefore, mutually exclusive indeed, as Jesus teaches in v. 13. People who, like the Pharisees, think otherwise, who pursue and are satisfied with the esteem of other men, only deceive themselves and stand under the judgment of God.

(2) Luke 16:16-18

Luke 16:16-18 are "notoriously difficult" verses.[51] The transition between vv. 14-15 and vv. 16-18 is abrupt, and on the surface the latter verses seem to bear little relationship to the former. V. 16 speaks of the law and the prophets, John the Baptist, and the kingdom of God; v. 17 affirms the permanency of the law; v. 18 introduces the topic of divorce. These verses seem to break the train of thought between vv. 14-15 and

---

Pharisees for greed (v. 39) and for neglecting justice (v. 42) and exhorts them to give to the poor (v. 41).

[47] Fitzmyer, *Luke* 2.1113; Sabourin, *Luc*, 284; and Summers, *Luke*, 192.

[48] In 1 Kgs 11:5, 7, the foreign gods Milcom/Molech and Chemosh are called "detestable" idols (*NASB*). It is worthy of note that the words *hypsēlon* and *bdelygma* in Luke 16:15 also occur together in the LXX of 1 Kgs 11:7, the former word being translated "a high place" (*NASB, NIV*).

[49] Summers, *Luke*, 192.

[50] Fitzmyer, *Luke* 2.1113.

[51] Easton, *Luke*, 247.

vv. 19-31,[52] and this fact has led not a few interpreters to conclude that little or no connection exists between vv. 16-18 and their present context. Fitzmyer, for example, says vv. 16-18 have "almost nothing" to do with "the topics of Jesus' comments in vv. 1-15."[53] Schmid expresses much the same opinion when he argues there is no logical connection either between vv. 16-18 and the preceding and subsequent verses or among the three verses themselves.[54] Even Marshall concludes the connection between vv. 14-15 and vv. 16-18 is artificial, the latter verses having been inserted into an "alien context."[55]

In the present section I will take exception to the prevailing opinion that Luke 16:16-18 is unrelated to the present context. The considerable difficulties notwithstanding, a plausible logical connection can be established among these three verses themselves and between them and the context. I would agree with Plummer that the discourse in vv. 16-18 is so condensed that the connecting links have been lost,[56] but I would also contend that with a little cautious reading between the lines plausible links can be reconstructed. Luke puts or leaves these verses in their present context for a reason. They are not extraneous to the context, but are an important element in the overall argument against the Pharisees in the preceding and following verses of Luke 16. Let me develop this thesis.

The underlying connection of Luke 16:14-15 and 16-18 is Jesus' polemic against the self-righteousness of the Pharisees, a theme also

---

[52]That there is a unifying train of thought between vv. 14-15 and vv. 19-31, at least on the redactional level, is recognized by many interpreters, among them Fitzmyer, *Luke* 2.1112; Rengstorf, *Lukas*, 195; and Schmid, *Lukas*, 262. That train of thought will be developed under the discussion of vv. 19-31.

[53]*Luke* 2.1114. Strictly speaking, Fitzmyer's statement refers to vv. 16-17. Given what he later says about v. 18 (it "seems to move to an entirely topic—even less related to the general theme of chap. 16" than vv. 16-17 [2.1119]), his statement about vv. 16-17 applies to v. 18 as well.

[54]*Lukas*, 262.

[55]Marshall, *Luke*, 625. If by this statement Marshall means that vv. 16-18 were not originally spoken together in this context, I would agree; such was not necessarily the case. If, however, he also means to suggest there is little or no connection, even of a logical nature, between these verses and the context, I must disagree. The latter does seem to be what he is suggesting for, in his discussion of vv. 16-18 (pp. 626-31), he makes little effort to connect those verses with the context. Such a conclusion seems to do less than justice to Luke's literary abilities, and is somewhat surprising in view of Marshall's usually strong defense of those abilities. That Marshall does come to such a conclusion about vv. 16-18 should alert us to the great difficulty of these verses. Other interpreters who, with various qualifications, see little or no connection between vv. 16-18 and their present context include Creed, *Luke*, 206; Koetsveld, *Gleichnisse*, 246 (his explanation of the present location of the three verses is that Luke perhaps had nowhere else to put them and happened to have room for them at this point on his parchment); Loisy, *Evangiles* 2.166; and Schulz, *Parabel*, 120.

[56]Plummer, *Luke*, 388.

behind his teaching in chapter 15. The Pharisees prided themselves on their righteousness, perhaps pointing, among other things, to their wealth as proof of God's blessing for careful obedience to the law. Jesus exposes the error of their reliance on and satisfaction with an outward image of piety in v. 15 ("God knows your hearts"; prosperity is an ambiguous sign). Vv. 16-18 then continue, even advance, the argument by providing a fundamental rejection of the religious claims of the Pharisees.[57] The Pharisees' self-righteousness is bankrupt not only because God knows the real condition of their hearts (that they are greedy hypocrites), but also because a change has taken place in redemptive history. "The Law and the Prophets were proclaimed[58] until John [*mechri Iōannou*]," v. 16 reads; "since then [*apo tote*] the gospel of the kingdom of God is preached, and every one is forcing his way into it" (*NASB*). Although H. Conzelmann surely "builds far too confidently and far too much" on this "particularly difficult verse,"[59] "there is an undoubted emphasis [here] on the new state of affairs brought about by Jesus' coming."[60] With Jesus' coming and the preaching of the kingdom of God a new epoch of redemptive history has begun. The old period of God's revelation (the law and the prophets) has ended; a new period of revelation has begun. The line of demarcation between the two periods is John the Baptist.[61] His preaching marks the end of the old period,

---

[57] This explanation of vv. 16-18 is suggested by Rengstorf, *Lukas*, 195.

[58] There is no verb in v. 16a; the *NASB* supplies "were proclaimed," Plummer suggests we are to understand *ēsan*: "they existed and had authority until John" (*Luke*, 389).

[59] Morris, *Luke*, 31. H. Conzelmann (*The Theology of Saint Luke* [New York: Harper, 1960]) refers to Luke 16:16 as "the clue" for distinguishing the epochs of salvation (p. 21), "the key to the topography of redemptive history" (p. 23). There is, of course, a measure of truth in this assessment. Difficulty arises, however, when Conzelmann absolutizes the distinction here between John and Jesus and uses it as part of his argument that Luke's geography is purely symbolical (e.g., pp. 20-23). The distinction in 16:16 is also cited by Conzelmann as evidence of Luke's transformation of the original eschatological scheme of two ages into a three stage structure (p. 17 n. 2). The resulting history of redemption consists of the period of Israel (indicated in Luke 16:16), the period of Jesus' ministry ("the middle of time"), and the period of the church (pp. 16, 26). Of Conzelmann's use of Luke 16:16 P. S. Minear writes, "It must be said that rarely has a scholar placed so much weight on so dubious an interpretation of so difficult a logion" ("Luke's Use of the Birth Stories," in *Studies in Luke-Acts* [ed. L. E. Keck and J. L. Martyn; Nashville: Abingdon, 1966] 122).

[60] Morris, *Luke*, 250.

[61] Rengstorf (*Lukas*, 195), H. Ridderbos (*The Coming of the Kingdom* [Philadelphia: Presbyterian and Reformed, 1962] 54), and Schmid (*Lukas*, 263) all refer to John as the "redemptive-historical boundary"; Grundmann (*Lukas*, 323) speaks of him as the eschatological boundary between the times. While several important interpreters argue that John is depicted here as belonging to the new era of redemptive history, to the kingdom of God (e.g., W. G. Kümmel, "'Das Gesetz und die Propheten gehen bis Johannes'—Lukas 16, 16 im Zusammenhang der heilsgeschichtlichen Theologie der Lukasschriften," in *Heilsgeschehen und Geschichte* [2 vols.; ed. E. Grässer and O. Merk; Marburg: Elwert, 1978] 2.84; Fitzmyer, *Luke* 2.1115-17; and Marshall, *Luke: Historian and Theologian* [Grand Rapids: Zondervan, 1970] 146),

Jesus' preaching inaugurates the new. The kingdom of God, the subject of expectation in the OT and in the preaching of John, is now present in the person and ministry of Jesus.[62] Because of this fundamental redemptive-historical change, any claims to righteousness the Pharisees may have thought they had on the basis of obedience to the law have now come to an end once and for all. The law, on which they staked their acceptance with God, has been fulfilled and transformed by the coming of the kingdom.

If the above analysis is correct, the relevance of Luke 16:16 for the context is obvious. In a profound and far-reaching way, the teaching of this verse eliminates any grounds for pride and self-confidence on the basis of obedience to the law, and thereby contributes significantly to Jesus' response to his critics. The argument is continued in vv. 17-18. Before we consider those verses, however, it is necessary to discuss briefly the last clause of v. 16.

V. 16c reads *kai pas eis autēn biazetai*, "and everyone is forcing his way into it" (*NASB* and *NIV*). Although this clause seems to state the results or effects of the preaching of the kingdom mentioned in v. 16b, the exact sense is far from clear. Fitzmyer calls this part of the verse "a *crux interpretum*,"[63] and Marshall voices the opinion of most interpreters when he says "few sayings in the Gospels are so uncertain in interpretation as this one."[64] The center of difficulty is *biazetai* which can be used in the passive and middle voices.[65] In the former case, the meaning would be "to be forced or pressed," in the latter, it would be "to apply force" (BAGD). While a few interpreters opt for the passive here,[66]

---

most seem to agree that although John is on the threshold of the kingdom he belongs essentially to the old era (e.g., Ellis, *Luke*, 202; G. E. Ladd, *The Presence of the Future* [Grand Rapids: Eerdmans, 1974] 202; as well as the first three interpreters mentioned in this note).

[62] Ridderbos, *Kingdom*, 55. Others who stress the presence of the kingdom in Jesus' teaching in Luke 16:16 include Kümmel, *Promise and Fulfillment* (Naperville, IL: Allenson, 1957) 123; Ladd, *Presence*, 202; and Marshall, *Historian*, 130-31.

[63] Fitzmyer, *Luke* 2.1117.

[64] Marshall, *Luke*, 630.

[65] For a full discussion of the various interpretations of this verb see G. Schrenk, "*biazomai*," *TDNT* 1.609-13; Fitzmyer, *Luke* 2.1117-18; and Ladd, *Presence*, 159-62. While Ladd's discussion of *biazetai* is focused on the occurrence of the verb in the parallel passage in Matt 11:12, his comments are relevant to Luke 16:16 because he makes a good case for both verses embodying the same fundamental idea. For bibliography on Luke 16:16 as a whole, see Fitzmyer, *Luke* 2.1118-19; Kümmel, "Gesetz," 76 n. 7; and Marshall, *Luke*, 627-28.

[66] E.g., Bailey, *Poet*, 116; Easton, *Luke*, 248; and Fitzmyer, *Luke* 2.1117. On this understanding of the verb the sense is "everyone is pressed to enter it [the kingdom]," i.e., "with a demanding urgent invitation (of the kingdom-preacher himself)" (Fitzmyer, *Luke* 2.1117). Ladd (*Presence*, 159-62) cites five different interpretations based on the passive of this verb.

most prefer the middle.[67] This preference alone does not alleviate the difficulty of the verse, however, as the middle voice itself can be used in both bad and good senses. Its use here, therefore, must be determined from the context, i.e., on the basis of which use makes better sense here.

The bad or negative sense of the middle voice of the verb ("to apply force on or against") issues in several different interpretations of v. 16c. The clause refers either to the opposition which the kingdom encounters (perhaps at the hands of the Pharisees and/or other groups),[68] to people's efforts to press into the kingdom without repentance,[69] or it echoes the Pharisees' own criticism of Jesus which he is using against them.[70] The meaning of "force against or violence to" the kingdom unites all these interpretations and does fit the context of Jesus' running controversy with the Pharisees in Luke 15 and 16. The majority view, however, is that the middle voice is used in a positive sense in Luke 16:16 ("to try hard, to make effort"). Contrary to the thinking of the Pharisees and Jews in general, all people (*pas*) now have access to the kingdom of God.[71] In order to enter the kingdom, however, resolute action is necessary, and this point is the emphasis of Jesus' statement.[72] The presence and dynamic activity of the kingdom (here more in preaching than in miracles) demands a radical response on the part of those who would enter it.[73] This interpretation of the verb and clause fits the context

---

[67] This conclusion is voiced by Marshall, *Luke*, 629, and is borne out by my own research.

[68] Ellis, *Luke*, 203, and Kümmel, *Promise*, 124.

[69] Arndt, *Luke*, 361, and Summers, *Luke*, 193.

[70] This intriguing interpretation is suggested by F. W. Danker ("Luke 16:16—An Opposition Logion," *JBL* 77 [1958] 231-43, esp. 234-36) and has been adopted by R. Banks (*Jesus and the Law in the Synoptic Tradition* [Cambridge: Cambridge University Press, 1975] 220) and Resseguie ("Instruction," 140). The gist of the argument is that v. 16c is really part of the Pharisees' own complaint against Jesus (for making the kingdom too accessible and thus doing violence to it) which Jesus picks up and uses as the springboard for charging them in vv. 17-18 with violating the law. Although this interpretation does have the advantage of making sense of this difficult passage, several criticisms can be lodged against it. First, it is certainly not the obvious reading of the text. There is nothing in the text itself, other than its difficulty, to suggest that this clause expresses a point of view other than that of Jesus himself. Second, there can be little question that, whatever the exact sense of the verb in the parallel passage in Matt 11:12 (*hē basileia . . . biazetai*), the words there are Jesus' own and not those of his critics. This fact would suggest the same is true of Luke 16:16.

[71] A number of interpreters call attention to the inclusiveness of the kingdom in this clause, especially in the substantive *pas*—e.g., Godet, *Luke* 2.172; Grundmann, *Lukas*, 323; Plummer, *Luke*, 389; Preisker, "Lukas 16:1-7," 89; Sabourin, *Luc*, 285; Schrenk, "*biazomai*," *TDNT* 1.612; and Talbert, *Reading Luke*, 157.

[72] Geldenhuys, *Luke*, 420-21; Godet, *Luke* 2.172-73; Kümmel, "Gesetz," 81; Ladd, *Presence*, 162-64, 166; Lagrange, *Luc*, 440; Marshall, *Luke*, 630; Ridderbos, *Kingdom*, 55; Sabourin, *Luc*, 285; and Schrenk, "*biazomai*," *TDNT* 1.612.

[73] Ladd, *Presence*, 163. Again Ladd's comment has specific reference to Matt 11:12, but applies with equal force to the present verse. Ladd argues that the dynamic interpretation of the kingdom in Matt 11:12 is supported in Luke 16:16 (p. 164); the kingdom of God is present in the preaching of Jesus (p. 166).

somewhat better than the negative sense. The stress on the inclusiveness
of the kingdom in this interpretation is particularly relevant to the
controversy with the Pharisees and to the redemptive-historical note in
v. 16. What is more, the emphasis on resolve to enter the kingdom recalls
vv. 1-13 where, as has been argued, the call is to decisive response to the
coming of kingdom. Lagrange may well be right when he suggests that
the response to the preaching of the kingdom Jesus has in mind in v. 16
includes using "worldly wealth to gain friends for yourselves [v. 9]."[74]

Jesus' response to the ridicule of the Pharisees is continued in vv. 17-
18. These verses guard against possible misunderstanding or allegations
of antinomianism because of the teaching in v. 16 that a new epoch of
redemptive history has begun.[75] They also charge the Pharisees themselves with misunderstanding and violating the law.[76] In v. 17 Jesus adds
a further comment on the relationship of the law and the kingdom of God
which he preaches.[77] "It is easier for heaven and earth to disappear," he
says, "than for the least stroke of a pen to drop out of the Law." By means
of hyperbole, Jesus stresses the permanency and abiding validity of the
law as transformed and fulfilled in his own teaching.[78] The OT as the
norm of ethical behavior is not abolished by the coming of the kingdom.[79] In the context of vv. 1-13, v. 14 ("lovers of money"), and vv. 19-
31, the OT law against the wrong use of wealth and avarice may be
especially in view here.[80] Although a new epoch of redemptive history
has begun (v. 16), there is continuity between the kingdom-preaching of
Jesus and the manifestation of God's will in the law of the OT. "The
former is but the logical and legitimate outgrowth of the latter."[81] Jesus'
attitude toward the law is not more casual than that of the Pharisees; his

---

[74] Lagrange, *Luc*, 440.

[75] This suggestion about the function of vv. 17-18 is made by Bailey, *Poet*, 82; Drury,
Design, 160; and Grundmann, *Lukas*, 324. It is also put forward, from a different perspective
on v. 16, by Danker, "Logion," esp. pp. 237-38; Banks, *Law*, 218; and Resseguie, "Instruction," 140.

[76] So, e.g., Arndt, *Luke*, 362; Danker, "Logion," 238; Goebel, *Parables*, 233; Seccombe,
Possessions, 179; and Rengstorf, *Lukas*, 195. This indictment is implicit in v. 17 and more
explicit in v. 18. With the exception of Arndt, the above interpreters' observation about the
charge of lawlessness has specific reference to v. 18.

[77] Fitzmyer, *Luke* 2.1116.

[78] Marshall, *Luke*, 627.

[79] Schmid, *Lukas*, 263.

[80] This application of the continuing validity of the law to the specific issue of care for
the poor is noted by Arndt, *Luke*, 361, and Talbert, *Reading Luke*, 158. With regard to the
OT teaching on this issue, see, e.g., Deut 14:28-15:11; 24:10-15; 25:13-16; Isa 58:6-7.

[81] Fitzmyer, *Luke* 2.1116. The element of continuity in v. 17 is, as Marshall points out
(*Luke*, 626), an important qualification of the ostensibly absolute distinction between the old
and new economies in v. 16. The qualification suggests the latter verse does not have the
programmatic significance for Luke that Conzelmann assigns to it.

teaching is not a new morality. If anything, his teaching deepens and broadens the demands of the law and perpetuates the law in a profound sense.[82] In the demands of the kingdom the law is fulfilled and validated.[83] If Jesus' claim in this verse is true, the implication is that his own teaching in vv. 1-13 about the beneficent use of possessions and the dangers of riches is in fundamental agreement with the OT. The Pharisees' ridicule of that teaching (v. 14), then, only shows that they themselves either do not understand the law or disobey it. Their lawlessness is illustrated in the logion about divorce in v. 18 and then, with more specific reference to the possessions theme, in the parable of the rich man and Lazarus in vv. 19-31.

At first glance, Luke 16:18 seems strikingly out of place in its present context. "Anyone who divorces his wife and marries another woman commits adultery, and the man who marries a divorced woman commits adultery." Jesus affirms monogamy and condemns "successive polygamy, which would have been made possible by divorce."[84] My purpose here is not to discuss Jesus' teaching on the topic of divorce per se, but rather to consider how the verse might be related to the present context. Although a few interpreters conclude v. 18 has very little to do with the context,[85] most regard the verse as a specific example or illustration of the continuing validity of the law just stressed in v. 17.[86] The retention or inclusion of the verse here by Luke seems particularly relevant to Jesus' controversy with the Pharisees for, as other synoptic tradition makes clear, the issue of divorce was one of the points of contention between Jesus and the Pharisees as to the meaning of the OT law (cf. especially Matt 5:31-32; also Matt 19:1-9 // Mark 10:1-12). Behind this verse, therefore, stands Jesus' criticism of the Pharisees for laxity and misuse of the OT with respect to marriage and divorce.[87] By

---

[82] Lagrange, *Luc*, 440. Cf. also Sabourin, *Luc*, 285.

[83] This point is made by Banks, *Law*, 218; Fitzmyer, *Luke* 2.1116; and Marshall, *Luke*, 627.

[84] Fitzmyer, *Luke* 2.1121.

[85] E.g., Fitzmyer, *Luke* 2.1119.

[86] E.g., Arndt, *Luke*, 362; Easton, *Luke*, 247-48; Grundmann, *Lukas*, 324; Marshall, *Luke*, 631; Meyer, *Commentary*, 232; Plummer, *Luke*, 389; Sabourin, *Luc*, 284; and Schmid, *Lukas*, 263.

[87] So Arndt, *Luke*, 362; Danker, "Logion," 238; Goebel, *Parables*, 233; Plummer, *Luke*, 389; Seccombe, *Possessions*, 179; and Rengstorf, *Lukas*, 195. Plummer, e.g., writes as follows about v. 18: "Perhaps this [verse] introduces an example of the durability of the moral law in spite of human evasions. Adultery remains adultery even when it has been legalized, and legalized by men who jealously guarded every fraction of the letter, while they flagrantly violated the spirit of the Law" (p. 389). Mention can also be made here of the almost passing suggestion of Grundmann (*Lukas*, 324) and Rengstorf (*Lukas*, 195) that v. 18 may have been included here because of Luke's familiarity with some link between

here prohibiting all divorce, Jesus exposes the Pharisees' failure to understand and obey the law at this point. The implication may be that they have failed similarly in their attitude toward and use of material possessions. Jesus also implies they stand condemned by the very law in the careful observance of which they so prided themselves. The point of condemnation by the OT itself is brought out in the parable of the rich man and Lazarus, Luke 16:19-31, to which we now come.

b) Luke 16:19-31

The second part of the immediate literary context currently under discussion (i.e., Luke 16:14-31) is the parable of the rich man and Lazarus (vv. 19-31). The purpose here is not to discuss this parable in detail, but rather to explain its basic thrust in relationship to the context and the overall argument of Luke 16. As Ellis observes, almost all commentators agree Jesus "does not intend here to give a preview of life after death.... It is probable, rather," Ellis continues, "that Jesus makes use of a well-known story to illuminate certain truths about the kingdom of God."[88] There also seems to be widespread scholarly agreement that, as Fitzmyer says, "the story [of the rich man and Lazarus] is a fitting conclusion to the theme of chap. 16."[89] Although the parable may not have been spoken originally in its present context, it is well suited to this context and thus demonstrates, at the very least, Luke's literary abilities. In this section it will be argued that the parable of the rich man and Lazarus is closely related to and illustrative of the teaching in both vv. 14-18 and vv. 1-13.

In its present context, the well-known parable of the rich man and Lazarus continues the rebuke of vv. 15-18 on the same occasion as introduced in v. 14.[90] The parable is, therefore, addressed to the Pharisees,[91] and, as a number of interpreters have noted, its presence here seems calculated to illustrate the teaching of vv. 14-18.[92] Since Talbert

---

money and divorce in the Pharisees' practice. As intriguing as this suggestion may be, it remains suspect because of the obscurity of the allusion and because of our lack of knowledge of any such link.

[88] *Luke*, 202.

[89] *Luke* 2.1125.

[90] Goebel, *Parables*, 234.

[91] Tannehill, *Unity*, 185, and Fitzmyer, *Luke* 2.1125, among others, make this point on the grounds there is no change of audience until 17:1.

[92] This relationship between Luke 16:14-18 and 19-31 is noted by Bultmann, *Tradition*, 178; Conzelmann (apparently), *Luke*, 112; Ellis, *Luke*, 201; Grundmann, "Fragen," 267; and Talbert, *Reading Luke*, 156-59. For a list of exegetes who call attention to this relationship, see Dupont, *Beatitudes* 3.164 n. 1.

develops the latter point quite persuasively and in some detail, let me summarize his argument. According to Talbert, Luke 16:14-31 is organized into a two-pronged group of sayings (vv. 14-15 and 16-18) followed by a double-edged parable (vv. 19-31). The first part of the parable (vv. 19-26) functions as the exposition of vv. 14-15, while the second part (vv. 27-31) illustrates vv. 16-18.[93] In Talbert's judgment, each part of the parable amplifies two principal themes in the corresponding group of sayings. The rich man's fate in vv. 19-25 (he regards v. 26 as transitional), first, drives home the point that wealth is not necessarily a sign of righteousness, and, second, shows that the God who looks on the heart regards proud men as an abomination.[94] The same sort of amplification also occurs in the second part of the parable, this time with respect to the two themes of vv. 16-18. Vv. 27-31 indicate, first, that there is "a universality in the kingdom's composition"; "if Lazarus succeeded [in getting into the kingdom], the kingdom is certainly inclusive."[95] Second, the law is still in force, especially with regard to the treatment of the poor. "Since in double-edged parables the second part receives the emphasis, the evangelist wants to accent the point about the continuing validity of the law and its teaching on the use of wealth on behalf of the poor."[96]

If this explanation of the relationship between Luke 16:14-18 and 19-31 is correct, several important implications follow. First, "this pattern gives unity to the section," as Talbert himself argues.[97] The juxtaposition here of vv. 14-18 and the parable of the rich man and Lazarus, though difficult, is not fortuitous or arbitrary. In a real sense, vv. 14-18 are the introduction or preface to the parable,[98] and both must be interpreted together. Second, love of money (v. 14) and the resultant neglect of the poor are an abomination in God's eyes. This point, implicit in vv. 14-15, is graphically illustrated in the rich man's fate. The dramatic change in his circumstances from v. 19 (his luxury) to vv. 22-24 (his torment in *haidēs*) is a clear expression of the reversal motif already seen in chapter

---

[93] Talbert, *Reading Luke*, 156. Ellis makes the same point (*Luke*, 201), but in less detail.
[94] *Reading Luke*, 156-57.
[95] *Reading Luke*, 158.
[96] *Reading Luke*, 159.
[97] *Reading Luke*, 156.
[98] This fact has been recognized by Bultmann, *Tradition*, 178; Easton, *Luke*, 246; Lagrange, *Luc*, 438; Plummer, *Luke*, 380; Sellin, "Studien," 213; and Stier, *Words* 4.201.

15 and especially in 16:15.[99] The Pharisees are thus warned about the consequences of loving money.[100]

A third implication of the relationship of vv. 14-18 and 19-31 is that the parable of the rich man and Lazarus (especially vv. 29, 31) is meant to reiterate the charge of lawlessness made against the Pharisees in vv. 16-18 (especially vv. 17-18).[101] In the parable Jesus sets before the Pharisees a basic requirement of the law which "for all their scrupulous attention to detail they failed to observe."[102] Evidently, they were, like the rich man of the parable, guilty of a lack of charity toward those in need. In calling attention to Moses and the prophets (vv. 29, 31; cf. vv. 16-17), Jesus makes the point, well expressed by Godet, that "the law on which the Pharisees staked their credit will nevertheless be the instrument of their eternal condemnation."[103] They are, therefore, exhorted to pay more careful attention to the law,[104] especially with regard to its instructions about caring for the poor and needy.

In addition to being related to vv. 14-18, the parable of the rich man and Lazarus is also linked thematically to vv. 1-13. As several interpreters have pointed out, the common theme of the two parables is that there is a connection between one's use of earthly possessions and one's eternal destiny.[105] In the parable of the unjust steward the theme is expressed positively, especially in v. 9; in the parable of the rich man and Lazarus it is expressed negatively (cf. also vv. 10-12). The note of commendation in the first parable stands in stark contrast to that of condemnation in the second.[106] The rich man's destiny seems designed

---

[99] Ellis (*Luke*, 200), Marshall (*Luke*, 632), Resseguie ("Instruction," 140-41), Sabourin (*Luc*, 287), Sellin ("Studien," 215), and Tannehill (*Unity*, 185-86) call particular attention to the reversal motif in Luke 16:19-31. Dods (*Parables*, 382), Easton (*Luke*, 247), Geldenhuys (*Luke*, 424), and Rengstorf (*Lukas*, 196) note the relationship of the parable to v. 15.

[100] Goulder ("Structure," 199) describes the parable of the rich man and Lazarus as portraying "the consequence of their [the Pharisees'] money-mindedness." Others who connect the parable to v. 14 include Goebel, "Gleichnisgruppe," 707; Summers, *Luke*, 194; and Volckaert, "Steward," 341.

[101] Resseguie calls particular attention to vv. 19-31 as an illustration of the Pharisees' lawlessness ("Instruction," 140-41).

[102] Banks, *Law*, 240. Banks's observation is about Jesus' teaching methods in general; I have applied it to the parable of the rich man and Lazarus in Luke 16.

[103] *Luke* 2.171.

[104] Seccombe, *Possessions*, 179. Seccombe adds that the warning of the parable is not limited to the Pharisees or even to the rich, but is relevant to all who neglect the poor. "The parable's strength is its description of a *relationship* which leads to perdition. Any reader rich or otherwise who is conscious of withholding help from a needy person is in such a relationship, and will feel the sting of the parable" (p. 179).

[105] Godet, *Luke* 2.160; Grundmann, *Lukas*, 325; Lagrange, *Luc*, 430; Plummer, *Luke*, 380; and F. J. Williams, "Steward," 372.

[106] The note of contrast between the two parables of Luke 16 is pointed out by many interpreters, among them, Derrett, "Dives," 370; Grundmann, *Lukas*, 325; Koetsveld,

to illustrate very pointedly the consequences of neglecting to obey the exhortation of v. 9,[107] of being unfaithful with worldly wealth (vv. 10-12), of serving mammon rather than God (v. 13).[108] The rich man of the chapter's second parable is condemned not because he is rich per se, but rather because he is so absorbed in enjoying the pleasures riches can buy that he neglects to care for poor Lazarus.[109] As Schmid suggests, the destinies of the rich man and Lazarus *are* ethically based, although this fact is not immediately apparent from the parable. The rich man represents those engrossed in the pleasures of the world, those not concerned with God.[110] His neglect of Lazarus is damnable, therefore, because it violates the law and the prophets (cf. vv. 29, 31) and also reveals his ultimate loyalty. He had made provision for the present life, but, to judge from his destiny, had made none for the life to come. He had made no friends by means of worldly wealth, had laid up no treasures in heaven. In neglecting Lazarus and using his riches only for himself he had been unfaithful in "the least" (cf. v. 10) and was therefore unqualified to receive the genuine and lasting goods of eternal life (cf. v. 11). He had served mammon, not God, and such service landed him in *haidēs*. The rich man's fate is a sobering reminder that one cannot serve God and mammon, and it spells out clearly the dangers of riches.[111] The parable warns the Pharisees (and other listeners) about the judgment awaiting a

---

Gleichnisse, 247; Marshall, *Luke*, 632; Martin-Achard, "Notes," 141; Morris, *Luke*, 252; Oosterzee, *Luke*, 253; Plummer, *Luke*, 390; Sabourin, *Luc*, 287; and Schlatter, *Lukas*, 363. This contrast is true on almost every interpretation of the parable of the unjust steward, except that which views it as ironic condemnation of the Pharisees. If, on the one hand, the steward's actions toward the debtors are just, the conduct of the rich man in the second parable surely stands in contrast to that of the steward. If, on the other hand, the steward's actions are unjust, the steward at least displays foresight, even if used for purely temporal goals. No such analogous quality exists in the conduct of the rich man in the second parable; he serves only as a deterrent example.

[107] This connection between v. 9 and vv. 19-31 is made by Drummond, *Teaching*, 324; Geldenhuys, *Luke*, 426; Hoyt, "Poor," 162; Klostermann, *Lukas*, 527; Krämer, *Rätsel*, 239; Lagrange, *Luc*, 442; Meyer, *Commentary*, 232; Milligan, "Parables," 119; Plummer, *Luke*, 390; Schulz, *Parabel*, 121; and Topel, "Steward," 221 n. 25.

[108] Fitzmyer (*Luke* 2.1111), Lagrange (*Luc*, 442-43), and Schmid (*Lukas*, 268) make special note of the connection between the parable of the rich man and Lazarus and v. 13.

[109] "The way in which the story is told," writes Tannehill, "strongly suggests that the rich man deserves torment because he did not share his wealth with the poor man who was in need. . . . It is not simply being wealthy but his callousness toward the suffering poor which is condemned in the parable" (*Unity*, 131). For a similar explanation of the rich man's fate, see Geldenhuys, *Luke*, 424 n. 16; O'Neill, "Steward," 240; and Sabourin, *Luc*, 287.

[110] Schmid, *Lukas*, 267. The emphasis of the parable is, it should be pointed out, on the rich man's unrighteousness rather than Lazarus's righteousness. As Lagrange observes (*Luc*, 443), the story is not told in the first place to promise paradise to the poor. Lazarus's presence in paradise is necessary for the rest of the story about the rich man.

[111] The latter point is stressed by Plummer, *Luke*, 390; Schmid, *Lukas*, 268; and Weiss, *Life* 2.248.

rich man who neglects the needs of the poor, and also instructs them on their social responsibility for the poor.[112] At the same time, it reinforces the teaching to the disciples in vv. 1-13 by revealing the ultimate issues at stake in stewardship and the consequences of indifference or disobedience.

2. Impact of Luke 16:14-31 on Interpretation of 16:1-13

Luke 16:14-31 broadens our understanding of vv. 1-13 in a number of important ways, several of which have already been noted. The context of the Pharisees' greed (v. 14), for instance, brings Jesus' teaching in vv. 1-13 into sharper focus, and the parable of the rich man and Lazarus (vv. 19-31) gives that teaching a note of solemnity and urgency. This context is significant for the interpretation of our parable in several other ways.

First, Luke 16:14-31 sheds light on our parable by clarifying the exhortation in v. 9. In that verse, Jesus exhorts his disciples to "use worldly wealth to gain friends for yourselves," but does not specify how they are to do so. The parable of the rich man and Lazarus supplies the answer. The figure of poor Lazarus in vv. 19-31 suggests the specific application of the exhortation in v. 9 includes using possessions for the poor. The figure of the rich man in torment in *haidēs* dramatizes the consequences of failing to do so.

Second, Luke 16:14-31 enhances our understanding of the parable of the unjust steward by making the eschatological background and motivation of the parable more pronounced. As noted in chapter two, vv. 1-13 are "impregnated with eschatological terminology," to use Seccombe's words.[113] V. 16, with its emphasis on the presence of the kingdom and the resolute effort required to enter it, brings the eschatological nuances of vv. 1-13 into sharper focus. As Grundmann observes, v. 16 makes clear the eschatological character of the decision between God and mammon demanded in the parable and in v. 13 in particular.[114] The exhortation of the parable to use one's possessions for the poor is urgent because the kingdom of God is present. The various eschatological nuances in vv. 1-13 themselves, in the context of v. 16, strongly suggest the former are "a fundamental evaluation of possessions in the light of the kingdom."[115] "By acts of humanitarian goodness" Jesus' disciples are

---

[112] Tannehill, *Unity*, 181 and 183, respectively.
[113] Seccombe, *Possessions*, 180.
[114] Grundmann, *Lukas*, 319.
[115] Seccombe, *Possessions*, 172.

"to actualize the values of the Kingdom in the present age."[116] In short, eschatology is to have an influence on ethics, specifically on stewardship of material possessions. The relationship between eschatology and ethics will be considered more carefully in the next chapter.

II. Broader Literary Context

Having considered the immediate literary context of the parable of the unjust steward in Luke 15 and 16, attention can now be directed to the broader literary context of the parable, the so-called travel narrative or central section of Luke's Gospel. Although many names have been given to the section,[117] "central section" is perhaps the best title for it. In the words of B. H. Streeter, who first suggested the title, it "states a fact but begs no questions."[118] Beginning at Luke 9:51 and extending probably to 19:44,[119] "this section makes up almost one-third of the entire Gospel,

---

[116] Seccombe, *Possessions*, 172.

[117] Among the names for it are the Perean Section, the Samaritan Section, the Great Insertion, the Travel Document, the Travel Narrative, and the Central Section. For a summary discussion of these various titles and their advocates, see especially H. L. Egelkraut, *Jesus' Mission to Jerusalem: A Redaction Critical Study of the Travel Narrative in the Gospel of Luke, Lk 9:51-19:48* (Frankfurt: P. Lang, 1976) 4-6; L. Girard, *L'Evangile des voyages de Jesus, ou la Section 9:51-18:14 de Saint Luc* (Paris: Gabalda, 1951) 20; and Resseguie, "Instruction," 3-4. "The very variety of names given to it . . . ," writes C. F. Evans, "shows that commentators have been at a loss what to make of it" ("The Central Section of St. Luke's Gospel," in *Studies in the Gospels* [ed. D. E. Nineham; Oxford: Blackwell, 1955] 40). Egelkraut echoes Evans's assessment, but adds that "at the same time such quarrelling about names is an almost amusing exercise in minutiae" (*Mission*, 6).

[118] B. H. Streeter, *The Four Gospels. A Study of Origins* (London: Macmillan, 1961) 203. Streeter's suggestion has been adopted by Evans, "Central Section," 41; C. C. McCown, "The Geography of Luke's Central Section," *JBL* 57 (1938) 65; and Resseguie, "Interpretation of Luke's Central Section (9:51-19:44) since 1856," *Studia Biblica et theologia* 5/2 (1975) 4. Along the same lines, N. B. Stonehouse refers to this portion of Luke's Gospel in passing as the "middle section" (*The Witness of Luke to Christ* [Grand Rapids: Baker, 1979] 114-15), and Ellis speaks of it as "the central division" (*Luke*, 146).

[119] There is little question that the section of Luke's Gospel to which our parable belongs begins at 9:51, but little agreement as to where it ends. Among the numerous suggestions about the end of the section, the following verses are the most frequently cited:

1. *18:14*—e.g., Bultmann, *Tradition*, 362; Evans, "Central Section," 40; E. Lohse, "Missionarischen Handeln Jesu nach dem Evangelium des Lukas," *TZ* 10 (1954) 2; and B. Reicke, "Instruction and Discussion in the Travel Narrative," in *SE* I [ed. K. Aland et al.; Berlin: Akademie, 1959] 206);

2. *19:27*—e.g., J. Blinzler, "Die literarische Eigenart des sogenannten Reiseberichts im Lukasevangelium," in *Synoptische Studien* (ed. J. Schmid and A. Vögtle; Munich: K. Zink, 1953) 20 n. 1; Conzelmann, *Luke*, 64; Godet, *Luke* 2.1; Grundmann, "Fragen," 254, and *Lukas*, 200; K. L. Schmidt, *Der Rahmen der Geschichte Jesu* (Berlin: Trowitzsch, 1919) 246; and J. Schneider, "Zur Analyse des lukanischen Reiseberichtes," in *Synoptische Studien*, 211; and

3. *19:44*—e.g., Ellis, *Luke*, 223-24; H. K. Farrell, "The Structure and Theology of Luke's Central Section," *Trinity Journal*, n.s., 7 (1986) 53; Geldenhuys, *Luke*, 46, 289; and Resseguie, "Instruction," 1 n. 4.

a good deal of its material is not found elsewhere, and it contributes not a little to the total picture which emerges from Luke-Acts."[120] Ostensibly, the central section recounts events and teaching in the period between Jesus' ministries in Galilee and Jerusalem, more specifically, while he is travelling from the former to the latter sphere of ministry.[121] In reality, however, this section of the Third Gospel is almost as controversial as the interpretation of the parable of the unjust steward itself. The purpose of the present discussion is not to enter into the details of this controversy, but rather to consider the impact of this level of context on the interpretation of our parable. Before this impact can be assessed, however, it will be necessary to outline the difficulties of the section and to survey the interpretations of it.

A. Outline of Difficulties of Broader Context

In addition to debates about what this large section of the Third Gospel should be called and what its limits are,[122] the more basic issues of its organization and purpose are also in dispute. At Luke 9:51 Jesus resolutely sets out to go from Galilee to Jerusalem, and a sense of movement is sustained throughout the remainder of the central section by repeated *Reisenotizen* or journey references.[123] Despite these references, the section is, however, characterized by an amazing lack of precise topographical, chronological, and personal data.[124] "Jesus is

Although the latter verse seems the best explanation of the end of the central section (because, e.g., Jesus is still en route to Jerusalem until this point and does not enter the city until 19:45), for our purposes it makes very little difference where the section ends. For a discussion and summary of the various views on this matter, see especially Egelkraut, *Mission*, 6-10, and Resseguie, "Instruction," 1 n. 4.

[120] Evans, "Central Section," 40. For a summary of the material unique to Luke's central section, see Kistemaker, "The Structure of Luke's Gospel," *JETS* 25/1 (1982) 33. A. T. Robertson lists eighteen parables of Jesus found only in Luke's Gospel; all but one (7:40-43) are in the central section ([assuming it goes at least as far as 19:27]; *Luke the Historian in the Light of Research* [New York: Scribner's, 1920] 150).

[121] According to Resseguie's count of verses in the *UBSGNT*, Mark devotes sixty-two vv. to Jesus' journey from Galilee to Jerusalem (Mark 10:1-11:10), Matthew has seventy-five (19:1-21:11), while Luke has 423 vv. ("Instruction," 2).

[122] Egelkraut calls these matters "external reflections of the internal problems of the text that give rise to the exegetical and theological dilemma" (*Mission*, 11).

[123] Luke 9:51, 53; 13:22, 33; 17:11; 18:31; 19:28, 41, all mention Jerusalem as the destination of Jesus' journey; 9:56, 57; 10:1, 38; 13:31-32; 14:25; 18:35, 36; and 19:11, 29, contain more general references to a journey.

[124] For full and helpful summaries of these data, see Egelkraut, *Mission*, 11-25, and Resseguie, "Instruction," 5-10. As Egelkraut notes, "this [lack of precise data] is amazing because Lk otherwise provides them in abundance" (p. 16). In a footnote to this statement (n. 2) he asks the reader to "compare 1:5; 1:26; 2:1-4; 2:15; 3:1-3; 3:23ff; 4:16; 4:38; not to speak of the references in the passion and resurrection story and the many geographical data in Acts."

always travelling toward Jerusalem," writes Schmidt in what is perhaps the classic summary of the difficulty of the section, "but he really makes no headway at all on this journey."[125] "One searches in vain in these pages to know where one is," says Lagrange; "one knows only that one is always in the land of Israel .... The scene is always simply somewhere."[126] Resseguie makes the same point about this section in more detail. He says,

> One is given the impression of a journey from Galilee to Jerusalem, but a journey which cannot be traced on a map. At 9:51 Jesus apparently leaves Galilee once and for all and arrives in the village of Mary and Martha at 10:38. Yet at 17:11 we read that he is still travelling between Samaria and Galilee, and the goal of the journey, Jerusalem, is not reached until 19:45.[127]

The vagueness characteristic of the topographical and chronological references in the central section is also found in the connections between its varied elements. These connections, particularly among the teaching units of the section, are often very loose.[128] "The general themes of the section are hard to define," Marshall notes, "and it is even more difficult to find any kind of thread running through it."[129] It is not surprising, therefore, that the section has the appearance of an "amorphous miscellany," a meaningless jumble.[130] Many interpreters would no doubt agree with C. L. Blomberg's conclusion that "no portion of the Synoptic gospels has proved as difficult to outline" as this one.[131] With justification, then, the central section of Luke's Gospel has been called a "most intriguing yet confusing contour in the Luke-Acts landscape,"[132] "the

---

[125] Schmidt, *Rahmen*, 269.

[126] Lagrange, *Luc*, xxxviii.

[127] Resseguie, "Instruction," 1. The lack of progress toward Jerusalem in this section has led several interpreters (e.g., Bailey, *Poet*, 82, and Schneider, "Analyse," 209) to reject what might, until Streeter's suggestion, be called the traditional title of the section, i.e., the "travel narrative." Ellis adds that "throughout the ministry from 4:42 onward Jesus is presented always without a home, always on a mission, always on the move. Therefore," he concludes, "it is improper in any case to call Luke's central division 'The Travel Narrative'" (*Luke*, 148). Cf. also Grundmann, *Lukas*, 198.

[128] Fitzmyer, *Luke* 1.825.

[129] Marshall, *Luke*, 401. F. Stagg says of the central section, "It does not move like a river; rather it spreads out like a lake" ("The Journey Toward Jerusalem in Luke's Gospel. Luke 9:51-19:27," *RevExp* 64 [1967] 499).

[130] Goulder, "Structure," 195.

[131] C. L. Blomberg, "Midrash, Chiasmus, and the Outline of Luke's Central Section," in *Gospel Perspectives. Studies in Midrash and Historiography* (vol. 3; ed. R. T. France and D. Wenham; Sheffield: JSOT Press, 1983) 217.

[132] D. P. Moessner, "Luke 9:1-50: Luke's Preview of the Journey of the Prophet Like Moses of Deuteronomy," *JBL* 102/4 (1983) 576.

central enigma" of Luke's Gospel,[133] "one of the greatest riddles of gospel study,"[134] "a scholar's puzzle."[135]

B. Survey of Interpretations of Central Section

Given the difficulties just outlined, it is little wonder that "a flood of essays" and at least three monographs have been published on the central section,[136] and "the opinions as to Luke's intentions are as diverse as the imagination allows."[137] To discuss all these opinions, many of which overlap, would take me far beyond the limits of this chapter and would in fact be unnecessary for my purposes. In this section of the chapter, I will survey the major interpretations of Luke's central section, highlighting the issues of debate, offering general criticisms in the notes, and drawing general conclusions about the character of the section. I will then suggest how the central section affects the interpretation of Luke 16:1-13.

The many interpretations of Luke's central section can be organized and surveyed in a variety of ways.[138] The outline to be used below is adapted from Resseguie's dissertation on the central section,[139] and consists of four main headings: chronological, literary, theological, and

---

[133] Reicke, "Instruction," 206.

[134] Drury, *Design*, 138.

[135] McCown, "Geography," 51.

[136] The reference to "a flood of essays" is from Egelkraut, *Mission*, 3 n. 2. Many of the essays on the central section have been or will be noted in the course of the present chapter. The monographs on the central section as a whole are Girard's *Voyages* (1951), Egelkraut's *Mission* (1976), and Moessner's *Lord of the Banquet: The Literary and Theological Significance of the Lukan Travel Narrative* (Minneapolis: Fortress, 1989). (The latter work, though valuable, appeared too recently to be included in any way other than passing reference in the notes.) For full bibliography on the central section, see Bailey, *Poet*, 79 n. 1; Blinzler, "Eigenart," 20 n. 3 (includes works between 1910 and 1953); Egelkraut, *Mission*, 238-40: (twentieth century) essays and monographs mainly devoted to the central section; 240-43: essays and books that give special attention to the central section within a larger context; Fitzmyer, "The Composition of Luke, Chapter 9," in *Perspectives on Luke-Acts* (ed. Talbert; Danville, VA/Edinburgh: Association of Baptist Professors of Religion/T. & T. Clark, 1978) 150-51 n. 38, and *Luke* 1.830-32; Girard, *Voyages*, 9-15 (includes works up to 1951); Moessner, "Preview," 575 n. 2; and Resseguie, "Instruction" (bibliography), and "Point of View in the Central Section of Luke (9:51-19:44)," *JETS* 25/1 (1982) 41 n. 1.

[137] Resseguie, "Interpretation," 4.

[138] For summaries and surveys of the various interpretations of Luke's central section, see Blinzler, "Eigenart," 22-25; Blomberg, "Midrash," 217-40; J. H. Davies, "The Purpose of the Central Section of St. Luke's Gospel," in *SE* II (ed. F. L. Cross; Berlin: Akademie, 1964) 164 n. 1; Egelkraut, *Mission*, 30-59; Kümmel, *Introduction to the New Testament* (rev. ed.; Nashville: Abingdon, 1975) 141-42; Moessner, "Preview," 577-82, and *Banquet*, 21-33; Resseguie, "Instruction," 12-43, and "Interpretation," 4-34; and G. W. Trompf, "La section médiane de l'évangile de Luc: L'Organisation des documents," *RHPR* 53 (1973) 141-42.

[139] "Instruction," 12-43.

practical interpretations. Each heading has several subheadings. The interpretations of the central section often overlap, and the line of demarcation between them cannot always be sharply drawn. While a number of interpreters thus fall into several different categories, I have categorized each according to his main emphasis.

1. Chronological Interpretations

For many years explanations of the central section have assumed that Luke here follows a chronological scheme of some sort. On the assumption that Luke's prefatory claim to have written *kathexēs* ("in order" [BAGD], 1:3) is to be taken literally, this section of his gospel is interpreted as recounting either several different journeys or a single journey by Jesus to Jerusalem.

a) Several journeys

A desire to harmonize Luke's Gospel with John's and/or an appeal to logic[140] have led some interpreters to conclude the central section must contain the accounts of several different journeys to Jerusalem. C. J. Cadoux, for example, notes the "indications of locality" in the central section do not lend themselves to one journey,[141] and argues that the section instead conceals three visits to Jerusalem and its neighborhood.[142] Luke 10:25-13:9 is one visit, 18:9-14 a second, the triumphal entry (19:28-44) introduces a third. Although Cadoux concedes it is futile to attempt a detailed harmony with John,[143] he believes that each of the alleged visits in Luke corresponds to visits mentioned in John's Gospel—the first to John 7:1-14, the second to John 10:22-29, and the third to John 12-20.[144]

---

[140] The sheer length of the section itself, e.g., or Jesus being in the vicinity of Jerusalem more than once are taken as evidence of several different journeys in this section. This summary of the appeal to logic is taken from Resseguie, "Instruction," 12.

[141] C. J. Cadoux, "The Visits of Jesus to Jerusalem," *Expositor*, ser. 3, 9 (1925) 182.

[142] "Visits," 184.

[143] "Visits," 185.

[144] "Visits," 184. It is noteworthy that at the outset of his article Cadoux makes the point that *kathexēs* in Luke 1:3 denotes a chronological plan in the Third Gospel (p. 177). Cadoux's approach to the central section is adopted and modified by E. J. Cook, "Synoptic Indications of the Visits of Jesus to Jerusalem," *ExpTim* 4 (1929-30) 121-23. Cook agrees that the central section of Luke can be harmonized (albeit not completely) with John's Gospel (p. 123), but is concerned to remedy what he views as the weakness of Cadoux's formulation. In order to avoid the difficulty of equating, as Cadoux does, the secret visit of John 7 with the public and leisurely progress described in Luke 9:51-10:42, Cook suggests a different harmony of the Third and Fourth Gospels. His outline is as follows: Luke 9:51-10:42 corresponds to the

Girard also detects several journeys in the central section. According to him, Luke 9:51-18:14[145] contains the accounts of three journeys to Jerusalem *during* Jesus' Galilean ministry.[146] This approach, of course, leaves room for harmonization with John's Gospel, but Girard's argument proceeds in a different direction. He contends the central section is an independent account, continuous with and parallel to the facts and discourses of Matthew, Mark, and even Luke 4:14-9:50. Luke's central section is, therefore, a sort of "fourth synoptic,"[147] the journeys of which coincide with those implicit in Matthew, Mark, and the earlier section of Luke.[148] On this hypothesis, Girard suggests the most exact title for this section is "The Gospel of the Journeys of Jesus."[149]

---

visit of John 5; Luke 11:1-13:9 to that of John 7; Luke 13:22-33 to that of John 10; and Luke 14:25-19:28 to that of John 12-20 (p. 122). The result of Cook's analysis is that Luke's central section includes four visits to Jerusalem rather than three.

[145] Girard's label for this section is L²; the rest of the Third Gospel, especially the Galilean ministry, he calls L¹ (*Voyages*, 20).

[146] *Voyages*, 69. The three journeys are 9:51-11:13, 11:14-13:35, and 14:1-18:14 (p. 65).

[147] *Voyages*, 74.

[148] *Voyages*, 105. On pp. 111-17 Girard does attempt to harmonize the three journeys of the central section with John's Gospel, but harmonization is not the emphasis of his approach.

[149] *Voyages*, 121. Girard assumes the central section is in chronological order, at least in its main lines (see esp. pp. 57-60). For other representatives of the position that the central section contains several journeys, see Girard, 51 nn. 1-3.

The interpretation that in the central section of his gospel Luke intends to recount several different journeys by Jesus is open to criticism at several points. First, it operates on the questionable assumption that the adverb *kathexēs* in Luke's preface (1:3; "in order," BAGD) denotes strictly chronological order. As Stonehouse, among others, points out, *kathexēs* can mean simply that Luke's interest is in a connected and orderly narrative in contrast to the piece-meal works of his predecessors, and not necessarily in the exact chronological sequence of separate events (*Luke*, 41). (For recent works espousing other possible interpretations of Luke's purpose as stated in his preface, see esp. Blomberg, "Midrash," 218 n. 10. For a summary of the various explanations of *kathexēs* in 1:3, see J. W. Scott, "Luke's Preface and the Synoptic Problem" [Ph.D. dissertation, University of St Andrews, 1985] 101. Scott contends that "while *kathexēs* may mean 'in orderly sequence,' the precise nature of that sequence is never part of the meaning of the word itself, but rather is indicated by the immediate context" [p. 101]. In 1:3, he concludes, the adverb means "in a narrative manner" [p. 105]). If Stonehouse's argument is correct, chronological order need not be assumed in the central section, at least insofar as Luke's preface is concerned. A second criticism of the "several journeys" interpretation is that the various journey references of the central section are so obscure and vague that it is dangerous to put too much weight on them. They are not, in short, reliable indicators of different journeys, nor, apparently, were they intended as such. Third, the interpretation in question generally relies too heavily on John's Gospel to reconstruct the chronology of this section of Luke's Gospel and fails to take Luke on his own terms. (The substance of the last two criticisms is from Resseguie, "Instruction," 17.) The differences in the correspondences suggested by Cadoux and Cook highlight how uncertain and tenuous such a procedure is. Plummer's advice on the matter of harmonization bears repeating. Noting that "although there is room in Lk.'s narrative for what Jn. tells us, we do not know where to place it," Plummer concludes that "it seems best, therefore, . . . to take his [i.e., Luke's] narrative with the indistinctness which he has left" (*Luke*, 261). For other criticisms of the "several journeys" interpretation as a

b) One journey

A second chronological interpretation of the central section regards the section as the account(s) of one journey to Jerusalem, i.e., Jesus' last. This interpretation can take several different forms.

(1) Multiple reports

One form of this interpretation is that the central section contains multiple reports of Jesus' last journey to Jerusalem. G. Mackinlay, for example, argues that this section is part of a threefold narrative of that same journey.[150] Each of the three accounts of the journey (4:31-10:42, 11:1-14:24, and 14:25-20:18) covers the same period, each is in chronological order.[151] G. Ogg also explains the central section on the basis of multiple accounts of the same journey, but finds here two accounts of that journey rather than three. He believes Luke utilizes two streams of tradition about Jesus' last journey from Galilee to Jerusalem—one in Luke 9:51-10:42, the other in 17:11-19:28.[152] As for the material in between (11:1-17:10), Ogg argues it records activities *during* Jesus' Galilean ministry which Luke has assigned to the period of the last journey because he was "deeply sensible of the preciousness of the teaching conveyed in these activities" and thus felt under divine compulsion to include them somewhere.[153]

(2) Perean ministry

A second form of the "one journey interpretation" of the central section is that Luke here narrates a prolonged Perean ministry which took place during Jesus' last journey from Galilee to Jerusalem. Godet espouses this interpretation. Insisting that Luke 9:51-19:27 recounts only one consecutive journey by Jesus to Jerusalem, Godet concludes that the three most prominent travel notices of the section (9:51, 13:22, and 17:11) are not indications of three different journeys but "way-marks set

---

whole, see Blinzler, "Eigenart," 23, and Egelkraut, *Mission*, 37-38. For specific criticisms of Cook (and Cadoux), see Resseguie, "Instruction," 14-15 (= "Interpretation," 8); for specific criticisms of Girard, see Blinzler, "Eigenart," 23, 25, 27; Evans's review in *JTS*, n.s., 3 (1952) 243-44; and Resseguie, "Instruction," 16-17 (= "Interpretation," 10).

[150] G. Mackinlay, "St. Luke's Threefold Narrative of Christ's Last Journey to Jerusalem," *The Interpreter* 7 (1910-11) 263.

[151] "Journey," 268-70. Mackinlay finds the literary clue to such an arrangement in Acts where important stories (e.g., Paul's conversion) are repeated three times to "draw attention and give emphasis" to the given theme (pp. 266-67).

[152] G. Ogg, "The Central Section of the Gospel according to St Luke," *NTS* 18 (1971-72) 40.

[153] "Central Section," 48.

up by the author on the route of Jesus . . . on account of the slowness and length of the progress."[154] "Jesus proceeds only by short stages," he explains, "stopping at each locality to preach the gospel."[155] Godet infers from Mark 10:1 and Matthew 19:1 that the route of the journey is through Perea,[156] and adds that the journey may have taken as much as six or seven months.[157]

(3) Samaritan ministry

On the premise that Jesus enters Samaria at the outset of the central section (cf. especially Luke 9:52, 56), several interpreters contend the section recounts a Samaritan ministry. Bultmann, for example, believes Luke takes Jesus through Samaria in 9:51-18:14. He adds, however, that this journey is a fictitious account created by Luke because "he probably felt the need not to leave the journey to Jerusalem so much in the dark as Mark had done, and found in it at the same time a background well adapted to receive all kinds of situationless units."[158] Lohse also explains the central section as the account of a Samaritan ministry, but stresses Luke's theological rather than literary motive. In 9:51-18:14 Luke supplies an account of Jesus' activities among the Samaritans in order to provide the theological foundation for the missions' mandate of the church. According to Lohse, the journey narrated here shows, among other things, that the gospel is to be taken to non-Jews and that a herald must not be dissuaded from his task.[159]

---

[154] Godet, *Luke* 2.3-4.

[155] *Luke* 2.1-2.

[156] *Luke* 2.2, 5.

[157] I.e., the period of time between Jesus' visit to Jerusalem for the Feast of Tabernacles recorded in John 7 and his last, passion visit (*Luke* 2.5-6). Plummer explains the central section in much the same way as Godet (cf., Plummer, *Luke*, xxxix [where 9:51-19:28 is entitled "The Journeyings towards Jerusalem: Ministry outside Galilee"], and 260-61). For a representative list of other advocates of the "one journey interpretation" of the central section, see Girard, *Voyages*, 56 n. 1.

[158] Bultmann, *Tradition*, 363. In Bultmann's judgment, Luke's editing in this section is not very skillful, "for though Jesus was journeying, by Luke's statement through Samaria, he was still surrounded by the same audience and questioned by the same opponents as he had been in Galilee" (p. 363).

[159] Lohse, "Handeln," 10-11, 13. Lohse's suggestion of a theological motive with practical meaning for the church makes him difficult to classify since his interpretation also falls under both theological and practical interpretations. Resseguie ("Interpretation," 15) includes R. H. Lightfoot (*Locality and Doctrine in the Gospels* [London: Hodder and Stoughton, 1938] 137-39) as a representative of the interpretation that the central section is "The Samaritan Section."

The interpretation that Luke's central section narrates one journey has several serious weaknesses. First, this interpretation, like the "several journeys" one discussed above, generally operates on the questionable assumption that Luke means to write in strictly chronological order. Second, this interpretation cannot adequately explain the striking absence of geographical and chronological references in most of the central section. Third,

2. Literary Interpretations

A number of interpreters depart from a chronological approach to Luke's central section, arguing instead that Luke's motive here is primarily, if not exclusively, literary.[160] Some believe the journey motif of the section is simply a literary framework for the inclusion of diverse and situationless surplus traditions; others are convinced Luke is here following a particular literary model.

a) Journey as literary framework

One of the first interpreters to break with chronological approaches to Luke's central section is McCown. In answer to his own question how a writer like Luke "who is so fond of geographical terms and settings is so indefinite, careless, and even mistaken in their use," McCown responds that the "inescapable" conclusion is Luke's geography and topography "serve merely as literary devices."[161] According to him, Luke derived the travel motif from Mark 10:1 or from already existing traditions about Jesus' last journey to Jerusalem, and used it as the basis for a collection of "materials for which Luke, or his source, had no definite local or historical situations and which he threw together into a very loosely organized mass."[162] The central section is, in short, "a *collectanea* around a travel motif."[163] Blinzler explains the central

---

the Perean and Samaritan forms of the interpretation overlook the fact that some material in the section presupposes a Jewish environment found neither in Perea nor Samaria. (For details of the latter criticism, see esp. McCown, "Geography," 57, and Egelkraut, *Mission*, 40 n. 1.) Fourth, this interpretation cannot account for the fact that Jesus is near Jerusalem at the end of chapter 10 (10:38-42), but apparently still on the border between Galilee and Samaria in 17:11. (The substance of the last three criticisms is taken from Resseguie, "Instruction," 22-23.) For other criticisms of this position as a whole, see Blinzler, "Eigenart," 22, and Egelkraut, *Mission*, 39-41. For specific criticisms of Mackinlay, see Resseguie, "Instruction," 20 (= "Interpretation," 11; Plummer says simply that "Mackinlay's theory is no help" [*Luke*, 261]); of Ogg, see Resseguie, "Instruction," 19 (= "Interpretation," 7); of a Perean ministry, see Resseguie, "Instruction," 21-22 (= "Interpretation," 14), and Stonehouse, *Luke*, 116-17; and of a Samaritan ministry, see Resseguie, "Interpretation," 16, and Stonehouse, *Luke*, 117-18.

[160] As we will see, many interpreters conclude the central section is a literary device. What distinguishes the interpreters included under the present heading is their almost exclusive emphasis on Luke's literary motive with little or no consideration of possible larger theological and/or paraenetic motives.

[161] McCown, "Geography," 56. McCown's attention to questions of theology and literary style leads Blomberg to credit him with beginning "a new trend which subsequent scholarship has almost unanimously followed" ("Midrash," 218).

[162] McCown, "Geography," 58.

[163] "Geography," 64. Among the "chief interests of the fictitious travel narrative" noted by McCown are the creation of "a sense of movement" so as "to hold the readers' attention

section in similar fashion. He contends the travel notices of the section provide the literary framework for the inclusion of situationless materials without injury to the collective character of Luke's work.[164] Since the central section can be accounted for on literary grounds, it is not proper to seek a particular theological motive here.[165]

b) Literary model

(1) Deuteronomy

The OT book of Deuteronomy is sometimes identified as Luke's model for the central section. The first person to suggest and develop this thesis seems to be Evans.[166] On the analogy of the apocryphal *Assumption of Moses*, Evans argues Luke may have selected and ordered his material in order to present this section of his gospel as "a Christian Deuteronomy."[167] Evans admits that some of the resemblances in subject matter and wording may be fortuitous, but is convinced, nonetheless, that the striking coincidence of order between Deuteronomy and Luke 9:51-18:14 confirms his thesis. Luke's motive for the "Deuteronomic sequence" of the central section, he asserts, springs from the conviction that Jesus was the prophet like Moses in Deuteronomy 18:15.[168]

---

to the crowded mass of teachings which the section collects" and the demonstration of what suffering meant to the early Christians (pp. 65-66). It is also noteworthy that McCown argues Luke intended the central section as the account of a "Samaritan ministry" (see esp. pp. 63-64).

[164] Blinzler, "Eigenart," 34. Cf. Bultmann, *Tradition*, 363, quoted earlier.

[165] Blinzler, "Eigenart," 35 n. 41. Other advocates of an almost exclusively literary interpretation of the central section include Bultmann (*Tradition*, 363), whom I included under the previous heading, and Schmidt (*Rahmen*, 269-71). For a list of additional representatives of this interpretation, see Egelkraut, *Mission*, 41-44 (esp. 43 n. 3), and Girard, *Voyages*, 56 n. 4.

As salutary as the literary emphasis of this approach may be, it is open to question on several points. First, not unlike chronological approaches to the central section, this approach regards the gospel writers as merely "uninvolved collectors" of tradition "who kept themselves out of the editorial and interpretive process" (Egelkraut, *Mission*, 44). As redaction criticism has shown, however, such was not the case at all. An exclusively literary approach to the central section, therefore, does not adequately appreciate other motives that may have been at work in Luke's production of this section. Second, this approach cannot account for the arrangement of the material within the central section. Why, for instance, is Luke 16 composed of two parables sandwiched around sayings about the law and the kingdom? Why is the material of that chapter juxtaposed to the three parables of chapter 15? These questions are difficult ones, to be sure, but it is hard to see how a purely literary approach to the central section can provide a satisfying answer to either.

[166] Evans first suggested the idea, almost casually, in the course of a review of Girard's *Voyages* in *JTS*, n.s., 3 (1952) 244. He later developed the idea in an influential essay in *Studies in the Gospels* (ed. Nineham; "Central Section," 37-53).

[167] Evans, "Central Section," 42. In his diagram of the correspondences between Luke and Deuteronomy (pp. 42-50), Luke 16:1-18 parallels Deut 23:15-24:6 (p. 48).

[168] "Central Section," 50. Evans's interpretation of the central section has been endorsed

(2) Chiasmus

Chiasmus is the second major literary model suggested to explain Luke's central section. The individual perhaps most responsible for introducing this theory into the discussion of the central section is Goulder.[169] Goulder contends that, much like rabbinic preachers, Luke here presents his main themes and then repeats them in reverse order.[170] According to him, the main chiasmus begins at Luke 10:25 and extends to 18:30, it intersects at 13:34-35 (Jesus' lament over Jerusalem), and is composed of seven parallel members.[171] Three main themes are developed in the chiasmus: prayer, money, and repentance.[172] Goulder's suggested parallel for Luke 16:1-14 is 12:1-34; both passages deal with the Pharisees' love of money.[173]

---

and/or adapted by Drury (*Design*, 138-43), Moessner ("Preview," esp. 580-82), Sellin ("Studien," 345), and Goulder (*The Evangelists' Calendar. A Lectionary Explanation of the Development of Scripture* [London: SPCK, 1978] 91-104). In a recent book, Moessner (*Banquet*, esp. 260-88) contends that "the Moses of the Book of Deuteronomy serves as a literary-theological model" both for "the words of Jesus (i.e., content) and for his journeying (i.e., form)" in the central section of Luke's Gospel (p. 285). Goulder is noteworthy here because he had earlier argued for the chiastic structure of the central section ("Structure," 195-202), an interpretation summarized in the next subsection. He apparently changed his view about this section.

Although "ingenious" (so Ellis, *Luke*, 147, and Resseguie, "Interpretation," 11), Evans's theory must be judged unproven at best. J. W. Wenham, summarizing scholarly response to the theory, lodges two criticisms against it ("Synoptic Independence and the Origin of Luke's Travel Narrative," *NTS* 27/4 [1981] 509-10). First, the overall appearance of the section is not at all like Deuteronomy. In Deuteronomy, for example, Moses gives a series of addresses to encamped Israelites, while in Luke's central section Jesus is on the move, doing things and talking to constantly changing audiences. Second, the supposed parallels between Luke and Deuteronomy are "often tenuous in the extreme." The law about escaped slaves in Deut 23:15-16, for instance, seems to bear little resemblance to the parable of the unjust steward. Wenham concludes that "the theory is ingenious rather than plausible" (p. 510). Similarly, Blomberg says the lack of close conceptual and verbal parallels makes Evans's theory "highly unlikely" ("Midrash," 228). To these criticisms two others might be added. Evans's theory of a Deuteronomic model breaks down or is incomplete if, as I have argued, the central section extends beyond Luke 18:14. It is surprising, furthermore, that there is no parallel in the central section to Deut 18:15, a verse which according to Evans is at the heart of Luke's arrangement of the section. (This last objection is raised by both C. H. Cave, "Lazarus and the Lukan Deuteronomy," *NTS* 15 [1969] 319-20, and Resseguie, "Interpretation," 13).

[169] Goulder, "Structure." Farrell ("Structure," 33 n. 3) notes that J. A. Bengel, N. W. Lund, and R. Morgenthaler had earlier called attention to Luke's chiastic structure.

[170] Goulder, "Structure," 195.

[171] "Structure," 196-201.

[172] Goulder, *Type and History in Acts* (London: SPCK, 1964) 136. Goulder repeats his theory of chiasmus in Luke's central section on pp. 133-41 of this book.

[173] "Structure," 198-99. Goulder's thesis is endorsed and modified by Bailey, *Poet*, 79-85, and Talbert, *Patterns*, 51-56. The former argues Luke 9:51-19:48 is chiastically structured with ten parallel members (16:1-8, 16, being parallel to 12:3-59 [pp. 80-81]), the latter that 10:21-18:30 is made up of 11 parallel members (16:1-31 being parallel to 12:1-48 [p. 52]). Talbert's argument and outline have been developed further in a recent article

3. Theological Interpretations

A third major approach to the central section is that it is primarily designed to make a theological statement. The advocates of this approach recognize the literary (rather than chronological) nature of the section, but stress in turn that the literary is used in the service of Luke's theology. Perhaps the most well-known and influential advocate of a theological interpretation of the central section is Conzelmann. His contention is that Luke has imposed the journey motif on existing material to express "his particular view of the ministry and nature of Jesus."[174] The motif symbolizes "Jesus' awareness that he must suffer," Conzelmann says. In this section "he does not travel in a different area from before, but he travels in a different manner."[175] A similar point is made by Stonehouse. Writing before Conzelmann and from a very different perspective on the gospels, Stonehouse emphasizes that, since

---

by Farrell who stresses the similarity of theological points in the seven corresponding members of the central section ("Structure," esp. 34-51).

Although the chiastic approach is suggestive and often helpful in calling attention to thematic connections within the central section, its overall plausibility is vitiated by several weaknesses. First, some of the alleged parallels are fortuitous and forced. As Resseguie points out, Luke 11:37-54 (seven woes), for example, has very little to do with money, yet according to Bailey's outline it is included under this theme (*Poet*, 80). In addition, Bailey has to disregard totally the stated audience of 16:1-13 to force vv. 9-13 into his chiasmus (Resseguie, "Instruction," 28). Second, this approach lacks rigorous criteria to determine parallels. Blomberg (who himself theorizes Luke arranged the material of the central section around a pre-Lucan chiastic parable source via topical links ["Midrash," 246]) suggests two criteria for a plausible chiasmus: (1) significant conceptual *and* verbal parallelism, and (2) parallelism close enough to exclude other equally reasonable parallels (p. 235). Without such criteria, chiastic theories run the risk of slipping into a study of thematic parallels, many of which can be so general as to allow for the discovery of parallels almost anywhere. (The latter criticism is, in fact, lodged by M. A. Tolbert [*Perspectives on the Parables* (Philadelphia: Fortress, 1979) 81-82] against Bailey's chiastic outline.) Third, "to be an effective literary device it [chiastic structure] must be fairly obvious. Yet only with concerted effort can one spot some of the parallels [in the central section]" (Resseguie, "Instruction," 28; the same criticism is made by Egelkraut, *Mission*, 58). Fourth, some outlines of Luke's alleged chiastic structure leave out significant amounts of material (Resseguie, "Interpretation," 14). Goulder's and Talbert's outlines, for example, omit 9:51-10:24 and 9:51-10:20, respectively; the former also omits 16:15-31, among other verses. It is interesting and perhaps telling against this theory that Goulder himself has apparently abandoned it in favor of Evans's thesis of a Christian Deuteronomy (see esp. Goulder, *Calendar*, 91).

[174] Conzelmann, *Luke*, 197.

[175] *Luke*, 65. As Marshall notes (*Historian*, 150 n. 4), Conzelmann does concede some didactic or paraenetic significance in the central section. This concession is found in the German edition of his book on Luke and not in the English translation. In the course of his comments on Luke 9:57-62 ("The Cost of Following Jesus" [*NIV*]), Conzelmann notes that the theme of discipleship ("Nachfolge") in these verses opens what he calls "the great paraenesis of the 'travel narrative' [die großen Paränesen des 'Reiseberichts']." Included in this paraenesis are mission instructions and comprehensive rules of Christian conduct (*Die Mitte der Zeit* [3d ed.; Tübingen: Mohr, 1960] 59).

the evangelists are not mere biographers but witnesses of the death and resurrection of Jesus Christ, the principal theme of all the canonical gospels is the passion theme.[176] This fact is reflected in Luke's central section. In this section one rarely loses sight of Jerusalem as the final destination, but, Stonehouse adds, "it is not legitimate to conclude that Luke represents Jesus as continuously en route to Jerusalem."[177] "The frequent mention of Jerusalem in this section is due not to a concern on Luke's part to mark the course of the journey to that city, but rather to disclose the inner conviction of Jesus that the messianic task was unthinkable apart from the programme of suffering and death which awaited him."[178]

Davies offers a different and slightly broader theological interpretation of the central section. According to him, the purpose of the section is to present Luke's theology of the ascension.[179] The journey to Jerusalem narrated here is "the first part of that ascent to heaven via death and resurrection which he [Luke] terms Jesus' *analēmpsis* [9:51]." The earthly journey prefigures "the real end—the journey via death into his heavenly kingdom, which brings Jesus to his glory and Jerusalem and the Jews to desolation and rejection." In the course of the journey to Jerusalem Jesus gives the disciples appropriate teaching.[180]

The note of judgment in Davies's interpretation is the keynote in Egelkraut's thesis about the central section. Egelkraut asserts that, writing after the destruction of Jerusalem, Luke's theological purpose in the central section is to explain God's judgment on Israel and Jerusalem.[181] The one leitmotif of the section,[182] the overarching theme that dominates it from beginning to end, is the confrontation and concomitant conflict between Jesus and the Jewish people which ultimately spelled

---

[176] Stonehouse, *Luke*, 110-11.

[177] *Luke*, 115-16.

[177] *Luke*, 118-19. Stonehouse seems to allow for the possibility that Luke's central section recounts Jesus' last journey to Jerusalem, but insists Luke does not portray it as a direct and hurried journey (see esp. pp. 116, 118, 126). The emphasis of Stonehouse's interpretation is, however, on the theological rather than the chronological interests of Luke. Others who maintain that the passion theme is highlighted in the central section include Lagrange (*Luc*, xxxviii: the whole section stands under the sign of Jerusalem and the passion) and Sabourin (*Luc*, 17: the journey motif accentuates the passion of Jesus).

[179] Davies, "Purpose," 164.

[180] "Purpose," 168-69. Davies emphasizes (p. 169 n. 1) that the journey sets the tone for the teaching, not vice versa (*pace* Reicke ["Instruction," 210], to whom I will come shortly).

[181] Egelkraut, *Mission*, 133.

[182] *Mission*, 199.

destruction for the nation and city.[183] Egelkraut insists the paraenetic material of the central section is subordinate to this conflict theme.[184]

4. Practical Interpretations

The title "practical" for the interpretations to be considered below should not be construed as a denial of a theological function for the central section. Such a function (particularly the presentation of Jesus as the suffering Messiah) is conceded, even stressed, in many of the following interpretations. What distinguishes these interpretations from those of the previous category is their emphasis that the primary function or purpose of the central section is to meet the practical needs of the church. Those needs may be to authenticate the witness of the apostles, to illustrate proper discipleship, or to instruct disciples and church workers.[185]

a) Authenticated witness

W. C. Robinson, Jr., suggests Luke's concept of authenticated witness is the theological context in which the central section is to be interpreted. As those who were with Jesus during his Galilean ministry and who followed him to Jerusalem, the apostles were thus prepared and qualified for their foundational role in the life and ministry of the church.[186] Much the same interpretation is advocated by Fitzmyer. The Travel Account, as he calls it, reveals Luke's theological concern to move Jesus resolutely toward Jerusalem, "the city of destiny."[187] It also presents Jesus as training Galilean witnesses for their later mission. This training serves as the basis of "assurance" for Theophilus (1:4), Fitzmyer suggests, by showing that the teaching of Luke's community is rooted in the teaching of Jesus himself.[188]

---

[183] *Mission*, 213.

[184] *Mission*, 199, 214. While a theological approach to Luke's central section generally represents a commendable advance from strictly chronological and/or literary interpretations, by itself it is weak on at least two counts. First, it cannot adequately account for the bulk of didactic material in the central section (Moessner, "Preview," 579, and Resseguie, "Instruction," 30-31, 33). Second, it often relies too heavily on the journey framework of the section, almost to the neglect of the content of the various pericopae (Resseguie, "Instruction," 33). The latter criticism is directed particularly against Conzelmann's interpretation.

[185] Resseguie, "Instruction," 34.

[186] W. C. Robinson, Jr., "The Theological Context for Interpreting Luke's Travel Narrative (9:51ff.)," *JBL* 79 (1960) 30-31.

[187] Fitzmyer, *Luke* 1.163-64 (= "Composition," 151).

[188] *Luke* 1.171; see also 1.826.

b) Discipleship

Contending that Luke's central section is concerned "less with geography than with theology," D. Gill suggests the *Reisenotizen* of this section lay special stress on the difficulties of true discipleship.[189] He writes,

> Jesus' journey is indeed a type of the Christian life, but, more than that, as a journey toward suffering it gives a rationale for the difficult things in the living of the Christian life, the things that are the biggest stumbling blocks and causes of misunderstanding for the community here and now.... We too, says Luke, must go the way of the cross.[190]

c) Instruction for disciples

A fairly large number of interpreters argue the central section is designed primarily to meet the practical need of providing instruction for disciples. Schneider and Reicke are the most influential advocates of this interpretation. Schneider asserts this section of Luke's Gospel is "distinguished by a didactic-paraenetic tendency." Luke has collected many pieces of tradition, removed chronological and topographical references from them, and arranged them so as to show the community of disciples and especially its leaders how to live and act according to God's will. The words of Jesus are thus made the basis for the thought and conduct of the Christian community.[191] Reicke takes a similar position, but argues his case differently. He argues that Luke, in order to fill the gap in earlier traditions, produced the central section by inserting two bodies of

---

[189] D. Gill, "Observations on the Lukan Travel Narrative and Some Related Passages," *HTR* 63 (1970) 208, 214.

[190] "Observations," 214.

[191] Schneider, "Analyse," 219-20. The influence of Schneider's work is evident in the interpretations of Grundmann and P. von der Osten-Sacken. Both explicitly endorse Schneider's didactic emphasis and combine it with Conzelmann's christological emphasis, with different results in each case. Grundmann contends Luke's central section portrays Jesus as a teacher faced with death. The teaching of the section is spoken in view of his death and is confirmed through his resurrection. Grundmann divides the central section into three parts, each of which contains long excursuses from Jesus' teaching ("Fragen," 259 [= *Lukas*, 200]). Our parable is part of the excursus 14:1-17:10, the focus of which is discipleship with warnings against false security and preoccupation with possessions ("Fragen," 266). Osten-Sacken argues this section occupies the central place in the process of christological clarification. Luke here deals with doubts about Jesus' messiahship caused by the delay of the parousia by showing that Jesus is the expected Messiah who must go the way of suffering to glory ("Zur Christologie des lukanischen Reiseberichts," *EvT* 33 [1973] 491-92). Noting that "an indissoluble relation" exists between christological and didactic interpretations of the central section (p. 494), Osten-Sacken writes that "Luke understands the journey of Jesus to suffering, resurrection and ascension at the same time as a time in which Jesus instructs the community for their own life in the epoch between his ascension and his parousia" (p. 495). Schneider's influence is also apparent in Stagg ("Journey," 501).

tradition (9:51-13:35 and 14:1-18:14) into the interval between the Galilean and Judean activities of Jesus.[192] This material, perhaps given its form in Antioch or another center of foreign missions,[193] has "an ecclesiastic-didactic character" which proved "valuable in answering practical questions discussed by the Church." In particular, it told Christians how they are to behave in relation to each other and to those outside the church.[194] The various pericopae of the central section therefore alternate between the main themes of instruction and discussion—instruction of the apostles regarded as ministers and missionaries, and discussion with adversaries and opponents.[195] "Each area would be important for the early Church," says Ellis in summarizing Reicke, "the former for those in congregational responsibilities and the latter for missionaries and others in contact with Jewish adversaries."[196] Reicke adds that this didactic material may have been put in the setting of a journey because "such pilgrimage [to suffering and glorification] is the lot of his [Jesus'] messengers on this earth."[197]

---

[192] Reicke, "Instruction," 207, 215.

[193] Reicke writes that in such places it would have been "valuable to recollect what the Lord had done and said in situations that corresponded to those in which Christian ministers and missionaries found themselves" ("Instruction," 215).

[194] "Instruction," 209.

[195] "Instruction," 210.

[196] Ellis, *Luke*, 147.

[197] Reicke, "Instruction," 216. Reicke's closing remarks (p. 216) about the character of the traditions Luke used in the central section is worth quoting, especially in view of the conclusions reached by some form critics. Having argued that the setting of the material contained in the central section "is to be referred to the practical needs of the missionary church," Reicke continues, "However, it may be emphasized with the greatest force that this ecclesiastic and didactic interpretation of the traditions in question does not at all eliminate the possibility of their essential authenticity. The fact that the traditions are supposed to have developed in the Church, and with regard to her interests, does not preclude our assuming that the Lord did indeed act or speak in a corresponding way. . . . Instead one should appreciate that the interest in the current problems of the Church led to the preservation of such traditions about Jesus as had especial importance for later generations of Christians." The influence of both Schneider's and Reicke's interpretations is seen in Ellis's commentary on Luke. Ellis mentions both men approvingly and himself describes Luke 9:51-19:44 as "The Teaching of Messiah," as distinct from "The Acts of Messiah" narrated in 4:31-9:50 (*Luke*, 146-47). "Luke's primary intention [in the central section]," writes Ellis, "is to present a theme not a chronicle, to present Jesus the teacher not Jesus the traveller" (p. 148). The journey motif of the central section is, therefore, "a scaffolding" on which the teaching aspect of Jesus' ministry is presented; one should not expect a chronological order in the content (p. 146). According to Ellis, the central section is arranged thematically in six sections of six episodes each (pp. 149-50; see his outline on pp. 34-35). Our parable is part of the section 13:22-16:13 (pp. 187-200) which answers the question "Who will enter the kingdom?" with "Not whom you think" (p. 187). For similar though differently outlined explanations of the central section, see Marshall, *Historian*, 152, and *Luke*, 401-2, 409-10, and Resseguie, "Instruction," 40, 180, 187-88, both of whom also endorse Reicke's approach. To the category of didactic interpretations of the central section might also be added the names of Kümmel (*Introduction*, 142), G. W. H. Lampe ("The Holy Spirit in the

From the foregoing survey of the interpretations of Luke's central section the reader can readily appreciate the difficulty of this context of our parable. The central section almost defies analysis, particularly if approached from a single perspective (e.g., only theologically). The complexities of the section notwithstanding, let me venture several conclusions by way of summary before proceeding to relate our parable to this level of literary context. It will be obvious from the following comments that I believe a practical interpretation, particularly a didactic-paraenetic approach like Schneider's and Reicke's, best explains Luke's central section.

1. The striking lack of precise geographical and chronological references in the central section strongly suggests Luke does not intend it to be read as a chronological record of a journey or journeys by Jesus. As Manson puts it, "whatever else" the section may be, "it does not appear to be a chronicle."[198]

2. Luke's interest in the central section is not in the journey per se, but the goal of the journey in view from 9:51 on.[199] The focus is Jerusalem and the things fulfilled there (cf. Luke 1:1). The whole section must, therefore, be seen in the context of Jesus' cross and resurrection.[200] Jerusalem is not merely the place where Jesus died; it is also the place where salvation is accomplished and from which witnesses carry the kerygma in Acts.[201]

3. The main concern of Luke in the central section is to present Jesus the teacher who alternately instructs his disciples and responds to his critics. The teachings of the section are given their proper perspective by the journey motif; they are the teachings of rejected Messiah, divinely destined to suffer in Jerusalem.[202]

4. If the above conclusions (especially one and three) are correct, it is likely that Luke has organized the material of the central section thematically or topically. While different thematic outlines are possible,[203] many advocates of a thematic arrangement of the central section

---

Writings of St. Luke," in *Studies in the Gospels* [ed. Nineham] 190), and Morris (*Luke*, 178)—all of whom argue Jesus here prepares his disciples for future ministry—, and Trompf, who argues for a threefold thematic organization of the didactic materials of the section ("Section," 144).

[198] Mansion, *Sayings*, 256, quoted by Resseguie, "Interpretation," 7.
[199] Ellis, *Luke*, 148-49, and Marshall, *Historian*, 151, and *Luke*, 401.
[200] Marshall, *Luke*, 401.
[201] Fitzmyer, *Luke* 1.164.
[202] Ellis, *Luke*, 147-48.
[203] Cf., e.g., Ellis, *Luke*, 32-36, and Marshall, *Luke*, 9-10, as well as various chiastic structures suggested for the section (e.g., Farrell, "Structure," 34-36).

would agree with Blomberg's assessment that "Luke was neither confused nor disorganized."[204] "In the final analysis, the dissonance between Jesus the traveler and the content that follows is more apparent than real, more a misreading of Luke's intent and procedure than an actual problem begging solution."[205]

5. The central section is designed by Luke to meet the practical needs of those to whom he writes. While the exact nature of those needs is a moot point,[206] we are justified in assuming, I believe, that at the very least Luke intends this section to contribute to his overall purpose of giving assurance to Theophilus and those like him (cf. 1:4). The central section may do so by reminding Theophilus of the cost and requirements of discipleship, and/or by confirming that what he has been taught already is in harmony with and is in fact based on Jesus' own teaching.[207]

C. Impact of Broader Literary Context on Luke 16:1-13

The broader literary context of Luke's central section clarifies our parable in several ways. First, the alternation of instruction and discussion which characterizes the section accounts for the change of audience at the beginning of our parable (cf. 15:1-2) and then again at 16:14, without resorting to the conclusion that Luke's introduction in 16:1 is too abrupt and/or inaccurate. As Sellin points out, the pattern of alternation is quite clear in Luke 15:1-17:10. Luke 15:1-32 and 16:14-31 are spoken to opponents, 16:1-13 and 17:1-10 to disciples. The purpose of this

---

[204] Blomberg, "Midrash," 247. Blomberg continues, "He was not attempting to trace Jesus' journey either chronologically or geographically and so cannot be accused of being a bad historian on either account. Of course Jesus' early ministry was in Galilee while his last weeks were spent in and near Jerusalem, so that he obviously had to travel from the one area to the other at some point. Many of the teachings of Luke's central section may well have been uttered by Jesus on this journey, but they need not have been, and certainly not necessarily in the order in which they now appear." Ellis writes in similar fashion. "This editorial arrangement [in the central section] is not 'erroneous' unless one insists on judging Luke as a 19th-century historian. . . . Nor is it arbitrary: the Evangelist shapes his materials for a particular literary purpose [i.e., to present Jesus the teacher]. Probably the bulk of Jesus' teachings did come in the latter stages of his ministry. And, of course, there is a very general chronological scheme common to all Gospel writers . . . But for Luke all this is quite secondary, almost as though it were taken for granted" (*Luke*, 149).

[205] This conclusion is from Moessner's summary of what he terms the "traditional-logical" approach to the central section ("Preview," 578-79).

[206] E.g., to train missionaries, combat heretics, alleviate doubts about Jesus' messiahship, authenticate the apostolic witness, and/or explain Israel's rejection of Messiah. See Resseguie, "Interpretation," 35-36, and "Instruction," 191-191d, for a summary of the explanations of the needs of Luke's readers.

[207] The latter suggestion is made by Fitzmyer, *Luke* 1.171 (= "Composition," 151).

literary device, Sellin believes, is to indicate the subsections of that larger context.[208] "The whole structure is dramatic," he concludes. "One could almost speak of act (main-section) and scene (sub-section)."[209] Whatever one makes of Sellin's conclusion, he is to be credited for pointing out that the broader pattern into which our parable fits is purposive. Change of audience alone is, therefore, insufficient grounds for questioning or disregarding Luke's introduction in 16:1. On the contrary, to judge from the pattern of Luke 15:1-17:10 a change of audience is quite expected at 16:1. This literary feature in Luke's central section thus confirms the argument in chapter two that Luke's introduction to our parable should be taken seriously. It is significant, furthermore, that although shifts of audience in the central section may signal shifts of topic, sometimes Jesus continues to speak on the same topic while relating it to a new audience. Such is the case in Luke 16, I have argued, and there is at least one other instance of this phenomenon in the central section, i.e., 12:13-34.[210] This precedent, along with the topical arrangement of the central section as a whole, lends further weight to my earlier contention that the theme of chapter 16, in general, and our parable, in particular, is the use of material possessions.

The topical structure of the central section suggests a second way in which this broader contextual level throws light on the parable of the unjust steward. A variety of topics are covered in the central section,[211] and Tannehill makes the following observation about Luke's method.

> The narrator prefers returning to major topics of teaching repeatedly, rather than grouping related teaching in a single discourse, thus reinforcing through recurrence and suggesting that Jesus was repeatedly engaged in this type of teaching. When Jesus keeps returning to the same topics, we realize that he is not dealing with momentary concerns but with weighty matters of lasting importance.[212]

Among the "weighty matters" thus dealt with in Luke's central section are the themes of possessions and discipleship. To judge from the prominence of these themes throughout the central section and the gospel as a whole, both must have been particularly relevant for Luke's goal of giving assurance to Theophilus. Both themes intersect in our parable. The theme of possessions, prominent in Luke's Gospel, is the

---

[208] Sellin, "Studien," 198-99.

[209] "Studien," 199.

[210] The phenomenon of change of audience without change of topic in both Luke 12 and 16 is noted by Tannehill, *Unity*, 241. The topic in both cases is material possessions.

[211] For a list of the prominent themes in the central section, see Ellis, *Luke*, 146; Farrell, "Structure," 34-37; and Tannehill, *Unity*, 242.

[212] Tannehill, *Unity*, 243.

subject of two major passages in the central section other than Luke 16 (12:13-34 and 18:18-30), as well as several smaller but important units (11:39, 41; 14:12-14, 33; 19:8). Since these passages are part of the Lucan theme of poverty and riches, discussion of them will be deferred until the next chapter where that theme will be considered.

While in a sense the theme of discipleship is implicit in every instruction to the disciples in the central section (cf., e.g., 12:4-12, 49-53), it is explicit in two passages—Luke 9:57-62 and 14:25-35. In both passages Jesus warns would-be followers about the cost of discipleship, telling them that discipleship demands undivided loyalty, wholehearted commitment to him. Of particular importance for our parable is the fact that in 14:33 Jesus singles out possessions as one of the threats or obstacles to such commitment. "So therefore," Jesus says to potential disciples in the crowds, "no one of you can be My disciple who does not give up all his own possessions" (*NASB*). Whether or not this statement is a universal demand for total renunciation of possessions and our parable must be similarly understood is a matter to be considered in the next chapter. What is worthy of note at this point is the recurrence of the topic of possessions in chapter 16. The proximity of our parable to this specific warning in 14:33 is striking and hardly seems fortuitous. It may suggest that Luke 16:1-13 is in a sense the positive counterpart to 14:33. In 14:33 Jesus warns would-be disciples that an attachment to possessions precludes discipleship; in 16:1-13, he instructs his disciples what discipleship involves, i.e., the use of worldly wealth for the sake of others (v. 9). There is, in a vein similar to 14:33, the added warning in 16:10-12 that unfaithfulness disqualifies one from greater privileges and blessings. Whatever the exact relationship of our parable to 14:33 may be, there is little question that Luke wants his readers to understand that a proper use of possessions is an integral part of true discipleship. The intersection of the two themes in our parable is perhaps best summed up by Ellis in the title he gives to Luke 16:1-13: "Faithfulness: The Badge of Acceptable Discipleship."[213]

A third way Luke's central section clarifies the interpretation of our parable is by reiterating the eschatological background of Jesus' teaching about possessions. It is widely recognized that the kingdom of God is the central topic of Jesus' preaching as a whole; it is, as Ellis notes, "the dominant motif" in the teaching of the central section.[214] Twenty of the thirty-two occurrences of the expression "kingdom of God" in

---

[213] *Luke*, 198.
[214] *Luke*, 12. Farrell makes much the same point ("Structure," 37-38).

Luke's Gospel, for example, are found on the lips of Jesus in this section.[215] While a more detailed discussion of Jesus' teaching on this theme must wait until the next chapter, it is worth pointing out here that the eschatological note is also present and pronounced in the two other major sections on possessions in the central section (Luke 12 and 18:18-30). It is not surprising, therefore, that we should find eschatological nuances in our parable as well as explicit reference to the kingdom in the immediate context (16:16). The pervasiveness of the kingdom in the central section confirms that the point of our parable is stewardship in an eschatological context.

III. Summary/Conclusions

In this chapter two levels of literary context of Luke 16:1-13 have been examined, the immediate context in Luke 15:1-32 and 16:14-31 and the broader context in Luke's central section. Both contextual levels bring the meaning of the parable of the unjust steward into sharper focus.

The immediate literary context, Luke 15:1-32 and 16:14-31, clarifies our parable in the following ways:

1. The emphasis on money and material possessions in Luke 16:14, 19-31, and the literary unity of the entire chapter confirms that material possessions is the theme of our parable as well. Vv. 1-13 give positive instruction on proper stewardship of the same, while vv. 14-31 warn about the consequences of unfaithfulness (cf. vv. 11-12), in particular, of neglecting to care for the poor.

2. The parable of the rich man and Lazarus in Luke 16:19-31 elucidates the meaning of the otherwise obscure exhortation in v. 9 of our parable. The life-situations and destinies of the rich man and Lazarus suggest that making friends by means of worldly wealth includes care for the poor.

3. The polemic context in which our parable occurs (cf. 15:1-2 and 16:14) emphasizes the parable's teaching by setting it against the background of the Pharisees' faults, in particular, their greed. The attitude toward and conduct with possessions enjoined in vv. 1-13 stand in stark contrast to the Pharisees in this area.

---

[215] Luke 9:60, 62; 10:9, 11; 11:20; 13:18,* 20,* 28-29; 14:15;* 16:16; 17:20 (2 times), 21; 18:16-17, 24, 25, 29; 19:11* (an asterisk indicates the occurrence of the phrase in connection with a parable). The statistics are taken from W. F. Moulton, A. S. Geden, and H. K. Moulton, eds., *A Concordance to the Greek Testament* (Edinburgh: T. & T. Clark, 1978), s.v., "*basileia*."

4. Luke 16:16 in particular reiterates the eschatological context of Jesus' teaching in vv. 1-13 and focuses the eschatological nuances in those verses. Further confirmation is thus supplied that the faithful stewardship taught in vv. 1-13 is eschatologically motivated.

5. The emphasis on the continuing validity of the law and the prophets in Luke 16:17-18, 29, 31, suggests Jesus' teaching in vv. 1-13 is in fundamental harmony with God's will as revealed in the OT. More specifically, care for the poor is not cancelled by the coming of the kingdom, but is to be an ongoing concern of God's people.

The broader literary context, Luke's central section, enhances our understanding of the parable in these ways:

1. The pattern of alternation between instruction and discussion into which our parable fits sets the teaching of our parable against the background of the running controversy between Jesus and the religious leaders of Israel. At least in chapter 16, where the topic remains the same although the audience changes, the discussion with the Pharisees in vv. 14-31 clarifies vv. 1-13 by contrasting the attitudes of the given parties.

2. The thematic connections between our parable and other passages in the central section—e.g., 14:25-35—indicate that the faithful stewardship exhorted in our parable is an integral part of genuine discipleship. Whether or not one shows charity to the poor is evidence of the true nature of one's ultimate loyalties. To judge from Luke's underlying didactic-paraenetic concerns, such teaching apparently would have special relevance for those to whom he writes.

3. The prominence of the theme of the kingdom of God in Jesus' teaching in the central section confirms the eschatological background of our parable. Jesus' teaching in 16:1-13 is eschatologically conditioned and motivated.

The two levels of literary context considered in this chapter confirm the basic thesis of this study, i.e., the parable of the unjust steward and its application(s) (Luke 16:1-13) teach charitable use of material possessions against an eschatological background. This confirmation does not, of course, answer all questions about the parable. Some loose ends remain to be tied up, in particular, how Jesus' broader teaching about riches and poverty and the kingdom of God affects the interpretation of this parable. These contextual matters are the subjects of the next chapter.

CHAPTER FOUR

THE THEOLOGICAL CONTEXT

Thus far I have examined Luke 16:1-13 in relative isolation (chapter two) and in its immediate and broader literary contexts (chapter three). In this final chapter the discussion will be expanded further by relating the parable to the theology of Luke-Acts, in general, and to two thematic strands of that theology, in particular.[1] Those themes are riches and poverty and the kingdom of God. My goal again is to show how this contextual level brings the meaning of our parable into sharper focus.

I. GENERAL SURVEY OF LUCAN STUDIES

During the latter half of the twentieth century a "revolution in Lucan studies"[2] has taken place in which the theology of Luke-Acts plays the central role. To sketch the general course of these developments and trends will set the background for the present chapter.[3]

As J. Kodell observes, "Luke has always claimed a large share of the exegetes' attention. For quantity, he is the chief contributor to the NT; and Acts is the only source for much information about the early development of the Church."[4] Until about 1950, most of that attention was focused on the sources of Luke the historian and the question of his

---

[1] Space constraints necessitate limiting the discussion of Luke's theology by and large to the Third Gospel.

[2] Marshall, *Luke*, 15.

[3] Of the vast literature that could be cited, the following works (listed in chronological order) are particularly noteworthy for their helpful summaries of and bibliographies on Lucan studies: C. K. Barrett, *Luke the Historian in Recent Study* (London: Epworth, 1961); W. C. van Unnik, "Luke-Acts, A Storm Center in Contemporary Scholarship," in *Studies in Luke-Acts* (ed. L. E. Keck and J. L. Martyn) 15-32; Marshall, "Recent Study of the Gospel according to St. Luke," and "Recent Study of the Acts of the Apostles," *ExpTim* 80 (1968) 4-8 and 292-96, respectively; Kümmel, "Luc en accusation dans la théologie contemporaine," *ETL* 46 (1970) 265-81(this article appeared in German translation in *ZNW* 63 [1972] 149-65, and in English in *ANQ* 16 [1975] 131-45; the latter is the source of the subsequent citations of the article); J. Kodell, "The Theology of Luke in Recent Thought," *BTB* 1 (1971) 115-44; W. W. Gasque, *A History of the Criticism of the Acts of the Apostles* (Grand Rapids: Eerdmans, 1975); Talbert, "Shifting Sands: The Recent Study of the Gospel of Luke," *Int* 30 (1976) 381-95; Fitzmyer, *Luke* 1.3-34; E. Richard, "Luke—Writer, Theologian, Historian: Research and Orientation of the 1970's," *BTB* 13 (1983) 3-15; and Gasque, "A Fruitful Field: Recent Study of the Acts of the Apostles," *Int* 42/2 (1988) 117-31, esp. 118 n. 2.

[4] Kodell, "Theology," 117-18.

reliability in that capacity. This state of affairs in Lucan studies is summarized and typified in the title and substance of C. K. Barrett's book, *Luke the Historian in Recent Study*. With the advent of redaction criticism in the late 1940s and early 1950s, however, the situation changed. The gospel writers came to be seen as creative theologians "writing with certain definite objectives [closely related] to [the problem situation of] a particular group of readers."[5] This fundamental change of perspective, which in the case of Luke-Acts owed much to the earlier stylistic and form-critical work of H. J. Cadbury[6] and Dibelius,[7] shifted the focus of attention from Luke the historian to Luke the theologian. The focus has by and large remained there ever since.

The individual most responsible for this shift in Lucan studies is H. Conzelmann.[8] In his book *Die Mitte der Zeit*, first published in 1954,[9] Conzelmann argued that Luke-Acts is, to use Perrin's words, "Luke's response to the central problem of his day, namely, the delay of the parousia and the subsequent necessity for the church to come to grips with its continued existence in the world."[10] To this end Luke allegedly abandoned the primitive eschatology of tradition in favor of a three-

---

[5] Seccombe, *Possessions*, 12. For discussions of the background and methods of redaction criticism, see N. Perrin, *What Is Redaction Criticism?* (Philadelphia: Fortress, 1969); J. Rohde, *Rediscovering the Teaching of the Evangelists* (Philadelphia: Westminster, 1968); S. S. Smalley, "Redaction Criticism," in *New Testament Interpretation* (ed. Marshall; Exeter/Grand Rapids: Paternoster/Eerdmans, 1977) 181-95; and Stein, "What is *Redaktionsgeschichte?*" *JBL* 88 (1969) 45-56. Cf. also Silva, "N. B. Stonehouse and Redaction Criticism," *WTJ* 40 (1977-78) 77-88, 281-303.

[6] H. J. Cadbury, *The Style and Literary Method of Luke* (Cambridge: Harvard University Press, 1920), and *The Making of Luke-Acts* (New York: Macmillan, 1928; repr. London: SPCK, 1958). As the title of the latter work indicates, it was Cadbury who popularized the phrase "Luke-Acts" to emphasize the historic unity of the two volumes to Theophilus (p. 11). The common authorship and unity of both books is almost universally accepted today, although whether or not the author is Luke, the physician and companion of Paul, is still a moot point in many circles.

[7] Dibelius, *Aufsätze zur Apostelgeschichte* (ed. H. Greeven; Göttingen: Vandenhoeck & Ruprecht, 1951; ET, *Studies in the Acts of the Apostles* [London: SCM, 1956]). This book is a collection of essays by Dibelius dating mostly from the 1920s, 1930s, and 1940s. The connection between redaction critical work in Luke's writings and the earlier work of Cadbury and Dibelius is pointed out by, among others, Kodell, "Theology," 117, and Richard, "Luke," 3.

[8] Other pioneers in Lucan studies during the period under consideration include E. Käsemann, P. Vielhauer, and E. Haenchen. See Kodell ("Theology," 116-17), Kümmel ("Accusations," 132-33), and Talbert ("Sands," 381-83) for bibliographic details and summaries of the influence of these individuals. Talbert ("Sands," 381) traces the roots of the shift from Luke the historian to Luke the theologian to Bultmann's *Theology of the New Testament*.

[9] Tübingen: Mohr. The English translation, from which all citations in this chapter are taken, appeared in 1960 under the rather prosaic title *The Theology of Saint Luke* (New York: Harper).

[10] Perrin, *Redaction Criticism*, 32.

staged redemptive history of his own making.[11] Conzelmann's work proved very influential in Lucan studies and, along with Haenchen's work on Acts, created something of "a temporary consensus" about Luke's purpose, structure, and method of composition.[12] Conzelmann did not go unchallenged, however. Reactions to his thesis increased to the point that by 1966 Unnik described Luke-Acts as "one of the great storm centers of New Testament scholarship."[13] In the opinion of Gasque, the very book in which Unnik's assessment appeared (*Studies in Luke-Acts*) illustrated "the malaise of contemporary Lucan research"; there was "no general agreement among scholars on even the most basic issues of Lucan research."[14]

The largely negative and somewhat chaotic situation in Lucan studies in the 1950s and 1960s gradually gave way to a decidedly more positive atmosphere in the 1970s and 1980s. While most of the scholarly attention in these two decades has remained focused on Luke the theologian, Luke was now taken on his own terms. Rather than being compared (often unfavorably) with Paul, as was the case in much of the scholarship of the 1950s and 1960s, Luke's writings began to be studied and valued in terms of their own contribution to New Testament theology. Kümmel and Marshall illustrate and set the tone for this more positive approach. In a well-known article Kümmel defended Luke against five common accusations raised by contemporary scholars, and concluded that "Luke remains, in the main lines of his theology, in agreement with the central proclamation of the New Testament."[15] Marshall argued much the same point in a book which came out the same year as Kümmel's article. He contended Luke was at one and the same time an essentially reliable historian and a major, orthodox New Testament theologian.[16] By the early 1980s the general mood in Lucan studies had changed to the point that Richard could assert "Luke-Acts can no longer be considered a

---

[11] For Conzelmann's own statement of the key points of his thesis, see *Luke*, 13-14, 16-17 (esp. 17 n. 2), 96-97, 131-32, 135. Conzelmann's thesis will be discussed further in the section on Luke's eschatology.

[12] Richard, "Luke," 3.

[13] Unnik, "Storm Center," 16.

[14] Gasque, *Acts*, 303 and 305, respectively.

[15] "Accusations," 143. The accusations to which Kümmel responded are the following (as summarized by Richard, "Luke," 4): "delay of the parousia, elimination of the salvific character of the cross, capitulation to 'early Catholicism,' and the historicization of both faith and kerygma."

[16] Marshall, *Luke: Historian and Theologian*. Marshall maintains the same perspective in his commentary on Luke. Other representatives of and contributors to this more positive assessment of at least the theology of Luke-Acts include Ellis (*Luke*; cf., e.g., p. 2, where he defends Luke as historian, theologian, and littérateur), Talbert (esp. *Patterns* and *Reading Luke*), and, more recently, Tannehill (*Unity*).

'storm center' of controversy. Instead," he concludes, "Luke's work is now viewed as one of several major contributions of the early community to Christian theology and history."[17] Much the same optimistic assessment has been offered even more recently by Gasque.[18] While it would be a mistake to conclude that all the issues and problems in Lucan studies have been resolved, it is nonetheless significant that Luke's two-volume work is now widely valued for the part it plays in both New Testament history and theology.

The issues in the past and present debates about Lucan theology are too numerous and complex to discuss in detail here.[19] To do so, moreover, is unnecessary for the purposes of this chapter. As suggested at the outset, however, two important thematic threads in the fabric of Luke's theology do warrant attention because of their relevance to the parable of the unjust steward. They are the themes of riches and poverty and the kingdom of God (or eschatology). The first has obvious connections with our parable and is the focus of the next section. The second, the kingdom of God, while not unique to Luke's gospel, figures prominently in debates about Luke's theology, and is present in Luke 16:1-13 itself as well as in the immediate and broader literary contexts. The eschatological theme in Luke's theology will be discussed more carefully in the third section. It will be shown that this theme has an important bearing on the teaching of our parable. In each section brief observations will be offered about the possible function of the respective themes for Luke's *Sitz im Leben*.

---

[17] Richard, "Luke," 12.

[18] Gasque, "Field." "One conclusion," Gasque writes, "that unites nearly all recent study on Luke-Acts is that Conzelmann's classic formulation of the purpose of the Lukan writings ... was incorrect. Luke-Acts was certainly not written to deal with the problem of the delay of the Parousia" (p. 118). Although no consensus exists about the exact formulation of Luke's purpose, Gasque suggests there has been "a movement toward an agreement concerning how to approach the problem" (p. 119). His article outlines this movement in terms of four questions. Gasque's recent assessment of Lucan studies is strikingly different from and more positive than his earlier work on Acts. This difference in tone and conclusions illustrates how much Lucan studies have changed in the last two decades.

[19] Among the major issues that have occupied and/or continue to occupy the energies of Lucan scholars are eschatology, soteriology, ecclesiology, christology, historical value, and Luke's purpose(s). For summaries and discussions of these and other issues, see Kümmel, "Accusations"; Kodell, "Theology"; F. Bovon, *Luc le théologien: Vingt-cinq ans de recherches (1950-75)* (Neuchâtel/Paris: Delachaux & Niestlé, 1978); Fitzmyer, *Luke* 1.3-29 (esp. pp. 8-29); and Richard, "Luke."

II. Riches and Poverty in Luke-Acts

Given the argument in chapters two and three that the parable of the unjust steward treats the disciples' wise use of material possessions, the well-known Lucan emphasis on riches and poverty is a natural place to begin a discussion of the theological context of the parable. As noted in the previous chapter, this theme is particularly prominent in the central section of Luke's Gospel.[20] It also pervades the rest of Luke-Acts.[21] The sheer quantity of material relating to riches and poverty indicates "the question of possessions clearly occupies a high priority on Luke's agenda of concerns."[22] "No other NT writer—save perhaps the author of the Epistle of James, and then only in an analogous way—speaks as emphatically as does Luke about the Christian disciple's use of material possessions, wealth, and money."[23] While gone are the days of attributing this emphasis to Ebionism in either Luke or his sources,[24] and many would agree with Fitzmyer that this teaching originates from the historical Jesus and not Luke himself,[25] it is striking nonetheless that Luke has retained or included so much material on the theme of riches and poverty. Why has he done so? What is he saying? To whom is he saying it? These are questions to be explored in this section, all the while keeping in mind how this theme, of which our parable is a part, casts light on our parable itself.

The literature on riches and poverty in Luke-Acts is extensive.[26] Despite this fact, however, the questions just noted are far from settled. The major source of difficulty is the apparent contradiction between teaching on renunciation of possessions and the dangers of riches, on the one hand, and positive exhortations to use possessions on behalf of others, on the other hand. In Johnson's opinion, "the problem we face is

---

[20] E.g., 10:34-35; 11:39-41; 12:13-34; 14:12-35; 16:1-31; 18:18-30; 19:1-10.

[21] Luke 1:51-53; 3:10-14; 4:18-19; 5:11, 28; 6:20, 24; 7:21-22; 8:1-3, 14; 20:45-21:4; Acts 2:44-45; 4:32-5:11; 6:1-6; 8:18-25; 9:36; 10:2, 4, 31; 11:29; 20:28-35; 24:17. Seccombe estimates "approximately 27% of the 600 odd verses of teaching material" in Luke 3-22 relate to the theme of possessions and the poor (*Possessions*, 12 n. 5).

[22] Pilgrim, *Good News*, 109.

[23] Fitzmyer, *Luke* 1.247.

[24] See Dupont, *Beatitudes* 3.150 n. 4 for references.

[25] Fitzmyer, *Luke* 1.248.

[26] A number of the more important works on this theme in Luke-Acts will be cited in the following pages. For bibliographies of literature on this theme, see Dupont, *Beatitudes* 3.152 n. 1; Fitzmyer, *Luke* 1.269; Hoyt, "Poor," 257-77; Keck, "Poor," *IDBSup*, 675; R. Koch, "Die Wertung des Besitzes im Lukasevangelium," *Bib* 38 (1957) 151 n. 1; D. L. Mealand, *Poverty and Expectation in the Gospels* (London: SPCK, 1980) 16 n. 1, 99-100, 103-4; Pilgrim, *Good News*, 16 (esp. n. 5), 193-98; and Seccombe, *Possessions*, 236-75.

that although Luke consistently talks about possessions, he does not talk about possessions consistently."[27] Luke appears to have both negative and positive attitudes towards riches and material possessions in general,[28] and the relevant passages will be discussed under these two headings. Closely related to this apparent contradiction, particularly the "negative"[29] attitude toward riches, is the widely held opinion that Luke's use of the material on this theme reveals a special bias on his part *for* the poor and *against* the rich. I will challenge this "dominant view"[30] that Luke is "the evangelist of the poor." The thesis I will argue is that Luke is neither inconsistent nor does he have a special bias for the poor or against the rich. He neither condemns riches nor glorifies poverty as such. His main concern in using the material on riches and poverty is to warn his rich readers of the potentially fatal obstacle riches pose for wholehearted discipleship and thereby to exhort them to faithful and charitable use of their possessions. Our parable is part of the latter instruction. While it is as much an overstatement to call Luke "the evangelist of the rich"[31] as it is to call him "the evangelist of the poor," the former description at least highlights his positive concern for the rich. The theme of riches and poverty is meant to serve Luke's basic reason for writing his two-volume work, i.e., to confirm Theophilus in the things he had been taught (1:4).

[27] Johnson, *Function*, 130. Cf. also Johnson, *Sharing Possessions: Mandate and Symbol of Faith* (Philadelphia: Fortress, 1981) 20: "If the ideals of total renunciation and almsgiving are not mutually exclusive, at least they are impossible to practice at one and the same time. To give alms on a continuing basis, one must have something to give; one must maintain some possessions." As the latter title implies, Johnson's way out of this difficulty is to suggest that the poor/possessions motif is used symbolically in Luke-Acts for a person's reception or rejection of Jesus. Although not agreeing with Johnson's premises about Luke's inconsistency, I do concur in large measure with his basic conclusion that sharing possessions is a mandate and symbol of faith.

[28] Fitzmyer (*Luke* 1.249) speaks of "a twofold attitude" in Luke: "(a) a moderate attitude, which advocates a prudent use of material possessions to give assistance to human beings less fortunate or to manifest a basic openness to the message that Jesus is preaching; and (b) a radical attitude, which recommends the renunciation of all wealth or possessions."

[29] "Negative," in quotation marks and/or unless otherwise qualified, indicates my conviction that Luke's attitude toward possessions is really not as negative as is sometimes thought or as may appear to be.

[30] Seccombe, *Possessions*, 13.

[31] This expression and concept is from Schottroff and Stegemann, *Jesus*, 117 (see also pp. 87, 91-92). The suggestion that the material on riches and poverty in Luke-Acts reflects Luke's concern for the rich rather than pity for the poor is made by Cadbury, *Making*, 258, 260-63. Much the same position is taken by Karris, "Poor," 116, 124 (= "The Lukan Sitz im Leben: Methodology and Prospects," in *SBL 1976 Seminar Papers* [ed. G. MacRae; Missoula, MT: Scholars Press, 1976] 228); Mealand, *Poverty*, 20, 91; Seccombe, *Possessions*, 3, 13 (esp. n. 8); and Stonehouse, *Luke*, 164. Even Pilgrim, who takes pains to qualify Cadbury's position (see *Good News*, 163 n. 4), comes to essentially the same conclusion (pp. 163-64). Also cf. Plummer (*Luke*, xxv-xxvi), who notes Luke is concerned to make the rich less worldly.

A. "Negative" Attitude toward Riches/the Rich

1. Bias for Poor and against Rich?

One aspect of Luke's "negative" attitude toward riches is an apparent bias for the poor and against the rich. Since this issue will affect our perspective on other teaching on riches and poverty in Luke-Acts, it is an appropriate place to begin our discussion of this theme. Although the question can be answered fully only after a thorough examination of all the material on riches and poverty in Luke-Acts, there are several key passages which give rise to the popular conception that Luke has these biases. They are Luke 1:50-53, 4:18-19, and 6:20-26. Each will be considered to see whether or not it in fact supports this conception.

a) Luke 1:50-53

The chords of the riches/poverty motif are struck for the first time in Luke's Gospel in the Magnificat (1:46-55). In this song of "a true Israelite,"[32] Mary praises God for the coming of Messiah. Of particular significance for the present discussion are vv. 50-53. In these verses Mary describes God's forthcoming salvation in terms of the reversal of the circumstances of the humble and the rich (vv. 52-53, respectively; cf. 6:20-26). The statement in v. 53 that God "has sent the rich away empty" has even been called "the *locus classicus*" for Luke's hostility to the rich.[33] While a great deal could be said about these verses, an observation about their structure will suffice to show they provide no evidence of either hostility to the rich or partiality for the poor.

The Hebrew-like poetic parallelism of the Magnificat is often noted.[34] The parallel members in vv. 50-53 suggest the basic contrast here is not economic or political in nature, but rather religious. On the one side, there are rulers (v. 52a) and the rich (v. 53b); on the other (note the chiasmus), the humble (v. 52b) and the hungry (v. 53a). Overarching and defining the respective kinds of people is the contrast in vv. 50-51 between those who fear God and those who are "proud in their inmost thoughts." While the various terms used here may reflect economic realities, and overspiritualizing must be guarded against,[35] the decisive

---

[32] Seccombe, *Possessions*, 81.
[33] Mealand, *Poverty*, 28.
[34] E.g., Godet, *Luke* 1.104, and Marshall, *Luke*, 78.
[35] Marshall, *Luke*, 85.

factor in the destinies of these people is their attitude toward God. Those who are humble and fear God will be lifted up, those who are proud and self-sufficient will be brought down. The same point is repeated elsewhere in Luke's Gospel (e.g., 14:11; 18:14).

b) Luke 4:18-19

The story of Jesus' rejection at Nazareth in Luke 4:16-30 is widely acknowledged as programmatic for Luke's description of the ministry of Jesus.[36] Fitzmyer expresses this consensus well in the following words.

> Luke has deliberately put this story at the beginning of the public ministry to encapsulate the entire ministry of Jesus and the reaction to it. The fulfillment-story stresses the success of his teaching under the guidance of the Spirit, but the rejection story symbolizes the opposition that his ministry will evoke among his own. The rejection of him by the people of his hometown is the miniature of the rejection by the people of his own *patris* in the larger sense.[37]

This story is significant for our purposes because of the way in which Jesus' ministry and mission is characterized in vv. 18-19. In those verses, in a quotation from the OT, Jesus defines his mission in terms of, among other things, having been anointed to "preach good news to the poor" (v. 18). This statement, perhaps more than any other single statement in Luke-Acts, is responsible for the opinion that Luke is "the evangelist of the poor."[38] We need to ask, then, who are the poor here?

---

[36] The programmatic character of Luke 4:16-30 is noted by, among others, B. Chilton, "Announcement in Nazara: An Analysis of Luke 4:16-21," in *Gospel Perspectives. Studies in History and Tradition in the Four Gospels* (vol. 2; ed. R. T. France and D. Wenham; Sheffield: JSOT Press, 1981) 150, 168; M. Dumais, "L'évangelisation des pauvres dans l'oeuvre de Luc," *ScEs* 36/3 (1984) 299 n. 8; Kodell, "Luke's Gospel in a Nutshell (Lk 4:16-30)," *BTB* 13 (1983) 16-18; Marshall, *Historian*, 118; H. Schürmann, *Das Lukasevangelium* (HTKNT; Freiburg: Herder, 1969) 1:225; and Seccombe, *Possessions*, 44. For bibliography on this passage, see Fitzmyer, *Luke* 1.539-40; Marshall, *Luke*, 180-81; and Schürmann, *Lukasevangelium* 1.225. One notable exception to the prevailing opinion about the programmatic character of Luke 4:16-30 is Stonehouse. He contends that to describe this passage as programmatic is misleading because it does not sum up the distinctive testimony of Luke to Christ (*Luke*, 76). What is more, the reserve here in disclosing Jesus' person, and the fact that the further actions and reactions are "unrepresentative" of Jesus' Galilean ministry as a whole, provide additional evidence that the passage is not intended to be programmatic (p. 88). These reservations notwithstanding, Stonehouse does agree the passage is generally indicative of the contents of Jesus' message (p. 89) and has important bearings on the understanding of his public ministry as a whole (p. 69).

[37] Fitzmyer, *Luke* 1.529. For other statements of the main themes of Luke-Acts contained *in nuce* in Luke 4:16-30, see Kodell, "Nutshell," 16; Marshall, *Luke*, 178; and Pilgrim, *Good News*, 64-65. Also see Ellis, who stresses rejection of the Messiah as the keynote of this inaugural address of the Galilean ministry (*Luke*, 96).

[38] Pilgrim, e.g., asserts that the theme of good news to the poor here "belongs to the heart and center of the Lukan story" (*Good News*, 64), by which he means Luke-Acts as a whole.

To answer this question, a consideration of the OT background and context is crucial.

At the risk of overgeneralization, *ptōchoi* in the OT[39] often combines the ideas of weakness and dependence on God, and draws attention to "the needy condition of the sufferer which God alone can cure."[40] In the Psalms especially, the word is used as the self-description of the pious man who calls on God to help him (e.g., Ps 86:1; 12:5).[41] While often associated with literal poverty, *ptōchoi* in the OT is not limited to people in this economic condition alone; depending on the context, it may have a spiritual meaning.[42] I would suggest the more-than-literal sense of *ptōchoi* is present in Isaiah 61, the passage from which the quotation in Luke 4:18-19 is taken.[43] As Stonehouse, among others, notes, the context of Isaiah 61 is eschatological, and the passage itself reiterates and reinforces the message of the redemption of God's people which is the dominant theme of Isaiah.[44] Isaiah 61 is, therefore, a prophecy of the eschatological salvation of the new age to come expressed in the imagery of Israel's release from captivity and of the Jubilee. Having read the passage and sat down, Jesus' declaration that "Today this scripture is fulfilled in your hearing" (v. 21) is an announcement that in his person and ministry the eschatological age, when the injustices and conse-

---

[39] In the LXX *ptōchos* is used to translate several Hebrew words, the details of which can be found in Marshall, *Luke*, 249. For a careful discussion of the OT background of poor/ poverty, the following are particularly helpful: R. J. Coggins, "The Old Testament and the Poor," *ExpTim* 99/1 (1987) 11-14; A. Gelin, *The Poor of Yahweh* (Collegeville, MN: Liturgical Press, 1964) 15-26; A. George, "Poverty in the Old Testament," in *Gospel Poverty* (ed. A. George; Chicago: Franciscan Herald Press, 1977) 3-24 (esp. 3 n. 1 for bibliography); Hoyt, "Poor," 13-61; Pilgrim, *Good News*, 19-38; Seccombe, *Possessions*, 24-43; and J. E. Weir, "The Poor are Powerless. A Response to R. J. Coggins," *ExpTim* 100/1 (1988) 13-15.

[40] Marshall, *Historian*, 122-23.

[41] Marshall, *Luke*, 249. Cf. S. Gillingham ("The Poor in the Psalms," *ExpTim* 100/1 [1988] 15-19, esp. 16), who argues the four main Hebrew words in the Psalter which describe the poor cannot be classified neatly in terms of economic deprivation, or even in terms of a particular religious group, but must each be taken in its given context.

[42] Even G. Gutiérrez, the theologian of liberation theology, admits that in the OT, particularly in the Psalms, poverty acquired a spiritual meaning as the opposite of pride. According to him, this spiritual poverty comes to its highest expression in Matthew's beatitudes (Matt 5:3) (*A Theology of Liberation* [Maryknoll, NY: Orbis, 1973] 296-97). In Gutiérrez's judgment Luke's version (6:20), to which we will come, is different than Matthew's, referring instead to concrete and material poverty (297-98).

[43] The quotation in Luke 4:18-19 is actually a rather curious combination of two different passages from Isaiah. Most of the quotation, including the phrase about preaching good news to the poor, is from Isaiah 61:1-2. Inserted into this passage, however, is the phrase "to release the oppressed" from Isaiah 58:6. For a discussion of possible explanations of this reading, see Seccombe, *Possessions*, 46-52.

[44] Stonehouse, *Luke*, 80.

quences of sin will be overcome, is in the process of fulfillment.[45] As will become clearer in the discussion of eschatology, this fulfillment shares in the tension between the present and future aspects of the kingdom of God. Jesus did bring at least a foretaste of the blessings of the promised eschatological salvation (e.g., his miracles, cf. especially 7:21-22), and it would be a mistake to interpret his mission in purely spiritual terms. Yet at best the fulfillment is only partial, and the fullness of the eschatological salvation prophesied by Isaiah awaits the consummation of the kingdom at the parousia. These matters will be discussed in more detail later. At this point, however, it should be emphasized that against the OT background just outlined the poor in Luke 4:18 are not simply all the poor as such, nor even Israel in need of salvation.[46] Rather the poor (and the other groups mentioned in vv. 18-19 as well) are the righteous remnant of Israel,[47] the true people of God.[48] "In contrast to those who have fastened their hope upon this world, they expect the salvation God has held out to his people as 'the consolation of Israel' [Luke 2:25]."[49] While *ptōchoi*, then, surely includes those who are literally poor and physically destitute (perhaps because their circumstances dispose them to trust in God), the word here in Luke 4:18 has more than socioeconomic connotations. Based on the OT background, the underlying connotation seems to be an attitude of dependence on God.

This conclusion about Luke 4:18 is borne out by another line of evidence. Given the programmatic character of Luke 4:16-30, an exami-

---

[45] Stonehouse, *Luke*, 153. Of v. 21, Seccombe writes, "The drama of the 'today' is that it transforms a mere reading of Scripture into a divine proclamation of the age of salvation" (*Possessions*, 66). As many have noted (e.g., Pilgrim, *Good News*, 66), here is realized eschatology. The note of fulfillment sounded in this verse leads Pilgrim to suggest "Jesus' announcement of the Salvation-Time" is a better title for the whole pericope (4:16-30) than the common title "Jesus' rejection at Nazareth" (p. 65).

Luke 4:21 is, of course, one of the pivots in Conzelmann's attempt to establish his thesis of a three-stage redemptive history. According to him, "today" and the salvation manifested at that time belong to the past, to the period of Jesus (*Luke*, 36-37, 195). Nothing in the text substantiates such a claim. As Marshall notes, the original "today" on which Jesus pronounced these words of fulfillment is and continues to be part of the era of fulfillment (*Luke*, 185).

[46] The latter is Seccombe's position (*Possessions*, 23).

[47] Ellis, *Luke*, 97.

[48] Ridderbos, *Kingdom*, 192. As Stonehouse points out, the transformation spoken of in Isaiah 61 is part of the radical and thoroughgoing renewal of the present order, and is the portion of a transformed people, not the poor as such simply because they are poor (*Luke*, 81).

[49] Ridderbos, *Kingdom*, 189. "Israel" is used in its ideal and spiritual sense, as in the psalms and prophets (Ridderbos, *Kingdom*, 194). Cf., e.g., Zechariah, Elizabeth, Mary, Simeon, and Anna in Luke 1 and 2. As Fitzmyer observes, the initial portrait in the opening chapters of Luke is of true Israel (*Luke* 1.188). Those waiting for the coming of Messiah are the pious poor (Pilgrim, *Good News*, 77).

nation of the beneficiaries of Jesus' ministry throughout the Gospel of Luke should cast light on the meaning of *ptōchoi* in Luke 4:18.[50] Among the people with whom Luke reports Jesus as frequently associating are tax collectors and sinners (e.g., 5:27-32; 15:1-2; 19:1-10), women (e.g., 7:36-50; 8:2-3; 10:38-42; 24:6-11), the sick, lame, blind, and demon-possessed (e.g., 4:31-41; 7:21-22). The common denominator in these groups is not that they are all physically poor and destitute (cf. 8:3), but rather that they are social outcasts aware of their need and coming to Jesus to have their needs met. It is particularly noteworthy that in several of the references to the sinners and/or tax collectors (some of whom may have been rich, like Zacchaeus and perhaps Levi as well), there is a strong contrast drawn between them and the proud religious leaders (e.g., 5:30-32; 7:29-30; 15:1-2). Generally speaking, the former respond to Jesus, the latter oppose him. The contrast between the humility implicit in repentance and response to Jesus' message, on the one hand, and the self-righteousness and pride of Jesus' opponents, on the other, suggests the poor to whom he preaches good news are characterized as much by their attitude toward him as by their economic circumstances. While there may often be a correlation between economic circumstances and responsiveness to Jesus, the correlation is not absolute, as Zacchaeus illustrates. In short, *ptōchoi* includes but is broader than the literally poor. Luke 4:18 is not, therefore, "a limitation of the promise of salvation to a specific circle of people."[51]

c) Luke 6:20-26

Another passage of importance for understanding Luke's attitude toward riches and poverty is Luke 6:20-26, the beatitudes and woes of the so-called Sermon on the Plain (6:20-49). These verses are of particular interest for the question of Luke's alleged biases since here the poor and rich are blessed and threatened in juxtaposition to each other (vv. 20-23, 24-26, respectively). The limits of space, as well as the overwhelming volume of literature on the sermon itself,[52] preclude detailed discussion of Luke 6:20-26 here. Several general remarks are in order, however, to indicate the bearing of these verses on the question at hand.

---

[50] This line of approach is suggested and pursued by Dumais, "Evangelisation," 301-3.

[51] Marshall, *Luke*, 249.

[52] Cf., e.g., Dupont's magisterial three-volume work on the beatitudes and Kissinger's helpful book, *The Sermon on the Mount: A History of Interpretation and Bibliography* (Metuchen, NJ: Scarecrow, 1975).

Luke 6:20-26 forms a single section of two contrasting parts describing two kinds of people.[53] One kind is described as poor, hungry, weeping, and persecuted (vv. 20-23), the other as rich, well-fed, laughing, and well spoken of (vv. 24-26). Both kinds of people are promised or threatened with, as the case may be, a reversal of their present circumstances.[54] As Ellis notes, "the 'beatitudes' and 'woes' are not blessings or cursings *upon* those groups but are insights into their true character . . . . By their present conduct and attitudes the disciples show to which group they belong (35)."[55] To postulate two different audiences for the beatitudes and woes, as many interpreters do,[56] is therefore unnecessary.[57] It may be, as Pilgrim argues, that "Luke addresses these woes to wealthy Christian adherents (or would-be adherents), who have not yet freed themselves from their love of possessions or status."[58] By thus warning such people of the dire consequences of the actions and attitudes portrayed in the woes, Luke calls them to repentance and wholehearted discipleship. The beatitudes comfort those who have already made such a commitment.

Although Luke 6:20-26 appears to support the impression that Luke (and Jesus before him) has a particular bias for the poor and against the rich as such, both kinds of people are qualified in important ways. The meaning of *ptōchoi*, for example, is qualified or narrowed as follows. First, it must be remembered that Jesus is speaking to and of people who are disciples already (6:20), not to all poor people in general. Since the happiness of which Jesus speaks in the beatitudes is "the result of a state of divinely given salvation," each of the statements of blessing is in effect "a statement predicating salvation."[59] The poor are blessed, therefore, not on the basis of their economic circumstances, but rather because of and in the context of their response to Jesus.[60] While the idea

---

[53] Marshall, *Luke*, 244.

[54] The reversal spoken of here is not a simple or immediate reversal (Marshall, *Luke*, 249-50). The fulfillment of blessing and judgment shares in the tension between the present and future aspects of the kingdom.

[55] Ellis, *Luke*, 112; cf. also Seccombe, *Possessions*, 86.

[56] E.g., Arndt, *Luke*, 190; Dupont, *Beatitudes* 3.34; Godet, *Luke* 1.317; Morris, *Luke*, 127-28; Plummer, *Luke*, 182; and Schürmann, *Lukasevangelium* 1.325.

[57] As Luke indicates in 6:20, the primary audience of the entire sermon is the disciples. Although it is striking that such strong words as the woes are spoken to disciples, it must not be forgotten that the disciples are a mixed group in constant need of warning about the extent of their commitment to Jesus. The mixed nature of the disciples is implicit in the passage on the wise and foolish builders with which the sermon ends (6:46-49; cf. Marshall, *Luke*, 244); it comes out very clearly in the story of Ananias and Sapphira (Acts 5:1-11).

[58] Pilgrim, *Good News*, 107.

[59] Marshall, *Luke*, 248.

[60] Pilgrim, *Good News*, 77.

of real poverty may be present in the beatitudes, it is not the basis or ground of the blessing pronounced in them. Second, the statement that the kingdom of God belongs to the poor already ("*hymetera estin hē basileia tou theou*," v. 20) indicates that a certain kind of attitude is presupposed in these people. As Jesus makes clear in Luke 18:15-17, only those who have childlike faith will enter the kingdom of God. If, then, the kingdom already belongs to *hoi ptōchoi*, it must be on this same condition. They are blessed because (*hoti*, 6:20) they have exercised such faith and thus share in the kingdom, not because of their poverty. Once again we see that one's attitude to God is the decisive factor in salvation.

A third qualification of *ptōchoi* is suggested in the parallel description of the poor in vv. 22-23 as those who are prepared to suffer with Christ.[61] The poor are those who have made the wholehearted commitment to Jesus elsewhere laid down as the condition for discipleship (e.g., 14:27). Taken together, these qualifications indicate no particular bias in the beatitudes for the poor as such.

Just as the poor as such are not blessed in the beatitudes, so the rich as such are not condemned in the woes. The key term, *plousioi*, is also qualified in several ways. First, the succeeding woes imply that what is being condemned here is the self-sufficiency and indifference to others which often characterizes the rich. "Woe to you who are well fed now" (v. 25a), for example, in contrast to "Blessed are you who hunger now" (v. 21), calls to mind the same contrast in the parable of the rich man and Lazarus (Luke 16:19-31, especially v. 25). It will be recalled from the discussion of that parable in the last chapter that the rich man's fate is likely determined by his selfishness and indifference to Lazarus. The same attitude and actions seem to characterize the rich in the woes of Luke 6; unless they repent, the same fate awaits them.[62] In addition, the word "laugh" in the next woe (*hoi gelōntes*, v. 25b) may have the nuance, present in the LXX, of evil, boastful laughter.[63] If so, the implication is that Jesus is here describing people who are self-satisfied and indifferent

---

[61] Marshall, *Luke*, 249.

[62] The connection between the woes and beatitudes in Luke 6:20-26 and the parable of the rich man and Lazarus in Luke 16:19-31 is often noted. Cf., e.g., Danker, *Jesus and the New Age* (rev. ed.; Philadelphia: Fortress, 1988) 142; Dupont, *Beatitudes* 3.199-200, and "The Poor and Poverty in the Gospels and Acts," in *Gospel Poverty* (ed. George) 46; Koch, "Wertung," 162-63; Pilgrim, *Good News*, 114-15; and Sabourin, *Luc*, 287-88. Particularly striking is the parallel between 6:24 and 16:25.

[63] Marshall, *Luke*, 256. Schürmann calls it "self-confident laughter" (*Lukasevangelium* 1.338).

to the needy.[64] Such attitudes and actions put these people in the class of the rich fool (12:13-21), the rich man in the parable of the rich man and Lazarus (16:19-31), and the rich ruler (18:18-30). In each case, as we have seen or will see, what is condemned is not the rich or riches as such, but rather an attachment to wealth or material possessions that effectively excludes wholehearted commitment to Jesus. What is at stake, then, in the woes is the truth of Luke 16:13: "You cannot serve both God and Money."

A second qualification of *plousioi*, similar to the first, is implied in the subsequent context of the Sermon on the Plain. As Dupont argues, Jesus' emphasis on love and generosity in Luke 6:27-36 may be designed to throw into relief an accusation of egotism and lack of charity in the woes.[65] If so, this fact is further confirmation that a certain kind of rich person is being spoken of in the woes, not all rich people. Although Jesus and Luke may be calling attention to the dangers and temptations inherent in riches, there appears to be no evidence here of a particular bias against the rich. In fact, the warning in the woes may even be evidence of a concern for the rich lest they, by a selfish attachment to and use of their riches, suffer the fate promised such people here. It perhaps bears repeating that the rich are here being called to repentance and wholehearted discipleship, not summarily sentenced to perdition.

There is, in conclusion, no clear evidence of bias for the poor and against the rich in Luke 6:20-26. This passage is not a blanket contrast between the poor and rich as such, but rather between two particular kinds of poor and rich people—those who trust God and respond to Jesus, on the one hand, and those who trust their riches and neglect the needy, on the other. While economic realities may be present in the contrast, the fundamental point of contrast is religious and ethical. One's attitude toward God and response to Jesus are of paramount importance. Any socioeconomic connotations here may serve to warn rich disciples in Luke's day, as it did in Jesus' day, of the dangers inherent in their possessions.

In summary, examination of Luke 1:50-53, 4:18-19, and 6:20-26 has revealed no particular bias on Luke's part either for the poor or against the rich. These verses cannot, therefore, be used to substantiate the claim that Luke is "the evangelist of the poor" or that he has a negative attitude toward material possessions. The fundamental religious issue of one's attitude toward God has come into focus at several points in the

---

[64] Marshall, *Luke*, 256.
[65] Dupont, *Beatitudes* 3.199-200.

discussion. The fact that economic realities are often associated with one's attitude toward God (either positively or negatively) is, however, not insignificant and must not simply be spiritualized away. The good news that the kingdom of God is open to the physically poor and destitute would no doubt comfort those of Luke's readers, especially Christians, who may find themselves in such circumstances. At the same time, this news, in conjunction with the Magnificat and the woes, may be intended to confront Luke's rich readers at several points. First, it may remind them that they must not judge or show partiality toward others on the basis of economic or social standing (cf. James 2 and 5). Second, it may warn them against both self-sufficiency and self-centered use of possessions which results in indifference to the needs of others. While riches themselves do not exclude one from the kingdom, they do pose a serious danger to wholehearted discipleship. Let us now consider the danger.

2. The Dangers of Riches

Another aspect of Luke's ostensibly negative attitude toward riches is his emphasis on the dangers of riches. This note is sounded in the woes of the Sermon on the Plain (6:24-26), as we have just seen. It is also especially prominent in the parable of the rich man and Lazarus (16:19-31), discussed in the previous chapter. Two other passages merit careful consideration here because of the important part they play in this particular emphasis. They are Luke 12:13-21 (the parable of the rich fool) and 18:18-30 (the rich ruler).[66]

a) Luke 12:13-21

The parable of the rich fool (Luke 12:16-21) and the verses that introduce it (vv. 13-15) are part of a long teaching section on material possessions (12:13-34).[67] In vv. 13-21 Jesus warns the crowds against attachment to riches, while in vv. 22-34 he exhorts his disciples to total confidence in God.[68] The unity of this section, noted by several interpreters,[69] has an important bearing on a proper understanding of the parable of the rich

---

[66] Other verses or passages in Luke-Acts which bear on the dangers of riches include Luke 8:14 and Acts 5:1-11.

[67] This point is noted by Arndt, *Luke*, 314, and Dupont, *Beatitudes* 3.183.

[68] Dupont, "Poor," 49. Note the alternation of audience here which, as noted in the previous chapter, is characteristic of Luke's central section and is present in 16:1-31.

[69] E.g., Dupont, *Beatitudes* 3.183; Godet, *Luke* 2.99; Plummer, *Luke*, 325; and Seccombe, *Possessions*, 146.

fool. The contrast between vv. 13-21 and 22-34 suggests that riches are dangerous because of the rivalry they pose for wholehearted trust in God. The fundamental issue in vv. 13-21 is, in other words, religious, not social or economic. This fact, implied by the context, is evident in the verses themselves.

In the course of his teaching on one occasion,[70] Jesus is interrupted by someone in the crowd who asks him to arbitrate a family dispute over an inheritance (v. 13). Jesus refuses the request, but uses the occasion to warn the crowds against the greed which lay at the root of the request. They are to be on their guard against "all kinds of greed [*pasēs pleonexias*]," Jesus says, because "a man's life does not consist in the abundance of his possessions" (v. 15). Possessions guarantee neither the quality[71] nor the length of life (cf. *etē polla*, v. 19). Jesus then reinforces this warning by means of a specific illustration of greed or covetousness at work,[72] the parable of the rich fool. Here he portrays the futility,[73] peril,[74] and sinfulness of greed. The rich landowner of the parable is judged (v. 20)[75] not because he is rich or has acquired his riches unjustly or because his planned project is immoral.[76] Rather he is judged because of the underlying selfishness[77] and godlessness revealed in his soliloquy (vv. 17-19).

---

[70] Luke 12:1-13:9 has the marks of being a connected teaching discourse belonging to a particular occasion in Jesus' ministry. Cf. Seccombe, *Possessions*, 146, and Tannehill, *Unity*, 240.

[71] Seccombe, *Possessions*, 140-41.

[72] Schottroff and Stegemann, *Jesus*, 97.

[73] Ellis, *Luke*, 178.

[74] Dupont, *Beatitudes* 3.184.

[75] The judgment pronounced in v. 20 ("this very night your life will be demanded from you") likely pictures eschatological judgment rather than the imminence of death, although the latter position is advocated by highly regarded scholars such as Dupont (*Beatitudes* 3.117), Fitzmyer (*Luke* 2.971), and Marshall (*Luke*, 524). Luke no doubt recognizes the possibility of God's judgment coming on an individual in the form of death (cf. Acts 5:1-11). It is not certain, however, that that is the point here; several considerations, in fact, suggest it may not be. As Seccombe notes (*Possessions*, 143), v. 21 promises the same fate to anyone who accumulates possessions without regard to God. Yet, he adds, it is "hardly imagined that all greedy people would meet with untimely death, and that those who are rich towards God would survive to old age" (p. 144). What is more, the larger discourse in which the parable of the rich fool is set (12:1-13:9, according to Seccombe) "majors on the inevitability and urgency of the coming Judgement" (p. 144; cf. esp. the call to watchfulness in 12:35-48). This fact suggests Jesus has the same thing in mind in 12:20.

[76] Schottroff and Stegemann, however, argue the man is guilty of an economic crime. By hoarding the produce of his fields, they contend, the man intends to drive up prices and thus ensure higher profit margins for himself at the expense of others (*Jesus*, 97).

[77] Cf., e.g., the striking repetition of the personal pronoun *mou* four times in vv. 17-19, and the man's stated goal: "Take life easy; eat, drink and be merry" (v. 19). The latter acts are, says Fitzmyer, "symbolic of carefree, even dissipated living," while the "egotistic assertions" implied in the pronouns mark "the superficial self-confidence of the speaker" (*Luke* 2.973). For similar assessments of the man as selfish, see P. Bemile, *The Magnificat within the Context and Framework of Lukan Theology. An Exegetical Theological Study of*

As Dupont argues, the man's fatal error is that he reckoned only with the present life. Not unlike the rich man in Luke 16:19-31, this man's error includes three inseparable aspects: he forgets God, eternal life, and his obligations to the poor.[78] The man's forgetfulness of God is conveyed in God's verdict, "You fool" (v. 20). "Biblically, the fool is the one who lives de facto without God (Ps. 14:1). The fool thinks and acts under the illusion that there is accountability to no one but self."[79] Such apparently is this man's attitude. His forgetfulness of eternal life is implicit in v. 21—he stores up things for himself, but is "not rich toward God." His barns are bulging, but he has no "treasure in heaven" (cf. v. 33).[80] He has given little thought to and made no provision for the life to come. The exhortation to the disciples in v. 33 to give alms to the poor suggests the rich landowner's forgetfulness of his obligations to the poor. The foolish conduct portrayed in the parable of the rich fool is strikingly similar to that of the rich man in Luke 16:19-31[81] and dissimilar to that of the unjust steward in our parable.[82] The consequences of such foolish conduct, though intended primarily as a warning to the crowds, serve a similar function for the disciples.[83]

b) Luke 18:18-30

Another key passage on the dangers of riches is Luke 18:18-30. This section, often entitled "The Rich Ruler" (cf. *UBSGNT* and *NIV*), falls into three parts: vv. 18-23, 24-27, and 28-30. In the first part, Jesus converses with the rich ruler; in the second, he speaks about him; in the third, he speaks to the disciples about themselves.[84] While Jesus' conversation with the rich ruler in vv. 18-23 has an important bearing on the understanding of Luke's attitude toward riches and poverty, considera-

---

Luke 1:46-55 (Frankfurt: Lang, 1986) 182; Marshall, *Luke*, 524; Morris, *Luke*, 212; and H. Rolston, "Ministry to Need. The Teachings of Jesus concerning Stewardship of Possessions," *Int* 8 (1954) 144.

[78] Dupont, *Beatitudes* 3.185.

[79] Pilgrim, *Good News*, 112. "This has been the grand illusion of the human race since its beginning," Pilgrim continues. "Yet the rich and the powerful are more tempted and trapped by this illusion than others. Hence the parable seeks to shatter its seductive hold upon the rich, so evident in the life of this land owner" (p. 112).

[80] Many interpreters have noted the connection between vv. 21 and 33, among them, Fitzmyer, *Luke* 2.974; Marshall, *Luke*, 524; and Pilgrim, *Good News*, 111. Note also the apparent equation of "eternal life" and "treasure in heaven" in Luke 18:18, 22.

[81] Dupont, *Beatitudes* 3.185, and Marshall, *Historian*, 142, and *Luke*, 524.

[82] Arndt, *Luke*, 316; Dupont, *Beatitudes* 3.197; and Tannehill, *Unity*, 247.

[83] Tannehill, *Unity*, 247.

[84] Godet, *Luke* 2.205.

tion of those verses will be deferred until the next subsection. My reason for doing so is that Jesus' demand in v. 22 ("Sell everything you have and give to the poor") better fits a discussion of total renunciation. Of significance for the present discussion of the dangers of riches are vv. 24-30. These verses expand the dangers from the story of one rich man (vv. 18-23) to all rich people. According to vv. 24-25 in particular, riches pose a nearly impossible obstacle to entering the kingdom of God. "Are wealth and discipleship at all compatible?" asks Pilgrim of these verses. "Or more bluntly, can the rich be saved?"[85] Several observations will indicate that both questions can be answered in the affirmative, but not without significant qualifications.

The first observation is that riches *are* a serious obstacle to entering the kingdom of God. While Jesus does not say it is impossible for the rich to enter the kingdom (cf. "How hard it is," v. 24), his hyperbolic comparison in v. 25 of "Palestine's largest animal trying to get through its smallest opening" implies it is virtually so.[86] The difficulty is clearly illustrated in the story of the rich ruler (vv. 18-23, esp. 22-23). Luke's attitude toward riches, particularly their dangers, should not be exaggerated, however, at least not on the basis of Luke 18:18-30. These verses are found in all the synoptic gospels (cf. Matt 19:16-29 and Mark 10:17-30). Jesus himself warned of the dangers of riches, and this warning fits Luke's emphasis on the riches/poverty theme.

A second observation is that riches themselves are not the problem, but rather people's attachment to them. This point is revealed in the response of the rich ruler to Jesus' commands to him. Luke reports he was "very sad" (and presumably did not follow Jesus—cf. Matt 19:22 and Mark 10:22) "because he was a man of great wealth" (v. 23). The man's response indicates that "his love for the things of this world is greater than his desire for the Kingdom."[87] The point of Jesus' teaching here on the dangers of riches comes into clearer focus when that teaching is seen in the context of Luke 18:9-17. In vv. 9-14, Jesus uses the parable of the Pharisee and the tax collector to warn the self-righteous;[88] in vv. 15-17, he declares that to enter the kingdom, one must receive it "like a

---

[85] Pilgrim, *Good News*, 119.

[86] Fitzmyer, *Luke* 2.1203. Cf. also Marshall, *Luke*, 687. Plummer notes that Jesus' statement in v. 27 ("What is impossible with men is possible with God") indicates that v. 25 speaks of impossibility, not just difficulty (*Luke*, 426).

[87] Seccombe, *Possessions*, 127.

[88] Marshall describes the contrast in vv. 9-14 as self-righteousness versus dependence on God (*Historian*, 143). Ladd writes, "The teaching of this parable is the same as the Pauline doctrine of free justification with the exception that there is no mention of the cross" (*A Theology of the New Testament* [Grand Rapids: Eerdmans, 1974] 79).

little child" (v. 17).[89] In neither case is the contrast between riches and poverty per se, but rather between pride and humility (cf. especially 18:14). One's attitude toward God is the decisive factor in entering the kingdom,[90] not whether one is rich or poor. The larger context in which Luke 18:18-30, in particular, and Luke's attitude toward riches and poverty, in general, must be viewed is thus religious.[91] Riches are dangerous, however, as vv. 18-30 emphasize, because of their ability to effect, often adversely, one's most basic attitudes and commitments. They often produce pride or self-trust,[92] either of which excludes the childlike faith essential for entering the kingdom; they intensify man's natural attachment to this age.[93] "The greater a person's stake in this world," writes Seccombe, "the harder it will be for him to take the decision to count this age as nothing in comparison to the Kingdom."[94] This fact accounts for Luke's (and Jesus') strong emphasis on the dangers of riches.

A third observation about Luke 18:24-30 relates to Jesus' tone in these verses. As Tannehill notes, the bitter denunciations of some earlier passages (e.g., 11:39-41) is replaced here by a sense of tragedy.[95] One can almost hear the pity in Jesus' voice as he says, having looked at the ruler, "How hard it is for the rich to enter the kingdom of God" (v. 24). There is also a note of hope in these verses that should not be overlooked. In response to the startled question of his hearers ("Who then can be saved?" v. 26)[96] Jesus replies that "what is impossible with men is possible with God" (v. 27). By not answering directly but "in a generic way," as Fitzmyer puts it, Jesus thus "gets across the all-important

---

[89] A number of interpreters call attention to the thematic contrast between vv. 15-17 and vv. 18-23 or 18-30; e.g., Dupont, *Beatitudes* 3.160; Hoyt, "Poor," 210; and Marshall, *Luke*, 683.

[90] It is worth noting here that in vv. 15-30, "entering the kingdom" is used interchangeably with "inheriting eternal life" and "being saved" (cf. esp. vv. 17-18, 24-26, 29-30). V. 14 may connect all these ideas to justification.

[91] Commenting on Luke 18:10-14, Marshall writes, "It is thus the attitude towards God which matters, and it in this context that the teaching on wealth and poverty must be seen. Luke does not present poverty as an ideal in itself, nor wealth as intrinsically evil. When his teaching on wealth and poverty is seen in the context of the Gospel as a whole, the underlying attitude to God is what really matters" (*Historian*, 143).

[92] Farrell, "Structure," 52.

[93] Seccombe, *Possessions*, 134.

[94] Seccombe, *Possessions*, 128-29.

[95] Tannehill, *Unity*, 187.

[96] The question in v. 26 perhaps reflects the popular equation between riches and righteousness, as several interpreters have suggested (e.g., Easton, *Luke*, 272; Geldenhuys, *Luke*, 460; Morris, *Luke*, 268; and Pilgrim, *Good News*, 121). As will be recalled from the discussion in the previous chapter, this equation may underlie Jesus' denunciation of the Pharisees in Luke 16:14-15.

message: salvation of human beings depends entirely on God. God can," Fitzmyer continues, "bring even the rich to the state that they are saved. For if a person, rich or poor, is saved, it is achieved only by what is impossible for human beings, but not for God. It does not depend on wealth."[97] That God does enable people to abandon their trust in possessions and to receive the kingdom "like a little child" is illustrated in Peter and the other disciples (apostles?) who "left all" to follow Jesus (v. 28).[98] It is also illustrated quite intentionally, as we will see, in the story of Zacchaeus (19:1-10).

The foregoing study of Luke 12:13-21 and 18:18-30 reveals that Luke is indeed very concerned about the dangers of riches. This concern is not, however, evidence of a "negative" attitude towards riches themselves. Instead Luke's concern must be seen in the fundamental religious context of people's ultimate loyalties. As the cases of the rich fool and the rich ruler indicate, these loyalties are often revealed in and hindered by the way riches are used and regarded. Perhaps Luke especially intends the warnings about the dangers of riches for rich Christians or would-be Christians among the community to which he writes. Such people may regard their riches as a sign of God's blessing and even use such reasoning as theological justification for selfishness.[99] They perhaps are also characterized by pride and arrogance (cf. 18:9). Whatever the exact circumstances of his readers, Luke's concern seems to be to warn rich people not to repeat the errors and share the fates of the rich fool and the rich ruler.

---

[97] Fitzmyer, *Luke* 2.1203.

[98] Peter and the disciples are, writes Pilgrim, "a living witness to Luke's readers that possessions can be abandoned by the grace of God for the kingdom's sake" (*Good News*, 121). Luke 18:28 cannot be used to support total renunciation as the necessary prerequisite for all disciples. There is nothing in the call of Peter or Levi (cf. Luke 5:11, 28, which 18:28 recalls) to indicate Jesus demands total renunciation of them. Even more to the point is Jesus' response to Peter in vv. 28-29. In Seccombe's words, "Jesus promises a many-fold reward not to those who leave *everything*, but to those who for his sake leave *anything* for the sake of the Kingdom (v. 29). Thus it is not a question of total renunciation, but of decision for the Kingdom in the face of the counter-pull of the world, from whatever source it comes" (*Possessions*, 129). Jesus' promise of reward "in this age" (v. 30) "is not," to quote Pilgrim again, "a guarantee of wealth and abundance in the tradition of Job, who received double of what he lost." Instead what is probably in view is "life in a new community where the needs of one person are met by the gifts of another, where a supportive community suffers and rejoices with one another, and one can trust God without fear or anxiety over earthly needs" (*Good News*, 122; cf. Fitzmyer, *Luke* 2.1206, and Godet, *Luke* 2.211, to the same effect). Just such community life is described in the early chapters of Acts (e.g., Acts 2:42-47 and 4:32-37). Such life is a foretaste of the life and conditions of the consummated kingdom of God.

[99] This suggestion, made by Karris in regard to Luke 16:1-31 ("Poor," 122-23), seems to apply with equal force to Luke 18:18-30 (cf. esp. 18:26).

3. Renunciation of Possessions

The most radical aspect of Luke's "negative" attitude toward material possessions is the apparent call for total renunciation. Three verses in particular seem to teach that one must give up all one's possessions in order to follow Jesus. Those verses are Luke 12:33, 14:33, and 18:22. While many different interpretations have been offered for these striking verses,[100] I will argue that the commands to give up one's possessions are conditional.[101] In other words, these commands are conditioned by the specific situation in which and/or the person to whom they are spoken, or are otherwise qualified by the context in which they occur. The focus of the following discussion will be to point out the conditional character of the respective commands, as well as the basic thrust of each.

a) Luke 12:33

Luke 12:33 reads, "Sell your possessions and give to the poor. Provide purses for yourselves that will not wear out, a treasure in heaven that will not be exhausted, where no thief comes near and no moth destroys." To understand this verse properly it must be seen in its context. This verse occurs as the conclusion of a section of teaching to the disciples on anxiety (12:22-34). That section itself, it will be recalled from the earlier discussion of 12:13-21, is part of a longer section on material possessions (vv. 13-34). In this context Luke 12:22-34 stands as the positive counterpart to the parable of the rich fool (vv. 13-21). In vv. 22-34 Jesus applies v. 15 ("a man's life does not consist in the abundance of his

---

[100] Among the interpretations of the command to renounce everything, the following can be mentioned by way of summary.

1. The command is literal, i.e., Luke is actually advocating total renunciation as the Christian ideal, if not the norm. Pilgrim (*Good News*, 98 n. 17) cites Schürmann as representing this interpretation (*Lukasevangelium* 1.324).

2. The command is intended for church leaders only. This is the position of Degenhardt, *Lukas*, esp. 215-16; it is critiqued by, among others, Karris, "Poor," 114; Marshall, *Historian*, 207-9, esp. 207 n. 1; and Seccombe, *Possessions*, 13-14.

3. The command is intended only for a specific situation of crisis. That crisis is, argues W. Schmithals, persecution ("Lukas—Evangelist der Armen," *Theologia Viatorum* 12 [1973-74] esp. 160-67). For a critique of Schmithals, see Pilgrim, *Good News*, 100-101, and Seccombe, *Possessions*, 15-16.

4. The command is limited to earthly discipleship in Jesus' time, but retains exemplary force for Luke's day. This interpretation is put forward by Schottroff and Stegemann (*Jesus*, esp. 108-13) and Pilgrim (*Good News*, esp. 101-2).

[101] Seccombe uses the word "situational" to describe this feature of the commands. The passages in question (in Seccombe's case, Luke 14:25-35 and 18:18-30) deal with "a specific individual situation intended to establish neither a general, nor a limited ethic of renunciation" (*Possessions*, 99).

Jesus' command is to test the sincerity of such persons, to sift superficial followers from genuine disciples. As Seccombe observes, "the emphatic appeal of v. 35b ['He who has ears to hear, let him hear'] stresses the public character of the discourse and calls for heart-searching on the part of the crowds to see whether their inward resolution matches their outward allegiance."[118] Jesus' audience in vv. 25-35, then, suggests v. 33 is not intended as a universal demand for total renunciation.

A second qualification of Luke 14:33, similar to the first, is implied in the connection between vv. 25-35 and the parable of the great banquet in the immediately preceding section (vv. 16-24). As a number of interpreters point out, the two sections are integrally related, especially by means of the excuses in vv. 18-20.[119] In the parable of the great banquet Jesus opposes "the comfortable self-complacency" of the speaker in v. 15 who apparently presumes on his own participation in the messianic banquet.[120] Jesus' response is, in effect, that what the speaker says is correct, "but the spirit in which he says it is quite wrong. Only those who are detached from earthly things, and treat them as of small account in comparison with the Kingdom of God, will enter therein."[121] Although the scenery and audience are different, much the same point is made in vv. 25-35. If the guests of the parable refused to pay the cost of discipleship, others may be tempted to underestimate the cost.[122] Hence Jesus stresses in vv. 25-35 the detachment necessary for true discipleship.[123] In this context, v. 33 is addressed to people in the crowd whose attachment to their possessions may be similar to that of the guests in vv. 18-19. If and when such attachment exists, it must be broken decisively if one is to be a true disciple of Jesus. Again we see that v. 33 is not intended as a universal requirement for discipleship, but is conditioned by one's attachment to possessions.

A third qualification of 14:33 is suggested in Jesus' arresting statement in v. 26: "If anyone comes to me and does not hate" his family and even his own life, "he cannot be my disciple." Virtually every interpreter of this verse qualifies the meaning of the word "hate" in some way. Jesus is taken to mean, for example, that a disciple's commitment to him must

---

[118] Seccombe, *Possessions*, 105.

[119] E.g., Danker, *Jesus*, 272; Karris, "Poor," 121; Marshall, *Luke*, 591; and Seccombe, *Possessions*, 117.

[120] Plummer, *Luke*, 360.

[121] Plummer, *Luke*, 360.

[122] Marshall, *Luke*, 591.

[123] Karris suggests detachment is the common theme which relates vv. 16-24 and 25-35 ("Poor," 121).

be so complete that all other commitments *appear* as hatred *by compari-son*,[124] and/or that such "hatred" applies only when one's family is opposed to Jesus.[125] The basic point of Jesus' statement, most would agree, is that all other loyalties must be subordinate to one's commitment to him.[126] Several interpreters also point out that this verse is an instance of Jesus stating a principle in a categorical way and leaving his hearers to find out the qualifications in the light of his other pronouncements.[127] These observations about v. 26 cast light on the meaning of v. 33. As G. Vos argues, the conflict of ultimate loyalties implicit in "hate" in the former verse indicates that in the latter verse Jesus is not condemning external possession "but the internal entanglement of the heart with temporal goods."[128] Where such entanglement exists, total renunciation is necessary if one is to be Jesus' disciple.

A fourth qualification of Luke 14:33 is implied by the tense of the key verb *apotassetai* ("renounce," "give up," BAGD). The present tense suggests Jesus' emphasis here is on a person's inner attitude.[129] Writes Marshall, "Just as one should not attempt a venture without having sufficient resources to complete it, but will need to put everything into it in order to be successful [vv. 28-32], so the disciple must be continu-ally ready (present tense) to give up all he has got in order to follow Jesus."[130] The decisive factor in Jesus' command, then, is an attitude of readiness to give up one's possessions. As the stories of the rich ruler and Zacchaeus illustrate (18:18-23 and 19:1-10, respectively), whether or not one will actually have to give up his possessions depends on one's

---

[124] Arndt, *Luke*, 344.

[125] Danker, *Jesus*, 272; Easton, *Luke*, 231; Fitzmyer, *Luke* 2.1063; Plummer, *Luke*, 364; and G. Vos, *The Teaching of Jesus concerning the Kingdom of God and the Church* (Phillipsburg, NJ: Presbyterian and Reformed, 1972) 94. "Hate," writes Vos, describes "the energetic determination of the will to forego even the pleasures of natural affection, *where they come in conflict with the supreme duty of the kingdom*" (emphasis added).

[126] Ellis, *Luke*, 195, and Geldenhuys, *Luke*, 398. Noting that "*miseō*" also occurs in Luke 16:13 (and parallel, Matt 6:24), Pilgrim explains the significance of the word as follows. "In both [Luke 14:26 and 16:13], he [Luke] uses it to emphasize the uncompromising character of the call to serve or follow Jesus. It is either/or. Either one leaves the old loyalties behind, or one does not" (*Good News*, 91).

[127] Geldenhuys, *Luke*, 398, and Plummer, *Luke*, 364. The latter is quoted approvingly by Fitzmyer, *Luke* 2.1063. Stein describes Jesus' method here as overstatement (*The Method and Message of Jesus' Teachings* [Philadelphia: Westminster, 1978] 8, 97).

[128] Vos, *Kingdom*, 94. Vos also observes that "the demand for sacrifice always presup-poses that what is to be renounced forms an obstacle to that absolute devotion which the kingdom of God requires" (p. 94). Cf. Easton, *Luke*, 232, who also qualifies v. 33 by means of "hate" in v. 26.

[129] Dupont, "Renoncer à tous ses biens (Luc 14,33)," *NRT* 93 (1971) 575-76.

[130] Marshall, *Luke*, 594. Cf. also Karris, "Sitz," 225.

all Christians, he is not inconsistent when he commends a positive use of possessions. Although the demand for renunciation itself is not absolute, the demand for wholehearted commitment is, however. The former demand, even though conditional, serves to emphasize the latter. Perhaps Luke intends the verses on renunciation, in their contexts, to make just this point for his rich readers, some of whom may be unsure what discipleship involves or halfhearted in their commitment. These verses make it clear that such halfheartedness is fatal to genuine discipleship. They also point to one means of the proper use of possessions, charity to the poor (cf. especially 12:33 and 18:22).

These conclusions about renunciation of possessions confirm the general direction in which the other material on Luke's "negative" attitude to possessions has led us. To judge from all this material, Luke's attitude is not as negative as it might appear at first glance. There is no evidence he has a particular bias for the poor and against the rich. He does emphasize the dangers of riches, but always in the context of pride and self-sufficiency which exclude wholehearted commitment to Jesus. The demand for total renunciation, though present, is conditional; it too is meant to emphasize the need for wholehearted commitment. Stonehouse's words perhaps best sum up the significance of this material. He writes,

> The issue is seen to be basically religious rather than basically social. Jesus [and Luke, *mutatis mutandis*, by including the material] is not so much concerned to assure the publicans and sinners of the love of God as to rebuke the self-righteous pride of the Pharisees and the complacency of the rich. The advantage which the poor and the publican enjoyed over the rich and the Pharisee was not a positive one, which assured him of the divine favour in this world or in the world to come. It was rather the negative advantage that he was likely to be more ready to receive the kingdom of God because he lacked the self-righteousness and complacency of those who trust in their religious preeminence or material wealth.[143]

Once the fundamental religious perspective of this material is recognized, it becomes very plausible to understand the material thus far considered as being primarily addressed to rich readers. The material warns such people against self-sufficiency, pride, greed, and selfishness. At the same time, it also alerts them to a proper use of their material possessions (especially 12:33 and 18:22). The religious issue does not exclude positive social implications. Let us now consider those implications.

---

[143] Stonehouse, *Luke*, 164.

B. Positive Attitude toward Possessions

While material possessions, particularly in abundance, can pose a serious obstacle to wholehearted discipleship, they can also be put to proper use by the Christian disciple. Luke has included a significant amount of material which bears on such use. This material is evidence of a positive attitude toward possessions on his part, and will be the focus of the present section. The discussion of this material will be much briefer than that in the previous section, not because Luke is less interested in a proper use of possessions, but rather because the relevant material is far less controversial than Luke's "negative" attitude. It is perhaps also worth noting that this material has special significance for the interpretation of the parable of the unjust steward because our parable is included under this (or a similar) category in most discussions of riches and poverty in Luke-Acts.[144] The thesis to be argued here is well expressed by Pilgrim, who writes as follows of the Lucan texts on a proper and prudent use of possessions.

> We believe that these texts reveal the primary and practical goal of Luke's presentation on the subject of possessions. What he seeks to create is a radically new evaluation of possessions and their proper use by Christians. His purpose is not to advocate some form of Christian ascetism [sic] on the one hand, or some kind of Christian communism on the other. Rather, Luke attempts to define and encourage a *discipleship* of one's material gifts in the service of love.[145]

Luke's message is of particular relevance for rich readers.

The primary use of possessions in Luke-Acts, "the dominant response called for,"[146] is almsgiving. The importance of this particular expression of charity for Luke is revealed by the fact that "apart from Mt. 6:1-4 the term *eleēmosynē* ("alms") occurs in the New Testament only in the Gospel of Luke and in Acts (Lk. 11:41; 12:33; Acts 3:2, 3, 10; 9:36; 10:24, 31; 24:17)."[147] The same point is made, although the term *eleēmosynē* is absent, in Luke 18:22 and 19:8; in both cases, giving to the poor is involved. The latter verse, part of the story of Zacchaeus, is especially important for understanding Luke's attitude toward posses-

---

[144] Pilgrim, e.g., discusses our parable in a chapter on "The Right Use of Possessions" (*Good News*, 123-46, our parable on 125-29); Seccombe does so in a chapter on "Possessions and the Christian Life" (*Possessions*, 135-96, our parable on 160-72).

[145] Pilgrim, *Good News*, 123. Much the same thesis is at least implicit in the works of interpreters, cited earlier, who emphasize Luke's concern for the rich. See, e.g., Karris, "Poor," esp. 116, and Schottroff and Stegemann, *Jesus*, esp. 87, 91-92, 117.

[146] Johnson, *Sharing*, 17.

[147] Schottroff and Stegemann, *Jesus*, 109.

way from that point on.[165] In determining to give half his possessions
(justly and unjustly acquired) to the poor, Zacchaeus "is not fulfilling a
rule, and Jesus has given no command."[166] Instead Zacchaeus's gift is a
spontaneous act of repentance, love, and gratitude.[167] "It is a thankoffering
expressive of a changed heart."[168] There is nothing here to suggest
Zacchaeus gives up all his possessions or even that he quits his profession.[169] As suggested already, this fact provides an important qualification to Jesus' command to the rich ruler in 18:22.[170] Total renunciation
is not the only nor even the primary solution to the problem of riches
either in Luke's day or Jesus'. The sheer size of Zacchaeus's gift,
however, while not mandatory or standard, is still significant for the
message of this story. Pilgrim brings out this significance well.

> By underscoring Zacchaeus' act of giving one-half to the poor, Luke force-
> fully informs his readers that the new way of discipleship goes beyond what
> any law can require, that it is much more than a token gift, that, in fact, it is
> a total commitment of one's wealth for the poor and needy. The consequences
> of such personal sharing in the life of the Christian community are pictured
> by Luke in the book of Acts. Here, Luke holds up the example of Zacchaeus
> for all his readers to consider.[171]

It is an example worthy of emulation. Herein lies the paradigmatic
significance of the story for Luke.[172]

---

[165] Marshall, *Luke*, 697-98, is representative of the majority opinion. See Fitzmyer, *Luke*
2.1220, for other representatives of this opinion. Cf. also *NIV*: "Here and now I give."

[166] Ellis, *Luke*, 221.

[167] Geldenhuys, *Luke*, 470.

[168] Ellis, *Luke*, 221. Dupont explains Zacchaeus's actions as an expression of sincere
conversion (*Beatitudes* 3.162).

[169] Easton thinks, rightly I believe, that had Zacchaeus eventually left everything Luke
would have included this fact (*Luke*, 278). Zacchaeus continues to go about his usual
business, Easton adds, albeit in a very different manner than before. For a contrary opinion,
see Plummer, who suggests Zacchaeus may eventually have left all and followed Jesus
(*Luke*, 435); cf. also Tannehill, *Unity*, 124.

[170] Cf. Arndt, *Luke*, 390, and Seccombe, *Possessions*, 132.

[171] Pilgrim, *Good News*, 133.

[172] While almsgiving or charity to the poor is the primary mode for the proper use of one's
possessions in Luke-Acts, with Zacchaeus as the paradigm, it is not, however, the only mode
for such use. As Pilgrim notes, Luke in his gospel also provides "a number of practical
examples, which illustrate further possibilities for Christian disciples" (*Good News*, 136).
These possibilities can be outlined as follows: debts and loans (lend gratis [Luke 6:27-36];
give and it will be given [6:37-38]; the two debtors [7:40-43]); inviting the ininvited (14:7-
24, esp. vv. 12-14, 21); doing love's deeds (10:25-37, an illustration of the love command);
and the fruits of repentance (3:10-14). The substance of the outline is from Pilgrim, *Good
News*, 137-46.

2. Acts Summaries

The charitable use of possessions called for in Luke's Gospel is illustrated in the life of the early church in the book of Acts. Of particular importance for our purposes are the summaries of that life in Acts 2:42-47 (especially 44-45) and 4:32-37. While these passages cannot be discussed in detail here, several comments or observations are in order.

The picture of the life of the early church in the Acts summaries is one of unity (2:44, 46; 4:32). That unity is expressed and fostered "through common meals, the practice of hospitality, worship, and the sharing of material possessions."[173] The accent in the summaries is on the charitable spirit which characterizes the early church, not on poverty itself.[174] The sharing is not for the sake of an ideal of poverty, but rather so there will be no poor among them (4:34).[175] The needy are supported from a central fund established by the contributions of Christians and administered by the apostles (4:34-35). Many of the contributions are substantial gifts from rich Christians who liquidate property to meet the general need (e.g., Barnabas, 4:36-37). There is no indication of compulsion or formal obligation, but rather "spontaneous generosity" (cf. Zacchaeus) such as "to cause it to be long remembered."[176] People sell their possessions and give the proceeds to the church as needs arise (2:45; 4:34-37). While private property continues in the early church,[177] it is not used selfishly nor does it become a barrier to the Christians' fellowship. When such barriers do arise on account of possessions, they are dealt with promptly and, in the case of Ananias and Sapphira, with severe divine judgment (Acts 5:1-11; cf. also 6:1-6).

A number of interpreters call attention to a possible apologetic note in the sharing motif in these summaries. The terminology Luke uses to describe the life of the early church here (e.g., *hapanta koina*, 2:44, 4:32) may be designed to exploit a point of contact with Hellenistic readers. In this way, Luke may be trying to commend the church by showing that

---

[173] Seccombe, *Possessions*, 208. Johnson argues that sharing possessions, especially in Acts, is an external manifestation of the spiritual fellowship of the Christian community (*Function*, 185 n. 3).

[174] Keck, "The Poor among the Saints in the NT," *ZNW* 56 (1965) 105.

[175] Dumais, "Evangelisation," 316. Cf. Dupont, "Poor," 34.

[176] Seccombe, *Possessions*, 208-9.

[177] Cf. Acts 4:37 where Barnabas sells a field, not everything he has. Cf. also 5:1, 4. For a brief discussion of these and other indications of the continuance of private property in the early church, see Seccombe, *Possessions*, 207-8. Seccombe provides a list of interpreters who likewise conclude "Luke does not mean to claim that the early church practised a form of economic communism" (p. 207 n. 52).

7. An eschatological note is often present in the material on riches and poverty or in the immediate context (e.g., the fulfillment of the beatitudes and woes; 12:33 and 12:31, 35-48). This fact suggests there is an important relationship between eschatology and ethics, in particular the ethics of stewardship. The nature of that relationship will be clarified in the next major section of this chapter. Before doing so, however, note should be made of the specific impact of the theme of riches and poverty on the interpretation of the parable of the unjust steward.

D. Impact of Riches/Poverty Theme on Our Parable

The theological context of riches and poverty in Luke-Acts broadens and sharpens our understanding of the parable of the unjust steward in several important ways.

1. The riches/poverty theme lends weight to the traditional interpretation that our parable treats the use of material possessions. The precise meaning of Luke 16:9 is unclear, it may be recalled, when taken in isolation. Jesus there exhorts his disciples to "use worldly wealth to gain friends for yourselves," but does not specify *who* those friends are or *how* they are to be gained. Vv. 10-12 make it clear the exhortation involves the faithful use of possessions, but they still do not answer the specific questions. The parable of the rich man and Lazarus in the immediate literary context (16:19-31) clarifies 16:9 to some degree. The rich man's apparent neglect of poor Lazarus, for example, implies that 16:9 is counselling the opposite behavior. That line of evidence, though important, is nonetheless still largely inferential. The pervasive and explicit emphasis on helping the poor throughout Luke-Acts, however, strongly confirms the presumption that Luke 16:9 is an exhortation to the same basic positive course of action. Luke 12:33 and 18:22 are of particular significance in this regard. These verses relate giving to the poor to having "treasure in heaven [*thēsauron (anekleipton, 12:33; cf. eklipēi, 16:9b) en tois ouranois*]." The parallel between this expression and being welcomed into "eternal dwellings" in 16:9 is striking, and suggests that charity to the poor is also in view in the latter verse. If so, the friends of 16:9 are the poor and the verse (as well as the whole pericope) is an exhortation to almsgiving. The conditions implicit in 12:33 and 18:22, as well as the thrust of 16:10-12, make it clear that 16:9 is about faithful

---

vols.; ed. P. J. Achtemeier; Missoula, MT: Scholars Press, 1979] 1.87-100), who warns against reading the life-setting of Luke-Acts too directly from the text, and uses the possessions theme as an example of the pitfalls of such a procedure.

stewardship of possessions, not total renunciation. The possible cross-reference between Luke 16:9 and the Acts summaries offers further confirmation that charity to the poor is the point of our parable.

2. The juxtaposition of the parables of the unjust steward and the rich man and Lazarus in Luke 16 fits a pattern found elsewhere in the Lucan material on possessions. Several times Luke illustrates wise and foolish uses of possessions in close connection with each other (cf. 12:22-34 with 12:13-21; 19:1-10 with 18:18-23; and Acts 4:36-37 with 5:1-11). This pattern, perhaps a literary device to highlight both uses, verifies the conclusion that Luke 16:1-13 treats the wise use of possessions. What is more, the corresponding positive members in each of the other juxtapositions (i.e., 12:22-34, 19:1-10, and Acts 4:36-37) offer further evidence that our parable, too, is an exhortation to show charity to the poor.

3. The religious issue at the heart of the Lucan theme of riches and poverty accentuates the importance of the wise use of possessions commanded in our parable. Because "no servant can serve two masters" (16:13), to make friends by means of worldly wealth, to show charity to the needy, is an urgent and crucial matter. As evidence of and testimony to one's ultimate commitment, such actions will have an important bearing on one's eternal destiny (cf. 16:9-12; 12:13-21, 33; and 18:22). Faithful stewardship of material possessions is, Luke reminds us, an integral part of true discipleship.

4. The eschatological note present in or near other material on possessions in Luke-Acts (e.g., 12:20, 31-32, 35-48) corroborates our attention to the same note in Luke 16:1-13 itself and in the literary context (especially 16:16). The not infrequent association of the two themes suggests that an important relationship exists between them. This relationship leads us to the next major section of this chapter, the eschatological theme.

III. Eschatology in Luke-Acts

A second thread of theological context of particular significance for the interpretation of the parable of the unjust steward is that of eschatology or the coming of the kingdom of God. The relevance of this theme for our parable has been suggested already in observations about the prominence of the eschatological note in the parable itself, in its immediate literary context, and in related material on the theme of possessions. In this section the relationship between eschatology and our parable will be developed in more detail.

Eschatology is, in Fitzmyer's opinion, "the most difficult and most controverted aspect of Lucan theology today."[182] Most of this controversy has been generated by Conzelmann's book, *The Theology of Saint Luke*. His thesis is that in order to explain the problem of the delay of the parousia Luke abandons the original belief in the imminence of the coming of the kingdom and replaces it with a three-phase redemptive history of his own making. In this way, the unexpected delay is accounted for as part of God's plan.[183] It is beyond the scope of the present chapter to discuss Conzelmann's thesis in detail.[184] Instead the main lines of Jesus' teaching on the kingdom of God as found in Luke-Acts will be summarized. By this procedure, Luke's own eschatology will come into focus; at the same time, it will become clear that Conzelmann's thesis does not do justice to the evidence and is therefore inadequate. In addition to summarizing Jesus' teaching on the kingdom, I will discuss the relationship of eschatology and ethics and draw conclusions about the impact of this particular contextual level on the interpretation of our parable. My thesis is that eschatology—the coming of the kingdom of God—is in a real sense the most basic context for understanding the parable of the unjust steward. The prudent use of material possessions counselled by our parable is both proof of one's citizenship in the kingdom and an actualization of the values of the kingdom in anticipation of its final manifestation.

A. Jesus' Teaching on the Kingdom of God

"Modern scholarship is quite unanimous in the opinion that the Kingdom of God was the central message of Jesus."[185] This assessment by Ladd is

---

[182] Fitzmyer, *Luke* 1.231. For bibliography on Lucan eschatology, see Bovon, *Luc*, 11-18; Dupont, *Beatitudes* 3.137 n. 1; Ellis, *Eschatology in Luke* (FBBS; Philadelphia: Fortress, 1972) 21-25; J. Ernst, *Herr der Geschichte. Perspektiven der lukanischen Eschatologie* (SBS 88; Stuttgart: Katholisches Bibelwerk, 1978) 114-17; Fitzmyer, *Luke* 1.262, 267; O. Merk, "Das Reich Gottes in den lukanischen Schriften," in *Jesus und Paulus* (ed. Ellis and E. Grässer; Göttingen: Vandenhoeck & Ruprecht, 1975) 203 n. 8; Richard, "Luke," 12-15; and Sabourin, "The Eschatology of Luke," *BTB* 12 (1982) 76.

[183] For Conzelmann's own statement of his thesis, see *Luke*, 13-14, 16-17 (esp. 17 n. 2), 96-97, 131-35.

[184] The literature on Conzelmann is staggering. For a long list of reviews of Conzelmann, see H. H. Oliver, "The Lucan Birth Stories and the Purpose of Luke-Acts," *NTS* 10 (1963-64) 202 n. 2. Among the many works that summarize and critique Conzelmann's theory are the following: Ellis, *Eschatology*, 5-11, passim; Gasque, *Acts*, 291-96; Kodell, "Theology," 127-34; R. Maddox, *The Purpose of Luke-Acts* (Göttingen: Vandenhoeck & Ruprecht, 1982) 100-57; Marshall, *Historian*, 77-80, 85-88, passim; Rohde, *Rediscovering*, 154-78; and Thiselton, "The Parousia in Modern Theology: Some Questions and Comments," *TynBul* 27 (1976) 44-46.

[185] Ladd, *Theology*, 57.

echoed by many other NT scholars,[186] and its truth is borne out by the frequent occurrence of the expression *(hē) basileia tou theou* in the synoptic gospels.[187] Luke shares this point of view on the importance of the eschatological theme for Jesus. In Luke 4:43, for example, Jesus summarizes his own ministry in these words: "I must preach the good news of the kingdom of God to the other towns also, because that is why I was sent."[188] The phrase *basileia tou theou* occurs thirty-one other times in Luke's Gospel and six times in Acts.[189] The kingdom is, then, the main focus of Jesus' teaching in Luke-Acts, including his parables.[190]

While scholars agree on the centrality of the kingdom in Jesus' teaching, the coming of the kingdom is explained in different ways. As is well-known, there are three main schools of interpretation of the kingdom of God.[191] "Consistent" or "thorough-going eschatology" argues that the kingdom of God as taught by Jesus is/was exclusively future, albeit imminent or near. This view, put forward by J. Weiss and developed by A. Schweitzer,[192] forms the basis of Conzelmann's thesis

---

[186] E.g., Chilton, ed., *The Kingdom of God in the Teaching of Jesus* (Philadelphia/ London: Fortress/SPCK, 1984) 1; Jeremias, *New Testament Theology* (New York: Scribner's, 1971) 96; Marshall, *Historian*, 128; Perrin, *Rediscovering the Teaching of Jesus* (New York: Harper & Row, 1967) 54; Ridderbos, *Kingdom*, xi; Stein, *Method*, 60; and Stonehouse, *Luke*, 152.

[187] About 110 times, by Merk's count ("Reich," 204).

[188] The proximity of Luke 4:43 to Jesus' sermon at Nazareth (4:16-27) and the similarity in vocabulary to 4:18-19 (e.g., *euangelisasthai* and *apestalken/apestalēn*) suggests the content of Jesus' "good news to the poor" (4:18) is "the kingdom of God" (4:43; cf. 6:20).

[189] The kingdom of God is, it may be recalled, the "dominant motif" in Luke's central section (Ellis, *Luke*, 12), the phrase occurring twenty times there. The statistics for Luke-Acts as a whole are my own count from Moulton, Geden, and Moulton, and agree with Koch, "Wertung," 159 n. 4. For slightly different figures, see Merk, "Reich," 204. The latter notes (p. 205) that Acts begins and ends with the preaching of the kingdom (1:3 and 28:31).

[190] The truth of this statement for the parable of the sower (Luke 8:1-15) and the kingdom parables themselves (Luke 13:18-21) is obvious. As a number of interpreters emphasize, however, the kingdom is also central to Jesus' other parables. Hunter, for example, praises Dodd and Jeremias for putting Jesus' parables "back into their true [i.e., eschatological] setting" ("New Look," 193), and asserts that the kingdom of God is "the theme of all his parables" ("Centrality," 73; cf. also 84). See also Hunter, *Parables*, esp. 52-91; Cranfield, "Mark 4:1-34," *SJT* 4 (1951) 404; Findlay, *Parables*, 19; Fonck, *Parabeln*, 48-49, 61-62, 66; Payne, "Metaphor," 36; and Perrin, *Jesus and the Language of the Kingdom. Symbol and Metaphor in New Testament Interpretation* (Philadelphia: Fortress, 1976) 1.

[191] For discussions of the history of interpretation of the kingdom of God, see Chilton, *Kingdom*, 1-26; Ladd, *Theology*, 57-60, and *Presence*, 3-42; Marshall, *Historian*, 107 n. 3; Perrin, *The Kingdom of God in the Teaching of Jesus* (Philadelphia: Westminster, 1963 [most of this book, a revision of Perrin's doctoral dissertation at Göttingen, is a history of interpretation of the kingdom in the teaching of Jesus from Schleiermacher to the late 1950s]); and Ridderbos, *Kingdom*, xi-xxxii. For additional bibliography, see Chilton, *Kingdom*, 154-57; Guthrie, *New Testament Theology* (Downers Grove: Inter-Varsity, 1981) 409 n. 1; and Ladd, *Presence*, 3 n. 2.

[192] J. Weiss, *Die Predigt Jesu vom Reiche Gottes* (Göttingen: Vandenhoeck & Ruprecht,

about the occasion and purpose of Luke-Acts.[193] "Realized eschatology," on the other hand, explains the kingdom of God as entirely present in the life and ministry of Jesus. Dodd is the best known advocate of this view.[194] A third school of interpretation is a synthesis of the first two. According to this group of interpreters the kingdom of God in Jesus' teaching is in some sense both present and future. The latter view is widely held and represents "an emerging consensus"[195] among NT scholars. For this reason, the following discussion of Jesus' teaching on the kingdom of God as recorded in Luke-Acts is organized in terms of the present and future aspects of the kingdom. Since the main lines of Jesus' teaching are clear, it will not be necessary to discuss this material in detail. In the course of the discussion I will, however, call attention to the implications of both aspects for Conzelmann's thesis.

1892); ET, *Jesus' Proclamation of the Kingdom of God* (Philadelphia: Fortress, 1971); A. Schweitzer, *Vom Reimarus zu Wrede* (Tübingen: Mohr, 1906); ET, *The Quest of the Historical Jesus* (2d ed.; London: Black, 1911).

[193] When the coming of the kingdom did not materialize in the near future as Jesus expected, it supposedly created a serious problem for the church. Luke responds to the problem of the delay of the parousia, Conzelmann thinks, by eliminating the early or imminent expectation from the traditions he transmits and thereby pushing the parousia into the distant future. According to Ladd, "few contemporary scholars view the Kingdom as exclusively eschatological [i.e., future]" (*Theology*, 58). He cites Hiers (*The Kingdom of God in the Synoptic Tradition* [Gainesville: University of Florida, 1970]) and Bultmann (*Theology of the New Testament* [complete in one vol.; New York: Scribner's, 1951, 1955; esp. 4-11]) as exceptions. For the latter, the imminence of the kingdom is existential, not temporal (cf. Ladd, *Presence*, 7-8, 20-22). "What is happening [in Bultmann]," writes Perrin, "is that he is accepting the *konsequente Eschatologie* of Weiss and Schweitzer and interpreting it in terms of the *Daseinanalyse* of Martin Heidegger's *Sein und Zeit*" (*Kingdom*, 115).

[194] Dodd, *The Parables of the Kingdom*, esp. 21-59.

[195] Ladd, *Presence*, 38. The kingdom of God as both present and future in the teaching of Jesus is, according to Perrin, "one of the points firmly established" by modern discussion (*Kingdom*, 185). Cf. also Chilton, who speaks of the recognition of both aspects of the kingdom as "the eschatological consensus" (*Kingdom*, 21). Among the representatives of this consensus are the following: O. Cullmann, *Christ and Time* (rev. ed.; Philadelphia: Westminster, 1964 [see p. 84 for his well-known D-Day and V-Day comparison]), and *Salvation in History* (New York: Harper & Row, 1967); Ellis, "Present and Future Eschatology in Luke," *NTS* 12 (1965-66) 27-41, and "Eschatology"; Kümmel, *Promise*, and "Futuristic and Realized Eschatology in the Earliest Stages of Christianity," *JR* 43 (1963) 303-14; Ladd, *The Pattern of New Testament Truth* (Grand Rapids: Eerdmans, 1968) 41-63, *Theology*, 57-69, and *Presence*; Perrin, *Kingdom* and *Rediscovering*; Ridderbos, *Kingdom*, esp. 61-184; and Vos, *Biblical Theology* (Grand Rapids: Eerdmans, 1948) 372-402, esp. 381-85. Cullmann (*Time*, 3), Stein (*Method*, 78-79), and Ladd (*Pattern*), among others, all note that the tension between the present and future aspects of the kingdom is the basic motif in the whole NT. For additional bibliography on scholars who share "the eschatological consensus," see especially Ladd, *Presence*, 38 n. 161. Notable exceptions to this consensus are Dodd (but see the next note) and Bultmann (cf. Perrin, *Kingdom*, 89).

1. The Kingdom as Future

Virtually all interpreters agree Jesus taught the future aspect of the kingdom, and it is clearly present in Luke-Acts.[196] The relevant material in Luke-Acts falls into three categories: general statements, imminence, and interval.

a) General Statements

A number of texts in Luke-Acts speak of the kingdom of God as a future reality. They do so in general terms without indicating either imminence or an expected interval. Among those texts are Luke 6:21-23 (recall the future tenses in the beatitudes); 11:2 ("your kingdom come"[197]); 13:28-29 (exclusion/inclusion at "the feast in the kingdom of God"); 14:14-15 (the resurrection of the righteous connected with the same feast); and 18:29-30 (the kingdom of God related to the age to come and eternal life).[198] The future aspect in these and other verses is beyond dispute.

b) Imminence

Several other texts suggest this future coming of the kingdom is imminent or near. Those verses are Luke 3:7, 9, 11 (the nearness of judgment—"the axe is already at the root of the trees," v. 9); 10:9, 11 ("the kingdom of God is near [ēngiken]"[199]); 13:6-9 (the parable of the fig

---

[196] Dodd comes to mind as an exception here, but there is some question as to Dodd's later views. Marshall notes that Dodd's position on realized eschatology apparently changes to allow for further eschatological events in the future (*Historian*, 107 n. 3, 129 n. 3; cf. Dodd, *The Coming of Christ* [Cambridge: Cambridge University Press, 1951] 17, 7). Ellis also mentions this change, but concludes that, since for Dodd the events themselves are "beyond history," it is doubtful that he allows for future eschatology any more than in his earlier writings ("Present," 27 n. 2; cf. Marshall, *Historian*, 107 n. 3, for a similar reservation). For a "summary of evidence for the Kingdom as future in the teaching of Jesus," see Perrin, *Kingdom*, 83.

[197] "If the kingdom were wholly present, the request for its coming in the Lord's Prayer would lose much of its force" (Guthrie, *Theology*, 416). Cf. also A. A. Trites, who describes this petition as a prayer for "the glorious fulfillment of the kingly reign of God" ("The Prayer Motif in Luke-Acts," in *Perspectives on Luke-Acts* [ed. Talbert] 178).

[198] Others verses on the future of the kingdom are Luke 9:26; 12:38-48 (note the uncertainty as to time, esp. vv. 38, 40, 46); 13:1-9, 18-21; 17:24; 21:27, 36; 22:16, 18, 29-30; also Acts 1:11; 3:19-21; 17:31; 24:25.

[199] Marshall disputes the perfect tense as a reference to "the nearness of the future, glorious manifestation of the kingdom." He argues instead that the reference is to "the actual presence of the kingdom in the ministry of Jesus" (or his commissioned disciples) (*Historian*, 132-34, and *Luke*, 422). Ellis writes, in similar fashion, "It is the local nearness of a present reality not the chronological nearness of a future reality" (*Luke*, 156). If this

tree—"leave it alone for one more year," v. 8—in the context of "repent or perish," vv. 1-5); 18:8 ("he [God] will see that they [his chosen ones] get justice, *and quickly*"[200]); 9:27 ("some standing here will not taste death before they see the kingdom of God"); and 21:32 ("this generation will certainly not pass away until all these things have happened"). The latter two verses are particularly significant because both figure in Conzelmann's thesis that Luke replaces the original imminent expectation of the kingdom with a timeless conception of it. As evidence of this alleged change in 9:27 Conzelmann cites the absence of the phrase *elēlythuian en dynamei* which occurs in the Marcan parallel (9:1). By omitting this phrase, which Conzelmann assumes is "a realistic description of the Parousia," Luke makes the saying "independent of any definite time."[201] The phrase *tōn autou hestēkotōn* then means "those who are standing by 'at the time,'" i.e., mankind in general alive at the time of the parousia, not those to whom Jesus speaks.[202] The latter conclusion is supported, Conzelmann adds, by the phrase *hē genea hautē* in 21:32.[203]

Several considerations speak against Conzelmann's interpretation of these verses. Since his emphasis is on Luke 9:27, I will restrict my comments to this verse. First, it may be, as Ellis suggests, that in 9:27 Luke omits the phrase "coming in power" because in his understanding the kingdom always comes in power.[204] Second, it is quite probable that this saying does not refer to the parousia at all in either Luke or Mark. The immediate context of the saying itself in both gospels suggests that seeing the kingdom is likely to be identified with the transfiguration "as a kind of proleptic manifestation of Jesus' future glory."[205] Other

---

argument is correct, Luke 10:9, 11 undermines Conzelmann's thesis. If the kingdom is already present in Jesus' ministry, the delay of its future manifestation is not the problem Conzelmann thinks it is. This difficulty for Conzelmann's whole reconstruction will become clearer in the discussion of the present aspect of the kingdom.

[200] Emphasis added. Cranfield ("The Parable of Unjust Judge and the Eschatology of Luke-Acts," *SJT* 16 [1963] 299 n. 1) and Marshall (*Luke*, 676) both contend the prepositional phrase means "soon, quickly"; hence imminence is present in Jesus' teaching here. This interpretation of the phrase is confirmed, Marshall adds, by the context of the parable of the unjust judge itself. The point of the parable is that God will vindicate his people and will do so soon.

[201] Conzelmann, *Luke*, 104.

[202] *Luke*, 104-5.

[203] *Luke*, 105, esp. n. 2.

[204] Ellis, "Present," 30-35.

[205] Ellis, "Present," 34. Others who interpret 9:27 as a reference to Jesus' imminent transfiguration include Plummer, *Luke*, 250, and Smalley, "The Delay of the Parousia," *JBL* 83 (1964) 46.

identifications are also possible, besides the parousia.[206] In addition, the use of "until [heōs]" in this verse "implies that the *tines will* experience death *after* seeing the *bas. t. Theou*, which would not be true of those who live to see the *parousia*."[207] Whatever the precise reference in Luke 9:27, it is likely not a reference to the parousia. The verse does not, therefore, prove what Conzelmann wants it to prove. It is important to add, however, that whatever is being referred to in this verse *is* an integral aspect of the kingdom of God and its manifestation is imminent. Jesus does promise some of his hearers they will see the kingdom of God before they die. Even if that manifestation of the kingdom has reference to the transfiguration rather than the parousia, the former is distinguished from the latter in time, not in kind. That this manifestation of the kingdom is probably something other than the parousia is also quite in line with the present aspect of the kingdom.[208] As we will see, this aspect also undermines Conzelmann's thesis about the purpose of Luke-Acts.

While imminence may not be Luke's major emphasis, he does retain this theme from tradition. The theme of imminence is "too prominent," writes Thiselton, "for Conzelmann to dismiss merely as careless editing, especially when he has portrayed him as one who is constantly concerned for every detail."[209] Luke does not abandon or eliminate the belief that the kingdom is imminent. Imminent does not mean immediate, however.[210] There are a number of texts in Luke that imply an interval is expected before the final coming of the kingdom. On several occasions, in fact, this note occurs side by side with the note of imminence.

c) Interval

Among the texts that suggest an interval before the parousia are Luke 9:27; 12:38 (the master may come in the second or third watch of the

---

[206] Marshall, e.g., explains Luke 9:27 as a reference to the events of the resurrection and Pentecost (*Luke*, 378). Cf. also Plummer's list of different interpretations of this verse (*Luke*, 249-50). The fact that Luke 9:27 can be explained as a reference to something other than the parousia makes it unnecessary to conclude, as do Cullmann (*Time*, 87, 148, 150) and Kümmel (*Promise*, 149), that Jesus is mistaken here in his own understanding of the time of parousia.

[207] Plummer, *Luke*, 250. See also Ellis, "Present," 32.

[208] See Marshall, *Historian*, 132, and *Luke*, 378.

[209] Thiselton, "Parousia," 46. Cf. also S. G. Wilson, "Lucan Eschatology," *NTS* 16 (1969-70) 344.

[210] Many interpreters emphasize this distinction, among them, Marshall, *Historian*, 131, 136; R. P. Martin, "Salvation and Discipleship in Luke's Gospel," *Int* 30 (1976) 373; and Schürmann, "Eschatologie und Liebesdienst in der Verkündigung Jesu," in *Ursprung und Gestalt* (Düsseldorf: Patmos, 1970) 286 n. 35 ("Jesu 'Naherwartung' ist gewiß keine 'Nächsterwartung'").

night); 18:8 ("when the Son of Man comes, will he find faith on the earth?"); and 19:11-29 (the parable of the ten talents).[211] In 9:27 and 18:8 the notes of interval and imminence occur together. The implication in 9:27 that some of Jesus' hearers will die before seeing the kingdom of God and that those who do see the kingdom will die after seeing it suggests an interval. Conzelmann himself admits the presence of this theme in Luke 9:27 by granting its presence in the Marcan parallel (9:1).[212] Even if, as argued earlier, Conzelmann is likely wrong in identifying either verse with the parousia, his admission is significant for the light it throws on his methodology. In order to avoid the difficulty that an expected interval here raises for his "consistent eschatology" and his thesis as a whole, Conzelmann excuses it as a community creation.[213] Such circular reasoning calls into question both Conzelmann's methodology and his conclusions.[214] Whatever the precise meaning of the manifestation of the kingdom in Luke 9:27, the note of an interval or delay in its coming is undeniable. The other texts cited above more clearly connect this interval to the parousia or the final coming of the kingdom.

The whole context of Luke 12:38, for example, is eschatological in the future sense of the word. The disciples' readiness for the coming of the Son of Man (vv. 35, 40) is compared to servants waiting for the return of their master. "It will be good for those servants whose master finds them ready," reads v. 38, "even if he comes in the second or third watch of the night." Writes Marshall, "The verse reckons with a certain interval before the parousia, although it springs naturally enough from the imagery of the parable."[215] The note of uncertainty about the time of coming is used as incentive for constant vigilance and faithfulness on the part of Jesus' disciples (cf. vv. 40, 42-46).[216] An interval of some sort is

---

[211] Other texts that suggest an interval are Luke 5:33-35; 9:23; 13:6-9 (note also imminence here); 17:20-30; 21:7-13, 24; 22:69; and Acts 1:6-8.

[212] Conzelmann, *Luke*, 104 n. 1.

[213] Conzelmann, *Luke*, 104 n. 1.

[214] Thiselton, "Parousia," 45. By such means Conzelmann overemphasizes "the distinctiveness of Luke's approach by exaggerating the note of imminence and immediacy in Matthew and Mark" (Thiselton, "Parousia," 45). Cf. also Mark 13:10, 32.

[215] Marshall, *Luke*, 537. Cf. also Arndt, *Luke*, 321.

[216] The phrase *ho pistos oikonomos ho phronimos* in 12:42 is particularly noteworthy because of its striking verbal parallels with the parable of the unjust steward. The only two places in the synoptics where *oikonomos* occurs are in this verse and our parable (16:1-3, 8); four of the five occurrences of *pistos* in Luke's Gospel are found in this verse and 16:10-12; *phronimos* is used only two times by Luke, both in the Gospel—12:42 and 16:8. What is more, in both Luke 12 and our parable faithful stewardship with possessions is prominent (cf. 12:31-33—seek his kingdom/sell your possessions and give to the poor; 16:9, 11, 13—*mamōnas*). This data is significant because it highlights the eschatological background of

also implied in Luke 18:8, the concluding verse of the parable of the unjust judge. Having promised his disciples that God will vindicate them, "and quickly" (v. 8a), Jesus then asks, "However, when the Son of Man comes, will he find faith on the earth?" Jesus' question assumes a delay. To again quote Marshall,

> The question as a whole presupposes a time of tribulation for the disciples in which they may be tempted to give up faith because their prayers are not answered; it is meant as an exhortation to take seriously the lesson of the parable that God will certainly act to vindicate them. Thus an interval before the parousia is presupposed, but the sense of imminent expectation is not abandoned.[217]

An interval is also presupposed in the parable of the ten minas in Luke 19:11-27.[218]

The foregoing evidence shows that Luke *and* Jesus presuppose an interval (of uncertain length) before the final coming of the kingdom of God. This fact makes it clear that the delay of the parousia is neither the problem Conzelmann makes it out to be,[219] nor does it exclude imminence as Conzelmann thinks it must. While Luke no doubt includes both strands in Jesus' teaching out of faithfulness to tradition, perhaps they at the same time serve his pastoral concerns and provide a response to church problems. Perhaps, as Ellis and Wilson suggest, one or both of these strands is intended to correct misapplications of Jesus' eschatology, e.g., an over-eager or false anticipation of the parousia.[220] Whatever the precise *Sitz im Leben* may be, the two strands in Luke's (and Jesus')

---

stewardship. The various parallels between our parable and Luke 12 (recall, e.g., 12:33 and 16:9) also provide further confirmation that our parable is about the wise use of material possessions in the context of the coming of the kingdom of God.

[217] Marshall, *Luke*, 676-77.

[218] The parable of the ten minas "presupposes the continuation of the world's time after Jesus' departure, and it lays special emphasis upon the vocation of believers during that interim" (Ridderbos, *Kingdom*, 515). Cf. Marshall, *Historian*, 132, and *Luke*, 703.

[219] Many critical analyses of the so-called delay of the parousia have been offered, often with particular reference to Conzelmann. Among them are the following: D. E. Aune, "The Significance of the Delay of the Parousia," in *Current Issues in Biblical and Patristic Interpretation* (ed. G. F. Hawthorne; Grand Rapids: 1975) 87-109; R. J. Bauckham, "The Delay of the Parousia," *TynBul* 31 (1980) 3-36; Ellis, "Eschatology," esp. 17-18, and *Luke*, 240; A. L. Moore, *The Parousia in the New Testament* (NovTSup 13; Leiden: Brill, 1966) esp. 85-88; Morris, "Luke and Early Catholicism," *WTJ* 35 (1973) 125-26; Smalley, "Delay"; Stonehouse, Review, 67-68; and Thiselton, "Parousia," 32-35, 44-46.

[220] Ellis, *Eschatology*, 18-19 (his emphasis is on the delay motif), and Wilson, "Eschatology," 345-47. Cf. also Ellis, *Luke*, 12-15, 61, 209-12, 239-47; Barrett, *Historian*, 62; Marshall, *Luke*, 702; Mattill, *Last Things*, 234; Morris, "Catholicism," 131; Richard, "Luke," 5; and Talbert, "Quest," 196. Could there be a relationship between a misapplication of eschatology (e.g., asceticism? dissipation?) and Luke's emphasis on the dangers and wise use of material possessions?

eschatology refute Conzelmann's thesis at several key points, as has
been noted. His thesis is also refuted by the present aspect of eschatology.

2. The Kingdom as Present

The distinctive feature of Jesus' teaching on the kingdom of God is that,
while future, it is also at the same time present in his person and
ministry.[221] Luke affirms "the two-stage manifestation of the kingdom,
and accents its manifestation in the present."[222] The presence of the
kingdom in Luke-Acts has been noted at various points in earlier
discussions. Luke 16:16, for example, stresses the presence of the
kingdom, as does 6:20 (the kingdom of God "*estin*" yours). One of the
clearest statements of this aspect of the kingdom is found in Luke 17:21.
"Having been asked by the Pharisees when the kingdom of God would
come" (v. 20), Jesus answers, "the kingdom of God is [*estin*] *entos
hymōn*." While the precise meaning of the latter phrase is difficult to
determine, there is widespread agreement that "in your midst" or
"among you" (*NASB, NEB*) makes better sense here than does "within
you" (*NIV*, but cf. marginal note).[223] If so, this verse is a reference to the
presence of the kingdom.[224] When would the kingdom come? It is already
in their midst, although in an unexpected form.[225] The assertion of this
verse is confirmed by a number of signs of the kingdom's presence in
Jesus' ministry. Among those signs are the following.

a) Healing Miracles

Perhaps the most striking sign of the presence of the kingdom is the
healing miracles of Jesus and/or his disciples. In Luke 7:22, for example,
Jesus points to his own miracles ("the blind receive sight, the lame walk,

---

[221] Among the interpreters who call attention to the distinctiveness of this feature of
Jesus' teaching are Ellis, *Luke*, 13; Guthrie, *Theology*, 412-13; and Ladd, "Eschatology and
the Unity of New Testament Theology," *ExpTim* 68 (1956-57) 269, and *Theology*, 70, 93.
For a helpful "summary of evidence for the Kingdom as present in the teaching of Jesus,"
see Perrin, *Kingdom*, 74-78.

[222] Ellis, *Luke*, 13. Others who call attention to Luke's emphasis on the present aspect of
the kingdom include Marshall, *Historian*, 134, and Stonehouse, *Luke*, 154.

[223] E.g., Ellis, *Luke*, 211; Guthrie, *Theology*, 413 (see esp. n. 20 for bibliography on
entos); Jeremias, *Theology*, 101; Kümmel, *Promise*, 34; Ladd, *Theology*, 68; Marshall, *Luke*,
655-56; and Stonehouse, *Luke*, 155. See also the literature cited in BAGD, s.v., "*entos*."

[224] Stonehouse also notes the present tense of the verb in this verse as implying the actual
presence of the kingdom (*Luke*, 155 n. 1).

[225] Ladd, *Theology*, 68.

those who have leprosy are cured, the deaf hear, the dead are raised") as proof that he is indeed "the coming one" (vv. 19-20), the Messiah. The clear echoes of Luke 4:18-19 in this statement connect these miracles to the fulfillment of the rule of God promised in the OT (cf. 4:21). The connection between this rule (or kingdom) and miracles is even clearer in Jesus' commission to the seventy-two in Luke 10. In v. 9 Jesus relates his representatives' ministry to their message—"Heal the sick who are there and tell them, 'The kingdom of God is near you'" (cf. v. 11). Healing the sick is proof of the nearness of the kingdom. The nearness of the kingdom here is, as Ellis puts it, "the local nearness of a present reality not the chronological nearness of a future reality."[226] Healing miracles are a sign of the presence of the kingdom of God.

Luke 10:17-18 indicates that an important part of the healing ministry of Jesus and his representatives is the exorcism of demons. The exorcism of demons, "one of Jesus' most characteristic miracles,"[227] is perhaps the clearest proof of the presence of the kingdom. The significance of exorcisms, either by Jesus or his commissioned representatives, is well expressed by Jeremias. He writes,

> Jesus enters this world enslaved by Satan with the authority of God, not only to exercise mercy, but above all to join battle with evil. . . . These victories over the power of evil [in exorcisms] are not just isolated invasions of Satan's realm. They are more. They are manifestations of the dawn of the time of salvation.[228]

This fact is explicitly stated in Luke 11:20. In response to criticism that he himself exercises satanic power (v. 15), Jesus responds, "But if I drive out demons by the finger of God, then the kingdom of God has come [*ephthasen*] to you" (v. 20). Although the meaning of the verb in this verse has been much debated, it likely connotes actual presence, not merely proximity.[229] "What was present," explains Ladd, "was not the eschaton, but the kingly power of God, attacking the dominion of Satan, and delivering men from the power of evil."[230] According to Ladd, Jesus' statement in this verse and in the two subsequent verses (vv. 21-22; cf.

---

[226] Ellis, *Luke*, 156.

[227] Ladd, *Theology*, 65. Cf. Luke 4:31-44; 8:26-39; and 13:10-17 (esp. 16).

[228] Jeremias, *Theology*, 94.

[229] Dodd, *Parables*, 28-29; Ladd, *Theology*, 66; and Marshall, *Luke*, 476. The latter offers a good summary of the debate about this verb.

[230] Ladd, *Theology*, 66. Similarly, Jeremias writes, in commenting on the same verse, "Every occasion on which Jesus drives out an evil spirit is an anticipation of the hour in which Satan will be visibly robbed of his power. The victories over his instruments are a foretaste of the eschaton" (*Theology*, 95).

Matt 12:28-29 and Mark 3:27) embodies the essential theology of the kingdom of God.[231] That theology is "one of conflict and conquest over the kingdom of Satan."[232] Such conflict and conquest, apparent in healing miracles and especially exorcisms, is proof the kingdom of God is present.

b) Table Fellowship

Jesus' table fellowship with his disciples and followers, especially tax collectors and sinners (Luke 5:29-30; 15:1-2; and 19:1-10), is another sign of the kingdom's presence. As Perrin points out, this "acted parable" is itself an aspect of Jesus' proclamation of the kingdom of God.[233] By means of table fellowship, and especially the acceptance it conveyed, Jesus symbolizes present forgiveness of sins and a new kind of relationship with God and one's fellow men. In such actions people "celebrated the joy of the present experience and anticipated its consummation in the future."[234] The religious significance of this table fellowship is reflected in Jesus' words, "I have not come to call the righteous, but sinners to repentance" (5:32; cf. also 19:10). "He was fulfilling his messianic mission when he gathered sinners into fellowship with himself."[235] Table fellowship is also an important ingredient in the life of the early church (cf., e.g., Acts 2:42, 46).

c) Forgiveness

The forgiveness of sins pictured in table fellowship is also proclaimed by Jesus as a present experience. In Luke 5, for example, Jesus pronounces a paralytic forgiven (v. 20, note the perfect tense of the verb—"apheōntai"), then heals the man to prove his divine authority to forgive sins (vv. 24-25). The same pronouncement of forgiveness also occurs in Luke 7:47. There Jesus explains that an infamous woman's lavish display of affection for him is proof "her many sins have been forgiven

---

[231] Ladd, *Theology*, 66.

[232] Ladd, *Theology*, 51. The note of conflict and conquest evident in exorcisms calls into question Conzelmann's theory about a Satan-free period during Jesus' ministry. For Conzelmann's statement of this theory, see *Luke*, 28, 170; for criticism, see, among others, Marshall, *Historian*, 137 n. 2; Martin, "Salvation," 274; and Stonehouse, Review, 69-70.

[233] Perrin, *Rediscovering*, 102.

[234] Perrin, *Rediscovering*, 107. The consummation of this fellowship is also pictured in terms of a banquet (cf. Luke 13:29; 14:15-24).

[235] Ladd, *Theology*, 75.

[*apheōntai*]."[236] The forgiveness of sins on earth is a sign of the inbreaking of the time of salvation in this age.[237] It is evidence of the presence of the kingdom.

d) Holy Spirit

Luke places a great deal of emphasis on the ministry of the Holy Spirit in the life and activity of both Jesus and the early church. It is as the anointed servant of Isaiah that Jesus proclaims the inauguration of the promised eschatological salvation (Luke 4:18-19, 21; cf. 3:22; 4:1, 14). It is by the power of the Spirit, described as "the finger of God," that Jesus casts out demons (11:20). The kingdom of God is also present in the eschatological powers of the Spirit operative in and through Jesus' disciples (e.g., Luke 3:16-17; 10:17-18).[238] The Spirit, given as an eschatological gift (Acts 2:14-21, 33), "constitutes a continuing presence of the kingdom of God in the post-resurrection Church. . . . Like Paul and Jesus, Luke regards the Holy Spirit as the mediator of the reign of God, 'the anticipation of the end in the present.'"[239]

e) Good Works

Good works themselves are a sign of the kingdom's presence.[240] Charity "declares the reality of the Kingdom and marks out those who are truly the 'sons of the Most High' (6,30-36; 14,12-14)."[241] As will become clear in the subsequent discussion, this fact is especially significant for understanding Jesus' ethics, in general, and our parable, in particular.

3. Conclusions

While Jesus' teaching on the kingdom of God is indeed complex, that teaching undeniably includes both present and future aspects. Luke

---

[236] The *hoti* clause is best understood as "the evidence of her prior forgiveness" rather than the grounds for it (Ellis, *Luke*, 122; cf. Zerwick and Grosvenor, *Analysis*). *NEB* makes this point explicit: "Her great love proves that her many sins have been forgiven." For other statements of forgiveness as a present experience, see, e.g., Luke 19:10; Acts 3:38; 13:38-39.

[237] Schürmann, "Eschatologie," 288.

[238] Ellis, *Eschatology*, 19-20.

[239] Ellis, *Luke*, 13. The latter quote by Ellis is from Cullmann, *Time*, 72. Ellis concludes by saying, "The Spirit's presence, therefore, obviates any anxiety about the time of the kingdom's glorious and public manifestation in the future (Ac. 1:8)" (*Luke*, 13).

[240] Ridderbos, *Kingdom*, 290.

[241] Seccombe, *Possessions*, 186.

reports and endorses both aspects. Both aspects of the one kingdom[242] are fatal to Conzelmann's thesis about Luke's purpose and methods. The sayings about the imminence of the kingdom show that Luke does not abandon this expectation in favor of redemptive history or a coming in the distant future. The note of an interval in the tradition proves that the delay of the parousia is not an unexpected embarrassment in need of explanation. Redemptive history is not, therefore, an improvisation by Luke. An anticipated interval undermines the whole basis of the "consistent eschatology" on which Conzelmann's thesis is built. The presence of the kingdom emphasized by Luke also suggests the parousia's delay cannot be a major problem for him. "Because the eschatological reality is present," writes Ellis, "the length of the interval until the consummation is of no crucial significance."[243] The certainty of the kingdom's presence makes the hope of final victory more vivid,[244] and provides incentive for watchfulness and faithful perseverance in the interim. Morris is surely correct when he says, "one cannot escape the impression that the delay of the parousia is more of a problem to some modern scholars than ever it was to the early Christians."[245]

Since the kingdom of God in Luke-Acts is both present and future, Conzelmann's dichotomy between eschatology and redemptive history must be judged false. It is not a matter of either eschatology or redemptive history; rather, "the eschatological events form part of salvation-history."[246] The kingdom of God in its dual aspects is the unfolding of redemptive history.[247] God's eschatological redemptive activity has been inaugurated in history in the ministry of Jesus (Luke 4:18-19, 21), and it moves according to the plan of God toward its consummation at the parousia (Acts 3:21). The structure of redemptive history in Luke-Acts is, therefore, that of promise and fulfillment.[248] The latter takes place in two stages, and corresponds to the two aspects of the coming of the kingdom. The tension between these stages, between the already and not yet of the kingdom, lies at the heart of Luke's theology. The teaching

---

[242] Ridderbos stresses the unity of the kingdom in its two aspects (e.g., *Kingdom*, 55).

[243] Ellis, *Eschatology*, 19. This point is emphasized by Cullmann, see esp. *Time*, 84-94, and *Salvation*, 174, 242-43, 290. Cf. also Bauckham, "Delay," 28-29.

[244] Cullmann, *Time*, 87, and *Salvation*, 179. Cf. Ridderbos, *Kingdom*, 521, and Schürmann, "Eschatologie," 287 n. 39.

[245] Morris, "Catholicism," 126.

[246] Marshall, *Historian*, 109.

[247] Ladd, *Theology*, 60.

[248] Ellis, *Luke*, 16. The fundamental continuity between promise and fulfillment speaks against Conzelmann's rigid division of redemptive history into three periods. Luke 16:16, for example, Conzelmann's key verse, indicates only two periods of redemptive history—

on the use of material possessions, including our parable, shares in that tension.

B. Relationship of Eschatology and Ethics

Having summarized Luke's account of Jesus' eschatology, we are now in a position to clarify the relationship between eschatology and ethics, in particular the ethics of stewardship. "In seeking to understand the essence of Jesus' ethical teaching," Stein rightly observes, "we must not divorce his ethical teaching from his teaching on the kingdom of God."[249] The former is integrally related to the latter. When viewed from the perspective of his central message, "the ethics of Jesus, then, are Kingdom ethics, the ethics of the reign of God."[250] Both aspects of the kingdom have an important bearing on ethics, in general,[251] and the wise use of possessions, in particular. On the one hand, the future aspect adds hope and incentive to Jesus' ethical teaching by reminding of reward and/or warning of judgment (e.g., Luke 7:35; 12:35-46; 14:13-14). On the other hand, "if the kingdom of God has already come, it must make a difference to the ethical standards of its members."[252] The reign of God, asserts Jeremias, "is inconceivable without the life of discipleship. For belonging to the reign of God transforms a man's whole life: not only his relation to God becomes new, but also his relation *to man*."[253] The standards of the kingdom are summarized in the command to love God and others (Luke 10:25-37; 6:27-36). Jesus' commandments are con-

---

the time of promise ("the law and the prophets") and the time of fulfillment ("the kingdom of God") (Ellis, *Luke*, 16; Bovon, *Luc*, 36; Fitzmyer, *Luke* 1.18; and Kümmel, "Accusations," 137-38). The stress on the continuing validity of the OT in 16:17-18 highlights the continuity between the two periods (Bemile, *Magnificat*, 214). Conzelmann's division is also contradicted by the infancy narrative of Luke 1-2 (Bemile, *Magnificat*, 205; Minear, "Birth Stories," 111-30, esp. 121-25; cf. Conzelmann, *Luke*, 16 n. 3, 118, 172, for his dismissal of these chapters.)

[249] Stein, *Method*, 106. For discussions of the relationship of eschatology and ethics, see Ladd, *Presence*, 278-304 ("The Ethics of the Kingdom"); Ridderbos, *Kingdom*, 285-333 ("The Gospel of the Kingdom [The Commandments]"); and A. N. Wilder, *Eschatology and Ethics in the Teaching of Jesus* (New York: Harper, 1950).

[250] Ladd, *Presence*, 290.

[251] Cf. Schürmann, "Eschatologie," 286-89.

[252] Guthrie, *Theology*, 895. "As the preaching *of the kingdom, as the proclamation of Father's will, all the imperatives of the gospel are always founded in the great indicative that the time has been fulfilled and the salvation has come*" (Ridderbos, *Kingdom*, 252, emphasis his).

[253] Jeremias, *Theology*, 204, emphasis his. In commenting on the social implications of the kingdom, Stonehouse writes, "The kingdom is a gift of the Father's good-pleasure, but as it comes in the midst of the world it comes as a rule of righteousness, demanding absolute righteousness of its subjects, and this includes the application, in a thoroughgoing fashion, of the principle of stewardship in all one's social relationships" (*Luke*, 164).

crete applications of "the one great principle of love."[254] As a response
of gratitude for present salvation (7:36-47; 19:8),[255] love manifests the
kingdom and gives evidence of one's membership in it (cf. 6:35-36 with
6:20).[256] Love produces, to use Seccombe's expression, an "anticipatory
realisation" of the conditions and values of the kingdom.[257] Charity is
"appropriate 'Kingdom behavior', anticipating the arrival of the age to
come and producing a foretaste of it now. . . . It is a living of the very
life of the Kingdom."[258] "If [eschatological] salvation means God will
put an end to the oppression of his people (Luke 4,18f), his people must
cease to oppress one another (3,12-14); if it means an end to hunger and
want (6,20f), his people will share what they have now with the hungry
and naked (3,11)."[259] While such behavior is incumbent on disciples
because the kingdom has already begun, it is not, however, foreign to the
OT; "it is after all only what the Law has always demanded."[260]

In light of the foregoing observations it becomes clear that eschatology is the fundamental theological context for the teaching on possessions in Luke-Acts, in particular their charitable use for the poor.[261] An

---

[254] Ridderbos, *Kingdom*, 329. The meaning of love, Ridderbos contends, is nowhere
clearer than in the saying that "no servant can serve two masters" (Luke 16:13//Matt 6:24).
From this statement (as well as Luke 14:26//Matt 10:37), he explains, "it appears that the
'love' which Jesus demands in the gospel is based on a radical *choice*. Properly speaking,
it is another word for 'conversion.' It consists in the complete surrender of the will, in being
at the disposal of the Lord in the same way as is a slave. This is why the battle that this love
is summoned to fight is the battle against 'competition,' against compromise, against that
which is 'an obstruction' to love in its service, against all other commitments which keep
love from this totalitarian service" (pp. 315-16).

[255] Love as an expression of gratitude is emphasized by, among others, Schürmann
("Eschatologie," 289) and Jeremias (*Theology*, 218). M. Hengel expresses well the connection between salvation and love. He writes, "Because men experience forgiveness of their
guilt, they themselves can forgive; because they receive the assurance that God's goodness
supports and sustains their life, they must no longer fret about their everyday needs, but can
pray like children, 'Give us this day our daily bread' (Luke 11:3 = Matt. 6:11). Because they
themselves have encountered the heavenly Father's boundless love, they must not relapse
into anxiety about asserting themselves; they can even dare to love their enemies and
renounce the compulsion of using force in return (Matt. 5:38-48; cf. Luke 6:27-36)"
(*Property and Riches in the Early Church* [Philadelphia: Fortress, 1974] 29).

[256] Seccombe, *Possessions*, 185-86, and Ridderbos, *Kingdom*, 250, 290.

[257] Seccombe, *Possessions*, 182.

[258] Seccombe, *Possessions*, 184. Seccombe also writes, "the ethic of the Kingdom is no
'Interimsethik' which is only practicable over a short period of time, but a making real of
what is to be the life of all men permanently in the new age" (p. 226).

[259] Seccombe, *Possessions*, 182-83.

[260] Seccombe, *Possessions*, 226. Cf. Ridderbos, *Kingdom*, 325, 329. Note the quotation
of Deut 6:5 and Lev 19:18 in Luke 10:27, as well as the emphasis on "the Law and the
Prophets" in Luke 16:16-18, 29, 31.

[261] Seccombe laments that while many interpreters recognize Luke's emphasis on
almsgiving "surprisingly little attention" has been given to how this emphasis relates to
Luke's eschatological understanding (*Possessions*, 182, esp. n. 216). Others who *have* called
attention to the close relationship of eschatology and possessions in the NT include Cassidy,

eschatological note is often present, as I have emphasized, in material on possessions or in the immediate context. It is present, for example, in Luke 12 where seeking the kingdom of God (12:31) entails using one's possessions to help the poor (12:33; cf. also vv. 35-48). It is also present in our parable. The totalitarian character of love at the heart of kingdom ethics is behind all the radical commandments on possessions in Luke-Acts (e.g., 12:33; 14:33; 18:22).[262] Love also highlights again the central religious issue, the issue of one's attitude to God, in all the teaching on riches and poverty in Luke-Acts. The inbreaking of eschatological salvation into this age brings about "a revision of all values," including material possessions.[263] In light of the kingdom of God, possessions become *elachistos* (Luke 16:10), they belong to the passing age (16:12). A person who, by virtue of his membership in the kingdom, recognizes this fact "will want to transform the wealth of this age into what counts as wealth in the value system of the world to come."[264] One way to do so, to have treasure in heaven, is by using possessions to help the needy (12:33; 18:22; 16:9). By concrete acts of love for the poor (e.g., alms) disciples give testimony to their own ultimate loyalties and also create a foretaste of the life of the kingdom in anticipation of its final coming. Such use of possessions actualizes the blessings of eschatological salvation in the present age, one of which is the relief of physical suffering and deprivation.[265] This "anticipatory realization of the life of the kingdom" is best illustrated in the life of the early church in Acts (e.g., 2:42-47; 4:32-37).[266]

Jesus, 154 n. 36, and Kümmel, "Der Begriff des Eigentums in Neuen Testament," in *Heilsgeschehen und Geschichte* (Marburger Theologische Studien 3; ed. E. Grässer, O. Merk, and A. Fritz; Marburg: Elwert, 1965) 272.

[262] See Ridderbos, *Kingdom*, 325-28.

[263] Jeremias, *Theology*, 223.

[264] Seccombe, *Possessions*, 227.

[265] Cf. Marshall, *Historian*, 144. Gutiérrez is surely right in insisting that the kingdom and social injustices are incompatible (*Theology*, 168). As citizens of the kingdom of God, Christians must by their individual and corporate acts of love work for the elimination of such injustices. Gutiérrez is wrong, however, in his expectation that injustices can or will be eliminated in this age and by merely human efforts.

[266] Seccombe, *Possessions*, 221. Seccombe calls attention to the echo of Deut 15:4 ("there shall be no poor among you") in Acts 4:34 ("there were no needy persons among them"). His explanation of the significance of this echo is worth quoting in full. "In Deuteronomy the absence of poverty is a characteristic of the faithful people enjoying the blessing of God in the land; i.e. it is consonant with salvation. The reality is recognized in Deut 15,11: 'the poor will never cease out of the land'. Luke does not echo Jesus' words in Mark 14,7, 'You always have the poor with you'. Thus in the summaries, and particularly in Acts 4,34, he may be saying that the Christians were enjoying the state of salvific blessing, and that their philanthropic activity was part and parcel of this" (p. 222 n. 126).

Before proceeding to consider the impact of eschatology on the interpretation of our parable, a final comment is in order about the redemptive-historical tension between the present and future aspects of the kingdom. That tension is also reflected in ethics. Ladd expresses this point well, and in the process also summarizes Jesus' (and Luke's) eschatology. He writes,

> There is an analogy between the manifestation of the Kingdom of God itself and the attainment of the righteousness of the Kingdom. The Kingdom has come in Jesus in fulfillment of the messianic salvation within the old age, but the consummation awaits the age to come. The Kingdom is actually present but in a new and unexpected way. It has entered history without transforming history. It comes into human society without purifying society. By analogy, the righteousness of the reign of God can be actually and substantially experienced even in the present age; but the perfect righteousness of the Kingdom, like the Kingdom itself, awaits the eschatological consummation. Even as the Kingdom has invaded the evil age to bring men in advance a partial but real experience of the blessings of the eschatological Kingdom, so is the righteousness of the Kingdom attainable, in part if not in perfection, in the present order. Ethics, like the Kingdom itself, stand in the tension between the present realization and future eschatological perfection.[267]

The teaching on possessions in Luke-Acts, and their charitable use in particular, shares in this tension. Charity actualizes the values and conditions of the kingdom, but it does not do so fully. As exemplary as the life of the early church is, that life is still disturbed by Ananias and Sapphira. The discrepancy between the ideal and the reality, the tension between the not yet and the already, creates, among other things, both a longing for the final coming of the kingdom and an incentive to be faithful in the meantime.

C. Impact of Eschatology on Our Parable

The intimate relationship between eschatology and ethics just outlined has significant implications for the interpretation of the parable of the unjust steward. Let me note those implications briefly.

1. The centrality of the kingdom of God in Jesus' teaching substantiates the eschatological note in our parable and its immediate context. This note is present, it will be recalled, in the image of eschatological judgment in the accounting the steward is called to give (16:2), in the master's commendation of the steward for having acted "shrewdly [*phronimōs*]" (v. 8a), in the contrast between the sons of this age and the

---

[267] Ladd, *Presence*, 291-92. Cf. also Guthrie, *Theology*, 896, and Marshall, *Historian*, 144.

sons of light (v. 8b), in the description of both the steward and mammon as "unrighteous" (*tēs adikias*, vv. 8-9, 11), in the reference to "eternal dwellings" (v. 9), and in 16:16. The eschatological note cannot be easily dismissed in our parable. Given its role in Jesus' other teaching it would in fact be very surprising if it were not present here. A non-eschatological interpretation of our parable is, therefore, ruled out.

2. Both aspects of the kingdom present in our parable have an important bearing on its interpretation. The note of imminent judgment in the steward's dismissal emphasizes the need for decisive response and imparts a sense of urgency to Jesus' exhortation. The seriousness of the issues involved is reinforced by the reminder that faithfulness/unfaithfulness will be rewarded/punished (vv. 10-12). The present aspect of the kingdom focuses more clearly the meaning and motivation for the exhortation to charity in our parable. Charity to the poor is important not only in view of inevitable judgment, but also because the kingdom is already present. The coming of the kingdom enables and demands such actions of its citizens. Possessions have become *elachistos* (16:10), they belong to the passing age (16:12). The values and currency of the kingdom are very different than those of this age. Real wisdom, therefore, entails a charitable, outgoing, generous use of one's possessions for the needy. Such actions create a foretaste of the life of the kingdom in advance of its consummation. As an anticipatory realization of the values and conditions of the kingdom, acts of charity like those illustrated in the life of the early church in Acts are concrete evidence the kingdom has come. They also provide proof of one's ultimate loyalties (16:13), they are a test of one's citizenship.

3. The fact that good works are a manifestation of present sonship (6:35-36) and an expression of gratitude for present salvation (7:47; 19:8-9) confirms my earlier contention that our parable does not teach works-righteousness. The charitable actions exhorted by our parable, and v. 9 in particular, must be seen in the context of what it means to be a true disciple, a son of God and member of the kingdom, not how one becomes a disciple.

4. The observation that the anticipatory ethic of the kingdom is not foreign to the OT but is only what the law always demanded accounts for the emphasis on the law and the prophets in the immediate context of our parable (e.g., 16:16-18, 29-31). The exhortation of our parable is of a piece with the OT law (cf. Deut 15:1-11). This fact emphasizes the fundamental continuity between OT promise and NT fulfillment.

IV. Conclusions

The elements of theological context discussed in this chapter broaden our understanding of the parable of the unjust steward and focus its meaning significantly. The thread of riches and poverty in the fabric of Luke's theology confirms, as interpreters have argued for a long time, that our parable does treat the proper use of material possessions. More specifically, our parable is an exhortation to show charity to the needy. The two-strand eschatological thread provides both the incentive and dynamic for such actions.

The substance of my findings in this chapter is summed up well by Seccombe. Luke 16:1-13 is, he writes, "a fundamental evaluation of possessions in the light of the Kingdom which will lead the wise disciple to use his possessions in the service of the needy."[268] The faithful stewardship thus enjoined in the parable of the unjust steward is, to paraphrase Ellis,[269] the badge of true discipleship; it is the mark of genuine wisdom. The message of this parable is one of particular relevance for rich Christians or would-be Christians in both Luke's day and our own.

---

[268] Seccombe, *Possessions*, 172.
[269] Ellis entitles Luke 16:1-13, "Faithfulness: The Badge of Acceptable Discipleship" (*Luke*, 198).

CHAPTER FIVE

CONCLUSIONS

While the parable of the unjust steward is difficult indeed and interpretive problems persist, the foregoing study confirms the traditional interpretation of the parable outlined in chapter one. That is, the parable gives positive instruction to disciples on the charitable use of material possessions. Though the steward of the parable acted dishonestly in authorizing the debt reductions, he nonetheless acted wisely in providing for his future. Jesus' disciples can learn a lesson from the steward at this point. Prudence for them includes using their possessions for those in need. The dual aspects of the kingdom of God provide the incentive and dynamic for such actions.

This interpretation of the parable of the unjust steward is justified on the basis of Luke 16:1-13 itself (chapter two) and is substantiated by the literary and theological contexts (chapters three and four, respectively). While the detailed conclusions reached in these chapters need not be repeated here, the major conclusions and contributions of each to this interpretation can be summarized as follows.

The exegesis of Luke 16:1-13 in chapter two demonstrated that the traditional interpretation of the parable is correct, even when the passage is temporarily isolated from larger levels of context in Luke's Gospel. Vv. 1-9 constitute the original parable, vv. 10-13 apply and amplify it. The emphasis of the entire pericope is on the faithful stewardship of material possessions; various eschatological nuances provide the background for the teaching. How one uses material possessions is indicative of one's ultimate loyalties and thus has a bearing on one's eternal destiny.

The immediate and broader literary contexts considered in chapter three focused the meaning of Luke 16:1-13 more clearly. Luke 15 sets our parable in the midst of controversy with the Pharisees and scribes, and suggests that Luke 16 in particular may be directed against their avarice. The positive instruction to disciples in Luke 16:1-13 is sharpened and reinforced in 16:14-31 against the dark background of the Pharisees' love of money and the rich man's selfish indifference. The eschatological context of our parable is particularly clear in 16:16. The emphasis on "the Law and the Prophets" in that verse and subsequent ones (e.g., vv. 17-18, 29, 31) also connects Jesus' teaching in our parable to the OT. The broader literary context of Luke's central section (9:51-19:44) clarifies the integral relationship between the charitable use of material possessions and true discipleship. The prominence of the kingdom of God in Jesus' teaching in the central section highlights again the underlying eschatological note in our parable.

The discussion of our parable in terms of Luke's theology in chapter four further enhanced our understanding of the parable. The material Luke includes or retains on the theme of riches and poverty may be especially intended to instruct rich Christians or would-be Christians on the meaning of discipleship for their use of possessions. Our parable plays an important role in that instruction. Though the material Luke includes on this theme is extensive and varied, he is not inconsistent. His fundamental and consistent concern is to make it clear that Jesus demands wholehearted commitment to himself and brooks no rivals, possessions included. The two-strand eschatological thread in Jesus' teaching provides the basic context for the exhortation in our parable. Christians are to use their possessions faithfully and for the sake of others not only because they will give an account one day, but also because the kingdom of God is already present and thus supplies the dynamic for obedience. By acts of charity like those that characterized the life of the early church in Acts Christians give evidence of their citizenship and actualize the values and conditions of the kingdom in anticipation of its final coming. The certainty of its final coming and the uncertainty about the time should create incentive to be faithful in the meantime.

The message of the parable of the unjust steward is surely relevant for both Luke's day and our own. The force of that message is captured well in a saying that came to mind in the early stages of my work on this parable. Someone has said, "He is no fool who gives up what he cannot keep to gain what he cannot lose." While this statement is not made (as far as I know) in the context of a discussion of our parable per se, it is nonetheless a fitting summary of its message. May God grant his people such wisdom, especially in the stewardship of material possessions.

BIBLIOGRAPHY

Arndt, W. F. *The Gospel according to St. Luke*. St. Louis: Concordia, 1956.

Arnot, W. *The Parables of our Lord*. London: T. Nelson, 1865; repr. ed., Grand Rapids: Kregel, 1981.

Arnott, W. "The Unjust Steward in a New Light." *ExpTim* 24 (1913) 508-11.

Aune, D. E. "The Significance of the Delay of the Parousia for Early Christianity." In *Current Issues in Biblical and Patristic Interpretation*, 87-109. Edited by G. F. Hawthorne. Grand Rapids: Eerdmans, 1975.

Bahnmaier, J. F. "Der ungerechte Haushalter Luc. 16:1ff. von Jesus keineswegs als Beispiel irgend einer Art von Klugheit aufgestellt." *Studien der evangelischen Geistlichkeit Wirtembergs* 1 (1827) 27-50.

Bailey, K. E. *Poet and Peasant and Through Peasant Eyes. A Literary-Cultural Approach to the Parables in Luke*. Combined ed. Grand Rapids: Eerdmans, 1983.

Banks, R. *Jesus and the Law in the Synoptic Tradition*. Cambridge: Cambridge University Press, 1975.

Barrett, C. K. *Luke the Historian in Recent Study*. London: Epworth, 1961.

Barth, M. "The Dishonest Steward and his Lord, Reflections on Luke 16:1-13." In *From Faith to Faith*, 65-73. Edited by D.Y. Hadidian. Pittsburgh: Pickwick, 1979.

Bauckham, R. J. "The Delay of the Parousia." *TynBul* 31 (1980) 3-36.

Bemile, P. *The Magnificat within the Context and Framework of Lukan Theology. An Exegetical Theological Study of Lk 1:46-55*. Frankfurt: Lang, 1986.

Bertram, G. *"phrēn, aphrōn, aphrosynē, phroneō, phronēma, phronēsis, phronimos."* In *TDNT* 9.220-35.

Bigo, P. "La richesse, comme intendence, dans l'Evangile, A propos de Luc 16:1-9." *NRT* 87 (1965) 265-71.

Blinzler, J. "Die literarische Eigenart des sogenannten Reiseberichts im Lukasevangelium." In *Synoptische Studien*, 20-52. Edited by J. Schmid and A. Vögtle. Munich: K. Zink, 1953.

Blomberg, C. L. "Midrash, Chiasmus, and the Outline of Luke's Central Section." In *Gospel Perspectives. Studies in Midrash and Historiography*, 3.217-61. Edited by R. T. France and D. Wenham. 6 vols. Sheffield: JSOT Press, 1983.

Bovon, F. *Luc le théologien: Vingt-cinq ans de recherches (1950-75)*. Neuchâtel/Paris: Delachaux and Niestlé, 1978.

Brauns, P. "Nun noch ein Auslegungsversuch von Lk 16:1-14." *TSK* 15 (1842) 1012-22.

Bretscher, P. G. "The Parable of the Unjust Steward—A New Approach to Luke 16:1-9." *CTM* 22 (1951) 756-62.

Bruce, A. B. *The Parabolic Teaching of Christ*. London: Hodder and Stoughton, 1882.

Bugge, C. A. *Die Haupt-Parabeln Jesu*. Giessen: J. Ricker, 1903.

Buttrick, G. A. *The Parables of Jesus*. New York: Harper and Brothers, 1928.

Cadbury, H. J. *The Making of Luke-Acts*. New York: Macmillan, 1928; repr. ed., London: SPCK, 1958.

—. *The Style and Literary Method of Luke*. Cambridge: Harvard University Press, 1920.

Cadoux, A. T. *The Parables of Jesus: Their Art and Use*. London: Clarke, [1930].

Cadoux, C. J. "The Visits of Jesus to Jerusalem." *Expositor*, ser. 3, 9 (1925) 175-92.

Caemmerer, R. R. "Investment for Eternity. A Study of Luke 16:1-13." *CTM* 34 (1963) 69-76.

Cassidy, R. J. *Jesus, Politics, and Society. A Study of Luke's Gospel*. Maryknoll, NY: Orbis, 1978.

Cave, C. H. "Lazarus and the Lukan Deuteronomy." *NTS* 15 (1969) 319-25.

Chilton, B. "Announcement in Nazara: An Analysis of Luke 4:16-21." In *Gospel Perspectives. Studies in History and Tradition in the Four Gospels*, 2.147-72. Edited by R. T. France and D. Wenham. 6 vols. Sheffield: JSOT Press, 1981.

—, ed. *The Kingdom of God in the Teaching of Jesus*. Philadelphia/London: Fortress/SPCK, 1984.

Clavier, H. "L'Ironie dans l'enseignement de Jesus." *NovT* 1 (1956) 3-20.

Coggins, R. J. "The Old Testament and the Poor." *ExpTim* 99/1 (1987) 11-14.

Compston, H. F. B. "Friendship without Mammon." *ExpTim* 31 (1919-20) 282.

Conzelmann, H. *Die Mitte der Zeit.* 3d ed. Tübingen: Mohr, 1960.

—. *The Theology of Saint Luke.* New York: Harper, 1960.

Cook, E. J. "Synoptic Indications of the Visits of Jesus to Jerusalem." *ExpTim* 4 (1929-30) 121-23.

Coutts, J. "Studies in Texts: The Unjust Steward, Lk 16:1-8a." *Theology* 52 (1949) 54-60.

Cranfield, C. E. B. "Mark 4:1-34." *SJT* 4 (1951) 398-414.

—. "The Parable of the Unjust Judge (Lk 18:1-8) and the Eschatology of Luke-Acts." *SJT* 16 (1963) 297-301.

—. "Riches and the Kingdom of God. St. Mark 10:17-31." *SJT* 4 (1951) 302-13.

Creed, J. M. *The Gospel according to St. Luke.* London: Macmillan, 1930.

Crossan, J. D. *In Parables: The Challenge of the Historical Jesus.* New York: Harper & Row, 1973.

—. "The Parable of the Wicked Husbandmen." *JBL* 90 (1971) 451-65.

Danker, F. W. *Jesus and the New Age.* Rev. and expanded ed. Philadelphia: Fortress, 1988.

—. "Luke 16:16—An Opposition Logion." *JBL* 77 (1958) 231-43.

Davies, J. H. "The Purpose of the Central Section of St. Luke's Gospel." In *SE* II, 164-69. Edited by F. L. Cross. Berlin: Akademie, 1964.

Davidson, J. A. "A 'Conjecture' about the Parable of the Unjust Steward (Luke xvi.1-9)." *ExpTim* 66 (1954-55) 31.

Degenhardt, H.-J. *Lukas—Evangelist der Armen.* Stuttgart: Katholisches Bibelwerk, 1965.

Derrett, J. D. M. "Fresh Light on St. Luke XVI. I. The Parable of the Unjust Steward." *NTS* 7 (1960-61) 198-219.

—. "Fresh Light on St. Luke XVI. II. Dives and Lazarus and the Preceding Sayings." *NTS* 7 (1960-61) 364-80.

—. *Law in the New Testament.* London: Darton, Longman & Todd, 1970.

—. "'Take Thy Bond . . . and Write Fifty' (Luke xvi.6). The Nature of the Bond." *JTS*, n.s., 23 (1972) 438-40.

Descamps, A. "La composition littéraire de Luc XVI 9-13." *NovT* 1 (1956) 47-53.

C. H. Dodd. *The Parables of the Kingdom.* Rev. ed. New York: Scribner's, 1961.

Dods, M. *The Parables of Our Lord.* Philadelphia: Westminster, 1904.

Drummond, D. T. K. *The Parabolic Teachings of Christ; or, The Engravings of the New Testament.* New York: R. Carter and Brothers, 1857.

Drury, J. *Tradition and Design in Luke's Gospel. A Study in Early Christian Historiography.* London: Darton, Longman & Todd, 1976.

Dumais, M. "L'évangélisation des pauvres dans l'oeuvre de Luc." *ScEs* 36/3 (1984) 297-321.

Dupont, J. *Les Beatitudes.* 3 vols. Paris: Gabalda, 1969-73.

—. "The Poor and Poverty in the Gospels and Acts." In *Gospel Poverty. Essays in Biblical Theology,* 25-52. Edited by A. George. Chicago: Franciscan Herald Press, 1977.

—. "Renoncer à tous ses biens (Luc 14,33)." *NRT* 93 (1971) 561-82.

Dutton, F. G. "The Unjust Steward." *ExpTim* 16 (1904-5) 44.

Eagar, A. R. "The Parable of the Unjust Steward." *Expositor,* ser. 5, 2 (1895) 457-70.

Easton, B. S. *The Gospel according to St. Luke. A Critical and Exegetical Commentary.* Edinburgh: T. & T. Clark, 1926.

Egelkraut, H. L. *Jesus' Mission to Jerusalem: A Redaction Critical Study of the Travel Narrative in the Gospel of Luke, Lk 9:51-19:48.* Frankfurt: P. Lang, 1976.

Ellis, E. E. *Eschatology in Luke.* FBBS. Philadelphia: Fortress, 1972.

—. *The Gospel of Luke.* NCB. Grand Rapids/London: Eerdmans/Marshall, Morgan & Scott, 1974.

—. "Present and Future Eschatology in Luke." *NTS* 12 (1965-66) 27-41.

Ernst, J. *Herr der Geschichte. Perspektiven der lukanischen Eschatologie.* SBS 88. Stuttgart: Katholisches Bibelwerk, 1978.

Evans, C. F. "The Central Section of St. Luke's Gospel." In *Studies in the Gospels,* 37-53. Edited by D. E. Nineham. Oxford: Blackwell, 1955.

—. Review of *L'Evangile des voyages de Jesus, ou la section 9:51-18:14 de Saint Luc*, by L. Girard, and *The Witness of Luke to Christ*, by N. B. Stonehouse. *JTS*, n.s., 3 (1952) 242-46.

Evers, M. *Das Gleichnis vom ungerechten Verwalter*. Krefeld: G. Hohns, 1901.

—. *Die Gleichnisse Jesu*. 4th ed. Edited by H. Marx. Berlin: Reuther & Reichard, 1908.

Farrell, H. K. "The Structure and Theology of Luke's Central Section." *Trinity Journal*, n.s., 7 (1986) 33-54.

Feuillet, A. "Les riches intendants du Christ." *RSR* 34 (1947) 30-54.

Fiebig, P. *Die Gleichnisreden Jesu im Lichte der rabbinischen Gleichnisse des neutestamentlichen Zeitalters*. Tübingen: Mohr, 1912.

Findlay, J. A. *Jesus and His Parables*. London: Epworth, 1950.

Firth, C. B. "The Parable of the Unrighteous Steward (Luke xvi.1-9)." *ExpTim* 63 (1951-52) 93-95.

Firth, H. "The Unjust Steward." *ExpTim* 15 (1903-4) 426-27.

Fitzmyer, J. A. "The Composition of Luke, Chapter 9." In *Perspectives on Luke-Acts*, 139-52. Edited by C. H. Talbert. Danville, VA/Edinburgh: Association of Baptist Professors of Religion/T. & T. Clark, 1978.

—. *The Gospel according to Luke (I-IX)*. AB, vol. 28. Garden City: Doubleday, 1981.

—. *The Gospel according to Luke (X-XXIV)*. AB, vol. 28a. Garden City: Doubleday, 1985.

—. "The Story of the Dishonest Manager (Lk 16:1-13)." *TS* 25 (1964) 23-42.

Fletcher, D. R. "The Riddle of the Unjust Steward: Is Irony the Key?" *JBL* 82 (1963) 15-30.

Fonck, L. *Die Parabeln des Herrn im Evangelium*. 4th ed. Innsbruck: F. Rauch, 1927.

Friedel, L. W. "The Parable of the Unjust Steward, Luke 16:1-13." *CBQ* 3 (1941) 337-48.

Gächter, P. "Die Parabel vom ungerechten Verwalter (Lk 16:1-8)." *Orientierung* 27 (1963) 149-50.

—. "The Parable of the Dishonest Steward after Oriental Conceptions." *CBQ* 12 (1950) 121-31.

Gander, G. "Le procédé de l'économe infidèle, décrit Luc 16:5-7, est-il réprehénsible ou louable?" *VCaro* 7 (1953) 128-41.

Gasque, W. W. "A Fruitful Field: Recent Study of the Acts of the Apostles." *Int* 42/2 (1988) 117-31.

—. *A History of the Criticism of the Acts of the Apostles*. Grand Rapids: Eerdmans, 1975.

Geldenhuys, N. *Commentary on the Gospel of Luke*. NICNT. Grand Rapids: Eerdmans, 1951.

Gelin, A. *The Poor of Yahweh*. Collegeville, MN: Liturgical Press, 1964.

George, A. "Poverty in the Old Testament." In *Gospel Poverty. Essays in Biblical Theology*, 3-24. Edited by A. George. Chicago: Franciscan Herald Press, 1977.

Gibson, M. D. "On the Parable of the Unjust Steward." *ExpTim* 14 (1902-3) 334.

Gill, D. "Observations on the Lukan Travel Narrative and Some Related Passages." *HTR* 63 (1970) 199-221.

Gillingham, S. "The Poor in the Psalms." *ExpTim* 100/1 (1988) 15-19.

Girard, L. *L'Evangile des voyages de Jesus, ou la section 9:51-18:14 de Saint Luc*. Paris: Gabalda, 1951.

Godet, F. *A Commentary on the Gospel of St. Luke*. 5th ed. 2 vols. Edinburgh: T. & T. Clark, 1976.

Goebel, S. "Die Gleichnisgruppe Luk. 15 u. 16, methodisch ausgelegt." *TSK* 48 (1875) 656-707.

—. *The Parables of Jesus: A Methodical Exposition*. Edinburgh: T. & T. Clark, 1883.

Goulder, M. D. "The Chiastic Structure of the Lucan Journey." In *SE* II, 195-202. Edited by F. L. Cross. Berlin: Akademie, 1964.

—. *The Evangelists' Calendar. A Lectionary Explanation of the Development of Scripture*. London: SPCK, 1978.

—. *Type and History in Acts*. London: SPCK, 1964.

Grundmann, W. *Das Evangelium nach Lukas*. 2d rev. ed. THKNT, vol. 3. Berlin: Evangelische Verlagsanstalt, 1969.

—. "Fragen der Komposition des lukanischen 'Reiseberichts.'" *ZNW* 50-51 (1959-60) 252-70.

Hampden-Cook, E. "The Unjust Steward." *ExpTim* 16 (1904-5) 44.

Hastings, A. W., and Hastings, E. "Notes of Recent Exposition." *ExpTim* 39 (1927-28) 532-33.

Hauck, F. "*mamōnas.*" In *TDNT* 4.388-90.

Hengel, M. *Property and Riches in the Early Church. Aspects of a Social History of Early Christianity.* Philadelphia: Fortress, 1974.

Hermaniuk, M. *La parabole évangélique.* Paris: Desclee, de Brouwer, 1947.

Hiers, R. H. "Friends By Unrighteous Mammon: The Eschatological Proletariat (Luke 16:9)." *JAAR* 38 (1970) 30-36.

Hof, O. "Luthers Auslegung von Lukas 16:9." *EvT* 8 (1948-49) 151-66.

Hofmann, J. C. K. von. *Die Heilige Schrift Neuen Testamentes zusammenhängend untersucht.* Vol. 8/1: *Das Evangelium des Lukas.* Nördlingen: Beck, 1878.

Hölbe. "Versuch einer Erklärung der Parabel vom ungerechten Haushalter, Lk 16:1ff." *TSK* 32 (1858) 527-42.

Hooley, B. A., and Mason, A. J. "Some Thoughts on the Parable of the Unjust Steward (Luke 16:1-9)." *AusBR* 6 (1958) 47-59.

Hoyt, T., Jr. "The Poor in Luke-Acts." Ph.D. dissertation, Duke University, 1974.

Hunter, A. M. "Interpreting the Parables. I. The Interpreter and the Parables. The Centrality of the Kingdom." *Int* 14 (1960) 70-84.

—. "Interpreting the Parables. III. The Gospel in Parables. The Men and the Crisis of the Kingdom." *Int* 14 (1960) 315-32.

—. *Interpreting the Parables.* Philadelphia: Westminster, 1960.

—. "The New Look at the Parables." In *From Faith to Faith*, 191-99. Edited by D. Y. Hadidian. Pittsburgh: Pickwick, 1979.

Ireland, D. J. "A History of Recent Interpretation of the Parable of the Unjust Steward (Luke 16:1-13)." *Westminster Theological Journal* 51 (1989) 293-318.

Jäger, G. "Noch einmal: Der ungerechte Haushalter." *Zeitschrift für kirchliche Wissenschaft und kirchliche Leben* 2 (1881) 111-12.

Jalland, T. G. "A Note on Luke 16,1-9." In *SE* I, 503-5. Edited by K. Aland, F. L. Cross, J. Danielou, H. Riesenfeld, and W. C. van Unnik. Berlin: Akademie, 1959.

Jensen, B. K. "Über das Gleichnis vom ungerechten Haushalter." *TSK* 2 (1829) 699-714.

Jeremias, J. *The Parables of Jesus.* 2d rev. ed. New York: Scribner's, 1972.

Johnson, L. T. *The Literary Function of Possessions in Luke-Acts.* Missoula, MT: Scholars Press, 1977.

—. "On Finding the Lukan Community: A Cautious Cautionary Essay." In *SBL 1979 Seminar Papers*, 1:87-100. Edited by P. J. Achtemeier. 2 vols. Missoula, MT: Scholars Press, 1979.

—. *Sharing Possessions: Mandate and Symbol of Faith.* Philadelphia: Fortress, 1981.

Jones, G. V. *The Art and Truth of the Parables. A Study in their Literary Form and Modern Interpretation.* London: SPCK, 1964.

Jülicher, A. *Die Gleichnisreden Jesu.* 2 vols. in 1. Tübingen: Mohr, 1910.

Kamlah, E. "Die Parabel vom ungerechten Verwalter (Luk. 16:1ff.) im Rahmen der Knechtsgleichnisse." In *Abraham unser Vater*, 276-94. Edited by O. Betz, M. Hengel, and P. Schmidt. Leiden: Brill, 1963.

Karris, R. J. "The Lukan Sitz im Leben: Methodology and Prospects." In *SBL 1976 Seminar Papers*, 219-33. Edited by G. MacRae. Missoula, MT: Scholars Press, 1976.

—. "Poor and Rich: The Lukan *Sitz im Leben.*" In *Perspectives on Luke-Acts*, 112-25. Edited by C. H. Talbert. Danville, VA/Edinburgh: Association of Baptist Professors of Religion/T. & T. Clark, 1978.

Keck, L. E. "Poor." In *IDBSup*, 672-75.

—. "The Poor among the Saints in the NT." *ZNW* 56 (1965) 100-29.

Kiehl, E. H. "The Parable of the Unjust Manager in the Light of Contemporary Economic Life." Th.D. dissertation, Concordia Seminary, 1959.

King, A. "The Parable of the Unjust Steward." *ExpTim* 50 (1938-39) 474-76.

Kissinger, W. S. *The Parables of Jesus. A History of Interpretation and Bibliography.* ATLA Bibliography Series, no. 4. Metuchen, NJ: Scarecrow Press and the American Theological Library Association, 1979.

Kistemaker, S. J. *The Parables of Jesus*. Grand Rapids: Baker, 1980.
—. "The Structure of Luke's Gospel." *JETS* 25/1 (1982) 33-40.
Klostermann, E. *Die Evangelien I: Lukas*. HNT, vol. 2. Tübingen: Mohr, 1919.
Koch, R. "Die Wertung des Besitzes im Lukasevangelium." *Bib* 38 (1957) 151-69.
Kodell, J. "Luke's Gospel in a Nutshell (Lk 4:16-30)." *BTB* 13 (1983) 16-18.
—. "The Theology of Luke in Recent Thought." *BTB* 1 (1971) 115-44.
Koetsveld, C. E. van. *Die Gleichnisse des Evangeliums*. Leipzig: F. Jansa, 1904.
Kögel, J. "Zum Gleichnis vom ungerechten Haushalter, Bemerkungen zu Luk. 16:1-13." *Beiträge zur Förderung christlicher Theologie* 18 (1914) 581-612.
Kosmala, H. "The Parable of the Unjust Steward in the Light of Qumran." *ASTI* 3 (1964) 114-21.
Köster, D. F. "Analekten zur Auslegung der Parabel vom ungerechten Haushalter, Luk. 16:1ff." *TSK* 38 (1865) 725-34.
Krämer, M. *Das Rätsel der Parabel vom ungerechten Verwalter, Lk 16:1-13*. Zürich: PAS, 1972.
Krüger, G. "Die geistesgeschichtlichen Grundlagen des Gleichnisses vom ungerechten Verwalter." *BZ* 21 (1933) 170-81.
Kümmel, W. G. "Der Begriff des Eigentums im Neuen Testament." In *Heilsgeschehen und Geschichte*, 271-77. Marburger Theologische Studien 3. Edited by E. Grässer, O. Merk, and A. Fritz. Marburg: Elwert, 1965.
—. "Current Theological Accusations against Luke." *ANQ* 16 (1975) 131-45.
—. "Futuristic and Realized Eschatology in the Earliest Stages of Christianity." *JR* 43 (1963) 303-14.
—. "'Das Gesetz und die Propheten gehen bis Johannes'—Lukas 16,16 im Zusammenhang der heilsgeschichtlichen Theologie der Lukasschriften." In *Heilsgeschehen und Geschichte*, 2.75-86. 2 vols. Edited by E. Grässer and O. Merk. Marburg: Elwert, 1978.
—. *Promise and Fulfillment. The Eschatological Message of Jesus*. Naperville, IL: Allenson, 1957.
Ladd, G. E. "Eschatology and the Unity of New Testament Theology." *ExpTim* 68 (1956-57) 268-73.
—. *The Presence of the Future*. Grand Rapids: Eerdmans, 1974.
Lagrange, M.-J. *Evangile selon Saint Luc*. 7th ed. Paris: Gabalda, 1948.
Lenwood, F. "An Alternative Interpretation of the Parable of the Unjust Steward." *The Congregational Quarterly* 6 (1928) 366-73.
Lohse, E. "Missionarisches Handeln Jesu nach dem Evangelium des Lukas." *TZ* 10 (1954) 1-13.
Loisy, A. *Les Evangiles Synoptiques*. 2 vols. Ceffonds: Pres Montier-en-der, 1908.
Lunt, R. G. "Expounding the Parables. III. The Parable of the Unjust Steward (Luke 16:1-15)." *ExpTim* 77 (1965-66) 132-36.
—. "Towards an Interpretation of the Parable of the Unjust Steward (Luke xvi.1-18)." *ExpTim* 66 (1954-55) 335-37.
Maass, F. "Das Gleichnis vom ungerechten Haushalter, Lukas 16:1-8." *Theologia Viatorum* 8 (1962) 173-84.
Mackinlay, G. "St. Luke's Threefold Narrative of Christ's Last Journey to Jerusalem." *The Interpreter* 7 (1910-11) 260-78.
Maddox, R. *The Purpose of Luke-Acts*. Göttingen: Vandenhoeck & Ruprecht, 1982.
Manson, T. W. *The Sayings of Jesus as Recorded in the Gospels according to St. Matthew and St. Luke Arranged with Introduction and Commentary*. London: SCM, 1949.
Marshall, H. S. "The Parable of the Untrustworthy Steward (Luke xvi.1-13). A Question Reopened." *ExpTim* 39 (1927-28) 120-22.
Marshall, I. H. *The Gospel of Luke*. NIGTC. Exeter: Paternoster, 1978.
—. *Luke: Historian and Theologian*. Grand Rapids: Zondervan, 1970.
—. "Luke xvi.8—Who Commended the Unjust Steward?" *JTS*, n.s., 19 (1968) 617-19.
—. "Recent Study of the Acts of the Apostles." *ExpTim* 80 (1968) 292-96.
—. "Recent Study of the Gospel according to St. Luke." *ExpTim* 80 (1968) 4-8.
Martin, R. P. "Salvation and Discipleship in Luke's Gospel." *Int* 30 (1976) 366-80.

Martin-Achard, R. "Notes sur mammon et la parabole de l'économe infidèle." *ETR* 28 (1953) 137-41.

Mattill, A. J., Jr. *Luke and the Last Things. A Perspective for the Understanding of Lukan Thought.* Dillsboro, NC: Western North Carolina Press, 1979.

McCown, C. C. "The Geography of Luke's Central Section." *JBL* 57 (1938) 51-66.

McFayden, J. F. "The Parable of the Unjust Steward." *ExpTim* 37 (1925-26) 535-39.

Mealand, D. L. *Poverty and Expectation in the Gospels.* London: SPCK, 1980.

Menoud, P.-H. "Riches injustes et biens véritables." *RTP*, n.s., 31 (1943) 5-17.

Merk, O. "Das Reich Gottes in den lukanischen Schriften." In *Jesus und Paulus*, 201-20. Edited by E. E. Ellis and E. Grässer. Göttingen: Vandenhoeck & Ruprecht, 1975.

Meyer, H. A. W. *Critical and Exegetical Commentary on the New Testament.* Part I, second division, vol. 2 [Luke]. Edinburgh: T. & T. Clark, 1880.

Michaelis, W. *Die Gleichnisse Jesu. Eine Einführung.* Hamburg: Furche, 1956.

—. "*skēnē*." In *TDNT* 7.368-81.

Miller, W. D. "The Unjust Steward." *ExpTim* 15 (1903-4) 332-34.

Milligan, W. "A Group of Parables." *Expositor*, ser. 4, 6 (1892 II) 114-26; 186-99.

Mitton, C. L. "The Unjust Steward." *ExpTim* 64 (1953) 307-8.

Moessner, D. P. *Lord of the Banquet: The Literary and Theological Significance of the Lukan Travel Narrative.* Minneapolis: Fortress, 1989.

—. "Luke 9:1-50: Luke's Preview of the Journey of the Prophet Like Moses of Deuteronomy." *JBL* 102/4 (1983) 575-605.

Moore, A. L. *The Parousia in the New Testament.* NovTSup 13. Leiden: Brill, 1966.

Moore, F. J. "The Parable of the Unjust Steward." *ATR* 47 (1965) 103-5.

Morris, L. *The Gospel according to St. Luke.* Tyndale New Testament Commentaries. Grand Rapids: Eerdmans, 1974.

—. "Luke and Early Catholicism." *WTJ* 35 (1973) 121-36.

Murray, G. "The Unjust Steward." *ExpTim* 15 (1903-4) 307-10.

Nägelsbach, F. "Noch einmal das Gleichnis vom ungerechten Haushalter." *Zeitschrift für kirchliche Wissenschaft und kirchliche Leben* 2 (1881) 481-86.

Nösgen, C. F. *Die Evangelien nach Matthäus, Markus und Lukas.* Nördlingen: Beck, 1886.

Oesterley, W. O. E. *The Gospel Parables in the Light of the Jewish Background.* New York: MacMillan, 1936.

—. "The Parable of the Unjust Steward." *Expositor*, ser. 6, 7 (1903) 273-83.

Ogg, G. "The Central Section of the Gospel according to St Luke." *NTS* 18 (1971-72) 39-53.

Olshausen, H. *Biblical Commentary on the New Testament.* Vol. 2. New York: Sheldon, 1862.

O'Neill, F. W. S. "The Unjust Steward." *ExpTim* 16 (1904-5) 240.

Oosterzee, J. J. van. *The Gospel according to Luke.* Vol. 8 in J. P. Lange's *Commentary on the Holy Scriptures Critical, Doctrinal and Homiletical.* 12 vols. Grand Rapids: Zondervan, 1960.

Osten-Sacken, P. von der. "Zur Christologie des lukanischen Reiseberichts." *EvT* 33 (1973) 476-96.

Paterson, W. P. "The Example of the Unjust Steward." *ExpTim* 35 (1923-24) 391-95.

Paul, G. "The Unjust Steward and the Interpretation of Luke 16:9." *Theology* 61 (1958) 189-93.

Pautrel, R. "Aeterna Tabernacula (Luc, XVI, 9)." *RSR* 30 (1940) 307-27.

Perrin, N. *Jesus and the Language of the Kingdom. Symbol and Metaphor in New Testament Interpretation.* Philadelphia: Fortress, 1976.

—. *The Kingdom of God in the Teaching of Jesus.* Philadelphia: Westminster, 1963.

—. *Rediscovering the Teaching of Jesus.* New York: Harper & Row, 1967.

Peters, R. "Der ungerechte Haushalter und die Gleichnisfrage." *Theologische Zeitschrift aus der Schweiz* 17 (1900) 128-44.

Pickar, C. H. "The Unjust Steward (Lk. 16:1-9)." *CBQ* 1 (1939) 250-53.

Pilgrim, W. E. *Good News to the Poor. Wealth and Poverty in Luke-Acts.* Minneapolis: Augsburg, 1981.

Pirot, J. *Paraboles et allégories évangéliques.* Paris: Lethielleux, 1949.

Plummer, A. *A Critical and Exegetical Commentary on the Gospel according to S. Luke*. ICC. 5th ed. Edinburgh: T. & T. Clark, 1922.

Porter, S. E. "The Parable of the Unjust Steward (Luke 16.1-13): Irony *Is* the Key." In *The Bible in Three Dimensions: Essays in celebration of forty years of Biblical Studies in the University of Sheffield*, pp. 127-53. JSOTSup 87. Edited by D. J. A. Clines, S. E. Fowl, and S. E. Porter. Sheffield: JSOT Press, 1990.

Preisker, H. "Lukas 16:1-7." *TLZ* 74 (1949) cols. 85-92.

Ragg, L. *St. Luke*. Westminster Commentaries. London: Methuen, 1922.

Reicke, B. "Instruction and Discussion in the Travel Narrative." In *SE* I, 206-16. Edited by K. Aland, F. L. Cross, J. Danielou, H. Riesenfeld, W. C. van Unnik. Berlin: Akademie, 1959.

Reimpell, J. C. "Das Gleichnis vom ungerechten Haushalter, Luk 16." *Zeitschrift für kirchliche Wissenschaft und kirchliche Leben* 1 (1880) 509-15.

Rengstorf, K. H. *Das Evangelium nach Lukas*. 6th ed. NTD, vol. 3. Göttingen: Vandenhoeck & Ruprecht, 1952.

Ressiguie, J. L. "Instruction and Discussion in the Central Section of Luke: A Redaction Critical Study of Luke 9:51-19:44." Ph.D. dissertation, Fuller Theological Seminary, 1978.

—. "Interpretation of Luke's Central Section (9:51-19:44) since 1856." *Studia Biblica et theologica* 5/2 (1975) 3-36.

—. "Point of View in the Central Section of Luke (9:51-19:44)." *JETS* 25/1 (1982) 41-48.

Richard, E. "Luke—Writer, Theologian, Historian: Research and Orientation of the 1970's." *BTB* 13 (1983) 3-15.

Ridderbos, H. *The Coming of the Kingdom*. Philadelphia: Presbyterian and Reformed, 1962.

Riggenbach, E. "Zur Exegese und Textkritik zweier Gleichnisse Jesu." In *Aus Schrift und Geschichte*, 17-34. Stuttgart: Calwer, 1922.

Ripon, W. B. "The Parable of the Unjust Steward." *Expositor*, ser. 4, 7 (1893 I) 21-29.

Robertson, A. T. *Luke the Historian in the Light of Research*. New York: Scribner's, 1920.

Robinson, W. C., Jr. "The Theological Context for Interpreting Luke's Travel Narrative (9:51ff.)." *JBL* 79 (1960) 20-31.

Rolston, H. "Ministry to Need. The Teachings of Jesus concerning Stewardship of Possessions." *Int* 8 (1954) 142-54.

Rücker, A. "Über das Gleichnis vom ungerechten Verwalter, Lc 16:1-13." *BibS(F)* 17 (1912) 1-64.

Sabourin, L. "The Eschatology of Luke." *BTB* 12 (1982) 72-76.

—. *L'Evangile de Luc*. Rome: Editrice Pontificia Universita Gregoriana, 1985.

Samain, P. "Le bon usage des richesses, en Luc XVI,1-12." *Revue Diocesaine de Tournai* 2/4 (1947) 330-35.

Schlatter, A. *Das Evangelium des Lukas aus seinen Quellen erklärt*. 2d ed. Stuttgart: Calwer, 1960.

Schleiermacher, F. *Ueber die Schriften des Lukas*. Teil 1. Berlin: Reimer, 1817.

Schlögl, N. "Die Fabel vom 'ungerechten Reichtum' und der Aufforderung Jesu, sich damit Schätze für den Himmel zu sammeln." *BZ* 14 (1917) 41-43.

Schmid, J. *Das Evangelium nach Lukas*. 4th ed. RNT, vol. 3. Regensburg: F. Pustet, 1960.

Schmithals, W. "Lukas—Evangelist der Armen." *Theologica Viatorum* 12 (1973-74) 153-67.

Schneider, J. "Zur Analyse des lukanischen Reiseberichtes." In *Synoptische Studien*, 207-29. Edited by J. Schmid and A. Vögtle. Munich: K. Zink, 1953.

Schottroff, L., and Stegemann, W. *Jesus and the Hope of the Poor*. Maryknoll, NY: Orbis, 1986.

Schreiter, M. J. C. *Historico-critica explicationum Parabolae de improbo oeconomo descriptio, qua varias variorus interpretum super Lucae 16, 1-13 expositiones digestas, examinatas, suamque ex Apocryphis Veteris Testamenti potissimum haustam exhibuit*. Lipsiae, 1803.

Schrenk, G. "*adikos, adikia, adikeō, adikēma*." In *TDNT* 1.149-63.

—. "*biazomai*." In *TDNT* 1.609-13.

Schulz, D. *Über die Parabel vom Verwalter, Lk 16:1ff. Ein Versuch.* Breslau: J. Max, 1821.

Schürmann, H. "Eschatologie und Liebesdienst in der Verkündigung Jesu." In *Ursprung und Gestalt*, 279-98. Düsseldorf: Patmos, 1970.

—. *Das Lukasevangelium.* Part 1 (1:1-9:50). HTKNT. Freiburg: Herder, 1969.

Schwarz, G. "'. . . lobte den betrügerischen Verwalter'? (Lukas 16:8a)." *BZ*, n.f., 18 (1974) 94-95.

Scott, R. B. Y. "The Parable of the Unjust Steward (Luke xvi. 1ff.)." *ExpTim* 49 (1937-38) 234-35.

Seccombe, D. P. *Possessions and the Poor in Luke-Acts.* SUNT, ser. B, vol. 6. Linz, Austria: A. Fuchs, 1983.

Sellin, G. "Studien zu den grossen Gleichniserzählungen des Lukas-Sonderguts. Die *anthrōpos-tis*-Erzählungen des Lukas-Sonderguts—besonders am Beispiel von Lk 10, 25-37 und 16,14-31 untersucht." Ph.D. dissertation, Münster, 1974.

Silva, M. "The Place of Historical Reconstruction in New Testament Criticism." In *Hermeneutics, Authority, and Canon*, 105-33. Edited by D. A. Carson and J. D. Woodbridge. Grand Rapids: Zondervan, 1986.

Smalley, S. S. "The Delay of the Parousia." *JBL* 83 (1964) 41-54.

Smith, B. T. D. *The Parables of the Synoptic Gospels. A Critical Study.* Cambridge: Cambridge University Press, 1937.

Stagg, F. "The Journey Toward Jerusalem in Luke's Gospel. Luke 9:51-19:27." *RevExp* 64 (1967) 499-512.

Steele, J. "The Unjust Steward." *ExpTim* 39 (1927-28) 236-37.

Stein, R. H. *An Introduction to the Parables of Jesus.* Philadelphia: Westminster, 1981.

—. *The Method and Message of Jesus' Teachings.* Philadelphia: Westminster, 1978.

Stier, E. R. *The Words of the Lord Jesus.* 8 vols. Edinburgh: T. & T. Clark, 1880.

Stoll, R. "The Unjust Steward—A Problem in Interpretation." *Ecclesiastical Review* 105 (1941) 16-27.

Stonehouse, N. B. Review of *The Theology of Saint Luke*, by H. Conzelmann. *WTJ* 24 (1961) 65-70.

—. *The Witness of the Synoptic Gospels to Christ.* Grand Rapids: Baker, 1979.

Summers, R. *Commentary on Luke.* Waco, TX: Word, 1972.

Talbert, C. H. *Literary Patterns, Theological Themes and the Genre of Luke-Acts.* Missoula, MT: Scholars Press, 1974.

—. *Reading Luke. A Literary and Theological Commentary on the Third Gospel.* New York: Crossroad, 1982.

—. "The Redaction Critical Quest for Luke the Theologian." In *Jesus and Man's Hope* 1.171-222. Edited by D. G. Buttrick. 2 vols. Pittsburgh: Pittsburgh Theological Seminary, 1970.

—. "Shifting Sands: The Recent Study of the Gospel of Luke." *Int* 30 (1976) 381-95.

—, ed. *Perspectives on Luke-Acts.* Danville, VA/Edinburgh: Association of Baptist Professors of Religion/T. & T. Clark, 1978.

Tannehill, R. C. *The Narrative Unity of Luke-Acts. A Literary Interpretation.* Vol. 1: *The Gospel according to Luke.* Philadelphia: Fortress, 1986.

Thiselton, A. C. "The Parables as Language-Event: Some Comments on Fuchs's Hermeneutics in the Light of Linguistic Philosophy." *SJT* 23 (1970) 437-68.

—. "The Parousia in Modern Theology: Some Questions and Comments." *TynBul* 27 (1976) 27-53.

Tillmann, F. "Zum Gleichnis vom ungerechten Verwalter, Lk 16:1-9." *BZ* 9 (1911) 171-84.

Tolbert, M. A. *Perspectives on the Parables. An Approach to Multiple Interpretations.* Philadelphia: Fortress, 1979.

Topel, L. J. "On the Injustice of the Unjust Steward: Lk 16:1-13." *CBQ* 37 (1975) 216-27.

Trench, R. C. *Notes on the Parables of our Lord.* 14th ed., rev. London: Macmillan, 1882.

Trompf, G. W. "La section médiane de l'évangile de Luc: L'Organisation des documents." *RHPR* 53 (1973) 141-54.

Unnik, W. C. van. "Luke-Acts, A Storm Center in Contemporary Scholarship." In *Studies in the Gospels*, 15-32. Edited by D. E. Nineham. Oxford: Blackwell, 1955.

Velte, D. "Das eschatologische Heute im Gleichnis vom ungerechten Haushalter." *Monatschrift für Pastoraltheologie* 27 (1931) 211-17.

Via, D. O., Jr. *The Parables: Their Literary and Existential Dimension*. Philadelphia: Fortress, 1967.

Volckaert, J. "The Parable of the Clever Steward." *Clergy Monthly* 17 (1953) 332-41.

Wansey, J. C. "The Parable of the Unjust Steward: An Interpretation." *ExpTim* 47 (1935-36) 39-40.

Weinel, H. *Die Gleichnisse Jesu. Zugleich eine Anleitung zu einem quellenmäßigen Verständnis der Evangelien*. Leipzig: Teubner, 1905.

Weir, J. E. "The Poor are Powerless. A Response to R. J. Coggins." *ExpTim* 100/1 (1988) 13-15.

Weiss, B. *Die Evangelien des Markus und Lukas*. MeyerK. 8th ed. Göttingen: Vandenhoeck & Ruprecht, 1892.

—. *The Life of Christ*. 2 vols. Edinburgh: T. & T. Clark, 1883.

Wellhausen, J. *Das Evangelium Lucae übersetzt und erklärt*. Berlin: Reimer, 1904.

Wenham, J. W. "Synoptic Independence and the Origin of Luke's Travel Narrative." *NTS* 27/4 (1981) 507-15.

Wiesen, G. *Die Stellung Jesu zum irdischen Gut mit besonderer Rücksicht auf das Gleichnis vom ungerechten Haushalter*. Gütersloh: Bertelsmann, 1895.

Wilder, A. N. *Eschatology and Ethics in the Teaching of Jesus*. New York: Harper, 1950.

Williams, F. E. "Is Almsgiving the Point of the 'Unjust Steward'?" *JBL* 83 (1964) 293-97.

Williams, F. J. "The Parable of the Unjust Steward (Luke xvi.1-9). Notes on the Interpretation Suggested by the Reverend R. G. Lunt." *ExpTim* 66 (1954-55) 371-72.

Wilson, S. G. "Lukan Eschatology." *NTS* 16 (1969-70) 330-47.

Wolf, C. U. "Poverty." In *IDB* 3.853-54.

Wright, A. "The Parable of the Unjust Steward." *The Interpreter* 7 (1911) 279-87.

Zahn, T. *Das Evangelium des Lukas*. Leipzig: A. Deichert, 1913.

Zimmermann, H. "Das Gleichnis vom ungerechten Verwalter: Lk 16:1-9." *BibLeb* 2 (1961) 254-61.

Zyro, F. F. "Neuer Versuch über das Gleichnis vom klugen Verwalter, Luk 16." *TSK* 5 (1831) 776-804.

INDEX OF AUTHORS

INDEX OF BIBLICAL PASSAGES

SUPPLEMENTS TO NOVUM TESTAMENTUM

ISSN 0167-9732

2. STROBEL, A. *Untersuchungen zum eschatologischen Verzögerungsproblem auf Grund der spätjüdische-urchristlichen Geschichte von Habakuk 2,2 ff.* 1961. ISBN 90 04 01582 5

6. *Neotestamentica et Patristica.* Eine Freundesgabe Herrn Professor Dr. Oscar Cullmann zu seinem 60. Geburtstag überreicht. 1962. ISBN 90 04 01586 8

8. DE MARCO, A.A. *The Tomb of Saint Peter.* A Representative and Annotated Bibliography of the Excavations. 1964. ISBN 90 04 01588 4

10. BORGEN, P. *Bread from Heaven.* An Exegetical Study of the Concept of Manna in the Gospel of John and the Writings of Philo. Photomech. Reprint of the first (1965) edition. 1981. ISBN 90 04 06419 2

13. MOORE, A.L. *The Parousia in the New Testament.* 1966. ISBN 90 04 01593 0

15. QUISPEL, G. *Makarius, das Thomasevangelium und das Lied von der Perle.* 1967. ISBN 90 04 01595 7

16. PFITZNER, V.C. *Paul and the Agon Motif.* 1967. ISBN 90 04 01596 5

17. BELLINZONI, A. *The Sayings of Jesus in the Writings of Justin Martyr.* 1967. ISBN 90 04 01597 3

18. GUNDRY, R.H. *The Use of the Old Testament in St. Matthew's Gospel.* With Special Reference to the Messianic Hope. Reprint of the first (1967) edition. 1975. ISBN 90 04 04278 4

19. SEVENSTER, J.N. *Do You Know Greek?* How Much Greek Could the First Jewish Christians Have Known? 1968. ISBN 90 04 03090 5

20. BUCHANAN, G.W. *The Consequences of the Covenant.* 1970. ISBN 90 04 01600 7

21. KLIJN, A.F.J. *A Survey of the Researches into the Western Text of the Gospels and Acts.* Part 2: 1949-1969. 1969. ISBN 90 04 01601 5

22. GABOURY, A. *La structure des Évangiles synoptiques.* La structure-type à l'origine des synoptiques. 1970. ISBN 90 04 01602 3

23. GASTON, L. *No Stone on Another.* Studies in the Significance of the Fall of Jerusalem in the Synoptic Gospels. 1970. ISBN 90 04 01603 1

24. *Studies in John.* Presented to Professor Dr. J.N. Sevenster on the Occasion of His Seventieth Birthday. 1970. ISBN 90 04 03091 3

25. STORY, C.I.K. *The Nature of Truth in 'The Gospel of Truth', and in the Writings of Justin Martyr.* A Study of the Pattern of Orthodoxy in the Middle of the Second Christian Century. 1970. ISBN 90 04 01605 8

26. GIBBS, J.G. *Creation and Redemption.* A Study in Pauline Theology. 1971. ISBN 90 04 01606 6

27. MUSSIES, G. *The Morphology of Koine Greek As Used in the Apocalypse of St. John.* A Study in Bilingualism. 1971. ISBN 90 04 02656 8

28. AUNE, D.E. *The Cultic Setting of Realized Eschatology in Early Christianity.* 1972. ISBN 90 04 03341 6

29. UNNIK, W.C. VAN. *Sparsa Collecta.* The Collected Essays of W.C. van Unnik Part 1. Evangelia, Paulina, Acta. 1973. ISBN 90 04 03660 1

30. UNNIK, W.C. VAN. *Sparsa Collecta.* The Collected Essays of W.C. van Unnik Part 2. I Peter, Canon, Corpus Hellenisticum, Generalia. 1980. ISBN 90 04 06261 0

31. UNNIK, W.C. VAN. *Sparsa Collecta.* The Collected Essays of W.C. van Unnik Part 3. Patristica, Gnostica, Liturgica. 1983. ISBN 90 04 06262 9

33. AUNE, D.E. (ed.) *Studies in New Testament and Early Christian Literature*. Essays in Honor of Allen P. Wikgren. 1972. ISBN 90 04 03504 4

34. HAGNER, D.A. *The Use of the Old and New Testaments in Clement of Rome*. 1973. ISBN 90 04 03636 9

35. GUNTHER, J.J. *St. Paul's Opponents and Their Background*. A Study of Apocalyptic and Jewish Sectarian Teachings. 1973. ISBN 90 04 03738 1

36. KLIJN, A.F.J. & G.J. REININK (eds.) *Patristic Evidence for Jewish-Christian Sects*. 1973. ISBN 90 04 03763 2

37. REILING, J. *Hermas and Christian Prophecy*. A Study of The Eleventh Mandate. 1973. ISBN 90 04 03771 3

38. DONFRIED, K.P. *The Setting of Second Clement in Early Christianity*. 1974. ISBN 90 04 03895 7

39. ROON, A. VAN. *The Authenticity of Ephesians*. 1974. ISBN 90 04 03971 6

40. KEMMLER, D.W. *Faith and Human Reason*. A Study of Paul's Method of Preaching as Illustrated by 1-2 Thessalonians and Acts 17, 2-4. 1975. ISBN 90 04 04209 1

42. PANCARO, S. *The Law in the Fourth Gospel*. The Torah and the Gospel, Moses and Jesus, Judaism and Christianity According to John. 1975. ISBN 90 04 04309 8

43. CLAVIER, H. *Les variétés de la pensée biblique et le problème de son unité*. Esquisse d'une théologie de la Bible sur les textes originaux et dans leur contexte historique. 1976. ISBN 90 04 04465 5

44. ELLIOTT, J.K.E. (ed.) *Studies in New Testament Language and Text*. Essays in Honour of George D. Kilpatrick on the Occasion of His Sixty-Fifth Birthday. 1976. ISBN 90 04 04386 1

45. PANAGOPOULOS, J. (ed.) *Prophetic Vocation in the New Testament and Today*. 1977. ISBN 90 04 04923 1

46. KLIJN, A.F.J. *Seth in Jewish, Christian and Gnostic Literature*. 1977. ISBN 90 04 05245 3

47. BAARDA, T., A.F.J. KLIJN & W.C. VAN UNNIK (eds.) *Miscellanea Neotestamentica*. I. Studia ad Novum Testamentum Praesertim Pertinentia a Sociis Sodalicii Batavi c.n. Studiosorum Novi Testamenti Conventus Anno MCMLXXVI Quintum Lustrum Feliciter Complentis Suscepta. 1978. ISBN 90 04 05685 8

48. BAARDA, T., A.F.J. KLIJN & W.C. VAN UNNIK (eds.) *Miscellanea Neotestamentica*. II. 1978. ISBN 90 04 05686 6

49. O'BRIEN, P.T. *Introductory Thanksgivings in the Letters of Paul*. 1977. ISBN 90 04 05265 8

50. BOUSSET, D.W. *Religionsgeschichtliche Studien*. Aufsätze zur Religionsgeschichte des hellenistischen Zeitalters. Hrsg. von A.F. Verheule. 1979. ISBN 90 04 05845 1

51. COOK, M.J. *Mark's Treatment of the Jewish Leaders*. 1978. ISBN 90 04 05785 4

52. GARLAND, D.E. *The Intention of Matthew 23*. 1979. ISBN 90 04 05912 1

53. MOXNES, H. *Theology in Conflict*. Studies in Paul's Understanding of God in Romans. 1980. ISBN 90 04 06140 1

55. MENKEN, M.J.J. *Numerical Litarary Techniques in John*. The Fourth Evangelist's Use of Numbers of Words and Syllables. 1985. ISBN 90 04 07427 9

56. SKARSAUNE, O. *The Proof From Prophecy*. A Study in Justin Martyr's Proof-Text Tradition: Text-type, Provenance, Theological Profile. 1987. ISBN 90 04 07468 6

59. WILKINS, M.J. *The Concept of Disciple in Matthew's Gospel, as Reflected in the Use of the Term "Mathetes"*. 1988. ISBN 90 04 08689 7

60. MILLER, E.L. *Salvation-History in the Prologue of John*. The Significance of John 1:3-4. 1989. ISBN 90 04 08692 7

61. THIELMAN, F. *From Plight to Solution*. A Jewish Framework for Understanding Paul's View of the Law in Galatians and Romans. 1989. ISBN 90 04 09176 9

64. STERLING, G.E. *Historiography and Self-Definition.* Josephos, Luke-Acts and Apologetic Historiography. 1992. ISBN 90 04 09501 2

65. BOTHA, J.E. *Jesus and the Samaritan Woman.* A Speech Act Reading of John 4:1-42. 1991. ISBN 90 04 09505 5

66. KUCK, D.W. *Judgment and Community Conflict.* Paul's Use of Apocalyptic Judgment Language in 1 Corinthians 3:5-4:5. 1992. ISBN 90 04 09510 1

67. SCHNEIDER, G. *Jesusüberlieferung und Christologie.* Neutestamentliche Aufsätze 1970-1990. 1992. ISBN 90 04 09555 1

68. SEIFRID, M.A. *Justification by Faith.* The Origin and Development of a Central Pauline Theme. 1992. ISBN 90 04 09521 7

69. NEWMAN, C.C. *Paul's Glory-Christology.* Tradition and Rhetoric. 1992. ISBN 90 04 09463 6

70. IRELAND, D.J. *Stewardship and the Kingdom of God.* An Historical, Exegetical, and Contextual Study of the Parable of the Unjust Steward in Luke 16:1-13. 1992. ISBN 90 04 09600 0